COMMUNISTS ON CAMPUS

THE UNIVERSITY OF GEORGIA PRESS | ATHENS AND LONDON

WILLIAM J. BILLINGSLEY

Communists on Campus

RACE, POLITICS, AND THE PUBLIC UNIVERSITY IN SIXTIES NORTH CAROLINA

© 1999 by the University of Georgia Press
Athens, Georgia 30602
All rights reserved
Designed by Kathi Dailey Morgan
Set in 10 on 13 Electra by G&S Typesetters
Printed and bound by McNaughton & Gunn
The paper in this book meets the guidelines for
permanence and durability of the Committee on
Production Guidelines for Book Longevity of the
Council on Library Resources.
Printed in the United States of America
03 02 01 00 99 C 5 4 3 2 1
Library of Congress Cataloging in Publication Data
Billingsley, William J., 1953–
    Communists on campus : race, politics, and the
public university in sixties North Carolina / William J.
Billingsley.
        p.   cm.
    Includes bibliographical references (p.   ) and index.
    ISBN 0-8203-2109-5 (alk. paper)
    1. Academic freedom — North Carolina — History —
20th century.   2. Universities and colleges — Law
and legislation — North Carolina.   3. Politics and
education — North Carolina — History — 20th century.
4. Anti-communist movements — North Carolina —
History — 20th century.   I. Title.
    LC72.3.N67B55   1999
    378.1'21 — dc21   99-11408
British Library Cataloging in Publication Data available

CONTENTS

ACKNOWLEDGMENTS

There are too many names and memories to properly thank all of those who contributed to the fruition of this study. The short list includes the various readers whose suggestions made this a better book, even if I did not always accept the advice. Special thanks go to Martha Topik and Ellen Goldlust-Gingrich, who expertly caught mistakes and omissions. To each I express my appreciation for engaged and meticulous readings.

I would like to acknowledge the courtesy and generosity of the staffs of the North Carolina Division of Archives and History in Raleigh, the Southern Historical Collection, the North Carolina Collection, and the Photographic Services Section of the University of North Carolina in Chapel Hill. I especially recognize Steve Massengill at Archives and History for his good cheer and tireless effort in helping track down source materials and photographs. At the Southern Historical Collection, Dr. Richard Schrader and John White were polite and professional in responding to my unceasing requests for files buried deep in the archives.

I am deeply appreciative of the support provided by the University of Georgia Press. Thanks there go to Karen Orchard, Kristine Blakeslee, and especially Malcolm Call, who never wavered in his understanding of the importance of the study, for giving me the freedom to do it in my own way.

Although centered on North Carolina, the project was conceived in California and I thank those denizens of the Golden State who figured in its gestation. I owe much to Jon Wiener, who taught me that history matters and to always keep my eye trained on core issues and problems. A collective acknowledgment is due the participants in the Graduate Seminar in Southern History at the Irvine and San Diego campuses of the University of California, who provided an exhilarating intellectual experience.

Each of the following persons offered intellectual and spiritual support and, most of all, friendship. My warmest appreciation goes to you: Alex Burckin, Peter Coclanis, William McKee Evans, Scott Howlett, Michael P. Johnson, Ralph Leck, Ann Rider, Greg Sutton, Steve Topik, Frank Towers, Stephen Vlastos, Mary Ann Rasmussen, and Harry Watson.

Finally, I need to recognize two people whose faith and support were incomparable. Colleen Tucker helped resolve problems great and small, and I thank her for her love and support throughout this endeavor. My mother, Margaret Brooks Billingsley, was the daughter of southern sharecroppers with a bare modicum of schooling. Her greatest gift to me was the example of great personal dignity and human decency retained amid struggle. This book is dedicated to her memory.

INTRODUCTION

During the 1960s, almost a decade after the tragedy of the post–World War II Red Scare had subsided nationally, it was reenacted in North Carolina, this time seemingly as farce. From 1963 to 1966 the state was gripped by a heated debate over the nature and purpose of communism and whether North Carolina's public university was being exploited by radicals bent on subversion. In this episode, unlike those of the previous decade, people did not lose their lives or suffer imprisonment, and only one person lost employment and faced banishment. But like the hearings chaired by Senator Joseph McCarthy and those of the U.S. House Committee on Un-American Activities (HUAC) of the earlier era, the North Carolina case was replete with political theater that provided absurd and ridiculous moments. During public hearings televised to a statewide audience, one witness called to testify on the extent of communist influence at the University of North Carolina stipulated that students had to "take a leftist tinge" to get high grades. When no communists or radicals of sufficient stature were present, they were imported. The most farcical moment of the Manichaean drama occurred when a member of the Communist Party USA's national committee, Herbert Aptheker, spoke to some 1,500 students assembled at the campus perimeter as he stood on a city sidewalk inches from university property, to which he had been denied access.

The focal point of this anticommunist episode was the passage of an "Act to Regulate Visiting Speakers" at state-supported colleges and universities. Enacted by the North Carolina General Assembly in the waning hours of its 1963 session, the "speaker ban" law resonated with themes reminiscent of the

McCarthy era. The law prevented from speaking on any of the campuses of the state's public colleges and universities any "known member" of the Communist Party or anyone using the Fifth Amendment in refusing to answer questions before any investigative panel. Although the law carried no criminal penalty for violation, it mandated that university officials vigorously enforce its provisions. For the next five years officials and liberal defenders of the university were locked in a struggle with conservative critics and anticommunists over the speaker ban and the nature of the relationship between the university and the citizenry. As cultural ideology the speaker ban had staying power; not until 1968, when a federal panel ruled the statute unconstitutional, was the issue put to rest.

This book began with an interest in the role of the university as a potential source of alternative cultural authority. How could an institution such as the University of North Carolina at Chapel Hill, renowned as a beacon of southern liberalism, exist in a political culture that in many ways reflected the hallmarks of southern conservatism? There undoubtedly would be periods of controversy and conflict as the hegemonic culture sought to limit the political space occupied by an institution that generated criticism from the host society. This book is not intended to be a traditional institutional history but rather a work that situates the university in society and examines the reciprocal influences on each other of the public university and the larger society during periods of social change and political reaction. This book also examines the ideological dimensions of anticommunism, especially its historic utility as a signifier of cultural fear and anxiety, as well as the democratic movements and protests of the 1960s. Foremost in this regard is the example of the African American struggle for civil equality, what one historian has called "the most significant social movement in all of American history." In the case of North Carolina, this concern is quite appropriate inasmuch as the era of the 1960s, a period defined in large part by the civil rights movement, began in North Carolina with the Greensboro sit-ins.[1]

All of these seemingly disparate interests coalesced in the speaker ban episode. Although the law included all tax-supported campuses, it was clearly targeted at the flagship campus at Chapel Hill. The speaker ban was not an isolated event disconnected from the larger contours of the relationship between the state and UNC; it marked the culmination of a long history, partially submerged or obscured, of attacks that charged the university with encouragement of subversive elements and of calls for investigation and tighter political oversight of the campus. Historically, these periodic outbreaks of anti-UNC sentiment alleged that communist influences had become entrenched at Chapel Hill and threatened to undermine North Carolina's social fabric. Although the content of the allegations was fueled by anticommunism, the specific context was usually provided by the politics of race. In this sense, a liberal Chapel Hill represented a threat to the structure of race relations that relegated black citizens to a subordinate status. The speaker ban was the product of a long history of cultural antagonism directed at liberal influences that in the popular mind were associated with UNC.

Despite a number of controversies, several of which conjoined allegations involving communist influences and racial liberalism, UNC had long avoided purges and maintained its reputation as a progressive institution in the South. The critical factor precluding purges at UNC was President Frank Porter Graham. Despite the controversies and allegations of subversion, during Graham's almost twenty-year tenure from 1930 to 1949 there were no politically inspired dismissals at Chapel Hill, largely because Graham was himself the personal embodiment of UNC liberalism. Graham's activism often courted suspicion, as he lent his name to groups and associated with causes that were unpopular and supported by radicals. Graham's liberalism was never understood or accepted by the state's economic elite. Nevertheless, no matter how much the conservative business establishment frowned on his activities, Graham was never publicly rebuked or politically threatened. From his "Labor-Capital Manifesto" of 1930 (which called for social-welfare legislation, an investigation of working conditions in textile mills, and recognition of the legitimacy of collective bargaining) to his chairmanship of the Southern Conference for Human Welfare, Graham embraced and acted on a distinctly liberal vision. In large part, UNC's reputation as a liberal, progressive institution rested on the political engagement and personal commitments of its president.[2]

In 1949 Graham left UNC after being appointed to fill an unexpired term in the U.S. Senate. The following year he sought election in his own right, and his candidacy became a referendum on his personal politics and, by implication, the political culture represented by UNC. Graham lost a close election to Willis Smith that revealed much about the state's political climate. In several eastern Black Belt counties that he carried in the first primary, in the general election he lost by large margins as a result of an openly racist campaign that urged "White People Wake Up." Among the advisers and workers for the Smith campaign was a young radio reporter name Jesse Alexander Helms. This campaign would be Helms's first brush with the UNC liberals; his antipathy toward the influence of Chapel Hill in the state's public affairs would eventually become a hallmark of his political career. Graham also lost in a number of pivotal Piedmont counties as the urban middle classes voted to protect their economic position against the possibility that Graham might promote social legislation that would threaten their relative comfort.

While the social and economic benefits of a modernizing university were discernible, the 1950 Graham-Smith election exposed the salience of race and, to a lesser degree, anticommunist imagery in North Carolina's political life. Despite decades of industrialization, the Tarheel State resonated cultural values that were distinctly agrarian, traditional, and southern. And these values were reflected in how the university was viewed. It was a source of pride and economic advancement, but it was not to be a laboratory for social engineering. In this manner, the verdict of 1950 categorically rejected the liberal values associated with Graham's university. But Graham's liberalism and his vision of a university pioneering social change and reconciliation had indeed found a receptive audience in some quarters of the state as well as in national circles. Thus, the university's role in public life revealed a tension between those social groups wedded to tradition and those viewing the institution as open political space from which to question and ultimately oppose the conventions of the larger society.[3]

What was the meaning of the 1950 election? How did it define the future of North Carolina politics at the dawning of the decade that saw the legal supports for Jim Crow brought down? The future was reflected in the past. It seems obvious that North Carolina was not nearly as progressive as its image. The election revealed sharply defined limits to the state's progressivism; social change would be contained within parameters that limited any threats to the position of the dominant interests and social classes. The balloting also demonstrated that race was a far more significant and potentially explosive organizing principle than previously thought.

In his magisterial rendering of southern politics, V. O. Key minimized the importance of race in North Carolina politics, largely on the basis of the state's comparatively small plantation district and its correspondingly fewer numbers of slaves. In the twentieth century, said Key, the state was governed by an economic oligarchy, in manufacturing and finance, located in the urban Piedmont. At the same time, the eastern counties that comprised the former plantation region were a "black belt in the minority." The smallness and putative weakness of the Black Belt thus meant for Key that racial considerations, although still present, were not a decisive factor in politics.[4]

As the election of 1950 demonstrated, Key underestimated the importance of race as a political lever. Although the industrial oligarchy certainly was powerful and ascendant, it was still not able to rule exclusive of the agrarian interests in the eastern Black Belt. The agrarians, including the remnants of a planter elite, and the urban bourgeoisie continued to govern as they had throughout the century, as a historical bloc, the industrial elite economically dominant but not yet able to break the agrarians' viselike grip on political power where it really mattered — in the General Assembly. During the 1950s, Black Belt politicos continued to wield considerable political clout. The legislature was egregiously malapportioned, with eastern politicians sitting in great numbers and often in positions of authority.[5]

The most prominent historian of the North Carolina response to the ramifications of the *Brown* ruling of 1954 agreed with Key that race was not the definitive aspect of Tarheel politics. In his masterful *Civilities and Civil Rights*, William Chafe stressed that while race was important, it was not the pivotal issue that produced Graham's defeat in 1950. The problem in North Carolina, said Chafe, was leadership, not a deeply held support for Jim Crow by poor whites, farmers, and workers. Business conservatives in state and municipal government created and exploited a myth of redneck rebellion to forestall meaningful social change that went beyond the image of moderation. According to Chafe's thesis, most white North Carolinians were ready to accept implementation of desegregation in a way that would have secured a progressive future for the state. That North Carolina did not do so was a manifestation of the "progressive mystique," a politics of appearance and style manipulated by an urban business elite.[6]

The best illustration of this influence and power was the state's plan created in response to the *Brown* decision. The plan certainly "postponed meaningful [school] desegregation in North Carolina for more than a decade," but what ideological and political interests drove the response? As Chafe notes, there was adequate support for implementation among the urban business class had Governor Luther Hodges been so inclined. This class, however, was not so deeply invested with the need to preserve racial privilege. But the eastern agrarians were, and their support was vital if Hodges was to entertain any prospect of moving his program through the General Assembly.

The most telling display of the ongoing power of regionally based racial politics in North Carolina rests in the coterie chosen to articulate the North Carolina response to *Brown*. The chairman of the Governor's Special Advisory Committee on Education was State Senator Thomas Jenkins Pearsall, whose name became synonymous with the plan eventually approved by Governor Hodges, the legislature, and the voters of the state. The Pearsall Plan provided for the continuity of segregation by sacrificing a few schools to integration and by creating a legal scenario that forced plaintiffs to wage a slow and costly district-by-district battle. Who were Pearsall and the other men who comprised the core of the committee? They were easterners, with deep attachments to the paternalism of North Carolina's racial hierarchy. They were not extremists or rednecks, but they were profoundly conservative in their adherence to segregation as a basis of social organization. Their strategy was simple yet brilliant: postpone indefinitely any meaningful integration by avoiding confrontation with federal authority.[7]

The social origins of the men designing the Pearsall Plan illuminate the political strength of the eastern Black Belt and the importance of race to that power. Pearsall was, first and foremost, a planter. Since 1935 he had operated a sprawling twenty-two-thousand-acre plantation that covered parts of four eastern North Carolina counties. At the time of the school desegregation crisis of 1956, some six thousand acres were under cultivation, worked by more than 130 tenant families, at least one hundred of them black. As one newspaper noted with ironic accuracy, "his farming operations, among the largest in the state, have given Pearsall some practical experience in race relations." Pearsall was not alone and was not the most committed to keeping North Carolina in company with the Deep South. The lawyers serving as special counsel to the committee were oriented toward a strong segregationist position, including a resolution of interposition. Two of the three lawyers, Armistead J. Maupin and W. W. "Tee" Taylor, were products of the Black Belt; the other, Thomas F. Ellis, although born in California, was "more southern in his thinking and accent than many a Tarheel born and bred."[8]

While most attention was focused on post-*Brown* racial developments and politics, the issue of communism was also a matter of public awareness and interest. At the center of this phenomena were the two highly visible trials of Junius Scales, which informed the public that the scion of a prominent family had been exposed to communism at UNC–Chapel Hill. But the Scales trials were by no means the sole putative association between the university and the Communist Party. In January 1954 informant Ralph Clontz told the Subversive Activities Control Board that he had known "far more than 20 Communists in North Carolina" since he had joined the party in 1948 as an undercover operative. In March 1954 Milton Abernathy was called to testify before the Senate Internal Security Subcommittee chaired by William Jenner. Abernathy (familiarly known to the students and townspeople in Chapel Hill as "Ab") had operated a Franklin Street bookstore in the 1930s that had served as a gathering place for radicals and social critics. In his discussion of the issues and personalities that became instrumental in shaping his early political views, Scales called Abernathy's Intimate Bookstore "the most interesting spot in town." Abernathy had operated a notary printing press in a back room of the bookstore, primarily to print *Contempo*, a literary magazine that published works by George Bernard Shaw, William Faulkner, Ezra Pound, and other prominent writers. Before the Jenner Committee, informant Paul Crouch alleged that Abernathy and his wife ran the press under the auspices of the Communist Party. An investigation yielded no revelations and seemed pointless inasmuch as Abernathy and his wife had sold the bookstore in 1950.[9]

The most significant exposé of communist activity at UNC and its support for desegregation and biracial organizing occurred in March 1956, when a

HUAC panel conducted three days of hearings on "Communist activities in the North Carolina area" at the federal court building in Charlotte. The panel questioned a variety of witnesses, black and white, about their activities and party functions. Most of those called to testify had been college students at the time of their involvement. Three informers asserted that they had attended meetings, been introduced to those under investigation or charged with subversion, or had encountered individuals implicated in testimony on the Chapel Hill campus of UNC.[10]

By the early 1960s, there existed a long association, perpetuated through popular memory, that linked UNC to a perception of radical activism. These associations were few and fleeting but were exposed and reemphasized by political figures and investigations amid the charged atmosphere of the emerging Cold War. Such acknowledgments were both a source of perverse pride for Chapel Hill in being somehow "different" and a source of cultural contagion. Still, there was no palpable contention that the university should be investigated or efforts made to quash the activism of its students and faculty. How did a speaker control law emerge in a state whose progressive image rested so heavily on the national reputation of its public university? Ellen Schrecker, the leading historian of academic McCarthyism, has noted that with the growing pressures of the Cold War, authorities were "increasingly reluctant to let Communist, and later merely controversial speakers address their students. Speaker bans were hardly new." What made the North Carolina case different was the timing and the political circumstances of its origins. Schrecker's observation described the late 1940s and early 1950s; other states, including Washington and California, had banned communists for several decades. But at a time when speaker bans were antiquated relics in several states, they were being reinvented elsewhere to serve quite different political purposes. In 1961 the City University of New York ended its long-held policy of proscribing communist speakers. On June 21, 1963, the Board of Regents of the University of California voted to abolish a twelve-year ban. Four days after the California action, the North Carolina legislature suddenly and without extensive discussion enacted a speaker ban far more draconian than those recently rescinded elsewhere.[11]

The significance of the North Carolina speaker ban rests in the historical context in which it occurred: the prominence of race in organizing social and political life. The greatest historian of the American South has observed that "even in its heyday Chapel Hill had never dared seriously to challenge prevailing Southern racial proscriptions and orthodoxies." By 1963 those proscriptions and orthodoxies were collapsing. The social tension in North Carolina during the spring of 1963 resulted from the impending collapse of Jim Crow. The streets of the state were filled not with communists but with young students, mostly black but with substantial numbers of whites, demanding an end to racial inequality. The uniqueness of the anticommunist movement in North Carolina was that it serviced the political needs of a moribund order at a time of crisis. Racialist ideology and segregation were finished, but anticommunism remained vital as protection against perceived threats to the social order. In this sense, the history of an anticommunist episode in one state suggests much about the entire history of anticommunism in America.[12]

COMMUNISTS ON CAMPUS

1 The "Speaker Ban" Law

Late on the afternoon of June 25, 1963, the North Carolina General Assembly prepared to close what had been a rancorous session in which the leadership and a coterie of influential conservatives had experienced disappointment, frustration, and defeat. In one telling incident during the session's final week, Senator Thomas J. White Jr., conservative spokesman and arguably the most powerful member of the legislature, had rushed from the Senate chamber onto the House floor to accost Representative Sneed High of Cumberland County, who had displayed the temerity to speak against funding for White's pet project — restoration of the grave site of revolutionary-era Governor Richard Caswell. In the aftermath of the measure's defeat, the two legislators argued furiously and had to be separated by House members.[1]

The frustrations of White and his cohort were rooted in a series of more substantial Assembly defeats compounded by their pent-up anger at the discomforting signs of social change in the streets of Raleigh and throughout the South. During the previous week, conservatives, led by Senate President Clarence Stone, had watched in shock as floor debate had devastated their effort to memorialize Congress to alter the U.S. Constitution. A Court of the Union proposal, had it been enacted, would have effectively prohibited the U.S. Supreme Court from ruling in apportionment matters as well as in other areas, such as school desegregation. This "Super Court" proposal would have enabled an ad hoc review of Supreme Court decisions by a special tribunal of the fifty chief justices of the state supreme courts. Here was a final effort to turn back the clock and preserve segregation and rural political power. Believing that the resolution would easily sail through the Senate, Stone and fellow ultras were shocked by its defeat—a loss that clearly resulted from opponents' ability to persuade their colleagues that the measure was dangerous and extremist.[2]

On the day prior to adjournment most Assembly members were conferencing in hopes of providing support for a plethora of local bills designed to meet a specific need in their counties or districts. When running for reelection, as most would, the legislators could offer the last-minute acquisitions as positive evidence of effective constituent service. The procedure was simplified and streamlined. After securing an adequate number of supporters and assuring their presence on the floor, the sponsor would move for a suspension of the rules, which, in the face of no opposition, would be granted and the bill "placed upon immediate passage." The second and third readings would follow expeditiously, and with a rising chorus of "ayes" the bill would be approved and ordered enrolled. Opposition was all but nonexistent. In the parlance of the process, it was everyone's turn to "feed at the trough."

The procedure was designed to handle noncontroversial measures as expeditiously as possible. Protocol demanded support, silence, or absence. At this point in the session, most members were getting in line to receive approval of their pet projects. Many members were not on the floor but were in the halls or conference rooms caucusing to produce a quid pro quo amenable to the legislators' specific needs. Following this fashion, on the late afternoon of June 25 House Bill 1392 authorized "the board of education of the Wilson City School Administrative Unit to convey certain property to the city of Wilson at private sale." House Bill 1394 authorized "the issuance of warrants by certain law enforcement officials in the incorporated cities and towns in Gaston County." House Bill 1396 did the same for "certain Law enforcement officials" in Pitt County.[3]

The 1963 session, however, would depart radically from the ceremonial exercise of pork barrel and localized legislation. On the afternoon of June 25, amid the welter of last-minute legislation, Secretary of State Thad Eure handed Representative Ned E. Delamar of Pamlico County a bill that the two had discussed several weeks prior to the end of the session and that was now ready for introduction. This was no ordinary bill; it called for a complete ban on designated speakers from the campuses of state-supported colleges and universities. Eure had heard of a similar measure enacted by the Ohio Assembly, had obtained the necessary information, and had the North Carolina bill drafted. Delamar carried the bill to fellow easterner Philip Godwin and asked him to introduce it after reviewing it for constitutional soundness. Godwin was aware that such a bill was in the works. He immediately agreed to act as the bill's chief sponsor and began to line up endorsements and orchestrate its rapid passage. Godwin carried the bill to House Speaker Clifton Blue and was granted a motion to have the rules suspended.[4]

House Bill 1395 was ready for action. It was entitled "An Act to Regulate Visiting Speakers at State Supported Colleges and Universities." It read:

> No college or university, which receives any state funds in support thereof, shall permit any person to use the facilities of such college or university for speaker purposes, who:
>
> A) Is a known member of the Communist Party;
>
> B) Is known to advocate the overthrow of the Constitution of the United States or the State of North Carolina;
>
> C) Has pleaded the Fifth Amendment of the Constitution of the United States in refusing to answer any question, with respect to communist or subversive connections, or activities, before any duly constituted legislative committee, any judicial tribunal, or any executive or administrative board of the United States or any state.[5]

The bill carried no criminal penalty for violation. It did, however, mandate strict enforcement by the Board of Trustees and the administrative officers of each state-supported college and university.

The bill encountered no opposition. With most members out of the chamber lining up support for their own last-minute proposals, there were few questions about the bill. Representative David Britt of Robeson County asked about the intent of the bill. Godwin replied that it was meant to "prevent card-carrying Communists from using the campus of the University as a forum." Any such means of expressing opposition to communism would scarcely be questioned in the Assembly during the most tranquil of times. Many members eagerly welcomed the opportunity to state their personal opposition to communism in any context. The few legislators willing to question or voice opposition to the bill found their patriotism impugned. As one such opponent, Republican Senator Charles Strong from Greensboro, noted later, "the implication was given that if you were against this bill you were not quite all true blue."[6]

With the rules suspended, House Bill 1395 was read a second and third time. It took fewer than ten minutes to sail through the lower chamber. Representative Godwin would justify the rapid passage by noting, "I had the Bill moving and didn't see any sense in stopping it." The bill was hand-carried by a page, accompanied by Godwin, to the nearby Senate chamber as a "special message." Stone was awaiting its arrival. Having discussed the measure with Delamar and Godwin, Stone enthusiastically supported its provisions.[7]

For the Senate president, it offered a good measure of retribution for recent defeats suffered by the states'-rights segregationists under his leadership. Equally important was the opportunity presented by the bill to sanction the institution that symbolized the liberal influences that he found so abhorrent — the University of North Carolina.

Godwin knew that the bill contained political dynamite. He entered the Senate chamber and walked to the rostrum, where he whispered to Stone, "Clarence, the bill is over here, whenever you want to handle it." Stone instructed Godwin to find a member to suspend the rules. Senator Garland Garriss of Northampton County moved for suspension, and Stone ruled it done. Stone then proceeded to steamroll the bill into law. It required a near-total abrogation of parliamentary procedure and senatorial courtesy for the bill to find its way into the General Statutes of North Carolina. A number of senators were out of the chamber as Stone quickly read the proposal and attempted to call for a vote. Before he could do so, several members scrambled to their feet, calling for recognition to speak on the bill. Lunsford Crew of Halifax County objected to Stone's heavy-handed attempt to rush the bill through without the benefit of discussion. Crew complained that he was leery of such last-minute bills. Stone agreed but conditioned his concern with a categorical "but this sounds like a good one to me." [8]

Having witnessed the power of extended debate in the Super Court defeat, Stone was determined that the scenario would not be repeated. He quickly called for a voice vote. In the words of one correspondent who witnessed the event, he "called loudly for ayes and noes and ruled that the ayes had it all in a single breath," despite a loud crescendo of "noes." As other senators called to speak, Stone drowned them out with repeated blows from his gavel. [9]

After the bill's rapid passage, two senators managed to speak against the measure. Senator Luther Hamilton of Carteret County, a leading opponent of the Super Court proposal, denounced the speaker control law as an abridgment of free speech and unworthy of the Senate. Perry Martin of Hertford County also vociferously criticized the bill. With little time to prepare an organized appeal, Martin spoke extemporaneously, condemning the maneuver as emblematic of the emotionally charged atmosphere that had characterized the Assembly in recent days. In his remarks, Martin pointed to the irony that the intended anticommunist law tended to reproduce and implement the feature that its proponents found repugnant about communism: the absence of open debate and free speech. "By passing this bill," said Martin, "you are dignifying communism and saying that you are afraid for the people of North Carolina to know about it. They have a right to be informed about any form of government." The speeches from the floor had no effect. Stone had already ruled that the "ayes" had carried the measure. House Bill 1395 was now virtually law; all that remained was to enroll the measure into the General Statutes.[10]

The anticommunist episode that was the speaker ban law was informed by ideological and political struggles internationally, in Washington, and in other southern states. As the Cold War intensified, especially in the underdeveloped postcolonial nations of Africa, Asia, and Latin America, news of guerrilla insurgencies and communist gains and victories came daily. American newspapers and electronic media were rife with stories and reports of communist-based issues that resonated with Cold War antagonisms.

The moral imperative of pursuing a Cold War victory over a demonic foe remained a key feature of a foreign-policy consensus that generated domestic repercussions. The rhetorical call to arms for an indefatigable commitment to resisting communism was provided by President John F. Kennedy. In his inaugural address, Kennedy established his bona fides as a cold warrior, as the speech emphasized foreign-policy issues and echoed the incipient warming of the war against international communism.[11]

Even as Kennedy spoke, plans were being made for a United States–backed invasion of Cuba that would oust Fidel Castro's revolutionaries. But the Bay of Pigs invasion would be an unmitigated disaster for the young president. With the ensuing U.S. program to isolate Cuba economically and diplomatically, Castro established closer relations with the Soviet Union, and when U.S. intelligence reported the installation of nuclear missiles in Cuba, the Cold War reached its zenith. In issuing an ultimatum that the missiles be withdrawn, President Kennedy indicated to an alarmed public that the threat from Soviet communism, through Cuban surrogates, was so serious that armed conflict might be imminent.

The Cuban Missile Crisis of October 1962 pushed the world to the brink of a conflict that might have culminated in a nuclear exchange. In North Carolina and other states, the potential for nuclear war was felt in preparedness drills that had schoolchildren crouching under desks and in halls to avoid shattering glass and the concussion of bombs. While the children often viewed the excitement as a strange form of play, their parents and teachers were confronted with the stark reality of the Cold War. The October events reinforced a fear of communism even as they offered a new sense this ideological rivalry could bring mutual annihilation. The crisis provided only one theater in which Kennedy called for militant vigilance against communism. It was not ironic that even as the speaker ban was being rushed into law, the president was emphasizing the confrontational character of anticommunism. On June 26, the day that the North Carolina anticommunist speaker law was enrolled, JFK visited the Berlin Wall, the foremost symbol of the confrontation with the communists.

The ideological ferment unleashed by the Kennedy administration's commitment to the Cold War coincided with a pivotal movement in the history of the United States: the collapse of the Jim Crow system. The critical developments that insured the success of the civil rights movement in ending de jure segregation and establishing the principle of civil equality occurred during the spring of 1963. In May came the Birmingham debacle as the pugnacious Bull Connor turned fire hoses and police dogs on children protesting racial inequality. With the viciousness of the segregation system exposed, a major political transformation took place as the world noticed. Jim Crow was ideologically and politically moribund. And the linkages to Cold War politics made segregation all the more expendable. The images of Birmingham were broadcast to the world, and propaganda from Moscow and Beijing made the most of the opportunity. Their message to the peoples of Asia, Africa, and Latin America was clear: how can the United States support your freedom and development while treating its own nonwhite citizens so badly? Segregation had become a major Cold War liability, and now, with the specter of domestic violence, Kennedy moved ever closer to swinging the full weight of federal authority behind racial equality in law.

The denouement was provided in early June, when the self-proclaimed leader of southern resistance to desegregation, Alabama Governor George C. Wallace, made his "stand in the schoolhouse door," refusing to accommodate the court-ordered enrollment of James Hood and Vivian Malone at the University of Alabama.[12]

In responding to Wallace's challenge from Tuscaloosa, President Kennedy proclaimed the moral incompatibility of racial inequality with American ideals. Placing the authority of the federal government behind the dismantling of segregation and de jure discrimination, Kennedy's act signaled the death knell of the Jim Crow system. The president's endorsement of a broad civil rights bill meant the end of an era that had governed southern race relations in the twentieth century.[13]

As segregation entered its death throes in the spring of 1963, defenders of the old order increasingly defined the social chaos and change that seemed inexorable as communist inspired. In Alabama, Wallace blamed the Birmingham demonstrations on communists. And the message resonated in listeners' ears. In every southern state, billboards posted by the John Birch Society showed a notorious photograph of Dr. Martin Luther King Jr. captioned "King at Communist Training School." The charge that communists were behind the civil rights movement received additional credibility from the nation's leading law enforcement official, Federal Bureau of Investigation Director J. Edgar Hoover, whose suspicions of King's political affiliations were also well known. The consequences were predictable: in the words of one historian, "No wonder a healthy minority of white Americans, north and south, believed that the Communist Party played a major role in fomenting civil rights disturbances.[14]

Communism was a nebulous entity for most Americans, who never encountered communists or understood communism as a political critique of capitalism. But for many, communism was a clear and present danger. And the events of 1962 and the spring of 1963 seemed to confirm that the profound social changes taking place exemplified a communist agenda. The forceful actions of the federal government in implementing desegregation seemed consistent with a particular understanding of what constituted communism: an omnipotent, central government. Thus, the Kennedy administration's declaration of support for sweeping social change in the form of desegregation and racial equality struck a responsive chord in this regard. The challenge or threat was external; it was coming from Washington. This perception resonated with a particular understanding of communism; it was, whatever its manifestations, a foreign intrusion into otherwise placid social relations. Such an understanding of communism and communists was remarkably synonymous with a regional myth of what was behind the civil rights demonstrations: "outside agitators" were responsible, and as segregation withered under the weight of civil rights protest and increasing federal pressure, the "outside agitators" were increasingly defined as communists.

The actions of the central state within the context of race relations and desegregation were not the only areas where a popular conception of communism was invoked. For many, communism represented atheism—that is, the threat posed to a Christian nation by a godless doctrine. This assumption was reinforced in 1962 and 1963 by another branch of the federal government, the Supreme Court. The federal courts, led by Chief Justice Earl Warren, had come under withering criticism and condemnation for their rulings in numerous segregation cases. But decisions by the Warren Court in several cases involving the establishment of religion were no less alarming to cultural conservatives, especially those in the southern Bible Belt. In 1962, in *Engel v. Vitale*, the Warren Court had declared unconstitutional a requirement by the New York State Board of Regents that sanctioned prayer in public school classrooms. In May 1963, at the time of segregation's deepest crisis, the Supreme Court, in *School District of Abingdon Township v. Schempp*, prohibited Bible reading in public classrooms. In many quarters of the South, the decision was met with shock and then derision. From such a perspective, the meaning of the Court's action was simple: God and religion were being driven from public life and supplanted by a secular, irreligious atheism. As the most visible and voluble spokesman for the embattled segregationists, Wallace provided the strongest condemnation: The "chief, if not the only, beneficiaries of the present court's constitutional rulings have been duly and lawfully convicted criminals, communists, atheists and clients of the NAACP." The *Abingdon* decision, in Wallace's view, provided the capper. The Supreme Court was now "ruling against God."[15]

Developments occurring internationally, in Washington, and elsewhere in the South were critical in providing a context of culture and politics that informed the origins and meaning of the anticommunist speaker control law in North Carolina. In particular, Senate President Stone was a devoted admirer of Governor Wallace, exchanging letters of support and encouragement with the Alabamian. In early July, scarcely a week following the enactment of the speaker law, Stone met Wallace at the centennial commemoration of the Battle of Gettysburg. But the speaker control law was not a result of concern with developments elsewhere. It was brought about by activities and memories specific to the political culture of North Carolina.

Stone had witnessed developments in the spring of 1963 that had left him badly frightened. Black demonstrators, with support from white collegians, had filled the streets of North Carolina's largest urban areas, pressing for an end to segregation. The residence of many legislators — the Sir Walter Hotel — had been picketed and partially occupied by black protesters demanding rooms. And the legislative building itself had been surrounded by the demonstrators. Concomitant with these developments, the record of the 1963 Senate under Stone's leadership saw few successes or accomplishments. With the session drawing to a close, Stone was determined to have a measure of revenge. The anticommunist law would become his political testament. The hegemony of white supremacy had reached its end, as signified by a frustrated and desperate act. "The train was coming," opponent Martin noted metaphorically, "and we were on the tracks. So we got run over." In the final act of his Assembly career, Stone's choice of legislative tactics demonstrated how the burgeoning civil rights movement and student protest had unraveled North Carolina's political culture.[16]

The opposition did, however, possess one final opportunity to block the controversial measure: the bill could be recalled before being enrolled into the General Statutes. However, this possibility was, at best, a long shot, requiring a two-thirds vote of the fifty-member Senate. The night of June 25, a group attempted to muster enough votes to effect recall, hoping to gain the support of Governor Terry Sanford. The Sanford administration was perceived as progressive and liberally oriented toward the state's institutions of higher learning. Sanford was himself a Chapel Hill product, a devotee of Graham's liberal vision. Sanford lieutenants had been instrumental in organizing opposition to the three states'-rights amendments when they entered the General Assembly. No one doubted that the governor and his closest aides adamantly opposed a bill that sought to quarantine an institution that represented their vision of the future.

On the night of June 25, several senators went to the nearby governor's mansion to enlist Sanford's support in persuading individual members to support recall. Though the governor was unable to veto Assembly action, the senators hoped that his moral authority would be sufficient to persuade the recalcitrant and the hesitant to recall the bill for further study. But Sanford refused to become involved, and the supplicants went away empty-handed. If the bill was going to be recalled, it would happen without the assistance of the governor of North Carolina.[17]

Sanford certainly recognized the law's potential to harm an institution that he revered as a vehicle of progressive change. It was ironic that the governor refused to oppose or take a public stand on a law attacking an institution with which he so strongly identified. Why did Sanford refuse to lend the prestige of his office to the recall effort? The question is significant because, to some extent, the bill was interpreted as a repudiation of Sanford's gubernatorial record by the conservative wing of the state Democratic Party. The governor's opponents were keenly sensitive to his weakening fealty to southern political traditions. Moreover, his adversaries were aware of his strong loyalty to his alma mater at Chapel Hill. In his initial statement claiming authorship of the bill, Eure had proudly declared, "we caught Terry unawares." This statement appeared to be a call to arms, as Eure assumed that the governor would be an implacable foe of such a restraint on the university.[18]

During the almost five-year life span of the speaker ban, Sanford failed to issue any public statement concerning the law's existence or effect, although state Democratic Party chairman Bert Bennett of Winston-Salem, a confidant and close supporter of Sanford, immediately criticized the law's potential for harm, and Bennett's statement was regarded as representing Sanford's view.[19] Despite the consensus of many observers that the episode animated the body politic of North Carolina unlike anything since the evolution controversy of the 1920s, Sanford remained mute, on the sidelines.

There is little doubt that Sanford opposed the law. In personal correspondence he emphasized his opposition as he attempted to remain noncommittal about its future: to a Massachusetts educator, he wrote, "I was out of town, and I am the only Governor in the country without the power of veto."[20] What, then, explains the glaring absence of involvement by the governor? As a lame-duck executive without the power of veto, Sanford could only rely on moral persuasion to oppose the law, and involvement would have entailed considerable risk: the Assembly was still in session, and Sanford did not want to antagonize a potentially vindictive Senate leadership that might use his opposition to wreak havoc on the pending legislative program that he favored. Sanford understood the negative ramifications of his intervention on the soon-to-be-called special session to redistrict the Senate. Proper redistricting would mean greater representation in the upper house for the urban constituencies of the largest Piedmont cities. Redistricting would empower legislators more sympathetic to a progressive agenda Sanford envisioned for state governance. This aspect of the governor's quandary possessed an impeccable logic: it was pointless to invest valuable political capital on an issue that would be difficult to win but that could produce disastrous consequences.

Another factor was his fear of the potential power of Red-baiting, anticommunist politics. One of Sanford's earliest campaigns had been the Willis Smith–Frank Porter Graham donnybrook of 1950, when Smith had overcome a substantial deficit in the first Democratic primary to win the nomination.[21] Although required to be formally neutral as an official in the Young Democrats, Sanford was an active Graham supporter. During the primary, Sanford witnessed the destruction of Graham's campaign, in part by charges that the former UNC president favored socialism and was irreparably tainted by involvement with communist-front organizations.

Even prior to the 1950 Senate race, Sanford had his own personal experience with anticommunist attempts to politically quarantine UNC. By 1949, the presence of a small contingent of communists, most notably Junius Scales and Hans Freistadt, prompted calls to clear up the question of UNC's relation to communist activity. The American Legion, through its local posts, responded with resolutions condemning communism and calling on the trustees to investigate "Communistic activities carried on at Chapel Hill."[22]

The legion's Red-purge activities reached their zenith in June 1949 at the state convention held in Raleigh. The legionnaires brought with them various resolutions related to the putative threat of communist subversion. Typical was the "Resolution Relative to Communistic Activities at the University of North Carolina," endorsed by American Legion Post 35 of Red Springs, a small town in southeastern Robeson County. The post members noted that press accounts confirmed the presence of communists at Chapel Hill. From this point the resolution moved swiftly from a demand for investigation to a call to "take any and all steps that are necessary to eradicate any and all activity, influence and/ or doctrine of the said Communist Party or any of its members or any other un-American group that may be found to be operating in or around the University of North Carolina at Chapel Hill."[23]

The resolution explicitly demonstrates how emphatic was the legion's obsession with communism, especially at Chapel Hill. There were communists present: they must be identified and eradicated. The legion proposal would have also required the trustees to mount a surveillance and "eradication" of those involved in certain activities off campus, apparently regardless of whether the participants had university connections.

As the legionnaires convened in Raleigh in late June 1949, a hodgepodge of proposals directed at UNC appeared before the Resolutions Committee.

The chairman of the committee was a young attorney and decorated veteran, Terry Sanford. Sanford and his committee confronted a difficult task: drafting a resolution sufficient to express effectively the membership's anticommunist credo but without punitive corollaries that might impair the reputation and function of UNC through a wild witch-hunt.

UNC officials were concerned that the legion might go beyond the trustees' anticommunist position. As a loyal alumnus reared under Graham's liberal influence, Sanford carefully orchestrated the resolution to read solely as the legion's desire to oppose communism in an "institution of learning." Furthermore, the resolution commended the trustees' formal anticommunist statement as a "positive approach to the presence of the spread of communism in our schools." [24]

The principal architect of the statement of the chancellor's position on communism and the university was elated. William Donald Carmichael, UNC's chief anticommunist watchdog, wrote a letter of effusive thanks on behalf of the administration. "We wanted to congratulate and thank you," said Carmichael, "for your very intelligent handling of the 'Communist Resolution' at the recent Legion Convention. Without loyal alumni and friends like you the University of North Carolina would not be the institution that it is today. God bless you." In this episode, occurring as the Cold War rapidly escalated, Sanford possessed the personal influence and administrative power to blunt the attacks on the university. As governor in 1963, Sanford's personal influence had waned following his identification with the Kennedy administration as it moved to embrace the goals of the civil rights movement. And without a veto, Sanford lacked the executive authority to nullify the speaker law. [25]

By 1950 Sanford had been personally exposed to the hysteria and demagoguery of anticommunism, witnessing its power and danger. But this alone could not explain his decision to avoid involvement with North Carolina's anticommunist moment as it occurred thirteen years later. The main reason for Sanford's silence at the outset of the speaker ban lay in his aspirations for higher office. Sanford had won plaudits around the nation for steering North Carolina through a difficult period of the civil rights struggle. Whatever the shortcomings of Sanford's record on civil rights and desegregation, the state refused to follow the path of resistance traversed by Mississippi and Alabama. Praising Sanford's leadership, some observers saw the "moderate" course navigated by the Tarheel State as a model for other states in the region. Equally significant was the continued prosperity and economic development enjoyed during Sanford's tenure. Sanford was feted and praised by prominent Democratic figures, who saw in him a rising star in the party. [26]

Despite rosy possibilities for the future, Terry Sanford's political career was at something of a crossroads in 1963. Unable to seek a second term as governor, his political vistas were focused on Washington, where the future — perhaps even the presidency itself—beckoned. Any aspirations for higher office, however, required broad-based support from within the state Democratic Party. Sanford had to steer a judicious middle path that avoided antagonizing the party's conservative wing. During the 1963 Assembly session, Sanford had refused to engage in any high-pressure tactics that might create lingering animosity. So eager was the governor to maintain sanguine relations with legislative leadership that the day following adjournment, despite the recent passage of the speaker ban, he called the term "one of the best, most progressive sessions in history." [27]

Sanford's rise to the governor's chair had been accomplished by winning support throughout the General Assembly. The Assembly was an essential power base that could not be ignored or alienated. To avoid disadvantaging his political future, Sanford decided to avoid the conflict engendered by the "Act to Regulate Visiting Speakers." The governor's only public comment was a passing note that the Assembly had begun taking "dangerous" actions during its last days.[28]

Even as he publicly ignored the speaker ban, Sanford sought to transform its repercussions into a possible political dividend for future campaigns. What remained vital to his ambitions was support from conservative elements within the state Democratic Party. He could be sure of support from the party's progressive, or nonconservative, element; there were no candidates of Sanford's stature who seemed as progressive and showed a legitimate chance of securing nomination. Accordingly, the governor's only response to the speaker ban was a curious letter of praise for Stone. In the aftermath of the law's passage, Stone was excoriated by the state's press for his quick-gaveled handling of the speaker bill and his subsequent rationale for its utility as a device for gagging politically active elements at Chapel Hill. This represented a political opportunity for Sanford, who quickly came to the aid of the embattled Senate president.

On December 6 the governor issued a statement entitled "A Word for Clarence Stone" in which Sanford declared that Stone had "been treated unfairly by the news media." The governor chastised the press for failing to report the numerous accomplishments of the soon-to-be-retiring Senate president. Among the items cited as evidence of Stone's statesmanship were his support for improved hospital facilities, better schools, highway safety, and higher faculty salaries at public colleges. Near the end of the statement, Sanford moved to cement his bond to Stone: "He has a most constructive record over the years. He has devoted much of his life to working for a better North Carolina. He is a warm-hearted, generous and kind man, extremely loyal to his friends. I like these qualities in a man and I like Clarence Stone. He has had far too much abuse." [29]

Nowhere in his effusive praise and defense did Sanford mention or allude to the primary reason why Stone had come under such withering criticism. Although one paragraph cited the 1963 session and praised Stone for providing "the necessary leadership to accomplish legislation which will continue to benefit North Carolina for many years," the statement lacked the slightest reference to the speaker ban law that Stone had rammed through the Senate. With his political antennae sensing the most propitious path out of a difficult situation, Sanford avoided the speaker ban issue while adroitly manipulating it for future political benefit. It was an impressive feat of political legerdemain. While the statement surprised the press, which was bewildered about its purpose, it brought praise from conservatives, just as it had been designed to do. Sanford received a number of letters of appreciation from eastern legislators for his public defense of Stone.[30]

Even Sanford critic Jesse Helms, the conservative editorialist at Raleigh's WRAL television, warmly commended the governor for his action and denied the press's contention that politics was behind the statement. "We prefer to believe," said Helms, "that the Governor was motivated by a sense of compassion and justice. And we admire him for it. Where is the politics? Governor Sanford and Senator Stone are not supporting the same candidate for Governor in next year's primary." On the surface, Helms's conclusion was indisputable: the governor was promoting protégé L. Richardson Preyer as his successor, while Stone was known to favor archsegregationist I. Beverly Lake. Still, such an explanation was badly flawed. The "politics" were more personal than those queried by the wily Helms. They involved the future ambitions of Sanford himself.[31]

On June 26, just hours before adjournment, Senator Hector McLean, a Robeson County banker and Sanford ally, moved to have House Bill 1395 recalled. By a standing vote, twenty-five senators voted "aye" on recalling the bill, thus indicating either opposition or reservations about it. Nineteen voted "no," indicating support or a refusal to renege on Stone's previous ruling. Despite a majority that favored reconsideration, the recall attempt narrowly fell short of the necessary two-thirds margin. With the same determination and swiftness that had characterized initial action on the bill, Stone moved to finalize the matter. "The chair is going to ratify that bill," he muttered, "bring it up here." House Bill 1395 to "regulate visiting speakers" was going to become law, the only one of its kind in the United States.[32]

Following defeat of the recall attempt, several members rose on a point of personal privilege to speak against the bill. Senator Robert Lee Humber of Pitt County, who had been absent from the floor when the previous day's voice vote had been taken, called the issue "one of the most important that can face our body." He urged discussion to "ventilate" the issue.[33] Many members desired to go on record so that their personal opposition to a measure that abridged free speech would be recorded for posterity. After several speeches, a statement of opposition was presented to Stone for entry into the permanent record:

> We, the undersigned, for reasons hereinafter appearing, respectfully request that the Senate journal show on the question of the adoption of House Resolution #1395, relating to Communism and those who believe in, practice or advocate it, that we voted against the said Resolution.
>
> We believe that it constitutes an abridgment or denial of free speech, a lack of due regard for the true purpose and meaning of the University of North Carolina and other public educational institutions in the life of the State and nation, a denial of Constitutional privileges, and that in other respects it violates our long recognized and generally accepted political and social principles of this Country. [34]

The following day brought adjournment of the 1963 General Assembly of North Carolina. Its final statutory product, the repressive speaker ban, would stand paramount as the historical legacy of the term. The otherwise undistinguished session would be remembered for little but the controversial passage of a curious bill representative of the earlier McCarthy era that seemingly had bypassed the state.

How could such an illiberal, retrograde measure appear in a state whose reputation emphasized moderation and progress? In his magisterial rendering of regional politics in 1949, political scientist V. O. Key Jr. labeled North Carolina a "progressive plutocracy" moving toward an "approximation to national norms" of political behavior. Central to Key's description was the absence of racial demagoguery in public political life and the putative weakness of race as an organizational factor in legislative affairs. In sum, Key attributed the state's progressivism to Black Belt weakness and, more prominently, to the liberalizing influence of the university in Chapel Hill. Here, said Key, was a key source of exceptionalism: UNC "has become famed for academic freedom and tolerance." [35]

The most obvious explanation for the appearance of the measure is that it was a straightforward response to an actual communist presence. If such were the case, perhaps it would have provided sufficient concern to prompt lawmakers to consider a draconian clampdown at the universities. In the weeks preceding the introduction of House Bill 1395, however, the General Assembly had not discussed or expressed concern about communism. Some Assembly members undoubtedly believed that communism presented enough of a clear and present danger to warrant such legislation. But rational concern with an overt communist presence did not motivate those sponsoring the speaker ban. "Communism" was a multifaceted ideological expression that could be cynically manipulated for a variety of purposes. Despite such manipulation, however, there had to be some association, recent or historical, that would focus on the university.

The two realities necessary to suggest to lawmakers that communism might be at work in North Carolina were present. The first of these was Scales's highly publicized Smith Act prosecution during the previous decade. During the trials it was revealed that Scales, the scion of a prominent Greensboro family, had been introduced to and joined the Communist Party (CP) while a student at Chapel Hill. Subsequently, as CP chairman for the Carolinas, Scales had operated from the Chapel Hill–Carrboro area. The logic was simple: Chapel Hill had been CP headquarters, and UNC students had served as party officers. Significantly, Scales's name had recently resurfaced, reminding legislators and others of the CP era in Chapel Hill. On Christmas Eve 1962 President Kennedy commuted Scales's six-year sentence, but Helms condemned the decision and reminded listeners of the earlier CP presence at UNC. In early June, just weeks before the sudden appearance of the speaker ban bill, Helms again invoked Scales's name, this time in conjunction with UNC professors and civil rights demonstrations.[36]

The news of Scales's release coincided with public exposure of a Marxist-Leninist Progressive Labor (PL) Club at UNC. Ostensibly, this could have provided the grain of reality needed to perpetuate the symbolic crusade against communism. But after the American Legion's call for investigation in October, the furor subsided. The explanations offered by UNC Chancellor William Aycock and Governor Sanford appeared to mollify critics and preempt any legislative concern. There exists no evidence that the matter of the "Red nest" described in the legion proposal was ever discussed in the Assembly.[37]

Despite the apparent absence of any open legislative concern about a communist-oriented student group at UNC, it was still possible that individual legislators retained a desire to take some action that would suffice as an anti-communist gesture. At its annual convention held in Charlotte in late June, the state department of the American Legion had passed resolutions condemning the UNC Progressive Labor Club and calling on the legislature to prevent members of the CP or Nazi Party from speaking on state-supported campuses.[38]

The second resolution resonates with the thinking and language of House Bill 1395, which was enacted just four days following the legion meeting. This possible connection is enhanced by the fact that many legislators were also legionnaires. Moreover, a significant number held office in their local posts, thus signifying a higher level of involvement and suggesting an even greater possibility of an Assembly presence at the Charlotte convention. One example of such an Assembly involvement was the election of L. J. Phipps, a representative from Orange County, as the next state commander of the legion. Unfortunately, the authorship of the anticommunist resolution cannot be verified, but at least three of the eight cosponsors of the speaker ban were legionnaires. Representative Delamar, a primary sponsor of the speaker ban, was both a devoted legionnaire and a staunch anticommunist, believing that Huey Long and the inquisitive students in Delamar's Sunday school class were inspired by communists. Delamar was a Cold War–era true believer in the reality of the Red Menace and subversion. He was sensitive to any nuance fitting his understanding of communism and its apparent synonyms, socialism and "extreme liberalism." Delamar seems to present the best possibility of a conduit between the legion resolution and the speaker bill. However, none of the cosponsors of House Bill 1395, including Delamar, commented publicly during the Assembly session about either the Progressive Labor Club or a fear of CP influence at Chapel Hill. Even in the aftermath of the speaker ban's passage, no concern with student radicalism was cited, and the sponsors offered no evidence or belief that any CP figures had spoken on campus in recent years.[39]

While there is no direct evidence linking the issue of student radicalism to the passage of the speaker ban, such radicalism nevertheless played an important indirect role. Television editorialist Helms had championed the propriety of the legion resolution when it appeared and continued to raise the issue as a general critique of the liberal influences at UNC. Helms was appalled by UNC officials' seeming indifference to "people in Chapel Hill with remarkably curious connections, past and present, with organizations officially listed by our government as Communist fronts." In December, two months after the earliest legion proposal fizzled, Helms told his viewers that the university was patently sympathetic to the Left. "The University campus has welcomed this Fall just about every conceivable type of extreme leftwinger," Helms claimed as he cited appearances by PL national chairman Milton Rosen and folk singer Pete Seeger as evidence of a pro-Left bias. In early April, as the civil rights movement intensified in North Carolina, UNC again came under withering attack as Helms revisited the issues of PL and "communist activities" on campus. The editorialist demanded that the "questions ought to be *cleared* up — or the University *cleaned* up."[40]

On April 18, Helms fired another salvo at the university, this time for its inadequate zeal in prosecuting the "Cold War against communism." Again, Helms contended that the legion charge of communist infiltration at Chapel Hill warranted investigation. The following week, PL — in the person of Rosen — was invoked as synonymous with the communists. Although mention of Progressive Labor would not recur prior to the passage of the speaker ban, its abatement in no way exhausted the accusation that colleges in general — and

UNC in particular—were breeding grounds for communist subversion, as numerous "Viewpoint" commentaries emphasized or dealt exclusively with the issue.[41]

For Helms, communism in its many guises never sprang from indigenous sources; it could never be a product of American social and economic conditions. Helms routinely dismissed or derogated as silly and ignorant the political thinking and behavior of students, emphasizing instead the influence of an outsider such as Rosen, Gus Hall, or Seeger. In this manner, communism was cast in the symbolic imagery that was often used to explain civil rights protests: the "outside agitator" was responsible for the troubles.

Helms was especially concerned with and unstintingly hostile to the concept of academic freedom. While stressing the legitimacy of "true academic freedom," he argued that it was being exploited by liberal-leftist professors and, more prominently, as a screen behind which communist outsiders and other subversives penetrated the campus. According to Helms, college officials had the public responsibility to remain vigilant in preventing abuse of an otherwise noble concept by screening visiting speakers.[42]

Ever the keen observer of political currents on campuses across the nation, Helms located a kindred spirit and model administrator in the person of Ohio State University President Novice G. Fawcett. Helms praised Fawcett as "a man of courage and decisiveness" following his cancellation of a campus forum critical of HUAC. Fawcett justified his unilateral action on grounds that any call for the abolition of a congressional committee was wholly illegitimate. What so enamored Helms of the Ohio State president was his refusal to define academic freedom as an inviolably sacrosanct principle of campus activity: "Dr. Fawcett was simply taking the position that academic freedom does not create an obligation to provide a public forum for the expression of views of those who would destroy freedom. His position, as a leading educator, is both refreshing and encouraging."[43]

In this assessment, the ideological imperative that became manifest as the speaker control law can be glimpsed. Communism was the antithesis of "freedom," and it was immoral not to defend freedom. "Academic freedom does not create an obligation to provide a public forum" would metamorphose into "No college or university which receives any state funds in support thereof, shall permit any person to use the facilities of such college or university for speaking purposes." And there can be no doubt that Helms equated communists with "those who would destroy freedom."

The connection between Helms's analysis of Ohio developments and the eventual anticommunist law in North Carolina became more obvious in late June. Reminding his viewers of Fawcett's proscription of the "steady stream of Communist speakers appearing on his campus," Helms reported an even more promising turn of events emanating from the Buckeye State. In what was its initial public exposure in North Carolina, Helms noted, "The Ohio legislature is now in the process of passing a law upholding Dr. Fawcett. The Ohio House of Representatives, by a four-to-one margin, voted to forbid Communists and Communist-fronters from speaking at any state-supported college or university in the state. . . . Ohio State was being overrun with characters espousing the Communist line, and apparently the University's faculty and student body failed to exercise any responsibility in making certain the situation did not get out of hand. . . . This should give the people of Ohio some comfort."[44]

The concluding sentence of Helms's editorial carried a stern homily that resonated as a call to action: the Ohio bill "should also provide a lesson for the rest of us who have been too timid, or too disinterested, or both, to take a stand."[45] This editorial was televised just four days prior to the sudden appearance of House Bill 1395.

The association between PL and the genesis of the speaker ban was expressed in Helms's celebratory commentary two days after passage: "No one can say [UNC officials] did not ask for it. No one can say they were not given adequate warning of the doubts and fears spreading throughout the state regarding things taking place on our tax-supported campuses. . . . [W]hen the Chapel Hill American Legion Post expressed concern about certain leftist activities at the University last year, the Legionnaires were impolitely rebuffed and ignored by the two top officials of the University — and by the Governor of North Carolina."[46]

Despite Helms's repeated claims that the speaker ban resulted from an overweening public concern with communism at Chapel Hill, in the days and weeks preceding the bill's introduction there had been no legislative discussions concerning PL and, apart from the legion recommendations, little or no public discourse on the matter. The stealthy introduction and rapid passage suggest something less than a cascade of public interest in the radical rhetoric of a handful of UNC students. As an ideological symbol, PL might have aroused the ire of some Assembly members, but in the brief and desultory discussion immediately preceding and following passage, no mention was made of the UNC group.

What is far more likely is that the presence of the Progressive Labor Club was manipulated as part of a more general attack on the real target of the speaker ban, the University of North Carolina itself. And Helms's role in creating an association between UNC and unsavory cultural influences in the public mind cannot be minimized. From the inception of the "Viewpoint" editorials in 1960, Helms continually criticized Chapel Hill as excessively tolerant of belief and behavior that he contended most North Carolinians found offensive. As he gathered a large audience, particularly in the conservative areas of eastern North Carolina, his portrayals of various phenomena ranging from civil rights to foreign affairs to collegiate issues were often linked to a concern with communism. In this manner, Helms initially suggested that a speaker control law might be needed to prevent speakers such as PL leader Rosen from visiting the campus. In an April editorial sent to the trustees, Helms warned:

> No sensible person would favor a law forbidding the appearance of men like Milt Rosen and other Communists on our university campuses. But sensible University officials, on the other hand, will see to it that a balance is maintained. . . . Let us not be deceived: Where they are able, the Communists impose their ideology by force and terror. Where they cannot do this, they seek to destroy freedom through subversion, through espionage, through poisoning the intellectual climate and the educational system. . . . We should not kid ourselves. This is happening. Several weeks ago, the nation's Number One Communist — Gus Hall — spoke at Yale University, and according to newspaper accounts he addressed an overflow audience of students and faculty members. . . . So you see: our campuses *are* susceptible. [47]

Critics of UNC such as Helms did not truly believe that the university was itself radicalized or sympathetic to a communist agenda. Rather, Chapel Hill's reputation as a bastion of liberalism drew their ire. In Helms's eye, UNC stood guilty of propagation of "socio-economic views foreign to the American tradition." This criticism encompassed a panoply of issues from Keynesian economics to criticism of segregation to support for a more active federal government. Here was the real source of the umbrage leveled at Chapel Hill: a tax-supported institution was neglecting to impart conservative values and traditional social views. In this sense, the purpose of institutions of higher learning, especially those dependent on public funding, was to inculcate the known and accepted "facts" pertinent to a hegemonic sociopolitical order. At a time when the most fundamental of traditional social arrangements and values were coming under frontal assault, this was a matter of paramount significance. With collegiate youth providing many of the insurgents, university administrators had a special role in quelling campus activism. For Helms and for portions of his audience, UNC was a too-liberal source of political authority that did not represent the traditional values of the region and state.

For the university to operate effectively as a research and teaching institution, it had to be granted a safe distance from prevailing political pressures. This relative freedom from direct political control suggested the possibility for the requisite open space to formulate and nurture social criticism. And few understood the oppositional possibilities embodied within the relative autonomy of the university as well as Helms, and these possibilities were the source of his complaints when he criticized a permissive "academic freedom" at Chapel Hill and elsewhere. And despite his citation of inferences of communist influences at the UNC campus, the fundamental concern was the open, tolerant atmosphere that spawned liberal values and, for some, liberal politics. Helms saw UNC as a liberal monolith, with a campus culture exclusively devoted to such beliefs and causes. That the university was capable of broadcasting its liberalism as a wider political influence alarmed Helms: "We are not so much concerned about a silly bunch of kids who prate about their far-left Marxist beliefs, even to the absurd point of saying that Communism is too 'conservative' for them. . . . What worries us is the constant advocacies of increased federal powers, of centralization of government, of downgrading of capitalism and free enterprise originating with those wearing the mantle of intellectual respectability."[48] In this view, academicians were legitimating social and political alternatives perceived as patently false and in stark contrast to those values that informed the worldview of Helms and those to and for whom he spoke in his evening broadcasts.

Helms was not alone in believing that UNC should conform politically and busy itself with the reproduction of the hegemonic culture. An increasing number of legislators, industrialists, and civic leaders harbored suspicions that the institution was too liberal for the society that sponsored it. As defenders of existing cultural parameters, these individuals, as voices of political factions, tended to identify unsettling social changes with the historic liberalism or "extreme liberalism" that putatively characterized the mythic environment of UNC. One state official, addressing the tensions that underscored the speaker ban, explained "all this talk about race, liberalism, and communism has bred some doubts about the University, including doubts by some legislators."[49]

The talk of "race, liberalism, and communism" produced more than "doubt." For those who identified UNC as representative of the fearful developments they had witnessed and the setbacks they had experienced, these linkages produced an antagonism that gave rise to the vindictiveness contained within the speaker law. Influential business and civic leaders also expressed this sense of suspicion giving way to irritation. Charles Reynolds, a textile manufacturer and recent president of the North Carolina State University Alumni Association, commented, "There is not a question but that Chapel Hill has an extremely liberal image. This has been so for a long time. It bothers me in more ways than one. There are a lot of institutions [of higher education] in the country that have images as liberal that concern me too."[50]

The residual and current suspicions about UNC's "extreme liberalism" and its association with matters of race and communism found expression and flowered in the speaker ban. And as suggested by the jeremiads of Helms and the worried observations of state leaders, the seed had been germinating for decades. Without a long-standing antecedent belief that Chapel Hill represented threatening cultural and political values, it is doubtful that the statute would have been as authoritarian and draconian as its drafters apparently intended. When a coterie of state officials were subsequently asked to identify how the measure came about, they pointed to the historic image of Chapel Hill as a repository of nonconformist — that is, radical — thought and politics. Often mentioned was the iconoclastic presence of former President Frank Porter Graham: "This all goes all the way back to Frank Graham, who *is* a well-intended fellow. I think he *is*. I don't think he *is* a Communist, but a socialist."[51] This conjectural exegesis of Graham's political ideas suggests how a memory from the past, imprecise and vague in substance, could be summoned forth to explain the anticommunist impulse of the early 1960s. The continual usage of the present tense in conjunction with phenomena several decades past illustrates how a certain view of history might have become instrumental in forging a punitive statutory restraint against the university.

But whatever his influence in focusing critical attention on the school or identifying a useful statute in Ohio, Helms did not introduce and sponsor House Bill 1395. Similarly, whatever misgivings certain industrialists might have had about UNC's reputation for liberalism, there is no evidence that the legislators who brought the speaker ban bill to the Assembly floor on June 25, 1963, did so at the behest of any constituent or non–Assembly member. From whatever source they learned of the related Ohio bill, the political motivations propelling the act were their own. They were not attempting to make a grandiose ideological statement about communism; while profoundly anticommunist, they had little analytical awareness of communism as a doctrine of political economy. Instead, they were responding to empirical events, trying to gain some understanding of the political reversals and social changes they and their colleagues were witnessing, along with a good measure of retribution. Although the speaker ban reflected ideological obsession, its sudden appearance was the product of actual social phenomena taking place in North Carolina, the South, and the nation.

2 | Student Radicalism and the University

There was little doubt that the speaker ban law was targeted at the university in Chapel Hill. The university was witnessing a renewal of student political activism following the relative quiescence of the previous decade. And students were becoming involved in activities that aroused anger in many observers, including segregationists and other traditionalists within the General Assembly.

The irritants necessary for the speaker ban law were present at Chapel Hill during the 1963 Assembly session. The core political issue in North Carolina and the South was the future of segregation, and UNC students were visible opponents of Jim Crow. UNC students were also evident as rhetorical adherents of leftist politics that embraced socialist ideology. But the socialist Left was small in size, and the legislature largely ignored it. The issue of the threat to segregation could not be ignored, however, as racist ideology had provided much of the underpinnings of the state's political culture throughout the century. And the upsurge of campus political activism, simultaneous with the massive push of the civil rights movement in the state, reminded some critics of the historic racial liberalism associated with Chapel Hill. Segregationists and their allies saw the university as the emblematic source of the setbacks they had suffered following the *Brown* decision and related political challenges continuing into the 1960s.

When the University of North Carolina opened its doors in September 1962 for its 169th year, the days of late summer seemed routine compared to previous years. The 1962–63 academic year, however, would be like no other in the school's storied history. From the opening of the term, student politics at UNC achieved an intensity as a centerpiece of campus life. This activity had few precedents in the school's history. UNC students had been aroused by the shocks that accompanied the direct-action protests of the civil rights movement. By the fall of 1962, many southern college campuses, including those with virtually all-white student bodies, were familiar with the increasing activities aimed at eliminating racial segregation. The example provided by black collegians, first in North Carolina and then suddenly all over the South, aroused sympathetic white students to action. This pattern repeated itself at the University of North Carolina, where small groups of concerned students embraced the movement's agenda. As civil rights protesters geared for the decisive struggles against the bastions of Jim Crow in the Deep South, small groups of UNC students expressed their willingness to confront the moral injustice of segregation in North Carolina. Most of these students were motivated by religious principles or a sense of civic idealism that viewed racial separatism as inherently unchristian or in violation of hallowed American liberty. Other students, however, opposed segregation on the basis of political ideology. Each of these points of view would be reflected in the speaker ban's attempt to control campus political activity.[1]

At UNC, much of the political debate and posturing was conducted in the pages of the student newspaper, the *Daily Tar Heel*. From September through May, the pages of the *Tar Heel* were awash in polemic as individual students and campus groups staked out positions on a variety of issues. The principal concern was whether segregation—in North Carolina and throughout the South—would be dismantled. This debate was highlighted by the James Meredith case at the University of Mississippi, where federal marshals compelled a recalcitrant Governor Ross Barnett to permit the registration of the black student. The paper had almost daily coverage of the Meredith crisis. Some stories were taken from wire service accounts, but others came from *Daily Tar Heel* reporters who drove to Oxford to investigate conditions in the aftermath of the rioting on the night of September 30, 1962. Student reporters also traveled to Birmingham during the following spring to cover events there.[2]

Another issue, while increasingly subordinate to the first, was the threat of nuclear confrontation, which seemed closer than ever following the Cuban Missile Crisis of October 1962. The nuclear threat constituted another issue that contributed to the political atmosphere that engendered the anticommunist law. The possibility that Fidel Castro's Cuba would become a base for a possible Soviet nuclear strike against the United States elevated public anxiety and antipathy to the suddenly palpable threat of communism.

The enormity of such issues produced sharp differences and testy exchanges between both individuals and campus groups. While many of the debates were contained within the framework provided by traditional campus politics, such as the Young Democrats and Young Republicans, several new organizations with different agendas, rhetoric, and tactics had arisen. As the academic year proceeded, each constituency forwarded its views and programs and made plans to invite to campus speakers who represented their thinking on the issues of the day.

A common assumption held that the political environment at UNC was dominated by the Left and was generally inhospitable to more conservative opinion. This belief was a perennial staple for university critics, who emphasized the visibility of the more radical individuals and tendencies. Such allegations were wholly inconsistent with the realities of the political scene at UNC. The ideological posture and programmatic creed of campus groups spanned the political spectrum from Right to Left. Not only was there a significant conservative representation at UNC, but it was vocal, articulate, and completely unencumbered in the public expression of its opinions. Conservative groups and voices were well positioned and audible, and prominent conservatives such as William F. Buckley Jr. and Fulton Lewis III had recently appeared on campus as student-invited speakers. The relative equilibrium between conservative and liberal speakers largely reflected the campus political culture. Despite small groups of liberal students and professors who were displaying a nascent activism, the student body was politically conservative and locked in southern tradition. Dorm rooms displayed Confederate memorabilia, radicalism was anathema, and most students were indifferent to the civil rights movement. This state of relative inactivity belied the popular belief that the campus was a site of political agitation. Chapel Hill's storied reputation for Left-liberal activism rested largely on the highly visible activities of small groups and individuals. Despite this reality, the image of UNC as a haven for radicals was essential for the creation of the speaker ban.[3]

It is ironic that despite the General Assembly's obsessive fear of communist subversion, conservative political groups had a well-organized and large following at UNC. The most conspicuous conservative group was the Young Americans for Freedom (YAF), affiliated with the national group founded in 1960 on the Connecticut estate of William F. Buckley Jr. as a counterpoise to insurgent student groups on the Left, particularly Students for a Democratic Society (SDS). YAF's principal inclination was the promotion of patriotic values and service as a student auxiliary in what was termed the war against the forces of international communism. The national organization's positions included a studied indifference to integration, support for Mississippi Governor Barnett's appeal to states' rights in the Meredith case, advocacy of an international effort to blockade Cuba and depose Castro, and the endorsement of the "good conservatives" of the John Birch Society. When SDS produced an organizing manifesto in the form of the Port Huron Statement, the conservative students reacted by producing the September 1960 Sharon Statement, named for the Buckley estate located near the town of Sharon, Connecticut. Nationally, YAF had no separate agenda. In large part, it existed to confront the initiatives of student groups on the Left.[4]

At UNC the group's goals were somewhat modest. The president of the chapter, a law student from Queens, New York, stated succinctly the purposes of UNC YAF: "We've made a start toward denting the liberal conformity for which Chapel Hill has been noted. UNC is basically a conservative school. Liberalism is the work of a small self perpetuating clique who are on the downgrade."[5]

One associate wrote a regular column called "A View from the Hill" for the *Daily Tar Heel*. In it, Armistead Maupin Jr., the son of a prominent conservative attorney, railed against Red China, liberals, civil rights activists, and anyone else threatening the proper order of things on campus and in the state, nation, and world.[6]

During the year, YAF brought a number of conservatives to campus or supported their appearances following invitations from university lecture boards. YAF sponsored an appearance by HUAC researcher Fulton Lewis III and endorsed lectures by Buckley and Russell Kirk. While YAF was primarily a debating society, the group occasionally gave public expression to its views. The most noteworthy political activity undertaken in this regard was a ten-person picketing of a benefit concert given by folk singer Pete Seeger, who had been a target of the far Right for many years. YAF also participated in a march by several hundred students down Chapel Hill's Franklin Street during the Cuban Missile Crisis. Shouting "Rip 'em up, tear 'em up, give 'em hell, Jack," "Castrate Castro," "Cuba no, Yankee si," and "Hold that blockade," the students burned an effigy of the Cuban leader before marching several blocks through downtown. When the event threatened to turn into a panty raid on the women's dormitories, police moved in and ordered the marchers to disperse.[7]

The frivolity of the anti-Castro event and the paucity of support during the Seeger protest, however, did not mean that the group was without influence. The student conservatives were as firmly committed to their ideals as their more iconoclastic classmates. The greatest influence exerted by YAF, as with several other UNC political groups, was felt off campus. Occasional letters from those students turned up in the *Daily Tar Heel* but also found their way with far greater effectiveness into the hands of television commentator Jesse Helms, who promptly put their numerous allegations to use in his own attacks on the corrupting liberal influences at UNC. Since 1960, Helms had served as the editorial voice of Raleigh television station WRAL. Each evening he read a brief statement called "Viewpoint" on issues of the day. Helms gathered a substantial audience as he hurled invective against liberals, communists, and the civil rights movement. A constant target was the nation's colleges and universities, with the University of North Carolina singled out for particular scorn. Helms occasionally read over the air letters from UNC students who complained about some unconventional aspect of campus life or policy.[8]

Activism by the student Left at Chapel Hill ultimately contributed to the morass of suspicions and antipathies that found expression in the speaker ban. The most prominent group of leftist student activists was the Student Peace Union (SPU), affiliated with the national group first organized in the Chicago area in 1959. The founders of SPU were longtime peace activists concerned with nuclear proliferation and the threat of such a war between the superpowers. The organization enjoyed a wide but short-lived influence on many college campuses during the early 1960s. It had radical albeit strongly noncommunist ties with the Left through the involvement of members of the Young People's Socialist League (YPSL).[9]

The Chapel Hill SPU affiliate differed from the national body in two important ways. First, its interests quickly transcended the limited agenda of peace activism in favor of the more energized and promising civil rights movement. Second, the small UNC contingent held political positions that reflected its religious ideology. Its activism was inspired by the Christian beliefs and by the sense of social justice of its most committed members. By the early spring of 1963 SPU was instrumental in organizing the initial attempts to eliminate segregated facilities in Chapel Hill. Despite its liberal reputation, the home of the university retained a number of segregated restaurants and stores. There were sporadic efforts to integrate restaurants and theaters following the 1960 sit-ins in Greensboro, but many establishments continued to bar black patrons. This prohibition would become the principal organizing issue for UNC's SPU.[10]

The Student Peace Union emerged at UNC largely through the efforts of two students from remarkably different backgrounds. The most visible member was Pat Cusick, an Air Force veteran from Gadsden, Alabama. Considerably older than most undergraduates, Cusick came from a family steeped in southern tradition and the memories of the Confederate past. Only after separating himself from direct familial influences, first at a private boarding school and then at Belmont Abbey College in North Carolina, did he begin to question the morality of racial segregation. On arriving in Chapel Hill in the fall of 1961, Cusick was psychologically prepared to engage in civil disobedience. He participated in several of the early efforts to challenge segregation, but when they produced no immediate results, he began to look around for stronger affiliations. In December 1961 Cusick applied for a local charter from the SPU.[11]

One of the charter members was John Dunne, a second-year student from Brecksville, Ohio. Recipient of a prestigious Morehead Scholarship and without any previous record as a social dissenter, Dunne seemed as unlikely to risk his future in civil disobedience as did Cusick, the scion of a white southern family. As a high school senior Dunne had been voted the "straightest arrow," an award given to the class member who disobeyed the fewest rules.[12]

The lives of Cusick and Dunne, however, would become tightly linked as their fledgling group began to attract members and to give visible expression to their convictions. Even as their concerns emphasized opposition to segregation, there were signs of growing political sophistication. The students began to establish linkages between freedom and oppression in their own society and elsewhere.[13]

In October 1963 SPU organized a campus protest against the impending U.S. visit of Madame Ngo Diem Nhu, the first lady of South Vietnam and sister-in-law of South Vietnamese President Ngo Dinh Diem. The UNC students were emphatic in their condemnation of the Diem government. Dunne, now acting as the campus chairman of SPU, issued a statement declaring, "We contend that the U.S. should withdraw all aid to the Diem regime; the United Nations should then be authorized to administer all economic aid to the peoples of both North and South Vietnam, and to hold free elections to determine the governments of both countries. We strongly urge all those who oppose U.S. support for this tyrannical dictatorship to join with us in protest."[14]

The protest was a part of a national effort organized to oppose continued U.S. economic and military support for the Diem regime. When Madame Nhu arrived at a scheduled appearance in Raleigh, she was greeted by several dozen protesters, chiefly students from Chapel Hill. The action by the UNC contingent became one of the first organized antiwar protests by college students during the Vietnam era.

The peace activists at Chapel Hill did not formally join the national SPU until December 1962. Before that time the small contingent, while in sympathy with the national group, steered clear of engagement with larger entities. In explaining the move, Cusick noted the advantages of being part of a more visible organization that already possessed national recognition: "The reason we had not planned to become a chapter originally was due to the financial burden it would place on our young chapter. However, the national told us they would not charge full dues until we become [sic] fully established." Cusick went on to recite the availability of speakers, films, and the "enhanced publicity" that could be obtained through formal SPU affiliation.[15]

In addition to these advantages, a more pressing concern militated in favor of SPU affiliation. Cusick acknowledged that his group sought to protect itself from any allegations that it was associated with other more radical groups that had recently been cast in the state's political spotlight: "We have already been the subject of criticism by some students who think we are associated with other campus groups that have been under fire recently. Because we are in no way connected with any other campus group, we think that affiliating with a national organization will exempt us from this undue slander." [16]

Cusick was referring to the New Left Club and the Progressive Labor group that had emerged during the previous year; SPU was staunchly anticommunist and took every precaution to distance itself from the dreaded communists. The declaration was illustrative of the continuing vitality of anticommunist impulses within the political culture. Despite an agenda that was, in numerous ways, implicitly radical, SPU's priority was to eliminate any suggestions of communist or radical influences. In renouncing any association with the New Left, Cusick emphasized the plurality of his group's membership; he sought to ensconce the movement within the acceptable parameters of American political culture. Cusick closed the interview with a statement intended to differentiate the SPU from the more ideologically conscious factions but also to anesthetize potential hostility from suspicious students and a public that had once again been told that the campus was harboring subversive elements: "The statement of purpose of the SPU does not bind any members to a specific policy and in our chapter the members have many different opinions and often agree only in that they are for peace and against war." [17]

By the spring of 1963, SPU had transformed its entire agenda into a crusade to abolish the practice of racial segregation in Chapel Hill. On March 17 the organization issued a manifest of its egalitarian principles entitled "A Resolution of the UNC Chapter of the Student Peace Union." The document's opening remarks indicated Cusick and Dunne's growing sophistication, especially with regard to their ability to identify a linkage between the problems of securing world peace and the reality of the violence of racial subordination at home: "The problems of world peace and the problems of civil rights and human freedom are not separate. They are both a part of our concern for the human community as a whole. . . . The continuation of racial discrimination in this community is an intolerable insult to the spirit of a free university and to the fundamental precepts of human freedom and dignity." [18]

The document then resolved to boycott a list of thirteen Chapel Hill establishments that practiced discrimination and promised to picket continuously those that refused to enter into negotiations. On April 15, SPU began a boycott of the College Cafe on Franklin Street. The protest began with a small handful of silent picketers who faced the occasional taunts of townspeople. The

SPU campaign took hold, however, and quickly expanded into a concerted effort to eliminate segregation in restaurants as well as UNC's North Carolina Memorial Hospital.[19]

A major ingredient in the reorientation of SPU to an antisegregation agenda was its linkages to black student groups in the Durham–Chapel Hill area that sought to expose the violent character of segregation. This association resulted in white liberal students being brought into an effective coalition with black students from area colleges and larger organizations such as the National Association for the Advancement of Colored People (NAACP) and Congress of Racial Equality (CORE) leading to the formation of the Committee for Open Business (COB). By the summer of 1963, COB and CORE would be responsible for organizing dozens of demonstrations aimed at desegregating downtown Chapel Hill. The protests gradually escalated until December 1963, when hundreds of people were arrested at sit-ins at Chapel Hill restaurants. Most of those arrested were students, and the protesters were an equal mix of blacks and whites.[20]

Dunne and Cusick, along with other members of SPU, participated in the protests. Dunne, now a CORE field-worker, was among those arrested. Dunne's conversion to direct-action protest had taken place the previous spring when he traveled to Birmingham as part of a UNC contingent to witness civil rights activists in the heartland of segregation. When the other students left Alabama to return to UNC, Dunne stayed behind and began an active role in the demonstrations. On May 11, while helping black parents locate their children who had been incarcerated during the Southern Christian Leadership Conference's children's campaign, Dunne was himself arrested and jailed. He spent several days in a cell with an ardent segregationist before being released on bond. Dunne was arraigned on charges of loitering and failure to obey the lawful command of a police officer and was subsequently found guilty of both charges, sentenced to a year in jail, and fined two hundred dollars. As his attorneys appealed the case, Dunne was set free on bail and returned to North Carolina.[21]

Dunne's Birmingham experience galvanized student opinion in Chapel Hill. Here was a student from a conservative background whose sense of moral duty compelled him to take up the cause of those he perceived as victimized by the violence of Jim Crow. Dunne's case quickly became a cause célèbre among the student body and propelled Chapel Hill's civil rights movement at a crucial juncture in its history. The *Daily Tar Heel* ran a series of stories on Dunne, his egalitarian idealism, and the Birmingham situation. On May 18 the student paper issued an editorial entitled "Concerning John Dunne" that praised Dunne while acknowledging that his actions might elicit retribution from the university's less idealistic and more traditional elements. The paper noted the rising surge of student activism: "[T]he leaders of our generation of war babies have new areas and methods of leadership. Instead of debating an issue in the Di-Phi [an ancient campus debating society], they act publicly on personal conviction. They believe this is the only kind of leadership which is significant today. . . . One need not agree with Dunne in all of his beliefs to respect and admire him for the conviction and sincerity with which these beliefs are converted into active expression." [22]

The editorial's tone was muted, however, with an inordinate concern that the members of the university's Morehead Foundation would rescind the scholarship that had brought Dunne to campus. This concern recognized the implicit radicalism of involvement by white students in the antisegregation movement. Prior to his arrival at Chapel Hill, Dunne had been completely immersed in the kind of rigorous intellectual pursuits required for consideration for such prestigious awards as the Morehead Scholarship. His brief stay at UNC, coinciding as it did with the accelerating commitment to civil rights, transformed Dunne from a Christian pacifist to a social activist. The members of the Morehead Committee had not had such transformative experiences; they remained steeped in the segregationist logic and traditions of the region. News that a Morehead scholar had been arrested as a civil rights "agitator" would provoke almost certain outrage among these traditionalists. [23]

The *Tar Heel* editorial astutely recognized the perilous contradictions in this episode and sought to win over the Morehead Committee as it praised Dunne's convictions: "There is often tension and misunderstanding when members of the 'older generation' fail to recognize leadership in actions they consider immature or irresponsible. This is an area where there should be more conversations." The student organ decried any action that might be taken against Dunne, saying such sanctions would make a "hollow mockery" of the leadership capacities that the foundation was created to identify and nurture through its financial support. [24]

The concern that the Morehead Committee would respond negatively was not an idle threat. Many of the Morehead scholars visited John L. Morehead, the foundation's president, and left convinced that there was a "strong possibility" that Dunne would be stripped of the prestigious scholarship. The Morehead students mobilized to defend one of their own, and dozens of UNC students and faculty felt sufficiently concerned by the possibility that they wrote letters and made telephone calls in Dunne's behalf. [25]

When Dunne returned to Chapel Hill, he was placed under the careful protection of campus authorities desirous of preventing retribution from those taking offense at the student's sojourn to Birmingham. Within a few days, the furor had subsided. In a letter to Dunne's mother, UNC Dean Charles Henderson expressed the administration's wishes: "I hope that the whole business will die down, and though I cannot say so with any authority whatsoever, I very much doubt that the Morehead Foundation will take any action." [26]

While the Alabama incident did "die down," it served to spur the Chapel Hill civil rights campaign to greater militancy. The COB gave way to Citizens United for Racial Equality and Dignity and was joined by the NAACP and CORE. By early 1964 the student government at UNC went on record endorsing student boycotts of all establishments practicing segregation. In February the civil rights coalition, now joined by the Student Nonviolent Coordinating Committee (SNCC) and the Southern Christian Leadership Conference (SCLC), began to block downtown intersections, resulting in dozens of arrests. [27]

Now under the umbrella of the Chapel Hill Freedom Committee, SPU was thoroughly immersed in and at the forefront of the local antisegregation movement. Cusick and Dunne were among fourteen members of the Freedom Committee arrested in conjunction with sit-ins and civil rights demonstrations around Chapel Hill. In April 1964 Dunne and Cusick, along with several others, were sentenced to one-year prison terms for their roles in the challenge to segregation in Chapel Hill. [28]

The tiny core of civil rights activists had come a long distance since the SPU's inception in 1962. Although suffering personal violence and incarceration, they had aroused the consciousness of UNC liberals. The activists had also served notice that the university was once again a locus of political forces that could challenge the state's conservative political culture, especially with regard to Jim Crow. The SPU's activities at UNC and the budding civil rights movement in Chapel Hill were not directly responsible for the draconian measure passed by the General Assembly in June 1963. But these activities were nevertheless essential in that they linked the university in the collective mind with an assault on the cardinal tenet of political life and behavior in North Carolina since the turn of the century, white supremacy. [29]

The UNC civil rights activists were more than a negative symbol to race-conscious traditionalists in the General Assembly. The students and several professors from Chapel Hill had become highly visible figures in Raleigh during the 1963 legislative session. The conspicuous white students caught the attention of angry and confused legislators who watched the nightly processions of demonstrations in the streets of the capital. Before the term had expired, Assembly conservatives would use the incidents to inflict punitive measures on the institution that represented subversion. Student radicalism, circa 1963, provided an essential dynamic for the fears that culminated in the effort to silence the university.

Since the Red Scare hysteria of the early 1950s, student leftist activism had all but disappeared from Chapel Hill. In this sense, the abeyance of UNC radicalism during the 1950s had closely mirrored the retrenchment and with-drawal from active political life of thousands of people across the country in response to the terror of the anticommunist crusade.[30] Following the publicity and harassment that accompanied former student Junius Scales's 1954 Smith Act arrest and subsequent trial and imprisonment, there was no political space for the Left at Chapel Hill between 1954 and 1960.[31]

Early in 1960 two developments established the necessary preconditions for a revitalized political climate at UNC. The first of these was the lunch counter sit-ins. As black students challenged the dominant political culture, they set an example of principled political activism. In the process, the climate of re-pression that characterized the previous decade was giving way to a democratic renewal that would find students at its forefront.[32]

The second and equally compelling development that resonated on numer-ous college campuses was the open repudiation of the House Un-American Activities Committee (HUAC) in May as it attempted to hold hearings on alleged communist activities in the San Francisco area. When HUAC con-vened, it was met by hundreds of demonstrators who came to protest the threat to political liberty that the committee represented. Although the protesters were treated rudely by police, the action galvanized opposition to the kind of congressional authority that had symbolized the repression of the previous de-cade. Before the 1960s ended, HUAC would become the object of intense criticism from civil libertarians.[33]

The sit-ins and the direct challenge to HUAC's role renewed political op-portunities at UNC. In their aftermath came the reemergence of a student Left on the campus. By the fall of 1962 there were two left-wing political organizations. Unlike earlier periods, however, neither group was aligned with the Communist Party. The first such group to appear was a New Left Club. Formed in 1960, "in response to a lamentable lack of political debate on cam-pus," the group comprised largely graduate students and junior faculty inter-ested in discussing contemporary political and philosophical issues.[34]

The New Left contingent received little attention or interest until the spring of 1962. It included approximately fifteen to twenty participants who met occasionally to discuss the meaning of domestic and international affairs. There quickly emerged important lines of cleavage between those favoring a less ideological New Left approach and other students interested in Marxism-Leninism. The tensions led to the dissolution of the club during the spring of 1962, but it was restarted in the fall. The club welcomed any interested parties to its meetings but expressed a special affinity for those considering themselves "to the left of Kennedy." The New Left Club eschewed sectarianism and sharp ideological focus. Instead, its activities were primarily educational and at-tracted a number of students interested in its intellectual orientation.[35]

The club's principal activities during the 1962–63 year consisted of a series of seminars, moderated by a law student, on Marxism, political economy, and problems of Third World development. In December, the New Left Club sponsored Seeger's concert, with the proceeds going to support SNCC's work. The concert drew more than a thousand persons, an impressive figure considering that the student body numbered fewer than ten thousand and that the event took place on the same night as an intercollegiate basketball game in the campus gym.[36]

That partisans of the New Left Club entertained radical notions with regard to the relationship between capitalism and various social and political situations, both at home and abroad, was undeniable. Such activities, however, elicited little attention as a palpable threat to principles on which the political culture rested. There were two reasons why such was the case. The first was that the New Left Club confined itself to matters that were largely intellectual — discussion groups and the like — and were therefore apparently consistent with the university's intended work. Second, the club confined its activities to the campus. Unlike the Student Peace Union, whose members traveled to Alabama and to Raleigh to challenge the strictures of racial discrimination, the New Left Club, although engaged in more radical thought, never crossed Franklin Street, the symbolic campus boundary. Its presence, however, was felt as publicity about its existence slowly filtered into public consciousness.[37]

The New Left Club's most important contribution to the reemergence of an active radicalism at UNC was its role in spawning a militant and ideologically driven cadre of students on the Left. This contingent consisted of perhaps ten persons, with the articulation of their political outlook provided by three students who would become the most visible components of the latest variant of UNC radicalism.[38]

By the spring of 1962, three core members of the New Left Club, Dennis King, Larry Phelps, and Nicholas Bateson, had grown disenchanted with the limitations of political discussion. They had become interested in a Marxist-Leninist politics emphasizing militant action. The problem was the absence of a vehicle in North Carolina for expression of such sentiments. A series of fortuitous developments in New York provided the Chapel Hill coterie with the affiliation that they were seeking. In 1962 a split had occurred in the Communist Party-USA (CPUSA). A more militant faction, calling itself the Progressive Labor Movement, broke away and began to call for support from those disenchanted with the quiescence of the CP in the face of a rising tide of social revolution around the world and the radical possibilities of black liberation in the United States.[39]

Led by Milton Rosen and Mortimer Scheer, PL borrowed heavily from the revolutionary program of Mao Tse-tung and the Chinese Communist Party.

Primacy was given to direct political action, with the purpose of mobilizing the urban working classes, especially the untapped reservoir of the black proletariat. In this sense, PL carefully modeled a strategy that could identify with the revolutionary fervor occurring in Asia, Africa, and Latin America as insurgent movements sought to topple regimes supported by Western governments. The emphasis on active political organizing among the most oppressed and exploited social classes appealed to a number of students, and PL made quick inroads on northern college campuses. PL eventually commanded a dominating position within SDS, largely by means of PL's ideological discipline within a larger movement bereft of such direction. As the movement developed into a party and dramatically increased its influence in the late 1960s and early 1970s, college students, radicalized by Vietnam, provided its most essential constituency and membership.[40]

Progressive Labor emerged from the factional disputes among the radical intelligentsia of the East Coast, particularly New York and Boston. Most of its organizational attention, like many other leftist parties, was directed at the northern working classes. Southern and rural workers were often considered politically backward, if not reactionary, and thus unlikely to be melded into a movement devoted to promoting social revolution. But two PL figures, Jacob "Jake" Rosen and Fred Jerome, strenuously argued against any strategy that devalued the potential role of southern workers. For Rosen, southern workers, black and white, were the linchpin of socialist revolution in the United States. Rosen thought that the most hideous contradictions of capitalist society were exposed in the South.[41]

Determined to demonstrate the possibilities of a southern strategy, Rosen went to North Carolina and began to familiarize himself with southern conditions. Once there, he took a job writing under the name "Jack Rose" for a local newspaper. By some means, possibly a story in the *Daily Tar Heel*, Rosen learned of the New Left Club at Chapel Hill and began appearing on campus, where he attended at least one of the club's meetings. After the meeting, a few of the members who considered themselves Marxists took Rosen to a Franklin Street bar, where they talked in detail about socialist politics.[42]

The students, idealistic and naive, were duly impressed with the New Yorker's grasp of issues and his level of political sophistication. Rosen had great influence on the students. Warning them on their "sectarian manners," he talked at length about the radical possibilities of effective mobilization in the South. The students were convinced that "this was the thing they had been looking for."[43]

In July 1962 the formal inception of the Progressive Labor Movement took place at the Hotel Diplomat in New York. Among the more than fifty delegates was a six-person contingent of UNC students. The conference called for the development of "a significant Marxist-Leninist program for a new party." Milton Rosen, the editor of *Progressive Labor* magazine, provided the plenary remarks for the session. His commentary illuminated the strength of the PL's identification with Third World revolutionary movements and the culpability of American capitalists and political leaders in perpetuating an imperial order: "The new world relationship of power favoring socialism, national and colonial liberation, and peace, has not fundamentally altered the basic characteristics of U.S. imperialism. [The Kennedy Administration is] the most dangerous clique that the ruling class has installed in government to date. Kennedy has shown himself willing to use every form of political ruthlessness to serve monopoly capital."[44]

The UNC cadre returned to Chapel Hill and began plans to organize the Progressive Labor Club (PLC). By August the new organization had taken shape. Its announced purpose was "developing a truly revolutionary national party based on improving the condition of the workers along Marxist-Leninist lines." The leaders of the fledgling group were King, Phelps, and Bateson. King, a history student, was the son of a high-ranking UNC administrator. Although influenced by the Beats, King possessed no conscious ideology on entering UNC and had spent much of his youth in a Methodist youth group. King eventually migrated to New York, where he reactivated his involvement with PL. He remained with the group until 1975, when he left because he "no longer believed in Marxism-Leninism." Larry Phelps, from Burlington, North Carolina, was also a history student. When he arrived at Chapel Hill, Phelps had brought no radicalism with him. In his freshman year he was a Free-Will Baptist. As he attended sessions of the campus debating society, he began thinking about a socialism that reflected the Social Gospel type of Christianity that had been a staple of his precollege experience. After graduation from UNC, Phelps accompanied a PL-sponsored delegation to Cuba in the late spring and early summer of 1963, in defiance of U.S. State Department restrictions. He eventually moved to New York, where he worked as an organizer out of PL headquarters in Harlem.[45]

While King and Phelps were North Carolina natives and without self-conscious political identities before arriving at UNC, Bateson was neither a native nor a political neophyte. A graduate student in psychology, he was the son of F. W. Bateson, an Oxford literary critic and left-wing Labour intellectual. After taking a degree at Oxford, Nick Bateson came to the United States in 1958 and worked for a year in the Yale University library before migrating south to UNC. Since 1960 Bateson had been engaged in graduate study while working as a research assistant in psychology. Well-versed in Marxist ideology, he was articulate and rhetorically forceful in a manner that made him an obvious spokesperson for the small band of radicals.[46]

The initial report of a Marxist-Leninist group in Chapel Hill failed to elicit critical attention, possibly as a result of the absence of a sufficient campus audience during the summer months. The publicity did draw the attention of UNC officials, including President William C. Friday. The administration's response was to minimize the activity as unrepresentative of the "excellent judgment" of most students. More important, the officials emphasized that PLC was not an official part of the university.[47]

With the beginning of the fall semester, PLC quickly became a subject of concern for both right-wing critics outside the university and for the UNC administration. The *Daily Tar Heel* published a story detailing PL's emergence from the New Left Club and noted the new group's Marxist-Leninist orientation. Bateson highlighted PL's direct-action tendency: "The purpose of the Progressive Labor Club is to act politically in an open and above board manner." When asked the all but inevitable question of PL's relationship with the CP, Bateson provided a surprising response. He disclaimed any affiliation between himself and the PL membership with the CP. His statement, however, was not predicated on a fear of being labeled a communist but on a repudiation of the political inertia that characterized the older group: "We don't object because they are communists, but because they are a bureaucratic organization, and because they are an organization that has made very few attempts to make meaningful contacts with the American people as a whole. Another reason is that it is sort of a corrupt organization. There are fewer than 2,000 members in America now. The leaders are reported to live at a degree of opulence incompatible with the ideals of socialism. The Communist Party hasn't been subversive, it's just been lazy."[48]

In distancing his group from the CP, Bateson stressed the democratic values by which PLC operated and how this belief was antithetical to the anti-democracy found throughout the United States: "We believe that the U.S. is a very anti-democratic nation. No true democracy can exist where there is any kind of economic anxiety." The PL spokesman articulated a program that stressed a planned frontal assault on racial separation and the low rate of unionization among the state's workforce: "Any union would have to be fully integrated before it could ever amount to anything. There must be some kind of unity among the workers. This basic disunity is harmful to both whites and Negroes."[49]

In publicizing its program of political work that emphasized unionization and racial integration, PL announced its intention to use the university as an organizational base from which to mount an assault on the entrenched social and political structures of American capital. In identifying integration and unionization as their foremost objectives, the young leftists challenged two of the underpinnings of southern political culture.

Such a declaration not only tested the parameters of legitimate political discourse but also called into question an implicit compact between the university and society at large. While heated rhetoric might be tolerated, the use of public facilities as a sanctuary from which to organize political action inimical to prevailing values was surely questionable. Such was especially the case as the hegemonic principle of racial segregation came under attack. Since the late 1950s and accelerating after 1960, the role of UNC liberalism in supporting more egalitarian race relations in the state had drawn sharp criticism from revanchist political figures, most recently from segregationist gubernatorial candidate I. Beverly Lake Jr., who lost to moderate Terry Sanford in the 1960 Democratic gubernatorial primary.[50] PLC's rhetorical militancy was probably sufficient to set off alarm bells, but the insistence that its work, by necessity, had to extend beyond campus boundaries made a critical response all but inevitable as the fabric of long-standing political arrangements unraveled throughout the South.

A response was not long in coming. Within a matter of days following publication of Bateson's statement, District 16 of the state department of the American Legion endorsed a resolution introduced by its Chapel Hill affiliate calling for a legislative investigation "to determine to what extent, if any, Marxism has permeated the University." The resolution was sponsored by Colonel Henry E. Royall, a retired army officer residing in Chapel Hill. Royall, the chairman of his post's Americanism Committee, had been a frequent visitor to the meetings of the New Left Club, where the students received his presence with an air of amused indifference.[51]

Royall was particularly concerned by the prospect of a growing militancy at UNC as he perceived a different orientation by PL. Unlike other campus activists, he noted that PLC members were ideologically driven by principles that were explicitly antagonistic toward American institutions. Although the legion proposal identified PLC as a likely target, it highlighted the more general contaminant of Marxism. This concern suggested that the university itself was culpable and had been insufficiently vigilant in preventing subversive tendencies from taking hold. In suggesting a core problem, the legion assault adroitly circumvented the students and targeted the university itself as the source of the problem. It was the public responsibility of UNC administrators to ferret out and dispose of any campus activities that smacked of "subversion." In addition to the legion, Jesse Helms provided frequent and caustic allegations of insufficient administrative vigilance against radical activity at UNC.[52]

The legion's recommendation expressed the importance of historical continuity in asserting that the university remained a suspicious "Red nest." The resolution resonated with the themes of the McCarthy era, citing "the past activities of Hans Freistadt and his Marxist Club and of Communist Junius

Scales." The application of historical antecedent resurrected a belief that the institution was incapable of restraining radical expression and thus required more direct political oversight from legislative authorities. In calling for "remedial legislation . . . in order that freedom loving North Carolinians may be saved from a possible academic Frankenstein of their own creation," the legion maintained that it was now incumbent on the state legislature to investigate and, if need be, take steps to restore public confidence in the institution. "The University Trustees, the University administration and Faculty," asserted the resolution, "have not succeeded in removing the causes for the appellation 'Red Nest' often applied to our University. . . . [I]n order that the investigation be as objective as possible, no member of the Board of Trustees, Administration or Faculty [should] be placed on any committee charged with the investigation."[53]

The legion proposal unleashed a torrent of criticism both of the university and of the proposal itself. UNC Chancellor William Aycock issued a statement saying that he "had no evidence of any 'Communist Cell' on campus, or any 'Communist' student in the University." The choice of language was disingenuous. In using the capital C, Aycock attempted to direct the issue to the question of whether or not there were members of the Communist Party on campus. Through subtly redefining the issue, the chancellor could assert that the legionnaires' concerns were specious and that there were "no grounds to warrant an investigation." Aycock recited this explanation long after he became aware of PL radicalism, emphasizing his absence of knowledge of "any student or faculty who holds membership in the Communist Party." In choosing this defensive strategy, the UNC administration began a journey down a path that abandoned an unfettered defense of free political expression.[54]

The concern of the American Legion and of many of the individuals writing to Aycock was not communism but rather the possibility that Marxism had permeated the campus. Critics believed that radical ideology had received legitimacy from campus officials. Moreover, the veterans' allegations specifically mentioned PLC as emblematic of conditions that were ominous and perhaps subversive. Aycock was aware of the action-oriented agenda declared by PLC in its renunciation of the CP, and he knew of the rhetoric attributed to Bateson in the *Daily Tar Heel*. On the day Chancellor Aycock dismissed the legion's claims and refused their call for investigation, the press also called on Phelps to make a statement. When asked about possible linkages to the CP, the student vehemently denied any relationship, stating that PL was "more activist and further left." He then proceeded to call on the legislature to investigate fascist tendencies in the legion. Such pronouncements did little to authenticate Aycock's assessment or mollify the accusers.[55]

The chancellor did acknowledge the existence of a campus group affiliated with the "so-called Progressive Labor Movement" but again displayed a remarkable legerdemain in producing a rationale by which to discredit the call for investigation. He noted that PLC was not an "officially recognized" student organization and was therefore, in accordance with university polity, ineligible to use campus facilities and buildings. This tactic, although ostensibly in the service of defending the university from outside criticism, surprisingly prefigured the speaker ban's prohibition of selected categories of speakers. At this juncture, however, such a statement did not indicate a desire by administrators to silence student groups. It was primarily an effort to sidetrack critics and to absolve the administration of responsibility. The implication was that since the group lacked formal campus standing, the chancellor had no power to act.

This was a specious explanation that had at best only a technical application. Recognition as a campus organization was routinely granted pro forma by the selection of a faculty adviser. Most student groups, as noted in a response by the *Daily Tar Heel*, did not possess such mentors. The New Left Club, which included several PLC members, quickly met the requirement by selecting a young professor, Bateson's research director, as its adviser. The student paper astutely recognized the issue involved and questioned the implication that the UNC administration had the prerogative to award or deny recognition to student organizations. Still, the administration persisted by attempting to create a facade to support its claim. Dean Henderson sent a letter to Bateson informing him that PLC was not recognized and "therefore [was] barred from the use of University facilities for meetings." The strategic importance of this development rested in its effect on the legislature: since state-owned facilities were not involved, an investigation could not be properly pursued.[56]

One critic, an implacable foe of the liberal university, would not be so easily assuaged—television editorialist Jesse Helms. Had it not been for Helms's remonstrations on the subject of UNC politics, it was possible that the furor would have subsided and the speaker law would never have been considered. But Helms quickly moved to repudiate Aycock's stance, announcing that while the charges had been made by the local American Legion post, they reflected a widespread sentiment throughout the state. He cited the "curious connections" of persons both present and past at UNC. Helms's principal allegation, however, was that the institution itself was "decidedly left-of-center" and, therefore, out of touch with the political sensibilities of most state residents.[57]

Helms contended that it was perfectly appropriate for taxpayers to insist on conformity to established patterns of political discourse and behavior by those at the university. Although careful not to impugn the honesty of Aycock's impression, Helms asserted that "it would be a healthy development if an intelligent study were made to determine, independently and without bias, just what the conditions are at Chapel Hill." Helms did not rest his complaint here: he called on Sanford to heed FBI Director J. Edgar Hoover's warnings of communist infiltration of the campus.[58]

At the time, Helms was not concerned about the presence of student radicals at UNC but about the authoritative voice of the university advocating political trends—from racial equality to Keynesian economics—that had become anathema to southern conservatives. "We are not so much concerned about a silly bunch of kids who prate about their far-left Marxist beliefs, even to the absurd point of saying that Communism is too 'conservative' for them. . . . What worries us is the constant advocacies of increased federal powers, of centralization of government, of downgrading of capitalism and free enterprise originating with those who wear the mantle of intellectual respectability."[59]

This reasoning reveals the editorialist's fundamental concern with the relationship between the university and the larger society. Any attempt to regulate or apply oversight by the state, especially authority emanating from Washington, was suspect. In this sense, the university's toleration of communists indicated a liberal bias endorsing state intervention, of which "far-left Marxist beliefs" was a logical extension.

While conservative critics such as Helms were genuinely alarmed about radical activities among the UNC student body, they were more concerned about the voice of authority symbolized by an institution whose history over the previous four decades was marked by the ascendancy of a liberalism out of step with southern values. The existence of radical students served as a convenient means to attack an institution that represented the abolition of segregation, support of a liberal interventionist state, and a closer involvement between federal and state agencies in resolving social and economic problems. This institutional characterization, which seemed ubiquitous at Chapel Hill, was anathema to conservatives, including the denizens of rural North Carolina, where change had been slow to penetrate and traditional views remained unquestioned.

Some observers have perceptively and accurately noted the hostility to the elitism that characterized UNC in the minds of many throughout the state. The university had taken on a cosmopolitanism reflecting a national cultural pattern. The institution's operation seemed distant and arcane. Only a select minority of the state's high school graduates, many of them sons and daughters of UNC alumni or from prominent families, could gain entry. The only comparable public institution was the Raleigh branch of UNC, which was at the time locked in a bitter struggle to secure a separate identity of its own that removed the stigma of a subordinate status to Chapel Hill. There were a plethora of reasons for both animosity and suspicion toward the university, many of them stored in the collective memory and summoned forth by critics such as Helms.[60]

Chancellor Aycock understood the precariousness of the university's political space. He had spoken of the ominous threats directed against UNC as he made his inaugural address in 1960. The incipient challenge came from traditionalists who feared the magnitude of social change rising on the horizon. Given the University of North Carolina's historical position as a bellwether of change and progress, it became all too likely a target for embattled traditionalists. It would be more ironic that Aycock's refusal to defend the legitimacy of dissent by the campus Left would play into the hands of the university's most insistent foes. Whereas Aycock began his tenure with a speech defending academic freedom, in the end he capitulated by purging the last symbol of the radical Left.[61]

In the face of a threat to its academic freedom and institutional integrity, the university was not without powerful defenders. The cautious attempt by Aycock to deflect the charges by conservative critics and anticommunist ideologues was reinforced by a vigorous renunciation of the proposed investigation from virtually all of the state's major urban newspapers. The *Raleigh Times* labeled it "forensic hogwash" that bordered on "slander." The paper pointed to the presence of conservative businessmen on the Board of Trustees as evidence of the "ridiculous" nature of the allegations.[62]

The *Winston-Salem Journal* saw the legion's action as a part of a larger attack on academic freedom at southern colleges and universities as conservatives sought to delegitimize support for various liberal policies — particularly opposition to segregation — that had become manifest on campuses throughout the region. The *Journal* saw the attack as consonant with the criticism by groups such as the right-wing John Birch Society, which condemned professors speaking in favor of the United Nations and a more integrated international order. The editorial criticized the resolution as a threat to both democratic principles and UNC's continued integrity as an academic institution: "The University, if it is to maintain academic freedom, cannot deny such groups an opportunity to assemble and express their opinions, so long as they otherwise behave themselves. There, in the tradition of our free society, reason must compete with error and truth must compete with falsity. This is the sort of democracy the University of North Carolina is endeavoring to maintain on its campuses."[63]

The *Durham Morning Herald* heaped stinging ridicule on PLC before dismissing the call for investigation. The tiny coterie of Marxist students was defined as analogous to an insect and lambasted as "hare-brained students" uttering "confused sophomoric nonsense." The *Herald*, however, recognized the true target and potential victim of the intended investigation: "It is the University that would be 'investigated.' And it is the University that would suffer pointlessly. [The investigation] would create suspicions that no final report would ever clear up." [64]

The final disclaimer dooming the legion's proposal was submitted by Governor Sanford. A UNC graduate and a former FBI agent, Sanford issued a statement saying that an investigation was unwarranted because there existed no threat to society or the university. Sanford premised this remark on information from no less an authority on communism than FBI Director Hoover. Sanford averred that as long as Hoover remained a careful monitor of communist activity on college campuses, such investigations were unnecessary. [65]

Without widespread, sustained concern, the specter of a Red Scare quickly dissipated. It did not end, however. Helms continued to remind his viewers of a leftist element at UNC, implicating the university as a source of political contagion. Following several months of dormancy, Helms reintroduced the PL and communist issue as it pertained to UNC and its responsibility to the taxpaying citizens of North Carolina. Beginning in April 1963 he began an ongoing series of editorials that demanded a "public examination" of the political Left at UNC. The renewal of the attacks on subversion at UNC largely coincided with the mounting intensity of civil rights protests throughout the state. UNC represented a manufactory of liberal values on race relations, and many of its students and faculty openly supported the egalitarian objectives of the civil rights movement. Any investigation, even one that failed to identify a "Red nest" and exonerated the university, would serve to stifle dissent and intimidate the university into a cautiousness that might stultify the activities of those social and political elements looking to the university for leadership. [66]

Student activism at UNC was an intrinsic factor in the appearance of a speaker bill. The presence of a small but vocal group of students identifying themselves as Marxist-Leninists committed to a socialist agenda was essential to the reenactment of a Red Scare episode in North Carolina. It is ironic, however, that the liberal student activists — those favoring nonviolent, direct action against segregation — also played a vital role in the inception of the law. To challenge directly white supremacy and segregation was, in many ways, the most radical act conceivable in 1963. To rural, conservative lawmakers, the distinctions between liberal, noncommunist civil rights protesters and the openly Marxist PL faction were obscured, if they mattered at all. For many southern segregationists, black protest and communism were synonymous. [67]

The students who took to the streets in the spring of 1963 alongside black students were committing a revolutionary act in the eyes of North Carolina's embattled conservatives. Such a disregard of states' rights and of established racial conventions required an explanation. The memory of UNC's historic role in championing unpopular social causes and harboring radicals was resurrected by the presence of a new generation of students and faculty that was challenging the sanctity of a racist system that had reigned almost unquestioned since the turn of the century. As the crisis of the old order intensified, so too would the suggestion that the institution apparently responsible for these difficulties be brought under control.

The American Legion also refused to let the issue fade away. At its annual state convention held in Charlotte in June 1963, the legion passed a resolution "condemning" PLC as "atheistic" and "hate-embittered." The resolution went on to censure UNC for allowing the group to have campus facilities. The wording and intent of the legion resolution are amazingly similar to the statute that was enacted in the General Assembly the following week.[68]

3 The Streets of Raleigh

In a fundamental sense it was the issue of blacks, not Reds, that was responsible for North Carolina's anticommunist episode of the 1960s. What particularly irked the legislators was the presence of whites, especially white students and professors, among the throng of black protesters. Despite the fact that whites never represented more than a tiny fraction of the demonstrators, that fact made for conspicuousness. Their presence was more troublesome to segregationists than the sheer weight of numbers. Had the demonstrators all been black, the legitimacy of racial separatism might have been maintained. The protests could have been contained by an ideological framework emphasizing alleged inherent racial differences had not sympathetic whites supported the moral legitimacy of black demands. In short, Jim Crow required near unanimity among whites to survive. As increasing numbers of whites, especially students and intellectuals, supported the protests, defenders of segregation were hard-pressed to make their claims along racial lines. Much of the most vehement animosity vented by prosegregation legislators was directed at whites participating in support of racial equality.

Herein lay the linkage between anticommunism and the political milieu of the public university. The allegations of subversion at UNC remained dormant through the spring of 1963. But they were by no means forgotten. In the minds of aroused legislators, especially those desperate to preserve segregation and rural political power, awareness of a new collection

44

of Chapel Hill radicals was conveniently stored alongside memory of Frank Porter Graham's racial liberalism and the communist presence of the 1940s and early 1950s. Anticommunism was an ideological vehicle sufficiently malleable to allow political expression of conservative anger. As it became apparent that segregation was waning in the state's metropolitan areas, racial traditionalists called forth a convenient anticommunist crusade in hopes of succeeding where segregationist appeals had failed.

During the spring of 1963 national attention focused on racial conflict in Birmingham, Alabama, and Danville, Virginia, where the SCLC organized major campaigns to break down segregationist barriers. Newspapers and television sets brought the vicious reality of Birmingham Police Commissioner Eugene "Bull" Connor into the homes of millions of Americans as he turned fire hoses and dogs on black demonstrators, many of them schoolchildren. The spectacle of Birmingham mobilized sympathy among increasing numbers of Americans for the civil rights movement's nonviolent goals. The resulting victory provided a breakthrough for the movement, demonstrating that change was possible in one of the bastions of segregation.[1]

While Birmingham and other sites of SCLC activity dominated the headlines and evening news, similar developments took shape in the cities of North Carolina. Despite the emphasis given to civil rights activities in the Deep South, North Carolina had already made historic contributions to the campaign to eliminate institutionalized racism from southern life. In February 1960 four students from North Carolina A&T State University opened a new phase of black protest by requesting service at the sandwich counter of a Woolworth's store in Greensboro. Refusing to move from their seats after being denied service, the students touched off a wave of sit-ins that quickly spread to other cities both in the state and throughout the South.[2]

The direct-action strategy of the sit-ins brought students, especially black college students, to the forefront of the civil rights movement. In April the momentum generated by the initial sit-ins took institutional form. Ella Baker, executive director of SCLC, called a conference on the campus of Shaw University in Raleigh to discuss future strategy. The result was a self-contained organization of students, largely independent from the cautious preachers of SCLC. A product of the North Carolina Black Belt, Baker sensed the students' energy and devotion and encouraged them to organize a separate and autonomous youth arm of the larger movement. Out of the conference the Student Nonviolent Coordinating Committee (SNCC) was born and with it a more activist phase in the civil rights struggle.[3]

The Greensboro students' influence was quickly felt as sit-in protests spread throughout the cities of the state's Piedmont region. At every location, students were at the forefront of an assault on the racial exclusion of southern tradition.

In the week following the initial Woolworth's action, a sit-in occurred in nearby Winston-Salem. Organized by Carl Matthews, a young black man who worked in the city, it included twenty-five others, mainly students from Winston-Salem State Teachers College. On the same day, February 8, black students from North Carolina College, accompanied by several white students from Duke University, conducted a sit-in at Woolworth's lunch counter in Durham. The protests spread to Raleigh as students from Shaw University organized a demonstration demanding full access to a suburban shopping center. By the end of February, similar sit-ins had taken place in Charlotte, High Point, Fayetteville, Concord, and Elizabeth City. Dozens of students were arrested, most for violation of local trespass ordinances. With few exceptions, this early phase of black protest against segregation in North Carolina was largely free of violence. One exception occurred in the town of Monroe, near the South Carolina border, where black residents led by ex-Marine Robert Williams attempted to integrate the town's only swimming pool and were met with threats and violence from the Ku Klux Klan. When blacks bought guns and prepared for self-defense, the Klan violence subsided. Williams was eventually charged with kidnapping a white couple during attacks on the black community in August 1961. Williams, who maintained that he had not kept the two against their will, eventually fled to Cuba.[4]

Although large crowds of whites often appeared to taunt the protesters, there were few attempts at physical assault. However opposed white authorities were to the black insurgency that demanded an end to segregation, there would be no scenes like those at Birmingham and later in Selma, where police wantonly attacked demonstrators. North Carolina officials carefully promoted a harmonious image of race relations even as they attempted to forestall and circumvent black demands for full equality. Taking a cue from leaders in state government, municipal authorities attempted to navigate a course suggesting an openness to reform while doing little to end racial discrimination.

In his study of the desegregation process in Greensboro, historian William Chafe noted that both state and local officials attempted to maintain the barriers of racial tradition at the same time they appeared to be cooperating with desegregation efforts. Chafe concludes that the continuous demonstrations were fundamental to securing a genuine willingness by white business leaders and public authorities to negotiate the termination of Jim Crow. Throughout the twentieth century, North Carolina had been led by governors whose allegiance was to business interests. This point is underscored by the preeminent study of the period, which noted that the state was dominated by an "economic oligarchy." In the years immediately following the Warren Court's *Brown* decision, North Carolina was governed by Luther Hartwell Hodges, a former textile executive and an ardent foe of desegregation. Still, Hodges typified a model of business conservatism that stressed economic development without dynamic social change. The Hodges administration went to great lengths to maintain the state's progressive "mystique" while simultaneously undermining the implementation of the Court's decree in *Brown v. Board of Education*. In general, white leadership in North Carolina responded to demands for civil equality only after pressure was applied that interfered with the normal course of business. Fearing that the state's progressive image would be sullied, white authorities sought to avoid the appearance that North Carolina was anything but a paragon of civic harmony. What mattered most was the maintenance of a salubrious climate for investment and industrial development. In this vision of progress, the needs and interests of all social sectors were virtually synonymous with those of business and industry.[5]

The drive for civil rights accelerated in North Carolina during the spring of 1963. Lacking the organizational support found elsewhere, the state's civil rights movement was truly an indigenous grassroots effort. Although NAACP and CORE chapters were present in a number of cities, local residents organized and carried out the crusade to dismantle Jim Crow. The most concerted and ultimately successful desegregation efforts came in the cities of the Piedmont crescent, a swath of territory (including Raleigh, Chapel Hill, Durham, Burlington, Greensboro, Winston-Salem, and Charlotte) that encompasses the state's urban and industrial heartland. Hotels, theaters, and restaurants were frequent sites of black students' attempts to gain admission to previously whites-only establishments. The sustained pressure of the demonstrations, along with a "fill the jails" campaign that stretched official resources to the limit, proved effective. In one city after another, merchant associations called for an end to segregation. Biracial committees were appointed to make recommendations to implement open access to public facilities for all citizens. As elsewhere, the process in North Carolina was in large part profoundly conservative. Existing patterns of social and economic activity remained largely undisturbed. In most cases, the committees included black and white elites and orchestrated the arrangements for integration with the active collaboration of chambers of commerce.[6]

In several cities progress toward desegregation took place with considerable speed. In Durham, major demonstrations sponsored by local chapters of the NAACP and CORE began in mid-May following the election of Mayor Wensell Grabarek. The protests at several area restaurants, in addition to City Hall, resulted in hundreds of arrests for violation of trespass laws. Most of the demonstrators were students at North Carolina College in Durham. The black students were joined by a few white students from Duke University. Unlike the recalcitrance shown by civic leaders in other southern cities, Mayor Grabarek and the city council expressed a willingness to negotiate open accommodations and fair employment practices with black leaders. In response to the massive demonstrations that accompanied the new mayor's election, Durham took steps to institute major changes in eliminating segregation in a variety of facilities throughout the city. Desiring to preserve its image, the city acted. These actions were direct responses to black protest and the threat of increasing demonstrations.[7]

Two days after the initial protests, seven eating establishments agreed to desegregate. Much of the work of reconciling the differences between opposing sides was assigned to an eleven-member Durham Interim Committee appointed by Grabarek. The breakdown of racial barriers in Durham came quickly. Important steps were taken to desegregate the city schools. The city's swimming pools were voluntarily desegregated without protest. On June 2, more than six hundred citizens lent their names to a "Pledge of Support to our Durham Merchants" that appeared in the *Durham Morning Herald*. The signers declared a belief in open business practices and "equal treatment for all without regard to race."[8]

The pledge was an attempt to comfort merchants who feared a loss of business from aroused whites if blacks were served as equal patrons. Those signing the document promised to patronize only those establishments refusing to discriminate. Two weeks after its inception, the committee issued a report on the pace of desegregation in Durham. More than fifty restaurants were now serving all customers, black and white. More than forty downtown stores had enacted fair employment standards in hiring clerks and other personnel. By the end of June 1963, all eleven of Durham's motels desegregated, and more than 90 percent of its food-service businesses did likewise. In many ways, Durham presented a model for how peaceful desegregation could be attained. As Aldon Morris has perceptively noted, the Durham protests were the result of "rational planning" and years of careful analysis of black contributions to the local economy. Although city leaders had to be prompted into action by widespread demonstrations, they displayed a willingness to negotiate differences. The situation in Durham not only resulted in a substantial dismantling of segregation in a major urban area but suggested that Jim Crow was moribund.[9]

Throughout the cities of the urban Piedmont, the demise of Jim Crow was negotiated by biracial committees comprised of business and civic leaders. In Winston-Salem, a Good Will Committee appointed by Mayor M. C. Benton announced on June 5, 1963, that most of the "larger and nicer" motels and nearly all of the city's restaurants had agreed to desegregate. The elimination of segregated theaters, hotels, and restaurants in Winston-Salem was a clear recognition of the city's progress in recent decades. Many of the larger manufacturing firms had been hiring blacks for years, foremost among them the R. J. Reynolds Tobacco Company and Western Electric, two of the largest employers in the area.[10]

A notable exception to the 1963 move toward desegregation by the Piedmont cities was Greensboro. In his study of race relations in that city, Chafe has stressed the reluctance of white city officials, led by Mayor David Schenck, to negotiate with a sincere intention of integrating public facilities. As in other cities, however, the massive pressure applied by black demonstrators with the sympathetic support of white liberals produced a crisis atmosphere by the end of May. The demonstrations had grown larger and more boisterous and threatened to get out of control. Led by Jesse Jackson, a young student from North Carolina A&T State University, demonstrators occupied the street in front of City Hall and promised to "take over the city of Greensboro" if their demands were not met. The demonstrations continued as thousands occupied the main downtown business district. Schenck was compelled to make concessions in the interest of maintaining the city's image. In early June the mayor spoke out forcefully in support of desegregation, and a number of restaurants, motels, and theaters announced their willingness to accept black customers. Schenck declared that the city would no longer use race as consideration for municipal employment and created a permanent commission on human relations to address racial grievances in the city.[11]

Greensboro remained far behind Winston-Salem and Durham in its pace toward desegregation. By the end of June fewer than 40 percent of its restaurants and motels were open to all persons without regard to race. Only token moves to comply with federal directives concerning school integration had been taken. Black patients in hospitals and other facilities continued to experience discrimination. Still, in many ways, Greensboro was a noteworthy exception to the progress made toward desegregation in central North Carolina during the spring of 1963. In most of the major urban areas — Charlotte, Durham, Winston-Salem — resistance to integration had been broken. Even in Greensboro, as Chafe acknowledges, the end of June brought a breakthrough of sorts as city officials were compelled by the ongoing demonstrations to publicly call for an end to segregation. Despite lagging considerably behind other cities, irreversible steps had been taken.[12]

By the summer of 1963, the major cities of the North Carolina Piedmont were well on the way to eliminating racially separate public accommodations. Although pressure was necessary, desegregation came with surprising suddenness, without the protracted acrimony that accompanied the process throughout much of the remainder of the South. In each of the Piedmont cities, agreement by white leaders to proceed with the integration of public and private facilities such as restaurants, swimming pools, and hotels would not have materialized without the pressure brought to bear by black protest. Had blacks not publicly expressed their unwillingness to tolerate second-class citizenship that denied them elemental privileges accorded whites, desegregation would not have taken place. Many whites, accustomed to deferential behavior from blacks, were dumbfounded by the protesters' strident demands. Accepting official pronouncements of racial harmony and achievement, many whites had perceived black quiescence to indicate satisfaction. The spring of 1963 shattered this comforting illusion. Nowhere were these illusions debunked with greater ramifications than in the capital of North Carolina, Raleigh.

The civil rights movement in Raleigh was afforded unique possibilities that could not be replicated in other cities. First and foremost, Raleigh was the seat of state government. The movement would have the opportunity to challenge not only the pattern of segregation in the city itself but also the statutory basis for segregation throughout the state. Protests would be directed at the legislature as it returned to the capital in early 1963 to begin a new session. Dominated by vociferous segregationists, the General Assembly offered a propitious target.

The possibilities also extended to the executive branch of government. As the recognized political leader of North Carolina, Governor Terry Sanford could be called on to take steps toward desegregation that would have far-reaching ramifications throughout the state. In his gubernatorial campaign against segregationist I. Beverly Lake, Sanford had promised "a new day for North Carolina" and used as his campaign slogan "massive intelligence, not massive resistance."[13] If state government leaders could be persuaded to endorse affirmative, nonrestrictive practices at the state level, changes would be sure to follow in numerous localities. A final consideration was the likelihood that public protests in support of desegregation at the seat of state government were likely to receive abundant attention from the state's press.

The capital city had witnessed sporadic sit-ins and demonstrations throughout 1962, but in the spring of 1963 two newly constituted civil rights organizations launched a concerted campaign of sit-ins, marches, and mass protests aimed at persuading establishments in downtown Raleigh to open doors to persons without regard to race. The first group was the Raleigh Student Movement (RSM), led by Charles Earle of Kingston, Jamaica, student body president at Shaw University. The group included students from area schools, primarily historically black St. Augustine's College and Shaw University, and provided an army of volunteers to protest and challenge segregation at restaurants, hotels, theaters, and other businesses. The black students were joined by a number of white students and professors, mainly from North Carolina State University. The leadership of RSM identified more than thirty downtown establishments that were to be boycotted. Four businesses, the Sir Walter Hotel, the Sir Walter Coffee Shop, the S&W Cafeteria, and the Ambassador Theater, were to be picketed. In addition, attempts were made to gain admission and service from each business. Dozens of students were arrested in the initial stages of the campaign, and in many cases they refused to leave jail.[14]

The civil rights movement in Raleigh did not consist solely of students.

Desegregation activities mobilized diverse elements throughout the black community. All participants, including the students, were brought under the aegis of the Citizens' Coordinating Committee, led by Dr. Charles Lyons, executive secretary of the North Carolina Teachers Association. In early May the committee issued a "Declaration of Principles and Intentions" defining the organization, its purpose, and its objectives. The manifesto announced as its primary goal "bringing about the conditions in which all people may enjoy equal opportunities in our city irrespective to race, creed, or color." It highlighted the pernicious effects of a segregated society and pointedly rejected the stigma of inferiority and the belief that blacks were not entitled to the same benefits of citizenship as whites. Change, the document emphasized, was possible, and it was needed immediately.[15]

The Citizens' Coordinating Committee sought to encourage blacks to seek entry to businesses servicing the public. Demonstrations would continue until complete desegregation was achieved in downtown theaters, restaurants, and motels. The committee also called for the elimination of racial discrimination in municipal employment and public schools. The declaration called on the Raleigh City Council to enact, as a demonstration of good faith and honorable intent, a civil rights ordinance that would forbid the licensing of businesses continuing to segregate.[16]

The pace of demonstrations increased dramatically throughout May and June. Among the early targets for integration were several downtown movie houses, including the State and Ambassador Theaters. The theaters were operated by a Charlotte-based company as part of a chain around the state. The district manager of the company was Raleigh Mayor William G. Enloe. On May 3 two black students were arrested while attempting to enter the Ambassador Theater's white seating area. The same evening, a contingent of white students from North Carolina State University picketed the State Theater, demanding an end to segregated seating.[17]

The first mass arrests took place on the afternoon and evening of May 8, as ninety-two students went to jail on charges of trespass at several venues, including the statehouse, the Ambassador and State Theaters, the S&W Cafeteria, and the Sir Walter Hotel Coffee Shop. Most of those arrested were students from Shaw University, with many young women among those incarcerated. Taken to the Wake County jail, the women were crowded into small cells, where they spent the evening praying and singing hymns. The following day, more than a hundred students chose to remain in jail despite an order by city judge Pretlow Winborne that they be released on their own recognizance. Lyons defended the students' actions, calling the protesters "very much under control" and stressing that "our students have good leaders and are responsible people."[18]

The Raleigh protests contrasted the viciousness of Birmingham with more peaceful possibilities in North Carolina. As the students picketed and marched in long processions outside segregated theaters in downtown Raleigh, they sought to bring events in the city into juxtaposition with developments in Birmingham. Singing and chanting their opposition to segregation, they were often greeted by jeers from crowds of whites lined up across the street. Despite the presence of policemen preventing outbreaks of violence, little progress occurred, and black demands grew more vocal. Protesters began to march with signs suggesting to white merchants, as well as to the city's political establishment, a dreaded comparison: "Will Raleigh Become Another Birmingham?" Raleigh's white leadership well understood the calumny that had accompanied the denouement of the massive demonstrations in Birmingham. By invoking the specter that Raleigh might be seen in the same light as the Alabama city, protesters were playing a trump card. For the white business and political elite, the risk to the city's progressive image was too great to ignore.[19]

The desire to maintain North Carolina's progressive mystique brought results in Raleigh, as it did in other cities. On May 9 Mayor Enloe announced the creation of a biracial Committee of One Hundred. The committee included business and civic leaders and sought to ameliorate racial discord and negotiate a resolution to the crisis. The concerns of the mayor and the business community were explicit. In announcing the committee, Enloe said, "The Committee of 100 should try to find, what, if anything, can be done to avoid another Birmingham. It's time to act. Something has got to be done or our entire city is going to be embarrassed nationwide." The possibility of violence in Raleigh and publicity about acrimonious racial relations sent shock waves through the white elite. As the demonstrations grew larger and brought out increasing numbers of white hecklers, the potential that Raleigh could degenerate into another Birmingham assumed greater urgency.[20]

The RSM was not content to apply pressure solely on city officials. Governor Sanford quickly became a target of its efforts. On May 10 several hundred demonstrators trooped to the governor's mansion, where Sanford was hosting a performance by the North Carolina Symphony. The students sang and chanted, "We want the Governor." They were ignored until the singing drowned out the symphony. Sanford, in formal attire and accompanied by a dozen state troopers, came out on the steps to address the students. The governor expressed irritation with the youthful protesters, and the confrontation turned into a testy exchange of words. Sanford said, "I have enjoyed [your] singing. You are not bothering me at all. You can stay here another hour or so if you like." A voice from the crowd answered, "We are not here to entertain you, Governor." Becoming more irritated, Sanford shot back, "You are not here at my request either, friend." Another demonstrator shouted, "You should have known our troubles without a request." Sanford retorted, "I'm not a dictator son, you're in a democracy," in response to which he received a solid chorus of boos.[21]

Sanford's answer epitomized the response of much of the white leadership of North Carolina. He voiced sentiments that appeared to offer support to black objectives and aspirations but never appeared to grasp the urgency blacks felt. Sanford had initiated limited reforms in state employment procedures, but they had produced few results. The principal problem inherent in this strategy of gradual reform was Sanford's unwillingness to apply the weight of prestige inherent in the governor's office to push for substantial changes in race relations.[22]

On June 25 Sanford met with black leaders from around the state. The governor had called for an end to the demonstrations, arguing that they had achieved their purpose and, if continued, might produce an antiblack backlash.[23] The black leaders cited the limitations of the desegregation that had been achieved. Many facilities remained closed to blacks, and various civic organizations still refused to accept black members. Taking issue with Sanford's contention that "the point had been made," the black representatives promised that the demonstrations would continue until negotiations yielded positive and lasting results. The statement presented to the governor closed with a list of fifteen items on which he could take action. The list included a public accommodations act, greater black employment in state government, and the complete integration of all state-owned facilities. The message was clear: a change in the state's racial system was going to take place, with or without Sanford's assistance.[24]

The absence of decisive action by Sanford did not simply reflect his personal preference. It was largely a matter of politics. The governor could not run the risk of antagonizing a state legislature in which the powerful offices were held by those clearly unsympathetic to the goals of the civil rights movement. The governor's legislative program, as well as his own political future, rested in large part on harmonious relations with influential members of the General Assembly.

The General Assembly served as the focal point of desegregation activities in Raleigh. In a state where the governor lacked a veto and was not constitutionally empowered to succeed himself, the legislature was invested with tremendous power. The upsurge of demonstrations coincided with the arrival of the General Assembly. As the Assembly organized itself for business, the legislators were confronted with the reality of black insurgency. Many of the legislators trekked to the capital from rural counties with substantial black populations. In these areas, especially in the Black Belt, white supremacy and a caste etiquette mandating the subordination of blacks remained an unquestioned social reality. The steady procession of demonstrators presented a fundamental challenge to the legislators' worldviews. Many representatives were of advanced years and were shocked by the strident demands for immediate change from those whose quiescence they had long taken for granted. The times were changing.

The existence of state-sanctioned separation by race in the capital of North Carolina allowed for acts of calculated provocation that placed increasing pressure on state officials to defend or change the system. A major contributor to the student protests in downtown Raleigh was Allard K. Lowenstein, who helped organize a series of demonstrations to end segregation. Lowenstein was not new to North Carolina politics. He had come from New York to the University of North Carolina, where he was strongly influenced by the liberal activism of President Frank Porter Graham. Graduating in 1949, Lowenstein served on Graham's staff during the latter's brief tenure in the U.S. Senate. Since his student days at Chapel Hill, Lowenstein had served as president of the National Student Association and had gone on to Yale for a law degree. After spending a year as a lecturer and administrator at Stanford, he returned to Raleigh during the fall of 1962 as an assistant professor at North Carolina State University.[25]

Lowenstein reappeared in North Carolina at a pivotal moment in the state's history. Long interested in civil rights and race relations, he played an instrumental role in bringing about an end to Jim Crow in Raleigh. He would also be a factor in the subsequent backlash from angry conservatives looking for someone or something to hold accountable for their misfortunes. An interesting manifestation of Lowenstein's utility as a scapegoat for segregationists was the preposterous intimation by WRAL editorialist Jesse Helms that Lowenstein was part of a far-flung communist conspiracy.[26]

Traveling to Africa in the late 1950s, Lowenstein had witnessed the racial oppression practiced in South and South West Africa.[27] A savvy political operative, Lowenstein was fully aware of the international ramifications of American race relations. In the struggle between the United States and the Soviet Union for the allegiance of the nonaligned nations, especially those in Africa, the South's racially oriented caste system was an embarrassment as well as a detriment to American policy interests during the Cold War. Realizing the potential to demonstrate the liabilities produced by segregation, Lowenstein seized on an opportunity to challenge southern race relations on a very vulnerable issue.

In April, Angie Brooks, Liberia's United Nations Ambassador, was scheduled to deliver an address at North Carolina State University. Brooks had been an undergraduate at Raleigh's Shaw University and was acquainted with Lowenstein from his investigative sojourn to Africa in the late 1950s. Following her campus appearance, Lowenstein escorted the Liberian official downtown for lunch. As he selected a place to eat, Lowenstein was fully aware that Raleigh establishments observing the color bar would likely refuse service to the black woman despite her diplomatic credentials. Moreover, the choice of restaurants — the S&W Cafeteria and the Sir Walter Coffee Shop — promised the likelihood that members of the General Assembly and the Council of State would be present as the drama unfolded. Most legislators resided in the Sir Walter Hotel during the session and frequently ate at the S&W or at the hotel coffee shop.

The first attempt at service was made at the S&W Cafeteria. Lowenstein and Brooks were accompanied by several North Carolina State students and Joseph Outland, a Shaw student and nephew of the ambassador. As the group requested to be seated, cafeteria manager John Lineberger closed the serving line and sent everyone away, including the forty whites who had queued for lunch. After nearly an hour, Lowenstein called the press and informed them of the imbroglio that was developing. Shortly after the reporters' arrival, Lowenstein's group went to the adjacent Sir Walter Coffee Shop. The reception at the Sir Walter was more confrontational than that at the S&W. When the group requested service, manager Arthur Buddenhagen proceeded to insult the two black members: "We do not serve Negroes. Did you want jobs as a chef or a waitress?" When presented with evidence of Brooks's ambassadorial status, Buddenhagen belittled her significance in remonstrating, "The 48 states still have the right to serve whom they wish." Undeterred by the overt display of racism, Brooks produced a business card and informed him, "If you are ever in my country, you can be my guest." When it became apparent that the management could not be swayed by the implications of an international insult, the group departed, but not before informing the press that a complaint would be lodged with the U.S. State Department.[28]

The State Department issued an immediate apology to both Brooks and the Liberian government. Concern that the episode would become a vehicle for anti-American propaganda by the Soviets left federal authorities with little choice. Lowenstein had successfully managed a propaganda coup with resonance at both the federal and state levels. The nefarious influence of regional racial standards on the United States's international interests had been clearly demonstrated. Segregation could not be continually tolerated as a concession to southern traditions; the stakes were too high. Similarly, the New South "progressive" image so carefully cultivated by North Carolina's business and political elite was called into question. The choice of restaurants could scarcely have been more telling, associated as they were with dining service for state officials.[29]

The incident embarrassed even Raleigh's ostensibly moderate elements. The News and Observer responded with a defensive editorial that castigated both Brooks and Lowenstein, accusing them of manipulating the ambassador's status for purposes of "agitation." Terming the incident "unfortunate," the newspaper ignored the blatant demonstration of racism in favor of an oblique criticism of confrontational politics: "[T]he fact should not be missed that the ambassador was not engaged in diplomacy or international affairs in this incident. She was involved in domestic American agitation. . . . A graduate of Shaw University, she was moving for change in the city in which she received her education. Clearly, however, she was not denied in surprise or insulted by accident. Perhaps what she sought was proper, but she asked for what she got. And the State College Professor and students who accompanied her were engaged with her in an incident obviously designed to serve a cause." [30]

The implication of the editorial seemed apparent enough: segregation might be questionable, but anyone engaging in direct challenge to Jim Crow was a provocateur and thus subject to deserved contempt and scorn. Lowenstein refused to allow such an allegation go unanswered. He denied that the event had been "staged," pointing out that the press had not been notified of the situation until the group had been kept waiting at the S&W for more than half an hour. In Lowenstein's view, the entire incident would not have taken place had the group been seated and served as it certainly would have been almost anywhere outside of the American South.

The Brooks affair elicited protests from individuals appalled by the blatant racism directed toward the Liberian ambassador. One letter sent to Brooks from a writer in Chapel Hill apologized for the discourtesy and labeled her treatment as "un-American." Another writer suggested that "the manager ought to be arrested and charged with endangering the life of our country." Such responses were few, however, and the semiofficial reaction engendered ominous threats against Lowenstein. The incident brought him to the attention of Clarence Stone, Helms, and various segregationists in the General Assembly. Stone immediately sought information on the professor from officials at North Carolina State. Chancellor John T. Caldwell responded to the request with a copy of Lowenstein's vita and a note describing him as "an exceptionally able teacher." Caldwell, however, was irritated by the activities of North Carolina State personnel and students on behalf of desegregation. Although not a segregationist himself, Caldwell sympathized with the status quo and nonagitation on racial matters. As the Raleigh campus was engaged in an important name-change controversy as well as a proposed enlargement of its football stadium and other facilities, the chancellor wanted to avoid antagonizing powerful Assembly figures, including Stone. Even as Caldwell noted Lowenstein's demonstrated ability as an instructor, the chancellor added a cryptic "I make no further comment at this time." Stone became a persistent antagonist for Lowenstein. When Lowenstein went to Mississippi to participate in organizing the Freedom Vote in that state, Stone promised to "do everything in my power to see that [Lowenstein] is dismissed and kept from teaching at any school in our state. We do not need his kind and certainly not on a state payroll."[31]

The sights and sounds witnessed in the streets of Raleigh during May and June left many of the 170 legislators bewildered, confused, and angry. On several occasions the demonstrators marched to the Legislative Building, chanting, singing, and calling on the lawmakers to support civil rights and desegregation. A selected target at the new statehouse was its cafeteria. Recently opened for its initial session, the building included a cafeteria beneath the Assembly chambers to accommodate not only members of the legislature but also visiting citizens. Of course, in this case, *citizens* meant "whites only." The chairman of the Legislative Building Committee was State Senator Thomas J. White of Lenoir County, an unreconstructed states'-rights segregationist. White had played a major role in designing the building and continued to view it as semipersonal property after its completion. When the session began, White was appointed to oversee the facility, playing a pivotal role in drawing up the rules for entry and use.

On May 9, two black ministers, John W. Fleming, educational director of the General Baptist Convention, and D. N. Howard, walked into the statehouse cafeteria crowded with legislators, including Senate President Stone and White. The black ministers sat down at a table and requested service. The cafeteria manager called the sergeant at arms, who asked the two men to leave. When they refused to do so, White and Stone called the governor's mansion to inform him of the situation. Sanford responded by dispatching members of the State Highway Patrol to the cafeteria, where they forcibly removed Fleming after he refused to leave.[32]

Sanford had realized the difficult spot in which the two conservative senators placed him. He could allow the two black men to be seated and served in support of the principle of public accommodations, thereby alienating the Assembly, or he could allow the segregationist rules governing the restaurant to remain intact. Sanford chose to avoid violating the sensibilities of the conservative lawmakers. But he also sought to maintain the state's peaceful image: before sending the state troopers to the cafeteria, he met with and instructed them about how to handle the potentially explosive situation. The two black men were forcibly evicted, but they were not roughly handled. Following Sanford's orders, the troopers did not arrest the ministers. Sanford attempted to placate the segregationists with rhetoric. He claimed that the action in the statehouse cafeteria was necessary: "We will not tolerate incidents which disrupt the work of government." But Sanford's logic was spurious: State business was not being conducted in the cafeteria, which was open to the public.[33]

The most concerted and dramatic protests, however, occurred at the Ambassador Theater and the Sir Walter Hotel, along Raleigh's Fayetteville Street. The Sir Walter, located just a few blocks from the capitol, was the residence of many legislators while the Assembly was in session and had been dubbed the "unofficial capitol of North Carolina." Many legislative particulars were argued and resolved in the Sir Walter's suites and restaurants. It was not surprising, then, that Lowenstein and the RSM targeted the hotel as a centerpiece of civil rights agitation. As legislators returned each night from the evening sessions, they were confronted by throngs of demonstrators singing and carrying placards demanding that the state abandon the segregationist path being navigated by the states of the Deep South.[34] Lawmakers were periodically compelled to wade through protesters while entering the hotel. As a race-related legislative agenda steadily unraveled in the statehouse, tensions grew outside the Sir Walter. The protests eventually came to symbolize a world turned upside down for many legislators, who had difficulty coming to terms with developments at home and around the world. An answer would have to be found.

The sit-ins at the Sir Walter had become routinized by early June. A typical tactic involved the occupation of the hotel lobby by students with suitcases requesting rooms for the evening. Usually, the students were black, but occasionally white students from North Carolina State would participate, often sitting for hours on suitcases as the hotel management and service personnel attempted to ignore them. When the singing became louder and more students arrived to occupy the entire lobby, Raleigh police made arrests. On June 10, ten students were arrested on trespass charges. The youths had sat in the hotel for several hours singing, "Tell Mayor Enloe we will not be moved." One student in the street was struck by a bag of water dropped from an upper floor of the hotel, possibly thrown by a legislator.[35]

After the Sir Walter sit-ins of June 10, however, the Assembly took swift action; no effort was made to camouflage or obscure the fact that its actions were intended as retribution for the protests. For some time, a bill providing limited state grants to students attending private colleges or universities had been under review. The bill, which had impressive backing among urban legislators, had been bottled up in the Senate Appropriations Committee, chaired by White. On June 11, an attempt was made to resurrect the bill and bring it out of the committee for a floor vote. As the committee deliberated the bill, Stone, who was observing the proceedings, pointed out to several of his colleagues that black students from Shaw University and St. Augustine's College would be eligible to receive the grants. Noting that students from the two institutions had been at the forefront of recent efforts against segregation, Stone thundered that if the bill passed, "you'll be giving every one of those demonstrators fifty dollars to march." The bill remained in the committee.[36]

The following day brought even sharper reprisal. Representative George Uzzell of Rowan County introduced an antitrespassing bill providing for stiff fines and jail sentences. The legislation's supporters exhibited no qualms in acknowledging that the bill was a response to the mounting demonstrations at the State Legislative Building and the Sir Walter Hotel. The law, which made violation of the rule adopted by the State Legislative Building Governing Commission a misdemeanor, was specifically targeted at the "NAACP and other social action groups." The following week the Assembly passed House Bill 1311, which provided for stiffer misdemeanor penalties throughout the state for violation of existing trespass statutes. The amended statute left the penalty for trespassing up to the discretion of the court. This measure was accompanied by a companion bill (House Bill 1310) to punish more harshly any contempt of court, but this legislation was defeated in committee.[37]

The issue of black demonstrations and their impact on the General Assembly had surfaced early in the session. Only after student protesters took to the streets of the capital did the legislature consider retributive measures. A harbinger of the animosity that would eventually be unleashed by the ultraconservatives occurred when black college officials made their appropriations requests.

On February 19, 1963, Dr. Lewis C. Dowdy, acting president of North Carolina A&T University, appeared before the Joint Appropriations Committee to present and respond to questions about the school's budget request. The mild-mannered administrator was criticized by committee members who were irritated by the political activism of A&T students. The sharpest rebuke came from John Kerr Jr., a representative serving his final term after many years in public life. Kerr came from Warren County, where more than 60 percent of the population was black and largely disenfranchised. As Dowdy quietly and deferentially responded to questions about various aspects of his budget, Kerr enlivened the proceedings by injecting his views on black protest. The veteran legislator began by demanding to know if "students from your college [took] part in the sit-in strikes in Greensboro, trying to do away with segregation?" When Dowdy responded in the affirmative, Kerr began a tirade that revealed his own paternalistic devotion to segregation as he ridiculed the educator: "You come down here begging the white folks to give more money to your school. . . . [S]ome of us are getting tired of this. . . . You can strike all you please, but don't come here and beg us. . . . Sit-ins are an action that is an anticipation of antagonism between the races." Kerr's intemperate remarks drew opposition from a number of state newspapers and produced a petition from A&T students protesting the treatment accorded their president. An editorial in the *Greensboro Daily News* raised what would soon become an important issue in its strong pro–civil rights criticism of Kerr, noting, "State college heads are not customarily threatened with a cut-off of funds because of the activities of their students — especially when they take place off-campus and after hours." On June 25, the state legislature took such action.[38]

Numerous other legislators shared Kerr's acrimony toward the street demonstrations. As the session wore on and the demonstrations increased in number and magnitude, the legislators' tempers grew short, and repressed anger began to surface. By mid-June the situation had become tense, and angry confrontation took place as the constant singing and chanting took their toll on the legislative residents of the Sir Walter. Returning to their rooms following a long day of legislative work, they found little peace and quiet. As one student noted late in the evening, "If we can't sleep nobody else will." Numerous legislators, unable to sleep, congregated in the hotel lobby and watched the proceedings taking place outside.[39]

Tempers reached the boiling point as segregationist legislators saw Jim Crow arrangements challenged with alacrity. On June 9, after another night of protests, a confrontation took place that suggested the forthcoming retaliation against the colleges. A contingent from UNC that included Student Peace Union activist Pat Cusick and professor of sociology Albert Amons was in the large group of demonstrators standing outside the entrance to the Sir Walter. As several legislators left the building, one angrily accosted the small cadre of white protesters. The unidentified man informed Kenneth Bode, one of the students, that if the legislator had the power, he would "cut off their school appropriations." When the student challenged the propriety of such a move, the legislator angrily responded, "There is one thing in my power, I can slap hell out of you." As he drew back the newspaper he was carrying as if to strike the student, a legislative colleague restrained him and led him away.[40]

The legislators expected college officials to quell the continuing protests. In the legislators' view, most North Carolinians favored continued segregation. As state officials, they perceived it within their public responsibility to insure that the state's colleges and universities did not stray beyond traditional parameters of thought and behavior. When such boundaries were breached, the aggrieved lawmakers considered the formal use of legislative authority to command obedience from those schools receiving state funding.

One of the regular observers of the protests at the Sir Walter was the venerable secretary of state, Thad Eure. Eure had become a permanent fixture in state government, having held his position on the Council of State for nearly thirty years. In many ways, he embodied the state's political traditions. He was a product of a Black Belt county and firmly believed in the sanctity of the state's system of race relations forged by the white supremacist campaign that had occurred at the turn of the century. With his many years of service, Eure had become an influential figure within the Democratic Party. Moreover, many legislators, especially those new to the General Assembly, frequently consulted him about how best to design legislation to insure passage. Eure particularly supported lawmakers from his native eastern North Carolina, and like them, he grew frustrated and angry as a result of the constant procession of civil rights demonstrators outside the Sir Walter and along Fayetteville Street. More than twenty years after the episode, Eure called it "one of the worst upheavals ever to take place in the state" and linked the developments with communism.[41]

The legislators who angrily surveyed the demonstrations each evening had internalized segregation and black inferiority as consistent with the natural order. Coming from counties with large black populations, they had also come of age politically during the McCarthy era. Eure acted as a senior adviser to Phil Godwin, Ned Delamar, George Uzzell, and other legislators. He understood and shared their concerns, and, like them, he believed that something should be done to get to the source of the disturbances. And the conspicuous presence of Lowenstein and other white professors and students seemed to suggest a locus for the assorted miseries that the legislators faced.

The idea for a bill that might facilitate the desire to silence the university surfaced as civil rights protesters took to the streets of Raleigh. Eure, a frequent visitor to the Sir Walter, discussed the situation in Raleigh on numerous occasions with various legislators. The precise trajectory of the discussions that resulted in the subsequent anticommunist measure is difficult to follow. There were, however, several scenarios — each with constituent elements linking them to the others — suggestive of the circuitous route followed by the eventual bill. Delamar, representing coastal Pamlico County, had approached Eure several weeks prior to the end of the session, requesting that a bill be drawn that would mandate that professors take loyalty oaths similar to those required of military officers. Believing the "international communist conspiracy" to be present in North Carolina, Delamar desired a bill that would "wake up" university officials and make them more vigilant about the threat in their midst. Despite his concurrence with the legislator's ideologically driven anticommunism, Eure took no action on the request, and the matter remained dormant.[42]

The question of a law that would draw a political quarantine around the university reemerged several weeks later as the demonstrations intensified and professors became more conspicuous. As Eure and Representative L. J. Phipps watched yet another line of demonstrators troop past the Sir Walter, Phipps identified one white man as a professor from the University of North Carolina. As a resident of Chapel Hill and an official in the American Legion, soon to become state commander, Phipps had participated in the attempt to obtain a legislative investigation of the UNC campus during the fall of 1962. Eure commented that there ought to "be a way to see that that man didn't appear in any more parades." In recalling the event, Eure was emphatic: "I would have been willing at that time to have done anything to tactfully see that what was going on in North Carolina *ceased*. I can't be more firm than that." The possibility that state authority could be used to enforce political conduct within the universities was coming closer to reality.[43]

By now the secretary of state was aware of a bill pending in the Ohio legislature that seemed to address the concerns of the angry legislators in North Carolina. In late May, a bill was introduced in Ohio that would award trustees of the state universities the prerogative of denying speaking privileges to several categories of persons. Among the list of potentially proscribed speakers were Communist Party members, those refusing to say in an affidavit that they did not advocate the overthrow of the government, and persons convicted of contempt for refusing to answer questions about possible communist affiliations. In its final form, the law was so watered down that its provisions could scarcely be discerned from the status quo ante. The measure did not mandate the prohibition of any speaker or attempt to remove from the trustees authority for campus speakers.[44]

When UNC officials refused to discipline or take action against professors involved in the Raleigh protests, members of the General Assembly, especially the cadre intimate with Eure, were outraged. When Eure informed them of the Ohio bill they urged that he find out its particulars. Eure called his counterpart in Columbus, inquired about the bill's language, and requested a copy. The information gathered by Eure was taken to the attorney general's office and remodeled, probably by Assistant Attorney General Ralph Moody, to suit the legislators' interests.[45]

On June 25, the bill designed to bring the state universities, particularly Chapel Hill, under tighter political control was introduced and passed by a legislature flush with frustrated conservatives eager to lash out at those perceived responsible for the numerous setbacks over the course of the 1963 term. While the anticommunist bill provided a means of retribution against the institution symbolizing many of the conservatives' fears and grievances, the disturbing presence of black demonstrators accompanied by white collegians mobilized the ultraconservatives into taking action. These concerns were best expressed by Stone's angry eloquence six months after the speaker ban was enacted: "I have not noticed any professor leading any demonstrations since we passed House Bill 1395."[46]

The anticommunist speaker ban law was the definitive product of the 1963 General Assembly. It emanated from outraged legislators' desire to drive the professors back to campus and, more important, to exercise direct political control over the university, some of whose students and faculty had been openly opposing the status quo. One legislator, speaking in retrospect, contended that the entire anticommunist episode could be traced to the visibility of white professors among the demonstrators: "If you have to single out one issue to say what triggered it, it was Al Lowenstein demonstrating in front of the Sir Walter filled with legislators from rural North Carolina."[47]

Most important, the exploitation of the anticommunist leitmotif obscured the social and political conditions in which the entire matter was grounded. While the passage of such a controversial statute aroused an endless array of critics, they concentrated their energies, for the most part, on the potential for damage to the university and on often arcane and supercilious debates over the meaning of academic freedom. The racial animus was quickly buried in an avalanche of issues focusing on the seriousness of the communist threat to North Carolina. Although several newspapers made the connection between a defeated conservative racial agenda and the sudden emergence of the anti-communist measure, by the end of June the debate had moved on to superficial issues.[48]

Two years after enactment of the anticommunist law, Representative Uzzell, who had vigorously supported the many anti–civil rights measures, recalled the original intent of the sponsors: "The Speaker Ban Law was originally passed more to curb civil rights demonstrations than to stop Communist speakers on state campuses. . . . [I] thought many of the demonstrations were Communist inspired, and this was primarily what the General Assembly was trying to prevent."[49]

Here was a common, trans-South means of explaining the civil rights insurgency during the death throes of Jim Crow. In several states the tattered ideology of segregation was supplanted with the far more flexible signifier of anticommunism. Even for those less than committed to preserving racial separatism, anticommunism possessed an almost visceral appeal. And it did not require deception or bad faith for some legislators to assume that their reversals could be traced to communism. Communists had previously been at UNC, the American Legion had recently spied another communist-oriented group on the campus, and it was widely understood that the Communist Party was active in promoting racial integration. Segregation was perceived as a hallowed and natural institution, and, more than anything else, communism implied activities that threatened the perceived harmony of existing social relations. The civil rights movement, with the conspicuous involvement of white collegians, seemed aptly suited to such a comprehension.[50]

Three days after passage of the speaker ban, an editorial appeared in an eastern North Carolina newspaper that attempted to clarify for its readers the issue of what a communist was:

> You may presume there are a considerable number of secret members, not to mention actual professional spies working for the Soviet Union. You can add identifiable persons who, while avoiding party membership, nevertheless unmistakably

serve the party's goals — as dictated by Moscow. Beyond these levels, identification becomes tricky, and presumption dangerous. For example the Reds often try to adopt as their own a flock of domestic proposals which may accord roughly with programs advanced by legitimate political parties in the free democracies. As practiced under Moscow's guidance this device is a conscious fraud. Its aim is to gain for communism an identity with certain causes the Kremlin believes either to be popular or provocative in the free countries. People in free lands who let the Reds get away with this nonsense are just playing Moscow's game. You don't prove a man a communist just because he favors six or eight or ten programs the Communist Party also pretends it wants for the country. It is more fundamental to remember that a Communist is a person of totalitarian mentality.[51]

Such a cornucopian explanation could explain many things that currently seemed either popular or provocative. A "communist" was a calculating conspirator whose activities bore close relation to those of the civil rights movement. Thus, the civil rights movement was symptomatic of and possibly synonymous with treason. The Communist Party was abstract, multifarious, and inclusive. Whatever the party was, it was illegitimate. And it was real. The speaker ban brought together a series of developments that produced accusations and political punishment for the university. The reason for the measure rested in Chapel Hill's putative lack of vigilance in preserving a public trust from dangerous elements.

These issues were indelibly linked to race and the implications of the civil rights movement. And within the North Carolina General Assembly, a cohort that included well-positioned and influential leaders was consumed by the movement's consequences for society and for their authority to govern.

4 The 1963 General Assembly

The year 1963 was the most critical in North Carolina's political life since the end of World War II. That year, the urban middle classes of the bustling Piedmont pressed their demand for more equitable representation in the state legislature. This was a moment of no small historical significance, for with it came the demise of the political values that had underpinned state government since the turn of the century. Foremost among them was the centrality of race as a factor in political organization. Of equal importance was the mounting civil rights insurgency that spread throughout the state during the spring and fall. As these developments took place, the General Assembly made plans to convene for its biennial session in Raleigh. The 1963 session would be one of the most rancorous and vitriolic ever. Senate reapportionment and race relations would inundate all other issues. The preeminent question confronting the General Assembly was that of power—who would possess and wield it—and, concomitantly, in what direction North Carolina would go: would the state identify its future with the other southern states, especially those that had chosen the path of defiance of federal authority, or would it move toward an approximation of national norms on matters of race and political development?

The General Assembly that convened in February 1963 reflected the tensions and uncertainties present throughout the state. While many citizens were demanding a fundamental rearrangement of social life and political structures, the legislature was under the leadership of a determined and strong-willed coterie of unreconstructed states'-rights conservatives who saw an opportunity to realign North Carolina alongside the defiant resistance of its southern neighbors. These legislators would attempt to restore a fading order through an admixture of fear, force, and the tyrannical use of parliamentary authority.

The seeds of acrimony had been germinating for nearly a decade. As other southern states had selected a strategy of defiant resistance to the federal mandate issued by the Warren Court in the *Brown* case, North Carolina had equivocated with a more cautious response that set it apart. There would be no "massive resistance" in North Carolina. Still, the state's model as it met its school desegregation crisis of 1955–56, the so-called Pearsall Plan, was a cleverly forged instrument intended to blunt the possibility that federal courts would compel the state to operate its public schools on a nonracial basis. The men who stood in positions of command in 1963 had actively participated in promulgating the "North Carolina way" as articulated by the Pearsall Plan. Some had openly advocated massive resistance through the doctrine of interposition. Two members of the 1963 Assembly, Senator Thomas J. White Jr. and Representative John H. Kerr Jr., had participated in the inception of the short-lived Patriots of North Carolina, a variant of the white supremacist Citizens' Councils that had emerged in the Deep South following the Supreme Court's repudiation of racially segregated public education. White made the defense of segregation a cornerstone of his politics and quickly moved to stake out a prosegregation position; Senate President T. Clarence Stone was no less an enthusiastic defender of segregation. But in 1960 a leading proponent of states' rights, I. Beverly Lake, had lost in a gubernatorial primary that hinged on the issue of how zealously the state would pursue segregation. Lake had been defeated by a cautious segregationist, Terry Sanford, who captured a substantial plurality of votes in the urban Piedmont. The General Assembly was the final stronghold of those who looked to the white supremacist past as the font of their political identity. From this power base, they would mount a desperate attempt to defeat their opponents and restore the battered hegemony that had belonged to their predecessors.[1]

Obsession with the specter of integration informed the varied legislative activities pursued by Assembly conservatives. The key issue of the session involved the need to reapportion the Senate. On this matter race, power, and the future of North Carolina politics appeared to conjoin. Reapportionment became the overweening concern as those from rural districts, in both the House and the Senate, vainly attempted to construct a formula that would palliate the urban clamor for greater representation. Of the host of grievances against federal authority none was more explosive or vexing than the spate of decisions handed down by the Warren Court as it entered the apportionment thicket. Of the apportionment cases, the most monumental impact was felt in *Baker v. Carr*. In *Baker*, the Court enunciated the principle of "one person, one vote" as a basis for legislative apportionment throughout the nation. Districts would have to be drawn and apportioned on the basis of population. The votes of urban areas, and the reorientation of political values that came with them, would now be felt.[2]

In southern states such as North Carolina, the impact of the apportionment cases suggested two results: first, black votes would become increasingly instrumental in determining who went to the legislature; second, and more important, rural politicos were in jeopardy of being supplanted by a majority of urban-based legislators. As the General Assembly of North Carolina began its work in 1963, the ultraconservatives were well positioned to effect changes that would benefit their own political fortunes and the interests of their constituencies. This strength was particularly pronounced in the Senate.

With the death of Lieutenant Governor Cloyd Philpott, Senator T. Clarence Stone of Rockingham County was elected to serve as Senate president. Stone had operated a family grocery business and an oil distributorship since the early 1920s. First elected to the General Assembly in 1935, Stone served several terms in the House before returning to his family businesses. In 1955 he reentered politics, winning election to the Senate. The 1963 session, over which he presided, was to mark the culmination of his long tenure as a public figure. Of irascible temperament, Stone was often given to personal attacks and profane outbursts against those with whom he disagreed. His selection as president over the ambitious and formidable Senator Lunsford Crew of Halifax County was the result of the many political alliances and loyalties he had forged during his career. Not merely intolerant of dissenting opinion, Stone was easily influenced by the banal flattery of those whom he trusted or who came to his defense when needed. His chief lieutenant, Senator Thomas J. White of Lenoir County in eastern North Carolina, tellingly influenced Stone's decisions as president. The other influential figure in Stone's presidency was not a member of the Assembly but a television personality. Stone had long been friendly with Jesse Helms, whom he often referred to as "my very good personal friend." Helms and WRAL President A. J. Fletcher offered constant counsel to Stone throughout the session and came to his defense in several episodes when Stone faced sharp criticism for his actions as Senate president.[3]

Stone brought to his role as Senate leader an unmitigated faith in white supremacy and the doctrine of states' rights. When Stone returned to the Assembly in 1955 after eight years of political retirement, he did so largely on the impetus of his militantly segregationist views, rekindled by the implications of the *Brown* decision. As the 1956 General Assembly began to consider how to meet the threat to its segregated schools from suits brought in federal court, Stone made his views known in a letter to U.S. Senator Sam J. Ervin Jr.: "The big vote that you got shows you how the people of this state feel on the segregation business. Most of the newspapers have joined the Yankees against us. I especially want to know something [from you] about our 'great Republican Chief Justice.' I may want to have something to say about him at the special session of the Legislature." [4]

Stone remained unreconstructed; his political sensibilities never transcended a South-versus-North regional conflict. On May 10, 1963, on the occasion of Confederate Memorial Day at the state capitol, Stone delivered an impassioned renunciation of the Supreme Court and a defense of anti-federalism: "We are still a conquered province. We do not have any states' rights any more—I want everybody to hear it—The Warren Court is a disgrace to any civilized people." [5]

Stone's advocacy of states' rights and defiance of federal power ossified between 1956 and 1963. Stone and other ultraconservatives sought to keep North Carolina a vital part of the "solid South" and to correct the apparent inconstancy and drift that had characterized the state's response to the conditions imposed by the Warren Court rulings. Stone's ascendancy to the Senate leadership gave him the opportunity to secure a long-sought objective: to move North Carolina into alignment with the Deep South states and their radical tactics to continue segregation, including massive resistance. Stone was an avid supporter and correspondent of numerous hard-line segregationists, including Georgia Senator Herman Talmadge, future Georgia Governor Lester Maddox, Arkansas Governor Orval E. Faubus, Alabama Governor George C. Wallace, Virginia Senator Harry F. Byrd, and Virginia Congressman William Tuck. In his letters, Stone conveyed his enthusiastic support for their efforts on behalf of segregation and states' rights. Concomitantly, Stone colored each missive with his own militancy and sense of urgency. By 1958, as Arkansas, Virginia, and Georgia adopted strategies of resistance, Stone was making known his preferences. In a letter to Ervin, Stone remarked, "I went to Richmond last Friday and heard Senator Talmadge make the best political speech I have heard in my life. . . . I wish that North Carolina would join hands with Georgia and Virginia in this integration business." [6]

Stone's devotion to white supremacy was as pronounced as his fealty to states' rights. These concepts had served as the twin pillars of southern politics: each had informed and reinforced the other to such an extent that they had become inseparable. As with many other southern legislators of his generation, Stone's political consciousness and worldview were infused by virulent racism. Such racism transcended mere racial contempt or hatred. It produced a genuine conviction that civil equality with blacks threatened white identity; racial distinctions as the basis of civilization had to be preserved, whatever the cost.

Stone passionately bemoaned the impending dangers to his South as he watched the revolutionary developments of the post-*Brown* period. Even within the Democratic Party, the bastion of southern power, alarming changes were taking shape. As he heaped scorn on Attorney General Herbert Brownell and the Eisenhower administration, Stone observed a similar reorientation taking shape in his own party. He responded in a familiar manner: Adlai Stevenson "was out in California a few days ago and it seems as if he wants to make Niggers out of us by 1963. I think they will have a hard time before they make us change our color."[7] The preservation of traditional social relations and the political arrangements governing them was paramount for an ardent segregationist like Stone.

While much of the nation fretted about growing Cold War tensions between the United States and the Soviet Union, Stone never relented in his adamant concern for the protection of regional prerogatives. To be sure, Stone and other Dixiecrats were staunchly anticommunist during the late 1950s as the Soviet Union began to endorse wars for national liberation among the former Western colonies. For southern conservatives, communism represented a cornucopia of values—among them atheism, racial equality, and insurrection among the subordinate classes—that were anathema to the perceived natural social order. During the late 1950s, however, conservatives had not yet discovered the transformative and obscurantist power of *communism* as a signifier that could be applied to virtually any issue, such as race. Segregationists were still attempting to rally support with a direct appeal to racial tradition and sectional identity. Enemies though Khrushchev and the Soviets might be, they remained a distant and indistinct threat. The real foes presenting a clear and present danger were much closer to home. In Stone's words, "I am NOT worrying about what is going on in Russia; Khrushchev does not bother me or any of us people here in the South. Our danger is from within, and this country has produced very few more dangerous men than Warren and Brownell." Stone closed his letter with "Yours for States [*sic*] Rights and the White Race."[8]

During the next six years Stone's thinking slowly metamorphosed as communism supplanted direct appeals to race in the arsenal of beleaguered segregationists. Stone never abandoned his belief in the sanctity of race as a foremost expression of political virtue. By 1963, however, his patience had been thinned by an inability to generate support in the General Assembly, and Stone blindly supported a younger cohort's vindictive effort to pin the communist label on an institution identified as a source of the setbacks experienced by the supporters of segregation and states' rights.

While Stone was the Senate's nominal leader, the power behind the throne was White, who influenced and attempted to dominate the proceedings of the General Assembly from its opening gavel to its controversial adjournment. The assertive senator had been instrumental in securing the presidency for his friend, Stone, and White was handsomely rewarded for his efforts. He offered unending advice to Stone on an assortment of problems, procedural and political, and the suggestions were rarely rebuffed. Stone admired White's intellect and determination to pursue a conservative agenda that reflected his own views. More important, the combative Stone recognized that he could not have secured his prominent post, the apex of his political career, without the ambitious White's Herculean efforts: "He is the man that helped me get the Presidency of the Senate. He went all out for me and telephoned and wrote letters all over North Carolina."[9]

Despite constant denials of the extent of his influence on Stone, when the legislature began its session on February 6, it was Tom White Day. One observer noted White's domineering influence by commenting, "usually there have been three or four big senators who wielded great influence, sometimes in different fields of legislation. . . . [I]n the 1963 state Senate, at least to date, the old quartet concept has been reduced to one individual, Sen. Thomas Jackson White of Lenoir County." White opened the proceedings with a glowing address nominating Stone for the presidency and then introduced the first two measures for consideration. Stone then reciprocated the support that had been extended him by naming White as chairman of the powerful Senate Appropriations Committee, thus providing his friend with critical leverage over the funding of a host of measures.[10]

Both Stone and White believed journalists to be inordinately biased against their politics and held the urban press responsible for breaking down a united front in the segregation controversy. Unlike the abusive Stone, White was shrewd and articulate. Rather than express a direct antagonism toward the press, he instead maintained that the taxpayers deserved to have laws considered "in an atmosphere conducive to calm deliberation." In White's view, journalists were a "distraction," but he believed the new rules keeping journalists from the Senate floor did not impose undue restrictions that prohibited reporters from doing their jobs.[11]

The press responded with irritation and puzzlement to the breach of precedent. The president of the state's Radio and Television News Directors asked White why "the people of North Carolina [should] submit to a dictator." The source of the difficulty was that White and Stone considered journalists a special interest, not unlike the liquor lobby or the schoolteacher lobby, and therefore undeserving of special privileges. Both men believed that the press, especially the large urban dailies, was hostile to conservative interests. Despite journalists' contention that their role was to report news in the public interest,

White was unmoved: "The argument that the Press is the 'guardian' of the people, leaves me rather cold." White saw the press as explicitly political, often complaining he had received threats to the effect that should he ever run for lieutenant governor, as he was considering, journalists would "cut me to ribbons." For White, the press had corrupted its freedom into license.[12]

The principal rebuttal to White's views came from an editorial in the *Charlotte Observer*. It noted that the abstract principle that White described was actually "an absolute necessity for a free people." The editorial strenuously denied White's intimation that journalists attempted to influence legislation as did lobbyists and interest groups. The antagonisms between the Senate's suspicious conservative leadership and the press could not be ameliorated. In late March Stone accosted a television newsman outside an empty committee room and denounced the reporter with angry curses. The incident demonstrated how strained the relationship between the press and the Assembly had become. Most of those defending Stone's conduct were eastern conservatives and prosegregation advocates. At least three of his defenders in this incident— Phil Godwin, Wayland Sermons, and Ed Wilson—were cosponsors of the eventual anticommunist measure.[13]

The issue of press access to General Assembly proceedings involved considerably more than the banishment of reporters to the galleries. As chairman of the powerful Senate Appropriations Committee, White acted as cochairman of the Joint Appropriations Committee. He quickly moved to hold all of the committee deliberations in executive session. Both the public and the press were prohibited from witnessing the committee's debates about how to spend the taxpayers' money. In response to the protest that ensued, White argued that the arrangement did not constitute an abridgment of democratic procedures because the committee doors were opened when the vote on appropriations took place. The public would be informed when votes occurred. The decision meant that a "complete news blackout" would obscure much of the discussion and actual work of the committee that played a vital role in shaping the state's budget every two years. Although there had been little dissent among the other committee members, the action had been conceived by White, who found himself and his committee assailed by Republicans, the public, and the press. Sam Ragan, news editor of the *Raleigh News and Observer*, spoke before the Durham Lions' Club and pointed out the implications of the action: "It is one of the worst abuses of legislative power I have ever observed. The drawn curtain of the legislature is pulling the wool over your eyes. They are spending your tax money, but they don't want you to know how they are doing it." The press was all but unanimous in its condemnation of the action orchestrated by White, calling it "a wall between taxpayers and spenders." Whereas Stone lambasted the press with invective and curses,

White became involved in physical confrontation. When the Assembly traveled to Wilmington in early April to conduct a session aboard the battleship USS *North Carolina*, White engaged in fisticuffs with a young United Press International reporter ostensibly because the reporter had used "profanity in the presence of ladies." White saw the incident as a deliberate provocation by a vindictive press determined to "destroy" him. Helms (White's close friend and supporter) quickly dispatched a letter to UPI headquarters in New York defending White's behavior and accusing the reporter of drunkenness and "vulgarity in the presence of ladies."[14]

Just as Stone and White led a phalanx of segregationists and states'-rights advocates in the Senate, the House also reflected the influential presence of ardent defenders of racial hierarchy and rural political power. Although not an ultraconservative in the mold of Stone and White, House Speaker Clifton Blue of Moore County was a veteran of state politics and was receptive toward those favoring preservation of established cultural norms. Blue was not likely to obstruct key bills introduced by House conservatives.[15]

Geography and racial demography played an instrumental role for the lower chamber's conservative leadership. Prominent conservative figures tended to come from the thinly populated rural counties of eastern North Carolina. Long holding pivotal influence in state politics, the eastern counties constituted the wellspring of conservative ideology, especially in relation to racial politics. With large black populations — in nine counties blacks comprised an outright majority — and almost bereft of substantial urban areas, the east served as the repository of traditional cultural values. Foremost among the ideological components informing eastern conservatives' politics was the primacy of "natural" and inherent racial distinctions. Segregation and the subordination of blacks to whites were the critical underpinnings by which politics were organized in most of the eastern counties. With black citizens all but disenfranchised, a small fraction of elite whites in these areas played a powerful role in state government that greatly transcended their numbers. This historic advantage had been perpetuated well into the twentieth century; racist and race-conscious politicians imbued with rural, agrarian values held critical levers of power.[16]

Despite a constitutional requirement mandating reapportionment after each census report, the North Carolina Senate had not been reapportioned since 1941 and, not unexpectedly, was egregiously malapportioned, with rural eastern districts enjoying as many or more seats as far more populous Piedmont districts. Reflecting the weight of past influence, the east in particular and small counties in general continued to exercise power far out of proportion to their population. And repeated attempts to reallocate seats to reflect altered demographic patterns had been turned down. Cities grew and the population of the urban Piedmont exploded, but the eastern/small-county districts continued to preempt any redistribution of political power. There had been no redistricting in 1951 or 1961, and sitting legislators, including Stone, had played an instrumental role in preventing any reconfiguration of district lines to assure that each senator represented an equal number of constituents.[17]

But change was in the wind. Recent Supreme Court decisions, especially the ruling handed down in *Baker v. Carr,* indicated a readiness by federal authorities to enter the apportionment thicket and assure fair and equal representation for all citizens. Redistricting could no longer be forestalled. With redistricting plans now subject to review by the federal courts, population equity would be the prevailing principle of acceptable reapportionment. Aware of the new federal mandate in apportionment issues, North Carolina's rural, small-county conservatives were trapped in a difficult situation. Unwilling to completely abandon the source of their hegemony, they were nevertheless compelled to participate in a reallocation of Senate seats that assured metropolitan areas increased power and influence in future Assembly sessions.[18]

The inequality of voting-age populations among districts was both startling and emblematic of the undemocratic representation within the Senate. Table 1 demonstrates the malapportionment among Senate districts. The Second District consisted of seven predominantly rural eastern counties. With a population of 102,711, the Second District had two seats. By comparison, the Twentieth District, comprised solely of Mecklenburg County, the state's most populous and urbanized county, was assigned a single seat from a population base of 272,111, more than two and a half times that of the Second District. As illustrated by the comparison of urban and rural districts, the 1963 North Carolina Senate, like its predecessors throughout the twentieth century, represented only a small fraction of the state's population.

This historical inequality was compounded by the virtual disenfranchisement of many residents of the eastern counties. Many of these counties contained large black populations; blacks comprised an outright majority in nine counties and numbered more than 40 percent in several others. In a number of these counties, blacks were systematically denied voting rights by procedural device or by intimidation. Several of these counties eventually came under federal supervision as the provisions of the 1965 Voting Rights Act were enforced in recalcitrant areas of the South where there was evidence that voter discrimination had taken place. In 1963, as in many previous years, the representatives sent to the Assembly from these counties were elected by a small fraction of voting-age persons. These representatives, in concert with other rural, small-county legislators from the west, had been able to exert a telling influence over legislative activities. The 1963 Assembly, especially the Senate,

Table 1. Population Characteristics for Selected State Senate Districts, North Carolina, 1963

District Number	Population	Percent Urban	Number of Seats	Nonwhite Population (Number)	Nonwhite Population (Percent)
1	115,118	15.6%	2	57,299	49.8%
2	102,711	12.6%	2	41,564	40.4%
3	78,465	12.3%	1	43,822	55.8%
4	113,182	37.8%	2	60,550	53.5%
5	69,942	42.8%	1	30,497	43.6%
6	147,173	29.4%	2	60,292	41.0%
7	172,735	19.8%	2	56,322	32.6%
8	144,995	30.4%	2	44,237	30.5%
9	178,533	21.2%	2	62,203	34.8%
17	246,520	76.0%	1	51,463	20.9%
20	272,111	77.9%	1	66,818	24.6%
22	189,428	69.2%	1	45,767	24.2%

Source: U.S. Bureau of the Census, *Eighteenth Census of the United States: Census of Population*, vol. 1, pt. 35, *North Carolina*, table 28, "Characteristics of the Population, for Counties, 1960" (Washington, D.C.: U.S. Government Printing Office, 1961).

reflected a profound rural influence, and traditional values informed a variety of political judgments. The burgeoning Piedmont cities such as Charlotte, Greensboro, and Winston-Salem — nodules of economic modernization and civic progress — were grossly underrepresented in Raleigh.[19]

What issues were implicit in the rural fear of reapportionment? The privileged position of eastern interests on a variety of tax issues might be jeopardized should the region lose representation to urban areas. Foremost among these possibilities was a tax levied on cigarettes and other tobacco products. The east had used its considerable leverage, in a bloc with western delegates, to block any attempts to tax tobacco. However, eastern influence made itself felt in a number of other tax-related issues. In 1955 a proposed tax on soft drinks was killed when an eastern representative — a prominent tobacco farmer — stood and announced that "a crate of soft drinks is a part of the standard pay for field hands." Thus signaled, small county delegates turned down the measure. With reapportionment, and added voting weight for the heavily urbanized Piedmont counties, tax legislation might be drafted and enacted to the detriment of such eastern interests.[20]

Of equal significance with economic matters that might be impacted by reapportionment and certainly more urgent were issues attendant to racial politics. Foremost among these considerations was the future of segregation. If and when the urban Piedmont counties obtained a preponderance of Senate votes, they would be positioned to make sweeping changes in the laws governing the state's pattern of race relations. This possibility gave the reapportionment issue its intensity and caused it to dominate the activities of the 1963 session. Committed to racial exclusivity and separatism, rural conservatives had reason to be concerned about what might ensue should urban districts come to exercise decisive influence in the Senate. As the session progressed, they witnessed, in city after city, biracial committees composed of business and civic leaders negotiating an end to racial segregation in most public facilities. The rural legislators were increasingly aware that their own cultural values, especially those rooted in racist assumptions, were losing currency in the urban Piedmont. There was also the likelihood that black voters in urban districts would play a more influential, perhaps pivotal, role as additional seats were awarded to those areas. For beleaguered eastern and small-county conservatives, the reapportionment issue portended dire consequences that spoke to the core of their worldview.[21]

Despite the numerous reapportionment bills, versions of which passed one chamber or the other, the Assembly raced toward adjournment without approving any plan. The urban delegates, led by the Republican-dominated Guilford County contingent, demanded that apportionment follow the principle of population equity among electoral districts. Small-county delegates, however, were just as adamant and refused to vote themselves out of office and their cultural hegemony into oblivion. One proposal that found favor among small-county conservatives was the so-called Little Federal Plan, a formula that would pattern the Assembly after the federal Congress, with one house based on population and the other on geopolitical unit. When adjournment came in late June, no apportionment bill had been approved. Eager to realign the institutional machinery needed to usher in more progressive politics, Governor Sanford announced that a special session to redistrict the state Senate would be convened in mid-October.[22]

The special session finally managed to construct a new apportionment scheme, increasing the Senate from fifty to seventy members and creating districts by population. At the same time, however, the Assembly endorsed a plan to redistrict the House by reducing its membership from 120 to 100. In this formula, each of the state's one hundred counties would receive one seat without regard to population, thus preserving rural, small-county dominance over at least one chamber. In the House, the state's most populous county, Mecklenburg, would have the same representation as Tyrrell County, the smallest. The rural politicos were not about to quiescently abandon a power base they had monopolized throughout much of the state's history. Believing the constitutional mandate and governor's directive satisfied, the legislators headed home to campaign for the Little Federal Plan.[23]

The Little Federal Plan was favored by small-county political leaders and by conservative figures such as Helms, who campaigned for its acceptance from his editorial perch in Raleigh. But was it favored by the people of North Carolina, an increasing number of whom resided in urban counties? Renovation of the means of allocating representation invoked a constitutional issue and thus required voter approval. In the referendum held on January 14, 1964, the Little Federal Plan went down to defeat under an avalanche of urban votes. By an almost two-to-one margin, voters indicated their dissatisfaction with a scheme that would preserve the power of small, predominantly rural counties at the expense of metropolitan areas. In Mecklenburg County, the measure lost by 40,322 votes to 1,533, a twenty-six-to-one margin. And the margin of rejection was no less impressive in other urban counties. Guilford County (Greensboro) defeated the measure 27,112 to 1,254, and Forsyth County (Winston-Salem) voted 19,225 to 1,374 against the scheme.[24]

The following year a federal suit was filed challenging both the U.S. Congress and state Assembly apportionment schedules. The court invalidated the two plans and issued a mandate, complete with deadline, for the restructuring of the legislative districts. In January 1966 a special session of the Assembly finally approved a schedule consistent with the population-equity formula required by the court.[25]

The fractious apportionment battles joined a variety of issues in the 1963 Assembly and engendered a tension that grew as the session progressed. The most critical social and political issues coming from the apportionment debates resonated with the question of whether the state would defend segregation. And legislative activity that addressed racial matters, in terms of both bills and individual rhetoric, was nothing if not ubiquitous. Throughout the session, issues that involved the ideology and institutional arrangements of racial separatism impinged on the Assembly's work.

From the outset, there were indications of smoldering frustration from those prepared to defend the hegemonic tradition of segregation, as defiant rhetoric occasionally erupted into openly racist condemnations of those forces opposing civil inequality and racial separatism. The more vituperative assaults on federal authority and civil rights protest came from the House. In late February, Caswell County Representative Ed Wilson stood before his colleagues and informed them that his county would do "everything legally possible" to restore segregation to its public schools. Wilson received a "heavy round of applause" from fellow members. In January the Caswell County schools had been desegregated following a seven-year legal battle. The suit had been launched in 1956 on behalf of forty-four black students charging that county officials were illegally applying the state's Pupil Assignment Law, which had been created to forestall implementation of truly desegregated public schools. In October 1962 a federal court ruled that the school board had to admit those black students petitioning for transfer. The decision came in the wake of a racist campaign to discourage the petitioners from pursuing the case. Individuals were threatened, and parents of petitioning children received letters bearing Ku Klux Klan emblems.[26]

As Wilson condemned the federal court and promised continued resistance to the judgment, he praised the obstinate school board, whose members were seated in the House gallery. Wilson proclaimed the suit the result of an attempt by "outsiders to destroy a good school program." Wilson believed that bringing black and white students into the same classroom would negate any possibility of study. The Caswell County case foreshadowed the increasing legal challenges to the pupil assignment strategy known as the Pearsall Plan. Formulated as a response to *Brown v. Board of Education*, the Pearsall Plan had effectively precluded any short-term efforts to desegregate North Carolina's public schools. The plaintiffs' success in the Caswell suit, however, suggested that the future of segregated schools was in serious jeopardy. As Wilson closed his address with "may this problem never happen to you," the loud applause offered compelling testimony that many Assembly members were keenly attuned to issues of race politics.[27]

The prosegregation speech was Wilson's most visible contribution to the 1963 Assembly. The event confirms his racist politics and his abiding belief that the problems of his county, state, and nation were caused by the presence of "outsiders," agents engaged in a nefarious effort to corrupt an otherwise peaceful and democratic social order. In his estimation, "90 per cent of the county's citizens approved of the school board's plans" to seek removal of the black students. Presumably, in Wilson's view, even the county's substantial black population favored segregated schools.[28]

Who were the "outsiders" seeking to interfere with an ostensibly popular arrangement? To this conundrum, Wilson offered no precise answer, but he seemed ready to affix some measure of responsibility to a symbolic influence identified with cultural dissent and racial liberalism—the University of North Carolina. Several months following Wilson's tirade, Representative Grace Rodenbough of Stokes County introduced two resolutions providing that former UNC Presidents Gordon Gray and Frank Porter Graham each be elected a "lifetime honorary member" of the UNC Board of Trustees. It was, in essence, a gesture to honor the accomplishments of two distinguished North Carolinians. The designations were to confer no formal authority but provided "honorary" recognition of Gray and Graham's service to the university. The resolutions were quickly approved, but their passage was not unanimous. For at least one representative, even Graham's honorary recognition was problematic. The *House Journal* noted, "Representative Wilson requests and is granted permission to be recorded voting 'Noe.'"[29]

What could have made Wilson so antipathetic to Graham that the legislator would vote to deny even honorary recognition to the former UNC president?

There is no record of Wilson's clarification of his opposition, but given the centrality of race to Wilson's previous rhetoric, Graham's widely known association with racial liberalism must have played a pivotal role. It is clear that the cultural memory of Graham's personal liberalism affected the antagonism directed toward the university. When House Bill 1395 suddenly appeared on June 25, Wilson was listed as a sponsor.

Like Wilson, Representative John H. Kerr Jr. was troubled and angered by overt challenges to the state's racial statutes and practices. The son of a veteran of North Carolina politics, Kerr was from rural Warren County, adjacent to the Virginia border. A plantation area, Warren County was located in the heart of the state's Black Belt region, and, at more than 60 percent, contained the largest percentage of black population of any county in the state. With many voting-age blacks prevented from participation in the electoral process, the county had historically elected to state and national office staunch conservatives whose politics were infused with a belief that blacks should forever remain subordinate to whites. The most famous of the Warren County politicos was Nathaniel Macon, who served as Speaker of the House of Representatives in the early nineteenth century and subsequently as a member of the U.S. Senate. Historian Hugh Lefler described this "Warren County tobacco planter" as the "guardian of the planter-slaveholders of his district, his state, and the South." Lefler also described the perpetuation of power by the slaveholding elite of the county: "A 'Hawkins' was a member from Warren County in forty of the fifty-eight General Assemblies from 1779 to 1835." [30]

Kerr was consistent with this historic trend in Warren County politics. Approaching the end of a long legislative career, he was increasingly frustrated by the almost daily encroachments on the racial strictures that had governed social arrangements throughout his public life, as evidenced by his harangue of Dr. Lewis C. Dowdy, the acting president of historically black North Carolina A&T State University, when he spoke before the legislature's Joint Appropriations Committee in February 1963. [31]

Kerr's outburst was quickly hushed by other legislators, and numerous letters to the editor criticized the aged conservative for being out of touch with a new social reality. Others objected to the implicit threat that unless administrators acted to forestall student demonstrations, appropriations might be jeopardized. A writer from Chapel Hill recognized a larger issue behind the controversy: "This incident clearly shows what happens when the votes of certain sections of rural counties like Warren are permitted to maintain their unconstitutional overweight over the votes of better-educated sections of the state's population. Redistricting is badly needed, if only to make sure that, as reason prevails over prejudice, the Kerrs' bark becomes worse than their bite." [32]

For Assembly traditionalists such as Kerr, race and power were closely aligned. Fearful that their political power and cultural authority were waning, they responded with vituperation and vindictive efforts to legislate against those forces challenging the underpinnings of power. Assembly conservatives would resist the effort to desegregate North Carolina's private and public establishments.

If the prosegregation forces saw reasons for alarm, they were also able to identify hope, however desperate it may have been. A beacon among the gloom was the resistance embodied in the defiance of Alabama Governor Wallace. Wallace's promise to "stand in the schoolhouse door" and his anti-federal rhetoric made him a cherished symbol to Tarheel conservatives, who found their own position increasingly tenuous. Senate President Stone and others seeking to preserve states' rights and segregation drew comfort from the realization that resistance was taking place elsewhere in the South. In their view, the chief legislative task was to bring North Carolina into line with its southern neighbors, as had happened a hundred years before.[33]

This desire received palpable support from the centennial commemoration of the Battle of Gettysburg. Slated to take place in early July, honoring the cultural memory associated with Gettysburg provided an undeniable symbol of regional pride that could be exploited for contemporary political advantage. Early in the session, two bills were passed that evinced legislative interest in preserving the Confederate memory of Gettysburg. In March, Senate Bill 170 provided thirty-five hundred dollars to commemorate the part played by North Carolinians at Gettysburg. Passed without fanfare, the bill provided the funds to assist in meeting the costs of rededicating the North Carolina Memorial. Aware that states' righters and segregationists hoped to exploit the occasion, Governor Sanford made an effort to defuse the event's political significance. In announcing that he would lead the state delegation, he proclaimed, "The only excuse for a commemoration of a bloody and tragic battle is the lesson we learn there." The lesson, in Sanford's view, was that "America is greater than any of its parts — North or South, East or West." Sanford clearly did not want the occasion to serve as a forum for regional chauvinism or a critique of current federal policy.[34]

Far more political in its overtones was House Bill 629. Introduced by eleven representatives from eastern counties, the bill proposed an appropriation of three thousand dollars for the United Daughters of the Confederacy and the Sons of Confederate Veterans to honor the last Confederate soldier to die on a Civil War battlefield. The funds were to pay for a statue that had been erected at Gettysburg in the aftermath of the Supreme Court's 1955 ruling in the *Brown* case. The United Daughters of the Confederacy requested that eleven southern states provide money to cover the costs of the politically en-coded shrine. Of the sponsors of the appropriation measure in the North

Carolina House, six were strong conservatives on issues of state-federal relations and race relations. Like the earlier measure, the last-Confederate-soldier bill passed without noticeable opposition in either house.[35]

The symbolic backdrop provided by the Gettysburg anniversary was seized on by the Assembly's ultraconservatives, who saw useful parallels between the Confederate rebellion and the current resistance to the Supreme Court's desegregation and reapportionment mandates. The week following adjournment, Stone traveled with the North Carolina delegation to Gettysburg. While some commemorated the battle as emblematic of a tragic event in the nation's history, Stone and others used the occasion to meet with fellow sympathizers and rally sectional sentiment in the undertow of identification with the region's martial ardor. Stone met with other segregationists and states' righters to commiserate and seek a means of establishing a united southern front in opposing federal intervention in regional affairs. Among those with whom Stone conferred was Wallace. Describing his meeting with the Alabama governor as the "highlight of my trip," Stone promised a copy of the recently enacted anticommunist bill. In acknowledging the meeting, Stone told Wallace, "You and I speak the same language and I want you to know millions are behind you in your effort to preserve States Rights."[36]

Legislative efforts for some measure of desegregation were few and lacked widespread support. The most positive measure in this regard to come from the session was the passage of a bill lifting the mandatory segregation of the state's National Guard units. Sponsored by twenty senators, only two of whom came from eastern districts, the measure was largely pro forma and noncontroversial. Because the agency received federal funds, maintaining segregated units could not have withstood any legal challenge. Recognizing this, the Assembly made a virtue of necessity. To assuage eastern conservatives, however, the state commander averred that actual desegregation would not take place in the foreseeable future.[37]

The few antidiscrimination bills that did appear received their strongest support from Republicans from urban districts. A key figure in these scant efforts was Senator Charles Strong, a cleric from Greensboro. One such measure, cosponsored by Strong and fellow Republican Thomas Story, was a resolution asking the Southern Association of Colleges and Schools to cease usage of discriminatory terminology in referring to black high schools. The Negro Hill School Bill was reported unfavorably by the Committee on Education. Strong also introduced legislation that would have lifted the legal requirement mandating employers to maintain segregated toilets for black and white employees. The bill would not have required a complete abandonment of segregated toilets but would have allowed employers leeway to maintain toilets without regard to race. This bill also failed to win committee approval. The legislature did, however, pass a substitute measure that allowed rather than required proprietors and employers to have nonsegregated toilet facilities.[38]

Senator Strong was also interested in eliminating the perceived threat of subversion of American ideals. He sponsored an Americanism bill that would have required public primary schools to teach a course on "freedom versus communism." The bill's ostensible purpose was to give the state's youth the necessary ideological apparatus to oppose communism. "I'm trying to point out," said Strong, "we're engaged in a worldwide struggle for mens' minds." This bill also failed in committee when Superintendent of Schools Charles Carroll reported that the bill would require teaching nothing that was not already part of existing curricula. However, the bill's limited support indicated how prepared some legislators — particularly easterners — were to accept the seriousness of inadequate safeguards against the infiltration of communist thought. Senator Henry Shelton of Edgecombe County voted to approve the bill: "I am in favor," he stated, "of something being done along these lines. I don't think it can be passed over lightly." The issue of communism and public education was destined to reappear, but Strong would oppose the bill to control speech at public universities.[39]

During May and June the pace and intensity of the civil rights demonstrations grew. Protesters ringed the legislative building, demanded service at the statehouse cafeteria, and staged demonstrations and sit-ins both inside and outside the Sir Walter Hotel. Increasingly angered by protesters' refusal to terminate their protests, rural legislators, led by those from counties with substantial black populations, demanded that action be taken to halt the endless unruly and provocative demonstrations. Representative Hugh Johnson of Duplin County responded with two "Negro bills." Clearly aimed at the demonstrations, one measure increased the maximum penalty for contempt of court from a $250 fine or thirty days in jail to a $1,000 fine, one year in jail, or both. Similarly, a trespass bill extended the maximum penalty for trespass to two years in jail. Both bills passed the House with "barely a whisper" of debate. In explaining their necessity, Representative George Uzzell from Klan-infested Rowan County firmly linked the measures to the demonstrations. These bills, he said, "will take care of things like this."[40]

Stone used his power as Senate president to prepare the Assembly for action on three states'-rights resolutions that had been introduced in the House by Representative Thorne Gregory of Halifax County. Intended to curb federal power in a number of areas, most prominently in the apportionment area, the measures would have put the state on record "memorializing Congress to call a constitutional convention." The resolutions had been introduced on May 22 and were scheduled for a committee report in early June. In anticipation of a favorable report, Stone had invited conservative California publisher William

Knowland of the *Oakland Tribune* to address a joint session of the Assembly. Although a Republican, Knowland earned considerable applause as he addressed the predominantly Democratic legislature. He advocated support for the constitutional amendments and inveighed against federal preemption of states' rights.[41]

The states'-rights amendments, as they were known, were part of a national campaign in various state legislatures to roll back the federal threat to rural power. Sponsored by the Council of State Governments, it was truly a national movement, as legislatures in almost every region considered the measures. The first resolution proposed a constitutional change permitting two-thirds of the state legislatures to amend the Constitution without congressional involvement. The second measure called for an amendment to prohibit federal involvement in the apportionment of state legislatures. The third proposition — perhaps the most radical in its implications — would have created a "Court of the Union" comprised of the fifty state supreme court chief justices. This body would be empowered to review and, if it so desired, overturn decisions of the U.S. Supreme Court. This was nothing less than an attempt by ultraconservatives to fundamentally alter federal-state relations in a manner that would produce a confederation in which decisive authority would reside with state judges. More than a dozen state assemblies approved at least one of the measures, but only Arkansas and Wyoming endorsed all three. Although not primarily racial in nature, the amendments indirectly addressed the racial politics of conservative white southerners such as those in the North Carolina Assembly.[42] Stone and his fellow ultraconservatives were certain that the three measures were headed for endorsement by the General Assembly as criticism of federal interference appeared ubiquitous and unanimous. In reality, the amendments represented a last desperate hope of salvaging some form of victory following a series of setbacks. Defeat on the resolutions would push the ultras to the edge and compel them to consider an even more desperate and reactionary measure.

As Assembly conservatives prepared to launch an assault on federal power, a principal component of their own cultural authority was unraveling as massive civil rights demonstrations took place in cities throughout the state. During the latter weeks of May and continuing into June, major demonstrations occurred in Greensboro, Durham, High Point, Fayetteville, Wilmington, and Raleigh (see chapter 3). And the actions were succeeding: in city after city, biracial committees negotiated plans for the complete integration of public businesses and venues. In North Carolina as elsewhere in the South, the formal demise of Jim Crow was fashioned by an urban, biracial bourgeoisie.[43]

Increasing numbers of whites also began to publicly distance themselves from naked racism and segregation. In Raleigh, a group of prominent citizens, including Allard K. Lowenstein and other faculty members and administrators from area colleges and universities, placed newspaper announcements attesting to their preference for open accommodations and calling on fellow citizens to join them.[44] Editorial pages overflowed with letters objecting to the treatment of blacks and decrying the repugnance of racism.

There was, to be sure, violent resistance to integration efforts. In Lexington, two people were killed, including a reporter, as young whites responded violently to attempts to desegregate a bowling alley. One hundred state troopers were dispatched to restore order as the town's mayor blamed the violence on "irresponsible whites." State police were also sent to the Granville County seat of Oxford to quell disturbances following four nights of race-related violence that occurred when blacks sought service at a cafe and attempted to purchase tickets at a movie theater. In late May, violence also flared in High Point for several days as black and white antisegregation picketers were attacked and beaten.[45]

Open violence against civil rights protesters was an exception, however; it never became generalized behavior and was quickly denounced by local political and civic leaders. Opposition to marchers and picketers most commonly took the form of verbal taunts. On Raleigh's Fayetteville Street, where demonstrators targeted the Sir Walter Hotel, silent groups of middle-aged white men would stand on the opposite sidewalk, watching as black and white protesters picketed. Letters opposing desegregation also appeared, but they were few in number and typically came from writers in rural eastern counties. One such writer from Halifax County commended Wallace's stand against federal intervention at the University of Alabama. The letter compared President John F. Kennedy, the attorney general, and the Supreme Court to "dictators and communism." "I don't see much difference here," it concluded, "from what [communism] is in other countries." For opponents of civil equality and desegregation, the association of federal authority and black insurgency with communism occurred with greater frequency as it became increasingly apparent that segregation, as a means of social organization, was crumbling. One letter to the *Raleigh News and Observer* complained, "unless there is something done and at once to curb the power of the Federal Government, we are going to be completely under Communist domination. It has been creeping up on us." Another writer was even more blunt about the source of the civil rights protests: "the Communists have infiltrated the colleges of the U.S. and sparked the Negro demonstrations."[46]

This shifting of ideological terrain to anticommunism and implicitly away from race per se cannot be solely attributed to a tactical maneuver necessitated by the bankruptcy and impending defeat of segregation. To be sure, as these letters indicate, there was an inseparable linkage between the two in the minds of many North Carolinians. And a political move was certainly required as it became apparent that segregationist rhetoric was falling increasingly on deaf ears. The anticommunist appeal, however, was not predicated on intellectual dishonesty and sheer demagoguery. There was conspicuous confirmation for segregationists, in terms of their meager comprehension of communism, that subversive and conspiratorial forces were at work.

The elemental presumption that communism was at the root of the demonstrations was fueled by the logic of racism. Blacks were perceived as happy and indolent; on their own, they possessed neither the skills nor the inclination to formulate such systematic challenges to segregation — someone else had to be directing them, giving them instructions. From this juncture it was but a small step to identify communist influences because the communists were known to favor complete integration and "social equality" between the races. The presence of whites among the demonstrators — often students and professors such as Lowenstein — tended to cast suspicion on colleges and universities as the locus of communist contagion. And there were those who had already decided to act on this belief. At the 1960 national convention of the American Legion, held in Miami Beach, the North Carolina Department submitted a resolution that stipulated, "There is evidence of a concentration of Pro-Communist expression in conferences, institutes, and seminars conducted in some of our educational institutions and a deliberate effort made to exclude pro-American expression, especially is this encouraged by those in the fields of political science and sociology."[47]

The resolution sought greater vigilance about the putative problem, but it raises the question of whether the state's universities were among those the North Carolina delegation had in mind. Such allegations, grounded in suspicion and anti-intellectualism, found fertile soil in the spring of 1963. The whites involved in fighting segregation came from UNC, North Carolina State, and Duke. UNC had a long, well-known history of student and faculty support for racial liberalism. For segregationists and others opposed to the sweeping changes that seemed to be taking place, this memory of the public university — as exemplified by Wilson's "Noe" vote against Graham — was not favorable.[48]

An additional putative indicator that communists were behind the protests was the commonly held definition of communism as synonymous with an omnipotent central government. In this view, the reach of an oppressive, all-powerful state compelling the behavior of citizens was a definitive characteristic of communism. When the federal courts issued rulings that conflicted with traditional social and political practices, or when federal troops were dispatched to enforce the fiat of Washington, it was perceived as symptomatic of the methods of a communist regime. Numerous complaints linking integration with communism pointed to recent Supreme Court and federal court decisions and presidential action as evidence that federal commands resembled communism. Emblematic of such trends that bore directly on the situation in Raleigh and other North Carolina cities were the Warren Court decision prohibiting state or municipal interference with sit-in protests occurring in public places of business and President Kennedy's announced support for a new federal civil rights bill. In the aftermath of these two developments, there appeared a surge in anticommunist rhetoric from elements of both the public and the Assembly.[49]

Religion constituted a final factor contributing to frustrated traditionalists' increasing tendency to conjoin civil rights and communism. On June 17, 1963, the Supreme Court issued an eight-to-one ruling that barred Bible reading and directed prayer from the nation's public schools as a part of any required classroom exercise. For those predisposed to antagonism and suspicion of federal action, the Bible-reading prohibition was interpreted as a blatant renunciation of God and religion. South Carolina Congressman L. Mendel Rivers declared that the Court had "officially declared its disbelief in God." And communism was, in the popular view, defined by its devotion to atheism. While many clerics accepted the propriety of the ruling, others did not, and their views reflected the opinion of many North Carolinians that if a majority of the population favored Christianity, there should be no ban on its public exercise.[50]

One example of this sentiment came at the annual convention of the state American Legion, which took place in Charlotte in late June. The Reverend Shelton Hutchinson, the legion chaplain, labeled the ruling a "trend toward atheism" in a service conducted for the four hundred legionnaires and their families. The legion's concern with atheism and communism became further evident when the group endorsed a resolution calling the UNC Progressive Labor Club an "atheistic and hate embittered group" and calling on the trustees to conduct an investigation. More ominously, an additional resolution asked the General Assembly to create legislation to "prohibit the use of any publicly owned building or property for any meeting or assembly" for anyone who was a "member of the Communist Party, the American Nazi Party or any organization advocating the overthrow of the government by force." Here was an immediate precursor of the bill introduced and enacted into law three days later.[51]

As the session approached adjournment, the ultraconservative coterie in both House and Senate watched with frustration and alarm as developments outside the Assembly signaled that core components of their political power — race, apportionment, states' rights — were being successfully challenged by forces representing different cultural values. The prospect of cultural defeat sharply accelerated in early June as the *Raleigh News and Observer* reported a "Historic Week of Racial Progress in the State": "Significance attaches to what happened at Winston-Salem, Durham, Statesville, Raleigh, and many other communities. Under community leadership, century-old traditions about Negro-white relations are being swept away." [52]

In Thomasville, public swimming pools were integrated. In Winston-Salem, Durham, Raleigh, and Statesville, virtually all public establishments were desegregated. And in a number of other cities, plans were being made for the dismantling of Jim Crow. Even in eastern North Carolina, the bedrock of racial conservatism, blacks were demanding change: 270 demonstrators were arrested at Kinston. [53]

Witnessing the demise of segregation and unable to make direct use of state power to restore their authority, conservative lawmakers grew increasingly angry. Returning to the Sir Walter Hotel each evening, members would be forced, on occasion, to avoid or step over sit-in protesters in the lobby. On most evenings, however, the legislators clustered to watch the demonstrations taking place in the street outside. As a result of the recent Supreme Court ruling that states and cities could not interfere with peaceful sit-ins in public places of business, there was little the legislators could do to offset or preempt the protests. The lawmakers were forced to watch impotently as the symbolic representation of the end of the era of white supremacy took place. Under these circumstances, tensions and anxieties accumulated.

The climax to the frustration and anger of the states' righters and rural conservatives came in late June. Following a week of unrelenting demonstrations in the capital, the final week of the session began. On June 20 the long-anticipated Super Court resolution came before the Senate. After a difficult session that included Stone's profane abuse of a television reporter and White's scuffling with a newspaperman, there appeared to be a final measure of redemption for the embattled conservatives. Although certain of passage, Stone was taking no chances with the resolution. Prior to the vote he allowed the "Citizens for Preservation of Constitutional Government," a local group of archconservative businessmen, to place a leaflet on each senator's desk urging passage of the controversial proposal. What transpired during the debate that followed surprised and shocked Stone and his fellow antifederalists. A coterie of speakers including Senators Perry Martin, Claude Currie, Luther Hamilton, and Lindsay Warren rose and characterized the measure as a dangerous abandonment of the federal-state framework embodied in the Constitution. The opponents noted widespread disagreement with recent Supreme Court decisions and federal actions but stressed that the Super Court proposal was an unwarranted and extreme response. [54]

The outcome of the ensuing vote indicated how eviscerated states'-rights ideology had become. Anticipating an easy victory, Stone was stunned by the twenty-eight-to-twelve margin of defeat that saw several expected eastern allies abandon the proposal. Debate and discussion from the floor had clearly caused several members to reconsider. Stone also recognized the debate's transformative impact on the Super Court resolution; he would not permit protracted debate to forestall passage of the last defiant gesture of his tenure as a public official — the anticommunist speaker ban law.[55]

The 1963 General Assembly session had been contentious and unproductive and had culminated in the spectacular defeat of the states'-rights resolutions. Segregation was at an end, and there was no manner of knowing where the civil rights movement might lead. The apportionment issue had not been resolved and constituted another source of frustration, fear, and anger. The day before adjournment, however, would offer a final opportunity for retribution against the dark forces assumed to be responsible for these reversals.

5 | Making a Case for Revision

Even as UNC carried on a quiet effort to line up support to question the application of the speaker ban, the university carefully examined those invited from outside the campus who appeared to come under the rubric of the law. The speaker law was not merely an object of debate; administrative instruments were put in place to assure conformity to the speaker policy necessitated by the statute. This screening took the form of a questionnaire required of sponsoring organizations before any speaking engagement would be approved and a venue made available. Given the vagueness of the statute and the administration's desire to avoid any action that might antagonize critics, enforcement was vigorous. Regardless of professional standing or academic credentials, any prospective visitor who was politically suspect would come under close scrutiny.

The case of the first official victim of the law to "regulate visiting speakers" confirmed opposition claims that the statute would have a deleterious impact on intellectual life at the University of North Carolina. In the spring of 1963, the internationally renowned geneticist and evolutionary biologist J. B. S. Haldane planned a lecture tour of the United States, including an appearance at UNC. The invitation had been accepted while the 1963 legislature was still in session, so Haldane's visit attracted little attention beyond the academic community. After the speaker law was passed, however, a faculty member recalled Haldane's earlier activities, including a stint as chairman of the editorial board of the *Daily Worker,* the organ of the British Communist Party.[1]

Haldane's editorial involvement with the *Daily Worker* had concluded in 1949, and there was no evidence that he remained an active CP member in 1963. More to the point, his scheduled appearance was entirely professional — a scientific lecture — and in no way involved the political speech implied by the speaker law.[2] Here was a propitious opportunity for the UNC administration to reaffirm the legitimacy of its academic mission regardless of a member's past or present political sympathies. Haldane's credentials were impeccable: member of numerous select and prestigious scientific groups, including the British Royal Academy of Science; holder of honorary doctorates from universities in several countries; and recipient of the Kimber Medal of the U.S. National Academy of Sciences. UNC could have maintained, with confidence, that Haldane's presence was purely professional and within the common intercourse of university activity.

With the political circumstances that faced President William C. Friday and Chancellor William B. Aycock and the strategic goal of persuading the Assembly to revise the law, such a course was implausible. When Haldane's past involvement was made known, the university demanded that he respond to questions about his political affiliations. Friday justified the action by acknowledging his intention to comply with every underlying mandate perceived to be a part of the statute: "Where there is apparent doubt as to whether the individual would be eligible under the law to speak on the campuses, then the university feels obligated under the law to make an inquiry." Rather than question or challenge this infringement on academic discourse, Friday and the university quietly acquiesced in the first test of the speaker ban.[3]

The issue of Haldane's appearance became irrelevant when he refused to respond to questions about his personal views and affiliations. The scientist maintained that he refused to answer on the basis of "principle." At this juncture, Friday considered the invitation "effectively canceled," and the matter was closed. The Haldane refusal presented such a bold-faced denial of academic freedom that it sparked a flurry of less publicized declinations by prospective speakers. Two Duke professors refused to speak to students at UNC-Greensboro and North Carolina State University in protest of the speaker law.[4]

UNC's capitulation to the ideological assumptions of the speaker law was reprised by editorialist Jesse Helms. Despite the absence of indications from any quarter that Haldane's talk was to be politically oriented, Helms averred that "it seems obvious that the gentleman is interested in spreading the philosophy of communism," and thus it was entirely appropriate to invoke the speaker law. Helms provided a hollow rationale for banning Haldane, but much of his editorial was devoted to transferring the issue of a foreign speaker,

Haldane, to domestic agents that had been associated with the university—in this case, Larry Phelps of Progressive Labor. In Helms's view, "since biology is the study of living organisms, then perhaps Dr. Haldane might have been able to explain the behavior of the absurd Mr. Phelps. But North Carolinians were probably more interested in how the University of North Carolina permitted Mr. Phelps' mind to become and remain so twisted." [5]

The editorialist refused to accept, however, the cancellation of Haldane's visit as conclusive evidence that UNC had fully accepted the requisite anticommunist faith: "The cancellation of Dr. Haldane's appearances is being presented as proof of academic righteousness. It is, of course, no such thing." Before Helms would give his blessing to the lifting of legislative controls, the university would have to go considerably further to demonstrate its commitment to the cause, a demonstration that would include nothing less than the ideological inspection of faculty and the purging of dissident elements. [6]

Perhaps the greatest tragedy was UNC's recognition that a grave injustice was being perpetrated not only on Haldane but also on students and faculty who might benefit from the appearance of a world-renowned scholar. Professor of classics B. L. Ullman, who had served with Haldane on the Balzan Awards Committee, referred to the result as a "great shame" and a vivid example of how the legislature had been "terribly misled" when it passed the law. The final verdict that UNC had suffered the biggest loss in refusing to allow Haldane's visit appeared some sixteen months later following the death of the scientist at age seventy-two. In reviewing Haldane's intellectual and professional achievements, Chancellor Paul Sharp noted that "he was one of the world's most interesting and influential personages. We can only regret that a legislative act keeps men of this renown from our campuses." The chancellor's statement, while true enough, failed to acknowledge an equally important reality of the Haldane affair: UNC's failure to insist on the unimpeded right to conduct the academic enterprise. [7]

After the Haldane case demonstrated that individuals with a suspect political record would be investigated, it would be some time before this particular application of the law would be called into question. Politically, it was important to those who desired repeal or revision that further demonstrations of the negative character of the law remain visible. If normal university operations and activities were unimpeded by the presence of the gag law, the imperative for amendment—to say nothing of repeal—would be markedly diminished. In a speech before the Greensboro Bar Association shortly after the Haldane cancellation, Chancellor Aycock used the episode to underscore the potential for damage to the university brought on by the law's presence. "We are being deprived," said Aycock, "of the opportunity to learn from visiting scientists who have something worthy to offer us in areas in which we need to catch up. We are in the process of losing our reputation as being a great institution, unafraid of the free flow of ideas."[8] Thus, unable to effect immediate repeal of the statute, UNC and its allies sought to initiate — and win — a propaganda war by demonstrating that, whatever the constitutional or libertarian issues, the law was a practical nuisance and threatened to ruin UNC's reputation in academic and professional circles.

The Haldane debacle opened a new vista of quiet activity by the faculty in support of revision of the speaker law. Realizing the political leverage that might be brought to bear from a far-reaching academic boycott of the state, faculty members began discussing the existence of the statute with colleagues in other states. This is not to say that there was a coordinated campaign to persuade organizations to avoid the state — there is no evidence that such was the case. Rather, individual members took it on themselves to make known to their colleagues the unique circumstances prevailing in North Carolina, an action they were certain would produce useful results in their campaign to focus critical attention on the law.

Results were immediately forthcoming. In late 1963, the American Physical Society announced that its planned 1965 national meeting, scheduled for Chapel Hill, had been postponed until 1966. UNC physics professor Eugen Merzbacher, the local coordinator for the meeting, noted that the society made no mention of the speaker law in announcing the postponement but added that had the law not been passed, "it seems certain that the meeting would have been held as planned." Thus, a national professional conference that would have brought some fifteen hundred of the finest scientific minds to Chapel Hill was jeopardized by the presence of the speaker law. Seizing on the obvious political ramifications of the postponement, Chancellor Aycock observed that "the timing of the thing indicates that the Gag Law was on their minds. They don't want to put themselves in the position of having to place restrictions upon whom they invite to the meeting."[9]

The speaker ban clearly had caused the postponement, and it was equally apparent that the meeting, along with other conventions, would be used as political leverage to persuade recalcitrant legislators that some adjustment would have to be made. Such a stratagem was apparent in Professor Merzbacher's parting comment: "I and my colleagues hope that by 1966 the Gag Law will be repealed. That would remove any obstacles which now stand in the way of unhindered communication between scientists."[10]

The newspapers responded editorially with consternation. They pointed to the postponement as evidence of the flaws in the law's construction and its subsequent muddled interpretation. The major dailies said that the law intended to apprehend communist subversives was actually netting legitimate scholars. More important, the law was bringing the state and its public institutions embarrassment and ridicule. "We can only wonder," said the *Durham Herald*, "how many slaps higher education in this state must take before the ban is repealed? It was predictable from the start that North Carolina's loyal students and faculties — not any Communist conspiracy — would be the real victims of this law." The abandonment of the state by the physicists and other expected cancellations offered sterling testimony that the law was badly flawed.[11]

The physicists' meeting was highly symbolic because it had been planned for Chapel Hill, but other professional organizations without formal plans to meet at UNC or in North Carolina announced preemptively that they would avoid holding conferences in the state until the law was rescinded. The Southern Political Science Association resolved in November 1964 that "until the Law (H.B. 1395) is repealed, the Southern Political Science Association agrees to abstain from holding any of its meetings upon state-supported campuses of higher education in North Carolina." A faculty panel appointed by the American Association of University Professors compiled a formal record of the episodes in which the university was adversely affected by the speaker law. The report, "The Impact of the 'Visiting Speakers' Law," identified nine examples of disruption during the nine months of the 1963–64 academic year and concluded that the law had been "hurtful" and that the "gradual erosion of our national prestige" was evident.[12]

Supporters of the law recognized immediately what was happening, but apart from allegations that the denials were contrived, they were powerless to combat the impact. Former House member L. J. Phipps of Chapel Hill, past president of the North Carolina Department of the American Legion, attempted to expose the refusals as part of UNC-backed plan to undermine support for the law. As a member of the Chapel Hill American Legion Post in 1962, Phipps had participated in the call for an investigation of communists, and at the State Convention held in Charlotte just days before the speaker bill was passed, he had supported a resolution calling for a proscription of all communists from state-supported institutions. Now Phipps wanted to determine if the American Association of Physics Teachers (AAPT) had genuinely refused to hold its annual meeting in North Carolina because of the speaker law or if the purported refusal was a fabrication designed to embarrass the state. In a letter to UNC Professor William Haisley, Phipps asked for information certifying the group's existence, the membership of individuals from the UNC Physics Department, and when the organization last met in North Carolina. Haisley's response confirmed that the idea to invite the AAPT to meet in the state was solely his own and that while the group had never met in the state, a conference in North Carolina was highly desirable because "the teaching of physics in this state needs all the help it can get." Phipps did not obtain the evidence of chicanery that he hoped for, and the matter was closed.[13]

The complicity of the professorate in manipulating the restrictions for political ends unsettled not only those who supported an unadulterated law but also elites who favored a revised law. The rising annoyance with faculty actions rested in a belief that the state was being unnecessarily embarrassed. Eager to maintain a progressive image, those charged with directing the affairs of state were not disposed to look favorably on the utilization of critical exposure as a tactic in securing the law's repeal.

Next, the American Society of Mammalogists decided to move its 1966 annual meeting from Nags Head, on North Carolina's Outer Banks, to Long Beach, California. The decision had been made at the group's 1964 meeting, and the speaker ban law was the exclusive reason for the relocation. How did the mammalogists, meeting in Mexico City, learn of the existence of the law? A member from North Carolina made a point of telling them. Dr. Frederick S. Barkalow, a professor of zoology at North Carolina State University, noted that "with reluctance and considerable personal embarrassment, [I] had to call attention to the Speaker Ban Law and how it might apply to some of our foreign members." Based on the results of the Haldane case, the society could scarcely sanction conditions that might put members in jeopardy as well as compromise the intellectual ideals of an academic organization.[14]

In a letter to Gordon Hanes, state senator from Winston-Salem and an appointee to a panel created to study the law, Barkalow articulated and defended the necessity of bringing the speaker ban to the association's attention. Hanes, the scion of a prominent textile and banking family, was vitally interested in resolving the speaker controversy while placating the core concerns of the various parties and interest groups. Like many of the elites involved, however, his primary objective was to forestall any unnecessary embarrassment to the state's progressive image. This meant keeping debate about the law's illiberal strictures in-house; greater publicity, in Hanes's view, would subject the state to the glare of national notoriety as well as intensify and polarize debate within the state.

Although nominally sympathetic to the UNC administration's amendment strategy, Hanes vociferously objected to Barkalow's action as well as the professorate's attempts to invite professional quarantine of the state. In responding to Barkalow's explanation, Hanes sharply criticized efforts to bring external scrutiny and pressure to bear and castigated the faculty members for their open opposition:

This responsibility [to see that taxpayers' wishes were followed] is made more difficult by the emotional attacks of the professorial fraternity in general and by actions such as that outlined in your letter. Having invited the American Society of Mammalogists in 1963 to meet at Nags Head in June 1966, I fail to see your reasoning for calling attention to the "Speaker Ban Law" since it does not apply to any meeting in Nags Head. You could have saved yourself the "considerable personal embarrassment" by simply not mentioning it. However, I strongly suspect that you called attention to the Speaker Ban Law with the specific purpose of causing this Society to remove their meeting from North Carolina to California, which was the ultimate result.[15]

The objection raised in Hanes's angry response was couched in the same assumption that had, in major part, informed passage of the law: professors should not engage in politics; they should limit their activity to scholarly research and teaching while studiously avoiding controversial subjects in the public domain. Hanes, like many others, considered himself a strong and committed friend of the university. His remonstrances about the professor's actions in bringing professional attention to the speaker ban were motivated by a belief that such actions constituted improper meddling in an area that was the exclusive domain of the taxpayers and their elected representatives in the legislature. However, as Hanes's uncharacteristically acrimonious charge confirms, the continuing stream of cancellations, although not decisive, was undeniably of immense propaganda value to those seeking change in the speaker law and corresponding adjustment of UNC policy. In fact, such actions were vital for any forthcoming movement on the law: without concrete, visible examples that the statute was detrimental to routine campus functions, opponents would have been increasingly hard put to find a convincing rationale for revision.

Apart from its ideologically and philosophically abstract dimensions, the speaker law did not appear to present a significant dilemma for the routine operations of a college or university campus. The students and faculty were not preponderantly engaged in any politics, much less enamored of radical politics. Just as most faculty members were concerned with research, teaching, and career advancement, students were consumed by course requirements and graduation. As long as questions and issues pertinent to the speaker law remained within abstract categories and inchoate forms, supporters of the law would hold the advantage. The seemingly impregnable fortress of anti-communism was sufficient to turn back most assaults predicated on abstract concepts such as academic freedom. When the cancellations began to register, the possible losses began to take on a more tangible veneer.

Another method of criticism pursued by individual faculty invoked a belief that under existing circumstances it would be difficult to recruit and maintain a nationally prominent faculty. Critics argued that the law would disillusion the faculty and that many professors, particularly younger academics, would seek positions elsewhere. There was no immediate avalanche of resignations or conclusive evidence that any individual either left or refused an offer to join the UNC faculty solely because of the speaker ban. The faculty attrition rate was not inordinate and resulted from a variety of factors; few resignations even mentioned the law. A faculty committee appointed to investigate the impact could identify only one case in which the intellectual conditions imposed by the statute were cited as contributing to faculty resignation. Professor Dudley Williams, chairman of the physics department at North Carolina State University, resigned his position to accept a position at Kansas State University, stating that the specter of the speaker ban had been a pivotal factor in his decision. However, there is reason to think that Williams's invocation of the speaker ban as a factor in his resignation might have been largely a propaganda missile. His move to Kansas State was not simply lateral but represented a substantial advancement to an endowed chair.[16]

When it became apparent in early 1965 that the General Assembly would not move decisively to modify the law, the incidence of speaker ban–related resignations began to rise. Evidence that faculty were leaving, ostensibly because of the speaker restrictions, raised the stakes concerning the law's future. While the actual number of resignations remained small, the exodus offered visible evidence of faculty disenchantment. More typical were entreaties like that directed to Governor Dan Moore from Lawrence Slifkin, a professor of physics at Chapel Hill. Slifkin pointed out the benefits he had brought to UNC — nearly four million dollars in federal research money — and how much he and his family enjoyed Chapel Hill and desired to stay. Still, said Slifkin, this was not enough: "I doubt I will be willing to compromise principles so much as to stay at a university fettered by a law such as now exists. I am just one case out of a great many who will surely drift away to other institutions if the present law remains intact. The point is that I would never have come here in the first place had the existing Speaker Ban been in effect."[17]

Slifkin was unique in putting in writing his unwillingness to remain. Although staunchly opposed to the law, most faculty members had decided to wait it out and put their faith in Friday's adroit political skills to remove the draconian prohibitions required by the statute. Unlike Slifkin, a full professor of demonstrated prominence, most faculty, especially untenured junior members, were not securely established enough to openly suggest to the governor that a law be rescinded as the price for their continuation in North Carolina. There was increasing evidence, however, that those faculty who did accept offers from elsewhere took advantage of the opportunity to link their departure to the presence of the speaker ban law. Jacques Berger, an assistant professor of zoology at North Carolina State, resigned his position after less than a year to accept a similar post at the University of Toronto. In a letter delineating his reasons for leaving, Berger noted "comparative academic opportunities" and "salary" as the two principal reasons. Toronto was indeed a prestigious location, and, as in most cases, salary and other forms of remuneration were typical factors. But Berger's letter quickly disposed of these circumstances to explain, "The academic opportunities at Toronto alone, were not enough to cause me to move; nor was the increase in salary anything but marginal considering the high cost of living in Canada. What greatly influenced my decision, however, was that I felt my future as a university professor of zoology would be far improved if I left a state university system which was obliged to operate under such a restrictive law." [18]

If some faculty members indicated the difficulty of remaining while the speaker law was in force, others evinced similar rationales in declining positions offered in the UNC system. Gerard Salton, a computer and information specialist from Harvard, turned down an offer to join the UNC Information Science Department to accept a similar offer at Cornell. In explaining his decision, Salton noted a fondness for Chapel Hill but averred that the town and the department "were not sufficient to overcome the many fears I had of the environment in North Carolina," thus identifying the climate imposed by the speaker law as a decisive factor. The loss of Salton was no small measure; department head F. P. Brooks Jr. noted that Salton's work in his field "is the best done to date anywhere. I do not know where to find another young teacher and scholar of such promise." Brooks also claimed that the loss delayed the creation of a Ph.D. program in information science at UNC. [19]

In the highly competitive academic job market in which UNC contended with upper-echelon schools for the best talent, growing awareness of North Carolina's political situation might well have been decisive in scores of other recruitments. In the case of Salton, only Brooks's dogged pursuit for clarification brought to light the speaker ban as a matter of concern.

Although faculty actions in focusing attention on issues threatening demonstrable harm to the state's reputation and the credibility of its institutions were essential, they were not, in themselves, sufficient leverage to compel the General Assembly to reconsider the law. While speaker ban opponents and business elites might be concerned with evidence of growing national embarrassment, loss of convention revenues, and, most important, the steady erosion of the state university system through faculty attrition, such ramifications did little to dissuade obstinate legislators and diehard supporters of the law.

Some UNC critics endorsed summary firings and expulsions for any students and faculty refusing to accept the reality of the law. J. Yates Bailey of Bald Creek believed that those who objected to the ban should be "given an opportunity to resign their position, and then if they would not resign, fire them because they are Communist thinkers and doers." F. D. B. Harding of Yadkin County was even more demonstrative in his lack of concern with academic disenchantment with the speaker law: "You talk about all the Students leaving? Well, maybe if we got rid of all those northerners and niggers, there'd be room for my kids to go to school." These statements were most remarkable because of their source: both Bailey and Harding were members of the state Senate. Although not as crude or obstreperous in their remarks, many other Assembly members were equally determined to turn back any attempts to rescind the law. Assured that anticommunism and its attendant manifestations had popular support, the General Assembly would take no precipitous action to address the controversy.[20]

Stronger evidence of the law's corrosive character, along with more assertive political leadership, would be required to effect revision of the speaker ban. And this leadership would not come from the legislature as a result of the remonstrations of UNC personae. Already angered at UNC opposition and eager to defend the fundamental integrity of their legislative handiwork, many lawmakers were further indisposed by the concerted civil rights protests occurring in Chapel Hill in 1963 and 1964. Using sit-in and sit-down tactics, student activists challenged establishments in the Chapel Hill area that still refused to serve patrons on a nondiscriminatory basis. With UNC students and faculty visibly at the forefront of the demonstrations, news reports brought the events into the homes and minds of many North Carolinians. As House Bill 1395 had its origins in reaction to civil rights demonstrations in 1963, vestiges of the animus that had engendered the law allowed for a revisitation of anti–Chapel Hill sentiment. The demonstrations represented lawlessness and disorder at the university and offered a convenient and practical opportunity to reassert the usefulness of statutory oversight of the campus.[21]

The Haldane case and the subsequent cancellations did not deter those who believed in the essential utility of the speaker law. The disruptions of academic inquiry were viewed at best as regrettable consequences. The statute had not yet been employed to apprehend the politically inspired orators that its drafters had in mind. However, the anticommunist antennae continued to identify suspects, and the UNC administration, ever eager to satisfy its critics' concerns and expectations, responded vigilantly to ostensible violators. In early 1965 an invitation to Arthur Miller was canceled on grounds that the playwright had "refused to answer certain questions when he appeared before the House Committee on Un-American Activities in 1956–57."[22]

The refusal to proceed with Miller's invitation demonstrated the lengths to which UNC would go to confirm its obedience to the speaker ban in an effort to secure a restoration of authority for its administrators. University officials could readily have ascertained, had they been so inclined, that Miller was immune from the particular categories established by the law. There was no question that Miller had never advocated "the overthrow of the Constitution" or the government, for that matter. And it had never been established that he was a Communist Party member. His refusal to answer certain questions before HUAC prompted his banning by UNC, and even here the law did not formally apply to Miller. While he had declined to name names, the author had cited the First Amendment rather than the Fifth in refusing to comply with the committee's directives. Not only had Miller never cited the Fifth, but his use of the First Amendment was not taken to avoid the issue of personal incrimination: Miller agreed to testify about his own experiences but refused to discuss the politics of friends and colleagues. By any estimation, there was scant reason that the award-winning playwright should not have been eligible to appear at the UNC Arts Festival.[23]

Why then, was the speaker law invoked and the invitation rescinded? The answer, in simplest form, was to avoid controversy. Controversy — in the person of a speaker who might have attracted the scrutiny of pro–speaker ban legislators or critics such as Jesse Helms —was to be avoided at all costs. Only if all questions pertinent to the sincerity of UNC's anticommunist resolve were removed could the conditions needed for the reestablishment of administrative authority be met. As benign and apolitical as the Miller visit appeared, no chances could be taken. The stakes were too great to risk offending those wielding effective power, the General Assembly. While such responses were serviceable for the administration's larger strategic interests, the damage done to UNC's reputation was palpable. One national publication somewhat facetiously claimed that "since the ban the most controversial speakers have been actress Jayne Mansfield and *Playboy* publisher Hugh Hefner."[24]

In pursuing this course of action, the UNC administration virtually capitulated to its critics' political agendas. As the university refused to exercise any discretion or prerogative in applying the speaker policy, it in effect and in substance called on elements supporting the law to make decisions. "I have felt," said Chancellor Sharp, "that administrative officers should not be called upon to define who is or who is not a communist. For that reason we consulted the attorney general of the state of North Carolina for such a definition."[25] Unwilling to aggressively confront critics, the administrators were determined to avoid anything that might engender controversy and, concomitantly, to do whatever was necessary to regain control of speaker policy.

For almost two years there had been no occasion to employ the provisions of the speaker law against the type of speaker anticipated by those who had created and supported the legislation. Despite the prevalence of unintended victims, the speaker law was not wholly ineffective in fulfilling its intended purpose: preventing campus access to domestic radicals. In May 1965 the law was wheeled into action against a figure who personified the type of individual the anticommunist lawmakers had in mind as they conceived House Bill 1395. The student chapter of the NAACP had invited Carl Braden to speak in

UNC's Gerrard Hall. A southern radical, Braden and his wife, Anne, had long been prominent activists in the civil rights movements and other campaigns to eliminate both segregation and political repression from American society. In 1954 a Kentucky court had convicted Braden of advocating sedition by inciting racial conflict. The Bradens had purchased a house in a white area of Louisville and then sold it to a black electrician, an unthinkable act during the era of restrictive covenants and Jim Crow. Public awareness of the sale resulted in a cross burning, shotgun blasts, and a bomb under the house. At the trial, much was made of the "seditious" literature found during a search of Braden's home, and a paid witness testified that Braden had recruited her into the CP. Convicted of sedition, Braden spent eight months in prison before an appeals court overturned the verdict.[26]

This was not the end of allegations of communist subversion against Braden as a consequence of his efforts to challenge segregation. In 1959 he was convicted of contempt of Congress for refusing to respond to questions from a HUAC panel regarding his political activities. Both Braden and Frank Wilkinson, executive director of the National Committee to Abolish the House Un-American Activities Committee, cited the First Amendment in refusing to discuss questions about alleged CP affiliation. For defying HUAC, Braden and Wilkinson served nine months in a federal penitentiary.[27]

By 1965 Braden was a speaker much in demand. As field director of the Southern Conference Educational Fund (SCEF), he had become a spokesman on the evils of segregation and how HUAC served as an instrument in perpetuating racial inequality. For tradition-minded white southerners, Braden was the embodiment of the "outside agitator" who ostensibly aroused blacks and naive white collegians.

When it was learned that the students planned to invite Braden, UNC administrators took immediate steps to establish a rationale for denying him campus access. The central figure in the attack on Braden and SCEF was, not surprisingly, Helms. The faculty adviser to the NAACP chapter notified Dean of Student Affairs C. O. Cathey and expressed the opinion that Braden might come under the terms of the speaker law. Cathey, ever vigilant to protect UNC's interest vis-à-vis the General Assembly, quickly determined that Braden was too controversial to risk legislative animosity. Cathey's initial response was predicated on a copy of a story appearing in a Knoxville, Tennessee, newspaper indicating Braden had been alleged to have a communist "connection." It was ironic that this story should have produced Cathey's anxiety over Braden's impending visit: the clipping had been sent by Braden himself as a publicity aid. Moreover, Braden had spoken directly about the issue in a letter to his UNC hosts: "Some people consider me to be a Communist but I do not feel that I would be in violation of the North Carolina Speaker Ban Law."

Braden's belief was well-founded; he had never been convicted of being a CP member, and he had not cited the Fifth Amendment before any governmental body.[28]

The confidence with which Braden claimed to be exempt from the speaker law did not dissuade Cathey: it had the reverse effect of convincing him that, under existing circumstances, Braden could not be permitted to speak. The problem, however, was to manufacture a plausible reason for invoking the speaker ban. In so doing, the UNC administration began a collaboration with anticommunist agencies as well as with forces supporting the restrictions of a law that began as an effort to silence dissenting speech at Chapel Hill. The effort began when the university contacted the State Bureau of Investigation (SBI) in search of information on Braden. An SBI official read to Cathey a quote he attributed to the state attorney in Kentucky: "There is no question but that these people are dedicated Communists." There was reason to suspect that Cathey was not merely seeking information but was looking for details that would be specifically useful as a basis to prevent Braden's intended appearance. The SBI man ended the conversation by hinting about what the UNC official was actually looking for: "I think you would be well within your rights to deny him the right to speak over there."[29]

Cathey then pursued a route of inquiry that was certain to confirm his intent: he contacted HUAC's offices in Washington. Cathey was told by telephone about Braden's sedition trials and about his having been labeled a communist. Cathey chose to focus on Braden's conviction for contempt of HUAC. A portion of Braden's "public" file from HUAC, along with a summary of SCEF, were also sent by committee Chairman Edwin E. Willis of Louisiana. The results were disappointing: although the file contained a thorough summary of Braden's legal record, there was no conclusive evidence that he had been a CP member or that he had ever taken the Fifth. Cathey was in a quandary as his need to invoke the ban conflicted with his sense of honesty and fair play. The statute applied to CP members and people who had pleaded the Fifth, and Cathey had not been able to establish the applicability of either criterion with regard to Braden.[30]

Despite the apparent contradictions, a decision had to be rendered, and Cathey now turned to a source that was sure to provide affirmation of his inclination to turn Braden away. In an effort to come to terms with the nagging legal questions, Cathey telephoned state Deputy Attorney General Ralph Moody. A zealous anticommunist, Moody had been the key figure in ascertaining the legal credibility of the statute by authoring the attorney general's opinion that the law did not violate any constitutional standards. Given the likelihood that the speaker law was his intellectual product, there was scant possibility that Moody would fail to provide the approval that the UNC official sought. Cathey asked Moody — segregationist and UNC critic — whether Braden should be allowed to speak. The attorney's directive was to the point: Cathey's answer should be that "pursuant to the Speaker Ban Act of the North Carolina General Assembly, the facilities of the University of North Carolina are hereby denied to Mr. Carl Braden." Moody's response revealed how loosely the law was applied: "It looked like [Braden] would come under the speaker ban." [31]

"Looks" or, more precisely, appearances were paramount to UNC administrators' objectives. On May 13, the NAACP chapter was informed that "Braden [would] not be acceptable as a speaker on this campus." No official reason was given for the denial. For his part, Dean Cathey pointedly refused to state that Braden's alleged communist affiliation had any part in the decision. [32]

What really mattered was that Braden was deemed politically controversial and, concomitant, that the General Assembly, a body that UNC officials were leery of offending, was still in session. In orchestrating the case against Braden, Cathey had stated the strategic imperatives in explicit fashion: "It might be highly inappropriate to have a controversial visitor speak on campus at this time for fear that programs of the University presently before the state legislature might be placed in jeopardy by such action. I impressed upon the students my view that whether Mr. Braden is in fact a Communist or not, his appearance on a public platform on this campus would be unwise from the University's standpoint." [33]

The NAACP agreed to move Braden to an off-campus venue, but not without first picketing the administration building in protest of the expanded and expressly political application of the speaker ban. For his part, Braden telephoned Cathey to inquire about the reason for the ban and was told, "it was expedient [because] the legislature is meeting and it was best not to have me on campus." Braden offered to defy the law by speaking from the steps of the administration building, but the students cautiously decided not to pursue confrontation. Braden spoke at the Chapel of the Cross Episcopal Church adjacent to the campus, where he labeled himself a "militant integrationist" and lambasted HUAC for using communism as "a smokescreen, a phony issue," to attack and discredit civil rights groups. [34]

In large part, the Braden invitation served as a litmus test of the sincerity and vigilance of UNC officials in conforming to both the letter and, perhaps more important, the spirit of the anticommunist law. Braden never became a controversial figure because the administration prefigured would-be critics' expectations. After two years, the university was policing itself, unilaterally putting a gag in the mouth of anyone whom it suspected might arouse umbrage in the legislature. Although there was clearly insufficient evidence to ban Braden under the formal conditions of the statute, the administrators had grasped that as a political activist, Braden was precisely the kind of speaker addressed by the law's implicit subtext. And as Cathey surmised, to have allowed Braden to speak would have raised the ire of UNC critics and perhaps stiffened the resolve of many legislators to maintain the speaker law intact. This concern was not imaginary; throughout the month of May, Helms had unleashed a series of speaker ban editorials beginning with a criticism of President Friday's commitment to enforcing the law and concluding with a blistering attack on Braden and the SCEF.[35]

Where Cathey had been mistaken was in assuming that imposing the ban was necessary to safeguard UNC's appropriation from the General Assembly. As the ultimate weapon to force compliance—the speaker law carried no criminal penalties—such a loss was always possible, but there had never been a hint or threat that the legislature would retaliate in this manner. The actual motive for banning Braden was less to avoid punishment than it was to encourage a reward—the restoration of authority over campus speakers to the trustees and administrative officers. As the Assembly session drew to a close, UNC officials hoped that some action toward statutory revision would be forthcoming. The administrators had meticulously applied the law in every conceivable instance where a speaker seemed questionable. After the Braden incident, it seemed that few members of the legislature could doubt UNC's renewed fealty to ridding the campus of communist activity. Finding the political commitment to reconsider the speaker law would be another matter.

6 | The Accreditation Threat

As the Braden affair unfolded, a special trustees' committee headed by former state senator and now federal attorney William Medford was presenting its report to Governor Daniel K. Moore and the one-hundred-member Board of Trustees. The Medford committee was created to formulate a trustee plan that would generate support for revising the speaker law in a way that would return campus speech policy to the trustees. At the same time, the Medford proposal would convey the necessary message that the trustees stood apart from UNC President William C. Friday and the administration. The report contained no surprises. Consistent with the earliest trustee resolution, the Medford report called the law unwarranted and injurious and "certain to reduce the attractiveness of the University to men and women of the learned world [from which] we must draw to our faculties." As expected, the fourteen-member committee, at Friday's urging and direction, called for amendment instead of repeal. Most prominently, the report did not challenge the banning of communists and persons pleading the Fifth Amendment. The core of the Medford recommendations was the UNC administration's cardinal objective in conceiving and pursuing a speaker ban strategy: the return to the Board of Trustees of "full power and authority on all matters relative to the administration of such university." [1]

The role and influence of President Friday, albeit obscured, nonetheless predominated in the formulation of the recommendations. Friday met with the Medford group and participated in its deliberations. More precisely, Friday provided a blueprint, and the special committee sanctioned it. A number of internal documents provided evidence that such was the case, most particularly a memorandum dated January 15, 1965, from UNC Vice President for Administration Fred Weaver to committee members that said "Amendment of the Act should be sought and it should be in the form presented to the committee by President Friday reflecting his consultations with the Chancellors and interested public officials." [2]

On May 24, the UNC Board of Trustees overwhelmingly voted to endorse the recommendations of the Medford committee and request commensurate action by the General Assembly. At the meeting, numerous trustees warned that the erosion — if not the destruction — of UNC's prestige would be a foregone conclusion should the law remain in its present form. Only four trustees voted against the Medford proposal, in effect announcing their support for maintaining legislative authority over campus speakers. Although decisively outvoted, the opponents forecast the political obstacles that any action on the speaker ban would face in the legislature. Three of the four "nay" votes belonged to trustees who were also members of the General Assembly. Led by Senator Tom White, an indefatigable supporter of an unamended speaker law, the opposition indicated that the resolution would be met by sharp criticism should it find its way to the Legislative Building in Raleigh. White warned his trustee colleagues to "postpone this thing" until a future date. [3]

The Medford recommendations, enthusiastically supported by the trustees, had little, if any, immediate influence on an increasingly recalcitrant legislature. Ever more wary of threats to their authority, Assembly members were not moved by the appeals of a body that sought, however unintentionally, to undermine the Assembly's previous work. Speaker ban partisans in both House and Senate remained exultant that their position had popular appeal and that repeal was a dead letter. "I think," said White, "that the people of North Carolina approve of the speaker ban law. It will never be amended or repealed with my vote." [4]

Representatives from rural, eastern counties were particularly supportive of the law and saw only political misfortune for those foolhardy enough to attempt to dismantle the statute. "The people down my way are very much disturbed about taking this law off the books," said Senator Dallas Alford Jr. of Nash County. "You can [vote to] take it off, and not come back to the Senate." Philip Godwin, a sponsor of the original bill, was even more emphatic in asserting the law's popular support. Repeal was, according to Godwin, "a dead issue. This is a law that the majority of the people want, but there are some people who just won't accept that fact. I'm still against repeal or any amendment." [5]

The previous spring, speaking before the Chapel Hill–Carrboro Chamber of Commerce, State Senator and Democratic Party Chairman Lunsford Crew stated, "I am convinced that in 1965 legislators and educators thinking and acting together will amend or repeal this law." This optimistic pronouncement was, however, largely intended for public consumption before a sympathetic UNC-oriented audience. In a follow-up letter to Chancellor William B. Aycock, Crew was far less sanguine: "I think that this is a matter which we must approach with a great deal of care and lay the groundwork very carefully for appropriate action in the next session of the General Assembly. It is very unfortunate that the major candidates for Governor have had to walk on their tiptoes in facing this issue." Crew's cautionary tone was well taken: the Assembly seemed to have little momentum toward or interest in taking any action. Despite the efforts of UNC and its supporters to closely adhere to and exceed the statute's requirements, most legislators appeared unmoved. Even those who sincerely desired to revisit the issue in hopes of providing relief for UNC were reluctant to become visibly involved.[6]

If the speaker law was going to be addressed by the 1965 Assembly, political leadership would be required. One person who might have provided a modicum of leadership was newly elected Lieutenant Governor Robert W. Scott. Scott had asserted that "the Law is not satisfactory" and called on the Assembly to take the necessary steps to reconsider the statute. Scott's prorevision position was simultaneously sincere and political: in appealing to "our Democratic tradition," he was reminding older voters that his father, popular former governor and senator Kerr Scott, had played a prominent role in the construction of that tradition. Moreover, Kerr Scott had been an ardent supporter of UNC's expanded influence within the state's political culture; he had appointed Frank Graham to the U.S. Senate in 1949. In taking his stand, Bob Scott catapulted himself into the leadership of the progressive wing of the Democratic Party. As a result, he received praise from the major dailies, most of which had come out strongly against the speaker ban.[7]

While Scott expressed disfavor with the law, he did not call for its repeal. Rather, his objections lay in his belief that the law lacked necessity as well as in the procedural questions surrounding its passage. His announcement studiously avoided any criticism of the legislature that enacted the law. Apart from the campaign calling for reconsideration by the Assembly, Scott was too poorly positioned to exercise decisive political leadership on the speaker issue. As lieutenant governor, he was consigned to a largely ceremonial role, one clearly subordinate to that of the governor.[8]

Any possibility for amendment rested in the hands of the one person with adequate political influence to persuade legislators that a reconsideration was useful: Governor Moore. This recognition was shared by speaker ban supporters and opponents alike. "It depends entirely upon the governor," said Senator Dallas Alford of Nash County. Fresh from resounding second primary and general election triumphs, Moore alone possessed the requisite political capital to convince the law's supporters in the General Assembly that its present construction was problematic. It was not, however, a simple task. It involved considerable risks as Moore would be forced to negotiate a path demarcated by his own predilections, the desires of speaker ban critics, and those of his diverse constituency.[9]

Possible resolution of the speaker dilemma was further complicated by Moore's own seeming ambivalence about the utility of a speaker law. During the primary campaign he had stated that he did not believe that the speaker ban law as passed in 1963 was needed. At the same time, however, he expressed strenuous objection to allowing communists and, by implication, those using Fifth Amendment protection, from speaking at state-supported colleges and universities. Moore's position left little hope that the new governor would provide the vital leadership needed for legislative action. While he did not think that such a law had been necessary, he indicated that, as governor, he would do nothing to effect amendment or repeal.[10]

In addition to Moore's personal abhorrence of the specter of communist speakers on state-supported campuses, there was the matter of fealty to the political forces and voters that put him in office. Moore had placed second to Richardson Preyer in the first 1964 Democratic primary. With votes from supporters of I. Beverly Lake, who had been third in the first balloting, Moore annihilated Preyer in the second primary. Lake, who had pressured Terry Sanford in the 1960 primaries, enjoyed considerable support, especially in the rural eastern counties, as an archsegregationist opposed to federal intervention in a host of areas. Lake had also campaigned as an ardent advocate of a strong and unadulterated speaker law. Cognizant of the pivotal role that Lake and his supporters had played in his victory over Preyer, Moore could not fail to uphold their expectations on this burning societal issue. Already viscerally committed to anticommunist sentiments, Moore's own perspective was reinforced by the political utility of supporting those who had supported him. Without new and compelling developments, Moore would not intervene on behalf of revising the speaker ban law.[11]

Another factor serving to buttress the governor's reluctance to move on the speaker law issue was the editorial encouragement he received from Jesse Helms. As a leading spokesman for the conservative rank-and-file across the state, Helms and WRAL had played a major role in certifying and sustaining the Moore campaign. Following its victory in the Democratic primary, Helms had offered his congratulations and suggestions as the Moore camp prepared for the Republican challenger in the general election. In doing so, Helms issued a warning: Moore "must naturally call for unity among the members of his party. . . . [S]till, there is no requirement, not even an implicit one, that he must now absorb or embrace the curious philosophies of those who fought him so bitterly. To the contrary, if these philosophies were repugnant to Dan Moore as a candidate — and he repeatedly said that they were — then he has an obligation to rid them from the backs of the people. This is Dan Moore's mandate!"[12] With the ever-vigilant Helms carefully observing the speaker issue, any appearance of a retreat by Moore would subject the governor to intense criticism from those who had been among his staunchest allies during the campaigns.

Despite Moore's unwillingness to initiate the amendment process, individual members of the Assembly pressed ahead with plans to bring a bill before their colleagues in hopes of securing revision of the law's draconian features. During the 1965 session, several bills were reported to be searching for sufficient support to enable a vote. The most serious of these efforts was led by Senator Jennings King of Scotland County. By the end of May, King had drafted a bill assigning "trustees the authority to do by regulation what the present statute does by law." The bill suggested by King was remarkably similar to the proposed recommendations for statutory relief that the UNC trustees had endorsed following the Medford committee report. The draft bill would have given the Board of Trustees "exclusive authority to determine the person or persons who shall be invited to speak upon the campus." It also proposed the publication of special rules and regulations to cover the possible appearance of "a known member of the Communist Party and [anyone who] had pleaded the fifth amendment."[13]

The King bill, had it been introduced and approved, would have transferred authority for visiting speakers to trustees and administrators, a provision central to UNC officials' desires. Such a bill would not, however, have satisfied pro–speaker ban legislators. Those favoring maintaining the speaker law were less than enamored with the prospect of yielding legislative authority to those who had unstintingly criticized the necessity of any speaker law. As if to confirm their suspicions, the King bill implied that under prescribed conditions communists and pleaders of the Fifth could — and presumably would — be permitted to speak on state-supported college and university campuses.

As the session drew to a close, King and other supporters of amendment were still twisting arms and cajoling in the hope of swaying the two or three senators who might prove decisive. The proamendment forces hoped for a positive outcome in the Senate, where an informal head count indicated that as many as twenty-three of the fifty members would support some measure of revision. In the end, the bill to amend Sections 116–199 and 116–200 of Article 22 of the General Statutes of North Carolina by restoring campus authority to the trustees never made it into the legislative hopper. As the issue of amendment intensified, views hardened, and it became more difficult for senators to indicate a public willingness to support a bill that would ostensibly enable communists to speak on North Carolina college campuses.[14]

If the situation was difficult in the Senate, it was nearly hopeless in the lower chamber. In the House of Representatives, every county, regardless of population, had at least one vote. The preponderance of legislators from rural counties where anticommunist sentiment ran especially high meant scant possibility of getting through a measure on the order of the King bill. Representative Donald Stanford of Orange County, the home of UNC, reported that he could count only thirty members at most who were willing to support amendment or repeal. With a total representation of 120, the chances of a bill clearing the House seemed infinitesimal.[15]

With Governor Moore unwilling to support any measure of amendment and with questionable support for revision in both houses of the General Assembly, it appeared that the much-anticipated session would conclude with the speaker law more firmly entrenched than ever. Much of the hope that opponents had invested in the session seemed to have produced little movement toward satisfactory resolution of the controversy. While Moore had implied, during the gubernatorial primary, his willingness to endorse a modest revision enabling certain scientists and academicians to speak, it was clear that such a prospect would not placate speaker ban opponents. For Friday and other prominent opponents, restoration of the trustees' authority over speaker policy was the crucial issue, and Moore's offer seemed to speak to such a possibility.[16]

As the session neared adjournment, however, momentum for a reconsideration of the speaker ban was gathering. On the morning of May 19, Moore and officials of the state's higher-education system had received a telegram from Emmett B. Fields, chairman of the Commission on Colleges and Schools of the Southern Association of Colleges and Schools (SACS), a regional accrediting agency. The association's executive council had been following developments linked to the speaker law and, in the telegram, noted that since the statute deprived the trustees of their "traditional authority" to devise and implement policy, it therefore raised "an issue of interference with the necessary authority of the Boards." Because the trustees' ability to "protect the integrity" of the university had been impaired and, the telegram inferred, since its educational mission had been "hampered by political interference," the Commission on Colleges would "determine the status of these institutions with respect to continued accreditation." The message seemed clear: unless remedial action were forthcoming to eliminate political meddling with academic processes, the UNC system faced loss of accreditation.[17]

The threat of a possible loss of accredited status immediately became the most serious complication visited on the state by the speaker law. None of the earlier episodes, where prospective speakers were turned away or declined to participate in the anticommunist drama, appeared to threaten the university's academic and institutional integrity in such a concrete manner.

And the sudden manifestation of the dilemma was by no means unanticipated. In late April, Fields and Gordon Sweet, executive director of SACS, had twice met with either Moore or members of his staff as well as officials from the State Board of Higher Education, an agency functionally aligned with UNC. On the first of these occasions, the two men met with Ed Rankin, Moore's chief of staff, and William Dees of Goldsboro and William Archie of Winston-Salem, the chairman and executive director of the board of higher education, respectively. Fields and Sweet explained the organization's purpose as a voluntary association whose members adhered to recognized standards of academic excellence. They detailed their concerns and reservations and those of the executive council with respect to the effect on academic standards of a law that deprived trustees of their prerogative to oversee campus activities free from political interference.[18]

Most of all, Fields and Sweet sought to encourage a process that would lead to a solution whereby the General Assembly would restore authority to the trustees. As the governor's surrogate, Rankin sought to explain the law's existence — and presumably its necessity — by pointing to its popularity and the widespread hostility to communism in the state. Ostensibly speaking for Moore, who was ill with a case of mumps, Rankin did little to convince Fields and Sweet that legislative relief would be forthcoming. For his part, Fields, dean of the College of Arts and Sciences at Vanderbilt University, gave no indication that SACS was on the verge of stripping the UNC system of accreditation, but he did reiterate that pending a report and subsequent approval by the executive council, the association did have the authority to apply probation or to impose the ultimate sanction of expulsion from membership.[19]

Within a matter of days SACS's interest in the speaker law and the possible loss of accreditation became a public issue. The law's critics had hoped that a serious consequence of this sort would materialize. The urban dailies, from the beginning ardent advocates of repeal or crippling of the ban, quickly seized on the dilemma. The state's press, generally against the law, argued that this problem could damage, perhaps irreparably, the state's public college and university system. Most particularly, the press pointed out, loss of accreditation would pose some very serious practical difficulties for students. The predicament threatened to hit close to home: few parents of students would prefer risking the future well-being that university credentials would confer to preserve a symbolic statement against communism. Should accreditation be rescinded, it might mean that teaching certificates and other professional credentials would lose reciprocal acceptance from other states. In an irony, since North Carolina mandated graduation from an accredited college or university as a requirement for teacher certification, the loss of accreditation would mean that UNC graduates would technically be ineligible to teach in the state's own primary and secondary schools. Critics also argued that loss of accreditation would jeopardize the acceptability of UNC alumni to graduate and professional schools in other states.[20]

Dees and Archie had attended the meeting at the governor's mansion with the SACS representatives. The two men were by no means neutral observers: both strongly opposed the law and were closely allied with the UNC administration as it sought a means of eliminating the legislative restrictions. A lawyer and UNC graduate, Dees echoed the concerns that had been raised about accreditation by SACS. In his statements to the press, Dees left no doubt that he concurred that the present situation placed the state-supported colleges in violation of association standards, which held that academic procedures should be unfettered by political interference.[21]

The initial visit by SACS representatives was intended to serve as a stimulus to prompt the governor to direct action by the legislature. There was no suggestion that a loss of accreditation was imminent or inevitable. The visit did, however, suggest to recalcitrant state officials that there existed a power beyond the boundaries of North Carolina that could apply effective leverage in the speaker ban debate. The visit was primarily a message for Moore, without whose leadership revision was only a faint possibility. In assessing the likelihood of successful legislative action, Senator Ralph Scott of Alamance County, chairman of the Senate Committee on Higher Education, concluded, "We are not going to get it repealed—or even amended—in this session unless the governor comes out for it." The visit from SACS was a tactical device aimed at subtly prodding the governor into providing the requisite leadership.[22]

Governor Moore saw little reason to support amendment. He had campaigned as a staunch anticommunist and owed his election in no small part to Assembly members and rank-and-file voters who refused to relent on the speaker law, whatever the consequences. For Moore, it was a matter of fidelity to constituents as well as of personal beliefs in the essential utility of any law designed to battle the communist foe. There was also a political dimension: Moore had recently won a landslide victory and the plaudits of those who admired the law-and-order conservatism of "Dan the Mountain Man." To suddenly endorse or, more precisely, to lead the forces of revision would appear as a breach of faith and weakness in the face of a threat from external interests.

The SACS and the accreditation issue would not disappear. With greater discussion about the ramifications of disaccreditation came greater anxiety that the reputation of the state's public colleges and universities was being unnecessarily compromised. The governor would have to address the nascent threat to state institutions. On May 16, at Moore's request, a second meeting was arranged with Fields and Sweet. For his part, Moore attempted to placate the SACS representatives along lines similar to those expounded by Rankin at the April meeting. The law, said Moore, enjoyed great popularity as an expression of the steadfast opposition to communism held by the people of North Carolina. He indicated that he had advocated limited revision to enable "speakers on scientific and cultural subjects to appear." In this putative gesture of conciliation, Moore intended that scientists such as J. B. S. Haldane and writers like Arthur Miller would be exempted despite their earlier affinities or associations with communist groups. Under this proposal, however, political speakers such as Carl Braden would continue to be proscribed. In this manner Moore proposed a formula for retaining ideological consistency with the intent of House Bill 1395 while providing access to "legitimate" speakers — those not engaging in critical or iconoclastic political speech.[23]

Moore made no mention of Fields and Sweet's fundamental requirement, restoration of full and unimpeded trustee authority over campus affairs. The governor received the fateful telegram on May 19 and the following day made his first public statement on the threatened loss of accreditation. For the first time, citizens became aware of the seriousness of the issue. In his statement, the governor refused to indicate what kind of response he contemplated. He simply acknowledged that the challenge could not be ignored. Moore expected the worst. He immediately began consultations with legislative leaders to determine how to resolve the SACS concern and, more important, to investigate the possibility for some movement toward amendment prior to the end of the session. The governor, however, adamantly refused to expend any of his own political capital to prompt Assembly action. Without forceful gubernatorial intervention, amendment at such a late stage was little more than a dream.

While Moore was reluctant to ask the legislature to revise the law, it was increasingly apparent that some action was necessary to satisfy SACS. The terms of the speaker ban controversy had been markedly transformed as opponents were infused with a newfound sense that at last an effective lever had been discovered to undermine the law. The *Chapel Hill Weekly* pointed the way, calling the loss of accreditation "a major disaster for the entire state." If SACS accreditation was lost, said editor Jim Shumaker, the other five accrediting agencies would withdraw their sanction, and UNC's vaunted graduate and professional programs would suffer loss of prestige and status. A long-term result, said the paper, would be the loss of grant money from federal agencies and private foundations. While other media sources were not as apocalyptic as the Chapel Hill paper, they were equally concerned that the loss of accreditation had to be avoided. The public obsession with anticommunism could not be indulged to the detriment of the state's educational institutions.[24]

On May 24, the UNC Board of Trustees voted to endorse Medford committee's recommendations and to approve a resolution calling on the General Assembly to restore authority over speaker policy to the trustees of each constituent campus.[25] Moore was simultaneously inundated with letters imploring him, as governor, to take decisive action — either to request amendment by the legislature or to affirm his support for the law. Pressure was building, and it was no longer possible to simply recite anticommunist homilies. It seemed that Moore would have to fully articulate a course of action that either promised resistance to SACS's indictment of the present law or preserved the integrity of the UNC system by safeguarding its status as a bellwether of academic process and principle.

While speaker law opponents were enthused by the possibilities presented by the accreditation controversy, supporters were deeply concerned that the advantage gained over the previous two years was being lost. Moore's open acknowledgment that loss of accreditation was a legitimate cause for concern left them worried. For the first time it appeared that Moore was beginning to waver in his professed support for the law. The governor received a torrent of letters pleading that he ignore the association and support retention of the law in its present form. The correspondents typically expressed a concern that repeal would expose the university to radicals. Most conspicuous in the letters, however, were anger and frustration. Something had to be done to insure public order from a welter of miscreants: permissive university administrators, student dissidents, civil rights protests, and so on. According to one writer, North Carolina needed to prevent a recurrence of the events that took place at the University of California, "where Communist, Socialist, and 'Freedom of Speech' speakers are given full opportunity," and "violent and riotous demonstrations on the part of students are distressingly frequent."[26] For the law's supporters, college campuses were emblematic of the social upheavals that were threatening the world as they knew it. In this view, statutory protection such as the speaker law would insure law and order by containing the problem at the source.

The possibility that the speaker law might be amended or repealed elicited protestations from a variety of quarters, including, ironically, college and university faculty. Wesley Critz George, a retired professor of anatomy at UNC, asked Moore to support the law to protect the university from those who would convert it into "an instrument for indoctrinating our youth with left wing dogma." George had well-known segregationist views (he was a founder of and officer in the Patriots of North Carolina) and had recently gained notoriety as he vainly sought to defend outdated postulates of genetic inferiority of blacks. Other faculty members, urging retention of the law, referred to the changing racial milieu as indicative of the disorder that the law to regulate visiting speakers was somehow designed to check: "[O]ne of the most suspicious and appalling aspects of the University administration," said two writers from UNC-Greensboro, "is its seeming desire to follow California, a desire reminiscent of the U.S. Supreme Court's dedication to one Gunnar Myrdal." The few faculty members openly supporting the law were older, often retired, and, most notably, had cultural ideologies that reflected a bygone era. These individuals tended to be angry and at war with their own institutions as faculty members, students, and administrators embraced more recent scholarly, cultural, and political developments. Because the handful of faculty members supporting the law generally had little influence or credibility within their own institutions, their entreaties for retention carried little weight.[27]

Most of the attention of those striving to bulwark the speaker law focused on the credibility of the implied threat from SACS. Godwin ridiculed the implied loss of accreditation as a "smokescreen" that represented "a last desperate effort to get something done about the law at this session of the legislature." Godwin believed, along with many others who supported retention, that opponents had deliberately manufactured the accreditation question to engender fear and thus create a stampede to action by the Assembly. This was not merely a point of curiosity: if it could be reliably determined that the SACS threat was prompted by in-state sources, then the opposition would be discredited, perhaps irreparably, as disloyal and reckless and the speaker law would be ensconced more firmly.[28]

There was, in fact, considerable veracity to suspicions that SACS acted with the complicity of North Carolina officials. Speaker ban supporters were not afraid to identify who they suspected had created the accreditation imbroglio by drawing the association's attention to the situation in North Carolina. Led by Dunn newspaperman Hoover Adams, fingers were pointed at Dees, who had early awareness that the Commission on Colleges was in the process of evaluating the state's accreditation status in light of the speaker ban restrictions. Moreover, in his public comments, Dees was overtly sympathetic to the accrediting agency's complaints. As a leading officer in the state's higher education system and an outspoken opponent of the law, Dees seemed to have both the opportunity through routine contact and the political motivation to have suggested the opportunity for SACS's involvement.[29]

A more likely suspect than Dees was Friday. It was widely known by both legislators and laypeople that the UNC president was at the forefront of the effort to amend or repeal the law. More than anyone else, Friday was well positioned to call attention to the statute through his professional memberships and contacts. Suggestions that Friday was responsible for alerting SACS were quick in coming, but he vigorously denied prior knowledge of the executive council's plan to consider withdrawal of the state's accreditation. At a meeting of the trustees on May 24, Friday denied being a party to or encouraging any pending SACS action. "I had no knowledge," said Friday, "of the fact that the executive council was meeting on May 19 to consider the action reported by their telegrams." He contended that he only learned of the threat on May 20, after receiving a copy of the telegram sent to the governor.[30]

Friday was perhaps disingenuous in his response. While he was likely unaware of the SACS executive council's impending action, he was not, by any means, fully extricated from probable complicity. No one was better positioned or possessive of the requisite political acumen to seize on the accreditation issue. In explaining his putative lack of involvement to the trustees, Friday acknowledged that the first time "an administrative officer of the University learned of the interest of the Southern Association of Colleges and Schools was in March, 1964." According to Friday, at that time "inquiries were made" about the law by an accreditation team.[31]

Friday neglected to mention that throughout most of 1964 he had been a member of the SACS Board of Trustees. Although he had resigned from the board in November, Friday had admittedly been aware of SACS interest, and, as a board member, he would certainly have had ample opportunity to bring the matter to the executive council's attention. Friday had taken careful steps to obscure and erase any linkage between himself and the SACS probe. By the summer of 1965, while possible revision was under deliberation, he falsely denied any awareness of SACS interest in the speaker control law during his tenure as a board member. Whereas he had informed the trustees of a March 1964 date, he stipulated, "My resignation from the Board of Trustees of the Southern Association took place before I had any knowledge at all of their interest in and concern over the accreditation of the University of North Carolina because of the so-called Speaker Bill."[32] In reality, nine months had passed between Friday's awareness of SACS's interest and his resignation.

Friday's comments were aimed at sustaining plausible deniability. He needed to demonstrate that he was not, during his tenure as a SACS board member, party to any clandestine plan to launch an accreditation probe in connection with the speaker law. While the accreditation threat did not manifest itself until after Friday's resignation in November 1964, the issue had certainly been raised and a logistical timetable suggested while Friday remained on the board.

In defending himself against charges of complicity, Friday noted that on several occasions in early 1965 he had asked the executive council to postpone any accreditation action in the hope that the Assembly would alleviate the problem. This action, however, largely sought to preserve the formality of not appearing to preempt the legislature. Although he might well have warned the council against premature or precipitous action, it is doubtful that he did so because he believed the legislature would act to repeal or relinquish its control. Friday had concluded early on that the issue ultimately "wasn't going to be won in the legislature. How in the world can you presume that the very body that enacted it is going to turn right around and repeal it?" At best, Friday hoped that Moore might be persuaded to lead a drive for amendment. When the governor chose not to intervene, SACS proceeded to apply the pressure of disaccreditation.[33]

Despite the disclaimers, Friday was certainly aware of and sympathetic to the political leverage of the SACS action. He had consistently raised the accreditation issue throughout early 1965, well before any disclosure that the executive council planned to raise the question. At the beginning of the Assembly session, Friday had warned legislators that unless the law was amended or repealed, accreditation might be adversely affected.[34] The report of the Medford committee, completed in April, had also emphasized the deleterious impact on accreditation should the law remain in its present form. Since Friday had been the strategist giving form to the recommendations of the Medford report, his association with the eventual accreditation threat was reiterated.

The application of the accreditation issue was a political masterstroke by Friday. Despite the allegations that he and others had manipulated the association's interest, none of the charges stuck. Friday had succeeded in introducing a pragmatic, less ideological question that appeared to present serious consequences for the future of higher education in North Carolina. Even as he continually maintained that the "possible loss of accreditation was serious," his somber warnings masked a larger political motive: to relocate the speaker ban away from arcane philosophical arguments to a more visible and imminent difficulty posed by the law. While Friday and his colleagues in higher education undoubtedly believed that accreditation was a serious matter, there was equally little doubt that they astutely wielded the issue for its political utility. Chancellor Sharp saw accreditation as the issue that would add "fuel to the fire that we hope to keep going around the speaker ban law." The administrators also did not delude themselves that the loss of accreditation, should it ever occur, would result in a diminution of institutional prestige. In a letter to the worried parent of a UNC student, Vice Chancellor J. Carlyle Sitterson was remarkably candid in assessing the possibilities attending the accreditation threat: "I do not think that the University of North Carolina is likely to lose accreditation and certainly no time soon. In my judgment the Association is not likely to do this. The University of North Carolina is so well known in the educational world that I do not believe, even if [loss of accreditation] occurs, it would prevent acceptance by a graduate school of work taken at the University." In Friday's assessment, the threatened loss of accreditation was "a hoped for attitude, but not the truth." UNC officials hoped that the issue would "temper some legislative attitudes."[35]

While the possible loss of accreditation was certainly cause for reconsidering the usefulness of amendment of some kind, the staunchest supporters responded quite differently. Ardent speaker ban supporters met the threat to the General Assembly's statutory integrity with recrimination. They were incensed that an outside agency would attempt to compel the elected representatives of a sovereign state to bow to the agency's wishes. In a stinging editorial, Helms called for an investigation of the association: "If the Southern Association of Colleges and Schools presumes now to set itself up as judge and jury, it is only reasonable that its qualifications be examined carefully." The SACS action, said Helms, was a demand "that our legislature yield in the face of a threat issued by a group of unstated size, without identification, and without stated qualification. . . . [I]nstead of proving ourselves worthy to them, they may have some explaining to do to us."[36]

The suggestion for an investigation of SACS was quickly taken up by Secretary of State Thad Eure, who assigned the task of accumulating evidence and researching the organization to Deputy Attorney General Ralph Moody. Both Eure and Moody had enthusiastically supported the speaker law since its inception. Together, they had been instrumental in drafting the features of House Bill 1395.[37]

The two officials quickly launched ambitious plans for an investigation of the accrediting agency. They were assisted by Representative Roger Kiser of Scotland County, who obtained a copy of the association's annual proceedings. In publicizing the report, Kiser evoked symbols and rhetoric reminiscent of the McCarthy era, claiming to have "disclosed" the "true nature" of the organization. Such an attempt to smear SACS as a clandestine if not subversive group was foolhardy. The major dailies noted that the association's published proceedings were completely open to public inspection. Dozens of North Carolina schools were constituent members, including, with notable irony, the school district in which Kiser taught. Furthermore, numerous Tarheel educators served on various SACS boards.[38]

Such exposure of the ill-fated effort to tarnish SACS's legitimacy did not dissuade Eure. By the end of the summer he had denounced the agency as a "monster" and derided local educators sympathetic to its agenda as "giving aid and comfort to the enemy."[39]

By invoking language suggesting foreign invasion, Eure and Moody sought to discredit the association. The two men were prepared to go further. Eure advocated that the state ignore the SACS and establish its own accrediting agency. In September, Moody submitted his findings, which called for requiring the association to "procure a certificate of authority from the secretary of state"; Eure promptly dispatched the incorporation forms to SACS headquarters in Atlanta. If North Carolina was successful in bringing SACS under the state's statutory auspices, the association could be sued in state courts if it attempted to withdraw accreditation. Eure's effort was largely greeted with sarcastic ridicule. The press labeled the effort a "pop gun" approach and suggested that the plan would merely squander state resources in dozens of lawsuits by professional organizations that indicated a willingness to follow the SACS lead. The press pointed out that since SACS was a voluntary organization of long duration—it had been founded in 1895 with UNC President George T. Winston serving as its first president—it was ludicrous to pursue a strategy that would subject the state to embarrassment.[40] The Eure plan never gathered legislative support, and SACS never returned the licensing forms.

More serious and purposeful than the quixotic attempt to license SACS for punitive purposes were the efforts to debunk the contention of the harshness of possible sanctions. A vigilant observer of any attempts to weaken the law, Dunn newspaperman Adams was alarmed by the implications of the SACS challenge. He was also troubled by Governor Moore's apparent vacillation in the face of a threat to what Adams considered was a sacrosanct law. After Moore's public announcement in response to the SACS telegram, Adams wrote to the governor and pleaded with him to defy the threat. Adams was adamant that the law remain intact whatever the consequences: "The threat of loss of accreditation by the Southern Association—and the actual loss of accreditation itself—does not frighten me one tenth as much as the mere thought that this law might be possibly weakened." Adams presented the issue in stark political terms. "This threat," he said, "is nothing but pure blackmail and a smokescreen. . . . [T]here is increasing evidence that William Dees is behind it and that Bill Friday is behind Dees." In closing, Adams appealed to Moore's sense of political retribution: "I realize that the campaign is over . . . but nobody in this state fought you harder than the Chapel Hill intellectuals. I think the sooner you tell them where to head in, the quicker Friday and the others will let up this pressure business."[41]

Adams was not content, however, to limit his appeal to the governor's anticommunist ideals and political sensibilities. In March, he had written to FBI director J. Edgar Hoover in hopes of enlisting the support of the nation's foremost "expert" on communism. In the letter, Adams introduced himself as a "very close friend of Jesse Helms" and briefly outlined the purpose of the North Carolina speaker law. In a summary analysis he told Hoover that the "trouble with Communists" in North Carolina "started at UNC during

Dr. Graham's presidency." Adams predicated his appeal for assistance on the impending possibility of amendment by the General Assembly. In describing the situation, Adams portrayed the opposing forces as surreptitious radicals. "We have it on good authority," he said, "that the left-wing bloc of the legislature very shortly will attempt to railroad an amendment to the law." Adams implored Hoover to "give us some help in our fight — either openly or confidentially. Anything that you can do will be warmly appreciated." [42]

Adams was hoping for a ringing endorsement of the speaker law from a widely respected law-enforcement official. Hoover did not disappoint the North Carolina editor. In a letter to Adams marked "personal" — Hoover did not want the actual contents to be divulged — the FBI man said that he could "readily understand the concern which prompted you to write." He described the CPUSA as "most anxious to expand its influence among the youth of our nation," hoping to do so by "infiltrating" college and university campuses. Communist "propagandists," said Hoover, "have made and are making recruits in our schools, colleges, and universities," ostensibly because students were not capable of "recognizing and exposing" CP propaganda. The response from Hoover seemed to conclude with precisely what Adams had requested. "I do not believe," said Hoover, "that Communist spokesmen should be allowed to speak on our campuses." [43]

Promising not to involve Hoover without his "specific permission," Adams did not immediately release the letter or its contents. The accreditation controversy, however, compelled speaker ban supporters like Adams to seek fresh ammunition. When the accreditation "propaganda" came out, the editor again wrote to Hoover informing him of the new offensive and requesting his permission to use the April letter. When Hoover responded that Adams was "free to use [the previous letter] in the manner indicated," the *Dunn Daily Record* published a series of selected quotes in which the FBI director appeared to affirm the utility of excluding "communist spokesmen" from the nation's campuses. The statement was quickly picked up and published throughout the state. By enlisting Hoover's direct endorsement, Adams believed that he had delivered a propaganda coup of his own that would rally pro-speaker ban forces and throw the opposition on the defensive. [44]

While Hoover's apparent support did result in certain advantages for those favoring retention, it did not represent an unmitigated triumph. Many North Carolinians undoubtedly were favorably disposed toward the man who symbolized the war against organized crime and internal subversion. One reason that the Hoover letter did not have a devastating impact on the accreditation issue was that it was not the unqualified endorsement that Adams had indicated. In reality, Hoover had made no mention of the accreditation controversy in his communication. And more important, Adams had apparently manipulated the FBI director's commentary by not divulging an aspect that implicitly supported precisely the amendment for which Friday and others had called. While Hoover certainly opposed communist speakers on campus, it was by no means clear that he had endorsed legislative fiat to effect such a result. In the same sentence of the original letter that concluded "I do not believe that communist spokesmen should be allowed to speak on our campuses," Hoover stipulated "but, this is a matter to be decided by college authorities."[45] The caveat appeared to affirm opponents' contention that authority over speaker policy rightfully belonged to the trustees and administrative officers.

In publicizing the letter's contents, Adams made no mention of the second clause of Hoover's concluding comment. On discovering what they considered a deliberate omission, UNC officials quickly pointed to the apparent duplicity in the Dunn editor's action. Arnold Nash, UNC professor of sociology and chairman of the campus AAUP, wrote two letters to Adams pressuring the editor to explain the rumored deletion. Adams apologized and denied that he had intended to willfully deceive or mislead the public. UNC Professor Lewis Lipsitz took umbrage at a federal official's apparent approval of such an illiberal law and wrote to Attorney General Nicholas Katzenbach's office, asking the administration to "clarify" its stand on the matter. Not surprisingly, the Johnson administration, striving to rally public opinion to fight a war against communism in Vietnam, was not eager to confuse the issue by opposing an anticommunist law at home and did not relish the prospect of a public political tussle with Hoover.[46] Nevertheless, the impact of Hoover's letter was markedly diminished and of no further value in the effort to staunch the anxiety generated by accreditation.

The ultimate reason for the failure to successfully enlist Hoover's support was that the speaker issue was being successfully transposed from the ideological terrain of anticommunism to the more pragmatic ground of accreditation. The prevailing concern was no longer whether it was worthwhile to make a state-mandated statement against communism but whether UNC would have its reputation jeopardized by a correctable flaw in the structure of the speaker law. And no matter how vigorously Adams and other supporters waved the flag of anticommunism, the issue of accreditation, unless discredited as a politically contrived effort, was going to redefine and relocate the nature of the speaker law debate.

The successful implementation of accreditation as a vehicle for reexamination of the speaker ban was nothing if not a brilliant victory for Friday and his associates. Almost immediately, speaker ban supporters realized that they had an issue they could not control. They were immediately thrown on the defensive by an issue that was not of their making and that they, as nonacademicians, could not anticipate.

The most visible manifestation of this worried defensiveness came from the most vociferous and pugnacious defender of the speaker law, Helms. In the first of several editorials attempting to undermine the accreditation issue and SACS, Helms appeared surprised and desperate at the accreditation strategy. Charging that the incipient effort was characterized by "falsehoods and distortions," Helms labeled it a "depressing development," meaning one that he and his allies could not hope to win.[47] If Helms and colleagues such as Adams could articulate and tap the ambiguous albeit perceived fear of communism, they were poorly prepared to position themselves — and surrogates like Hoover — as experts on the accreditation question.

Helms's initial comment on accreditation indicated that while he knew that the issue was manufactured for a political objective, he and others would be helpless to prevent eventual reconsideration. In an almost pleading tone, Helms appealed to opponents to admit that the accreditation issue was false and that the university faced no such harm.

> It is to be hoped that University President William Friday, and other honorable men who have conducted a spirited fight against the speaker ban law, will promptly disassociate themselves from current efforts to imply that unless the law is repealed or amended, the state's educational institutions may lose their accreditation. The implication is simply not true, and President Friday and his associates know it. They cannot afford the luxury of silence if this unworthy effort continues. As men who contend they are dedicated to the search for truth, they are obliged to remove themselves from the company of those who substitute distortion in the place of reasonableness.[48]

Helms's sophistry could scarcely hope to dissuade Friday and "other honorable men" from continuing to affirm the seriousness of the impending SACS action. Like Helms, Friday was a consummate politician. He had long realized that the speaker ban was about politics, not truth. And in a political struggle, truth was usually the first casualty. A skilled strategist, Friday had adroitly plumbed the logic of the speaker ban and realized that the accreditation issue would guarantee additional pressure for amendment. He had realized early on that since the speaker ban was the result of resentment and frustrated political goals, patience and shrewdness would be required to mediate the law's draconian character.[49] Despite his call for fair play, Helms would get no reprieve from Friday.

In witnessing the fear and uncertainty that the accreditation controversy brought to their adversaries, speaker ban opponents knew they had located the issue for which they had been searching. The *Chapel Hill Weekly* gleefully noted Helms's exasperation and reprinted a partial text of his plea to Friday to disclaim the SACS effort. Rather than the barbed criticism it usually leveled at the Raleigh broadcaster, the paper playfully jabbed at "Judicious Jesse's" appeal to "honesty and morality." The editorial observed that while "invective, distortions, and sneers" were expected from "Old Jesse," it was laughable for him to appeal to "honesty and fairness." [50] The Chapel Hill paper, like Friday, realized that the speaker ban issue, as evinced by Helms's conciliatory remarks, was being transformed in such a way that made formal reconsideration inevitable. And Helms knew it as well.

On June 1, Governor Moore announced his proposal for dealing with the accreditation threat. He concluded that he did "not believe that it would be in the best interest of higher education for the General Assembly to consider repeal or amendment of the speaker ban law at this time." While the governor's statement decisively eliminated the last possibility for legislative action prior to the close of the session, it also contained an assurance that the law would receive a rehearing and rethinking. Moore recommended that the Assembly "authorize the appointment of a commission of nine members to study this specific problem in all of its complexities." While the governor refused to assume a role in the forefront of the drive to reconsideration and, presumably, revision, suggesting a special study commission indicated that he considered some changes to be in order. [51]

Moore's preference for an ad hoc study commission received a mixed response. While pleased that the speaker law would finally receive a long-anticipated review, many of the state's newspapers were disappointed with the governor's "abdication" of leadership. In recommending a commission, the governor appeared to be choosing a course that exposed him to little risk. Moore and his assistants argued that in the absence of any meaningful chance that the legislature would approve an amendment, the commission idea remained the last best alternative. Speaking at the UNC commencement on June 7, Moore received a polite, if strained, response as he attempted to explain the circumstances behind the commission idea. He reiterated that "the lieutenant governor, the speaker [of the House], and other leaders of the legislature agreed with my conclusion. It was our collective opinion that any effort to amend or repeal the law at this session would be futile." [52]

Moore would not or could not acknowledge the political motivations behind his decision to request a study commission. As a candidate who had personally and sincerely supported the speaker law's basic intent of denying political speech to communists, Moore was philosophically unsuited to assertively press for revision. In addition, having just emerged from the rigors of a competitive campaign, the governor understood that the great majority of North Carolinians harbored bitter animosities toward the idea of communism. To make what might be perceived as a sudden about-face might risk his recently won popularity. Moore favored limited revision, primarily to placate SACS. He was not, however, willing to go public with that preference.

On June 16, a joint resolution creating the special study commission was ratified and signed into law by Senate President Bob Scott and House Speaker Pat Taylor. The nine-member panel was empowered to collect evidence, conduct hearings, and, most important, submit a report of its findings along with recommendations to the governor. That the commission would provide recommendations all but assured that a special session of the Assembly would be called to resolve the speaker law dilemma.[53]

The speaker ban had entered a new phase. In Chapel Hill, Friday was pleased that his strategy had finally paid dividends. He had been convinced that if the speaker law ever received the critical scrutiny and full hearing it deserved, authority would be returned to the trustees.[54] Friday's paramount objective — power — was now on the horizon.

Collegians and others protest on Raleigh's Fayetteville Street, May 1963.
North Carolina Collection, University of North Carolina Library at Chapel Hill;
reprinted by permission of the *News and Observer* of Raleigh, North Carolina.

Civil rights demonstrators ring the new Assembly building, May 1963.
North Carolina Collection, University of North Carolina Library at Chapel Hill;
reprinted by permission of the *News and Observer* of Raleigh, North Carolina.

Liberian Ambassador Angie Brooks and her nephew, Joseph Outland, waiting in the whites-only Sir Walter Coffee Shop, April 1963. North Carolina Collection, University of North Carolina Library at Chapel Hill; reprinted by permission of the *News and Observer* of Raleigh, North Carolina.

The "unofficial capitol" and local residence of numerous legislators, Raleigh's Sir Walter Hotel was a primary target for civil rights demonstrations in the spring of 1963. North Carolina Collection, University of North Carolina Library at Chapel Hill; reprinted by permission of the *News and Observer* of Raleigh, North Carolina.

A state patrolman preparing to evict black ministers John W. Fleming and
D. N. Howard from the statehouse's segregated cafeteria, May 1963.
North Carolina Collection, University of North Carolina Library at Chapel Hill
reprinted by permission of the *News and Observer* of Raleigh, North Carolina.

Young civil rights activists in the Wake County (Raleigh) jail, May 1963.
North Carolina Collection, University of North Carolina Library at Chapel Hill;
reprinted by permission of the *News and Observer* of Raleigh, North Carolina.

Governor Terry Sanford, 1963. North Carolina
Collection, University of North Carolina Library at
Chapel Hill; reprinted by permission of the *News
and Observer* of Raleigh, North Carolina.

Senate President Clarence Stone *(seated)*
and Senators Thomas J. White *(right)* and
Ralph Scott *(left)*, 1963. White Papers,
Southern Historical Collection, University
of North Carolina Library at Chapel Hill.

UNC President William Friday *(seated)* and
UNC–Chapel Hill Chancellor William Aycock,
1964. North Carolina Collection, University
of North Carolina Library at Chapel Hill.

Senator Robert Morgan of Harnett
County, 1965. *Raleigh News and
Observer.* North Carolina Collection,
University of North Carolina
Library at Chapel Hill; reprinted by
permission of the *News and Observer*
of Raleigh, North Carolina.

Representative David M. Britt, chairman
of the Speaker Ban Study Commission,
August 1965. North Carolina Collection,
University of North Carolina Library
at Chapel Hill; reprinted by permission
of the *News and Observer* of Raleigh,
North Carolina.

The Speaker Ban Study Commission, 1965. North Carolina Collection, University
of North Carolina Library at Chapel Hill; reprinted by permission of the *News and
Observer* of Raleigh, North Carolina.

Governor Dan K. Moore, 1965. North Carolina Collection, University of North Carolina Library at Chapel Hill; reprinted by permission of the *News and Observer* of Raleigh, North Carolina.

On a Franklin Street sidewalk, Frank Wilkinson speaks to students sitting behind "Gov. Dan K. Moore's (Chapel Hill) Wall," March 1966. North Carolina Collection, University of North Carolina Library at Chapel Hill; reprinted by permission of the *News and Observer* of Raleigh, North Carolina.

Dr. Herbert Aptheker,
CPUSA figure and historian,
1965. AP/Wide World
Photos.

Students protesting the UNC administration's decision to deny campus access
and facilities to speaker ban opponents and invited speakers, March 1966.
North Carolina Collection, University of North Carolina Library at Chapel Hill;
reprinted by permission of the *News and Observer* of Raleigh, North Carolina.

Jesse Helms is elected to the Senate, November 1972. North Carolina Collection, University of North Carolina Library at Chapel Hill; reprinted by permission of the *News and Observer* of Raleigh, North Carolina.

7 Rethinking the Speaker Ban

The decision to forgo a campaign for amendment by the General Assembly in favor of a commission to consider the issue was astute and inherently political: Governor Daniel K. Moore created a forum in which his own risks would be minimized yet his personal preferences, while obscured, would nonetheless be felt. Such a medium would service several desirable political outcomes. First, each side would receive a full hearing, which would, it was hoped, release some of the intense pressure and shrillness that the debate had recently provoked. Second, the commission, if carefully selected, would receive the respect and support of the contending parties as well of a strong majority of citizens interested in the speaker law. The commission would then be well positioned to recommend acceptable proposals to resolve the persistent firestorm of accusation and controversy that had accompanied the law since its inception.

Moore planned to insure that the creation of a commission would ultimately, if indirectly, reflect his own views on how to end the fractiousness by arriving at a solution amenable to each side. The resolution creating the panel—entered in the House at the behest of the governor—stipulated that Moore would have the decisive role in determining the group's makeup. The commission members were crucial to the desired outcome; the resolution enabled Moore to select five of nine commissioners, including the all-important chairperson, who would give direction to the deliberations and identify a method of resolving the dispute. Lieutenant Governor and Senate President Robert Scott would select two members of the panel, and the remaining two would be tapped by House Speaker H. Pat Taylor of Anson County. The commission would reflect the assumptions of the leaders of the executive and legislative branches, with the governor's selection of a chairperson pointing the way.[1]

In Moore's assessment, amendment but not repeal was required. For political purposes, the anticommunist components of the law needed to be retained. By the same measure, the formal mechanism of trustee oversight would have to be reaffirmed by significant changes in the law necessitated by the accreditation flap. Joseph Branch, the governor's legislative liaison, noted the pivotal factor militating in favor of revision: "This is, in the last analysis, an academic affair." In Branch's view and, implicitly, Moore's, a "way [would have] to be found to satisfy the accrediting association."[2]

Scott had long been on record favoring amendment but not repeal. He realized the potential explosiveness of the communist issue and decided it was unwise to risk antagonizing voters who were otherwise likely to support him. Two days following the naming of the study commission, Scott articulated his views about the situation and what revisions were required. Speaking in Winston-Salem, the lieutenant governor acknowledged that the people of the state favored keeping the law "just like it is." "It's an emotional thing," said Scott, "the average citizen is against communism and that's all there is to it. Accreditation doesn't mean a thing to the man on the street—and he doesn't know what it is."[3]

House Speaker Taylor made his preference known prior to the public announcement of commission members, and his words resonated with the same imperative expounded by Moore and Scott—amendment. For Taylor, the answer rested in compromise: the two polarities—those wanting to end the restraint on academic freedom and those not wanting to see communists on the campuses—somehow had to be reconciled. "This controversy must be ended," said Taylor, "we can't afford to let it go on."[4]

The appointment of panel members was expedited by the knowledge that the Southern Association of Colleges and Schools was meeting in Richmond, Virginia, in November 1965 to review recent developments and perhaps decide the status of UNC's accreditation. Assuming that a special session of the Assembly was needed to amend the law, the committee would have a scant five months to conduct an investigation, hold hearings, and report its recommendations. Governor Moore set a target date of July 1, at which time the commissioners would be named and organized to begin work.[5]

On June 24, the announcement was made. Moore stressed that he had "used no particular criteria other than seeking the best commission he could find for the job." "They are," said the governor, "outstanding citizens of North

Carolina and [were chosen] because of the interest they have shown over the years—and will continue to show—in North Carolina."[6] And, indeed, the appointees were "outstanding citizens" with proven records of accomplishment in business, education, journalism, politics, and the legal profession.

The governor appointed Representative David M. Britt, an attorney from Robeson County, as chairman of the Speaker Ban Law Study Commission. Moore also selected Charles Myers, the president of Burlington Industries; Colonel William T. Joyner, a Raleigh attorney; Elizabeth G. Swindell of Wilson, immediate past president of the North Carolina Press Association; and the Reverend Ben C. Fisher of Wake Forest, chairman of the State Baptist Convention's commission on higher education. Scott chose two members of the state Senate, over which he presided, Gordon Hanes of Winston-Salem and Russell Kirby of Wilson County. Taylor named two House members, Lacy Thornburg of Jackson County and A. A. "Gus" Zollicoffer of Vance County.[7]

The panel's composition seemed balanced and varied. These terms are, of course, relative, referring to who or what is included rather than excluded. There were no blacks appointed to the commission. During this period of development in North Carolina's political culture, it was highly unlikely that any were considered. North Carolina had only recently begun to recognize the social legitimacy of blacks entering public life alongside whites, and it was predominantly an urban phenomenon. In many areas of the state de facto segregation remained a reality of life. Ku Klux Klan activity had risen sharply in 1964 and 1965: a cross had been burned on the lawn of the governor's mansion, and the Klan was permitted to operate a booth at the state fair in Raleigh, where "vicious anti-black taunts" were broadcast to the crowds. For many rural and small-town whites, the presence of a black man or woman would have tarnished the study commission's image. And legislators from these areas had numerous and strategically important seats in the General Assembly. Race was, after all, a critical subtext of the speaker ban controversy. Resentment of the surging civil rights movement had helped engender a belief among some legislators and their supporters that the hidden specter of communist influence was somehow responsible.[8]

Most of the state's demographic regions were represented—the coastal east, the sand hills, the urban Piedmont, and the mountains. The eight men and one woman had a median age of forty-eight. One woman among eight men may not appear balanced, but Swindell was not selected as a representative of women but as a conservative publisher from eastern North Carolina. If a black agenda vis-à-vis the civil rights movement was beginning to question the absence of civil equality and the exclusion of blacks from authoritative public roles, the question of gender equality remained for the future. Women's issues were, however, present amid the tension of the 1963 Assembly that produced the speaker law. The most vivid example was the submission of a bill by Representative Martha Evans of Mecklenburg County that called for pay equalization for male and female state employees with similar job classifications. When the proposal was voted down in committee, Senator Thomas J. White, although not a committee member, attended the hearing and announced that he would have voted "no" had he been so empowered. The female members of the House recognized issues other than communism when House Bill 1395 passed by a voice vote. Four of the five female legislators—Evans, Nancy Chase of Wayne County, Grace Rodenbough of Stokes County, and Rachel Davis of Kinston—were among the fourteen House members who entered a statement of dissent against the new statute into the official record.[9]

The commission included two industrialists, a publisher, an educational administrator, and five attorneys. The state press, with few exceptions, endorsed the appointments and lavished praise on each member. The group was, said the Greensboro Daily Record, "a good commission," capable of "detachment and objectivity." The Greensboro paper came close to anointing the anticipated outcome of the panel's effort: "If these men and women decide something should be done—either amendment or repeal of the speaker ban law—their opinion will carry great weight in North Carolina's legislative and executive chambers."[10]

The study commission appointees were all selected for political reasons. Each possessed some affiliation or basis of opinion that was deemed useful to a satisfactory resolution of the speaker law problem. But Moore, Scott, and Taylor did not simply audition prospective appointees for a willingness to act as surrogates, thereby allowing the three men to impose a predetermined solution. The commission was granted the freedom and autonomy to choose how best to meet and resolve the issues raised by the ban law. While the individuals were independent agents in terms of how to redesign the language and terms of the statute, they were committed to just that—amendment.

Both Scott appointees were his friends and political allies from the Senate. Hanes's appointment acknowledged the governmental influence exerted by the state's preeminent industrial and financial interests. The scion of an affluent and socially prominent family of textile manufacturers, since 1958 Hanes had served as president and chairman of the board of the Hanes Corporation, one of the state's textile giants. Prior to the emergence of the accreditation problem, Hanes had ardently supported the speaker law. He was also a friend and confidant of UNC President William C. Friday. As such, Hanes was acutely aware of the university's position on the law. During the recent General Assembly session, Hanes had been among those exploring possible avenues for amending the law.[11]

Kirby was a certain vote for amendment. Like Hanes, Kirby had been among those desiring legislative action during the past session. Perhaps more telling was the fact that Kirby had been one of the fourteen senators protesting the passage of the original bill in 1963. In a statement entered into the *Senate Journal*, Kirby and the others had declared that the law "constitutes an abridgement or denial of free speech, a lack of due regard for the true purpose and meaning of the University of North Carolina and other public educational institutions in the life of our state and nation, a denial of Constitutional privileges, and that in other respects it violates our long recognized and generally accepted political and social principles of this Country." In the intervening period, Kirby had come to accept the position that outright repeal was not politically possible.[12]

Taylor selected two close friends who, like himself, favored compromise through amendment. From the mountains, Thornburg had operated a law firm in Sylva, Jackson County, where the governor had been reared. Zollicoffer was Taylor's longtime friend and associate. They had attended the exclusive McCallie School in Chattanooga, Tennessee, together. Thinking that "on the face it sounded all right," Zollicoffer had voted for the original speaker bill. Since that time, however, he had come to have reservations about the law, especially after the accreditation threat became known. During the recent Assembly session, Zollicoffer had worked to line up the votes necessary for amendment.[13]

In assessing the composition of the commission for his audience, Jesse Helms was adamantly displeased at what he found. Helms was convinced beyond doubt that "outright repeal" or "crippling amendment" was a certainty. He refused to accept the superlatives that the governor and the press had assigned to the members. Helms concurred that the members were, in the words of the governor, "excellent citizens" but quickly pointed out that "excellent citizenship was hardly the only test to be applied to possible appointees to this important committee." In Helms's tally, Hanes and Kirby had been "discreetly vocal" in their opposition to the law. The appointment of Thornburg and Zollicoffer, said Helms, "served the purpose of providing two more votes for repeal or amendment."[14]

From Helms's vantage point, the commission was tantamount to a stacked deck, with the decision a foregone conclusion. Helms carefully omitted Governor Moore from the suggestion that the panelists had been deliberately chosen to amend or repeal the law. For political reasons—Helms had invested strong support in Moore's social conservatism—the governor could not be excoriated as were Scott and Taylor. But Helms was no more satisfied with two of the governor's selections. With such an unsatisfactory commission, there seemed but one possibility left to the combative television personality: discount the commission's significance while emphasizing the next line of defense, the General Assembly: "Any substantial public interest in the work of the committee will of necessity be strictly artificial. It seems clear that the eventual recommendations of the committee can be forecast with reasonable certainty. Thus, the next round of any significance in the communist speaker ban law controversy will take place in the General Assembly. Fortunately, that will be the round that counts." [15]

Helms could not acknowledge that Moore, with whom the editorialist had staked his hopes, also favored amending the speaker ban law. The accreditation issue had dramatically transfigured speaker law politics. Moore's selection of proamendment panelists was not a matter of the governor's naïveté. The governor believed that amendment was necessary and chose members who would work to that end while ensuring perpetuation of the original law's anticommunist hallmarks. [16]

One of Moore's choices for the commission was concerned with the mere existence of the speaker ban law. As the president of Burlington Industries, the world's largest textile manufacturing firm, Myers represented the state's powerful industrial establishment. When the commission began its deliberations, Myers favored outright repeal, the sole member to take such a position, according to Chairman Britt. The presence of one of the state's preeminent economic leaders among the commission's ranks indicated the momentum toward significant amendment. [17]

Fisher, who served as executive director of the Baptist State Convention's Council on Christian Education, brought two noteworthy associations to the commission. Reared in the small mountain town of Webster, in Jackson County, Fisher was a longtime friend of Governor Moore. In addition, Fisher was the only member enjoying close professional contact with SACS. Personally acquainted with the association's executive secretary, Gordon Sweet, Fisher was well positioned to serve as a conduit of information between the two bodies. The *Raleigh News and Observer* surmised, "Fisher's commission role may well be one of an intermediary between the commission and the Southern Association." In naming him "Tar Heel of the Week" in February 1963, the Raleigh paper cited Fisher as "one of the top clerical PR men in North Carolina." With a background as a moderator and a close working relationship with many SACS officials, Fisher, like the others, was prepared to establish a means for compromise. [18]

Surveying the likely positions of Hanes, Kirby, Thornburg, Zollicoffer, Myers, and Fisher, Helms concluded that the "game is over before it begins." In his exegesis on the absence of objectivity by the first six members, Helms attempted to preserve the assumed neutrality of the remaining members without exploring their likely positions. With the vote already predetermined, said the commentator, "it is unnecessary to evaluate the possible positions of Mrs. Elizabeth Swindell of Wilson, or Colonel W. T. Joyner of Raleigh. It is highly unlikely that the chairman of the committee, Representative David Britt, will even have to cast a vote."[19] Helms chose this strategy because he expected or hoped that each of the final three members would be a voice for retention. He had ample reason to believe that Swindell, Joyner, and Britt supported the speaker ban and might oppose any move to return authority to the trustees.

Swindell had followed her father, editor John Gold, and her grandfather, founder and publisher P. D. Gold, into the family newspaper business at the *Wilson Daily Times* after the death of her husband. In August 1963 Helms celebrated her election as president of the North Carolina Press Association: "She is a lady whom we have long admired," said the commentator, "and we have frequently noted Mrs. Swindell's apprehension about the trend of thinking in her country. She is not blind to the perils of communism, or the breakdown in American principles." But as a member of the study commission, Swindell also represented the state's press association, and many dailies vehemently opposed any speaker control law. The Gold family had maintained a long friendship with Frank Daniels, the publisher of the *News and Observer* and a chief patron of the university.[20]

If there was a person on the committee with a conservative pedigree acceptable to Helms, it was Joyner. The two men had first joined forces in the notorious 1950 Senate primary pitting UNC President Frank Graham against Willis Smith. With the enterprising journalist playing an important role in persuading Smith to ask for a second primary, Joyner assisted in campaign strategy and delivered a series of radio speeches denouncing Graham's liberalism and his positions on "deficit spending," "socialized medicine," and "Federal abolition of segregation and the increasing of Federal Control over the personal lives of citizens." Joyner had played a prominent role in a spirited and successful campaign, and the friendships he established—including ties to Helms and Hoover Adams—would be long lasting.[21]

In the ensuing decade, Joyner had served as the legal counsel of the Pearsall committee, which addressed the question of North Carolina's response to the requirements of *Brown v. Board of Education.* Joyner was a staunch conservative who desired some means of preserving a substantial measure of racial segregation. But as an architect of the Pearsall Plan, Joyner demonstrated judgments that reflected an ability and willingness to compromise. He opposed as ill-fated any attempts to pursue a strategy of massive resistance.[22]

In 1964 Joyner had been among Moore's earliest and most eager supporters, assisting in the payment of the candidate's filing fee in Raleigh. Consistent with his desire to oppose segregation while avoiding the application of blunt instruments, Joyner sharply criticized opposing candidate I. Beverly Lake's support of massive resistance. Like Moore, Joyner was a business conservative.

Although implacably opposed to communism, he was inclined to seek compromise and social peace as a means of safeguarding long-term conservative interests.[23]

There was also abundant reason for Helms and others to believe that Britt might support retention of the speaker law. Britt had voted for House Bill 1395 and had continued to voice support for the measure.[24] A quiet but committed anticommunist, Britt held that no circumstance existed under which political speakers such as Gus Hall or Milton Rosen should be allowed to appear on a state-supported campus. As the chairman of the new commission, Britt was well positioned to oversee its agenda and insure, regardless of amendment, that the speaker law would continue to resonate with a resolve to oppose communism.

Despite Britt's ability and savvy, there were others of more established reputation who might have served as the leader of the commission. Why did the governor select Britt? Three factors made the selection of Britt compelling. First, Britt was expected to be the unanimous choice as the next House speaker. His widespread support and network of allies could be useful in securing amendment in a body where there remained substantial support for the original law. Second, Britt was held in high esteem by conservatives both in and outside of the legislature. As chairman, Britt could mute the criticisms of those opposing any amendment and blunt charges that the commission was insensitive to the threat of communism. Many conservative supporters of the ban law reacted with enthusiasm to the news of Britt's selection. Said Adams in a letter to Britt, "I was delighted when I learned about [the appointment] today. Frankly, I had been quite concerned as to who would be named and I feel much better now. With people like you, Col. Joyner, and Mrs. Swindell on the committee, I am confident that the right thing will be done."[25]

The principal factor in Britt's selection was his closeness to Governor Moore. Moore desired that the committee chairperson understand the governor's own position and, equally important, be loyal. On receiving the telephone call from Moore, Britt reassured his friend and sponsor, "Governor, I rise and fall on your fortunes." Britt was not simply a surrogate who performed a directed task. He had Moore's trust that the "right potential answer" would be found. Britt was aware of the limitations: "To repeal this cussed thing would be politically difficult. From the outset, I was looking for a middle ground."[26]

Helms was correct in his forecast of the study commission: the speaker law would be restructured by means of amendment. Had the conservative commentator carefully examined the inclinations of the three unexplored panelists, he would have been led to an interesting discovery: all nine members came to the commission, each in his or her own manner, to work for an acceptable amendment. Without an a priori understanding that some form of amendment was necessary, the study commission would never have been created. But what also went unmentioned was that a majority of the commission were staunch anticommunists who agreed with a basic tenet of the law: UNC should be off-limits to communists. Herein lay the dilemma faced by the Britt commission as it began work: how to alleviate SACS's concerns about accreditation yet preserve the core requirement of keeping communists away from the campus.

The Britt commission held its first organizational meeting on July 14 at the Legislative Building to identify what issues would be studied. With the exception of several days of public hearings, the study commission met in executive session away from the press and public scrutiny. At the July meeting, held before an audience, the panel created a subcommittee to examine the law's constitutional aspects. Many of the state's legal minds, including members of the General Assembly, continued to have grave doubts as to the ban's constitutionality. This issue was especially important in the aftermath of several state and federal court decisions directly bearing on the North Carolina law. Constitutional issues were not, however, paramount to the commission's deliberations. Members assumed that if the functional operations of the statute could be improved, revisions could be made to address lingering legal difficulties. "I quite agree," said Hanes in a letter to a Senate colleague, "that standing alone the constitutionality of the law will not govern our decision or that of the General Assembly." Nearly all parties in the proceedings realized that the accreditation controversy was the central issue involved. However, those desirous of retaining the law fundamentally intact attempted to downplay the problem. At the initial meeting, Joyner declared that while he "certainly thought that it would be wise to investigate the accreditation aspect . . . it would not be wise to let the idea get out that this was the most important thing."[27]

Prior to the first official meeting, commission members swung into action, seeking information that would shed light on various questions of concern. Letters were sent to the executive officers of the flagship public universities of neighboring states, inquiring about their speaker policies. The responses indicated that on matters of visiting speakers, regional state universities either had minimal requirements or adhered to policy positions that left the decision to "the integrity and wisdom of the Trustees and the administration." The president of the University of South Carolina, Thomas F. Jones, averred that "the only rule in effect has been that speakers can be invited to the campus only by recognized student organizations. We are particularly glad that our legislature did not see fit to pass a speakers' ban law. We don't see how an institution can function as effectively in the law with it." But the University of South Carolina was no bastion of free speech where dissenters and radicals were welcomed. Jones stated that Carl Braden had been recently turned away by informing the sponsoring student group of his record. Jones pointed out the usefulness of executing a ban without a formal policy or state law: "Without a law, we were able to see that Braden was not an acceptable speaker. With the law, we could not have banned him as a Communist because he does not admit being one." The informal ban was justified: "We want our young people to be able to know the facts about what's going on in the world, but we feel the campus is a place for scholars rather than a place for agitators!"[28]

Finding no similar bans at neighboring universities, the commission looked to the source of the North Carolina speaker law as a possible guidepost for resolving the problem. Swindell, who had been designated the panel's secretary, sent an inquiry to President Novice G. Fawcett of Ohio State University. The North Carolina legislation had been modeled after an Ohio bill, and Helms had heaped accolades on Fawcett for his opposition to radical speakers at the Columbus campus. Fawcett explained that although the Ohio legislature had enacted a speaker law, it was "rather redundant since the same authority is vested in our Board of Trustees in the statutes that were on the books before the recent law was passed." The matter of accreditation was not a concern in Ohio, said Fawcett, "since our statute vests authority in our Board which is where authority belongs. Many faculty people would consider a regulatory law on this subject as constituting unwarranted political interference."[29]

If the spate of inquiries increasingly revealed the singularity of North Carolina's legislative ban, news in August confirmed the total isolation faced by the state. Near the end of its session, the Alabama legislature rejected a bill to ban communists from the state's public campuses. Supported by Governor George C. Wallace, the bill was closely patterned after the North Carolina measure. Wallace had been encouraged to promote the bill after receiving a copy of the bill from Clarence Stone, an admirer of the Alabama segregationist. Unlike North Carolina, the Alabama legislature held discussions about the bill's advisability, and the press debated the matter. In the end, the measure was withdrawn after it became clear that key members of the Senate would hold up passage of a pending appropriations bill rather than let the speaker bill go through. Thus, Alabama, where assumptions ran strong that communism and racial integration were indelibly linked, refused to jeopardize the integrity of its public universities. As in South Carolina, opinion in Alabama rejected the need for a speaker law but held that communists should not be allowed to speak on campus. In the words of the Birmingham Post-Herald, "The burden now is upon college presidents of the state to see that such speakers do not appear. We believe they will do a good policing job." The members of the study commission discovered that North Carolina was the only state that as a matter of law denied its university officials the authority to administer campus speaker policy.[30]

The Britt commission resolved to determine how deleterious a possible loss of accreditation might be. Inquiries were forwarded to federal agencies and foundations that administered "a variety of loan, scholarship, contract research and other higher education programs." The organizations were asked what effect, if any, accreditation or lack of accreditation had on grants. The answers Britt received, although neither conclusive nor categorical, tended to indicate that the foundations' officers would take a dim view of a withdrawal of accreditation because of the speaker ban. The Ford Foundation's response noted that while there was "no simple answer," the legislature should consider whether an outside agency would view the law as "a legislative expression of confidence in the integrity and judgement of the institutions that may be applying for a Foundation grant. This problem would occur to any foundation that might be considering an institution for a grant." The Carnegie Corporation, despite not having a formal policy about unaccredited institutions, reported that "it has been many years since we have made a grant to such an institution." Carnegie research grants went to individuals and experimental groups, typically at accredited colleges and universities.[31]

The responses from federal agencies also lacked encouragement. Although some stated that the lack of accreditation by itself would not affect the awards process, the circumstances attending the loss of accreditation would be considered. Other agencies indicated that the withdrawal of accreditation would have a significant impact on grant decisions. In some cases, accreditation was a mandatory requirement. The State Department's Bureau of Educational and Cultural Affairs indicated that the absence of accredited status would, in effect, disqualify internationals from receiving grants to study or work at a school so affected: "Citizens of other countries under our educational exchange program are given grants to study, teach, or pursue research in accredited institutions. This accreditation is effected by appropriate regional organizations such as the Southern Association of Colleges and Schools."[32] The loss of accreditation by North Carolina would thus present the probability of a serious diminution in the quantity and caliber of international students on the state's campuses. As a research institution drawing substantial numbers of foreign students and researchers, the impact at Chapel Hill would be particularly dramatic.

The Department of Defense responded that while each military branch had its own requirements, accreditation was a major consideration in terms of tuition assistance to students enrolled in military-science and officer-training programs: "The Army authorizes tuition payments to any accredited college or university and to unaccredited schools if they can show documentary evidence that their credits are recognized as fully transferable by any fully accredited college." U.S. Air Force requirements were even more exacting: "they require documentary evidence from at least three accredited schools certifying that credits earned at non-accredited institutions are fully transferable toward a degree." The department's spokesman closed with a candid and ominous appraisal: "We would be less than frank were we not to advise that such a loss of accreditation would raise serious questions as to the availability of such institutions to participate in [department] programs."[33] Thus, a host of statewide programs would be affected by the loss of accreditation. Reserve Officers' Training Corps programs would be badly compromised, and prospective applicants to national military academies would face greater complications in gaining admission.

The Vocational Rehabilitation Administration of the Department of Health, Education, and Welfare noted the exclusive status of UNC's relationship with the agency. "The University of North Carolina is at the present time the only public institution of higher education which is receiving training grants. These grants are in the fields of medicine, surgery, physical therapy, recreation, and mental retardation." The respondent cited the dire repercussions of a withdrawal of accreditation: "In any field which the requirements for approval by the professional association include a requirement that the institution must be accredited by the appropriate regional accrediting authority, it would be necessary for us to discontinue support."[34]

The Britt commission convened its first public hearing on August 11 before a statewide radio and television audience. The morning session was devoted to testimony from Dr. Emmett B. Fields and Gordon Sweet of SACS. Fields began with an overview of the association's organization, membership, and standards. He stated that 411 constituent members comprised the College Delegate Assembly, membership was completely voluntary, and the members were "united to preserve and foster education of quality in the Southern region." The criteria for accreditation, Fields noted, were set forth in the association's *Standards for Colleges*. The standards were approved by the delegate assembly, and compliance was determined by the fifty-four-member Commission on Colleges, which Fields chaired.[35]

Fields stated that SACS had become aware of the situation in North Carolina as a result of a self-study conducted by UNC in 1963–64. In February 1963 a visitation committee was selected to visit the school to observe and evaluate its educational operations within the standards observed by the association. The SACS visitation team became aware of the law in October 1963, when Friday and William B. Aycock forwarded documents including faculty resolutions and statements by the president and chancellor. When the visitation team arrived in Chapel Hill in March 1964, it surveyed the situation and reminded UNC administrators of Standard 2 of the delegate assembly, pertaining to organization and administration: "The responsibilities of the governing board include establishing broad institutional policies, securing financial resources to support adequately the institution's program, and selecting the chief administrative officer and, upon his recommendation, the other administrative officers of the institution. The governing board should not be subject to undue pressures from state officials or other outside political or religious groups; furthermore, the governing board should protect the administration from similar outside pressures."[36]

In its report, the visitation committee emphasized the "position taken by the University faculty and administration" and endorsed the "steps aimed at corrective action" by the trustees and the State Board of Higher Education. The executive committee of the Commission on Colleges considered the report at its June 1964 meeting in Atlanta and again at the annual meeting of the delegate assembly, held in December in Louisville, Kentucky. After the Louisville meeting, Sweet informed Friday of the council's concern and notified him that the association would "maintain interest and concern in the subject." At this juncture, Fields explained, SACS hoped that the authorities in North Carolina could work out an amenable resolution; if not, however, the commission "stands ready to protest in the name of academic integrity, when the educational effort is hampered by political interference, or in any way menaced by those who would subvert the search for truth." When it became apparent that the 1965 Assembly was not likely to move to alleviate the cause for concern, Fields and Sweet visited Raleigh to talk with the governor. When those meetings yielded no firm commitment to altering the law, the executive committee approved the statement informing North Carolina officials of the committee's intention to begin discussions that would "determine the status of these institutions with respect to accreditation." And these discussions were the raison d'être of the Britt committee.[37]

Fields affirmed that in no way did the executive committee of the Commission on Colleges challenge the right of the legislature to "pass, amend, or repeal any law it wishes, including the one which is the basis of the present controversy." SACS's authority, said Fields, resided with its constituent members "with respect to the conditions for membership and accreditation as set forth in the *Standards for Colleges*." Routine procedures were followed, Fields stressed, and at no time had the association addressed itself to the General Assembly of North Carolina. The executive committee had not commanded the legislature to take any action.[38]

Still, the council had concluded that the situation in North Carolina constituted an egregious violation, both in spirit and in substance, of the association's standards regarding undue outside interference. Fields summarized: "Political interference has occurred, and [the executive council] believes that the evidence for this finding is *prima facie*. It inheres in the language of 'An Act to Regulate Visiting Speakers at State Supported Colleges and Universities.' . . . [T]he Executive Council has concluded that higher education cannot function most effectively in the midst of this bitter spectacle, and that detrimental effects have ensued."[39]

With these remarks, Fields provided the strongest indication to date that SACS had every intention of acting to remove North Carolina's public colleges and universities from its roster of accredited schools. The executive council, led by Fields and Sweet, appeared thoroughly committed to a course of action that would result in the Commission on Colleges voting to revoke the University of North Carolina's accreditation.

After Fields's statement, the members of the study panel questioned him at length about the association's intent, the origins of its concern, and, most prominently, what the accrediting agency expected the commission and ultimately the legislature to do. The questions were often pointed and hard-hitting; at times the scene resembled a courtroom interrogation, as the panelists peppered Fields with questions. Many of the questions seemed politically motivated and inspired by a desire to ensnare Fields in one trap after another.

Joyner turned his legal ingenuity to the task of preserving as much as possible of the state's rigid anticommunist law. He asked if the people of North Carolina, as represented by the Assembly, constituted outside influence, thereby implying that the SACS action challenged the authority of a democratically elected body. This was a loaded question. Fields readily acknowledged the sovereignty of the state's polity, but he noted that the people's prerogative consisted of electing a governor and legislature that must then be "responsible" to the needs of the institutions.[40]

Joyner questioned the association's seemingly late interest in the speaker ban issue. He noted that according to the proceedings of the association's annual meetings in December 1963 and December 1964, there had been no reference to the situation at UNC or to the law. Did not this omission indicate that the quality of instruction had not been affected by the law? Did it also intimate that the accrediting agency's late interest reflected political shenanigans put into motion at the behest of UNC officials? Fields responded that the executive committee's investigation had not been completed at that time, and it was hoped that UNC officials, working in concert with the legislature, would be able to find a satisfactory solution.[41]

Most of all, Joyner wanted to know, "What is the result of the loss of accreditation?" Several of the panelists raised this pivotal question, and each time Fields politely declined to speculate about his group's expectations: "This is not a question that I can give a complete answer to." "Have you ever observed a case?" asked Joyner. "Loss of accreditation? I have not myself, personally, observed this," answered Fields. Joyner persisted: "I am very interested as to what would be the consequences, the inevitable consequences, or the probable consequences of loss of accreditation." Fields continued that because the association did not issue edicts to its members, "there would be no routine mode" for forecasting a definitive outcome.[42]

The questions from the other members, while not as sharp as those from Joyner, were also directed toward the same conclusion: what did SACS expect the commission to recommend? Fields's answers seemed evasive as he continuously refused to speculate. The panelists became exasperated with his persistent refusals. Swindell reflected the panel's increasing annoyance: "Well then, let me ask just one more [question], then I'll give up. If the Board of Trustees made some guidelines and rules and regulations, that more or less included this: speakers from designated political groups, and speakers that were so-called Communist political speakers would not speak on a university campus. But for the sake of argument, cultural and scientific speakers of any political thinking could speak, how would your accreditation association view that? Now that action would be taken by the Board of Trustees?" Fields's appeared to struggle for a response: "Here again you are asking me to comment on a set of facts that don't exist. I would say only this, that we have at no point insisted —I hope this is abundantly obvious to the study commission — we have at no point insisted that Communists be required to speak on university campuses."[43] Fields had gone as far as he possibly could given the circumstances. He had indicated the source of the problem as SACS viewed the matter: removal of campus authority from the trustees. Implicit in his exegesis of the SACS's concern was his solution: the accreditation issue could be summarily resolved by a restoration of authority.

The afternoon session of the first public hearing saw a revisitation of the accreditation issue. Dr. Howard Boozer, the acting director of the State Board of Higher Education, testified about the effect of loss of accreditation on grants and financial assistance from federal agencies and private foundations. Boozer's presentation revealed that the results of losing accreditation were serious and were likely to be felt over time rather than immediately. The loss of grants might lead to a loss of top researchers and teachers. Should such a reduction in the caliber and prominence of faculty occur, it would likely mean lower ratings for the colleges and universities involved. Boozer testified that the U.S. Office of Education was expected to grant more than forty-three million dollars over the next two years for purposes of upgrading primary and secondary schools. Each recipient school was required to be accredited or provide substantial documentation that its credits would be accepted by other schools. This accumulation of information, following on the heels of a portended withdrawal of accreditation, confirmed for the committee the task that it was to perform. Whatever else might appear in its report, the commission would have to recommend that authority be restored to the Board of Trustees.[44]

The overtones of the initial day of testimony upset the committee. While some members expressed irritation over Fields's nebulous responses, most admitted their worries that accreditation would be lost. Kirby noted that while he had expected "the Southern Association to give us more direct answers," he had "a feeling in my bones" that accreditation would be lost. Hanes was particularly put off by Fields's apparent evasiveness: "Dr. Fields proved that the Southern Association is a self-controlled, self-authoritative, self-disciplined organization that doesn't blush at all to take paths of complete inconsistency." Still, Hanes acknowledged that he thought it "extremely likely that we either lose our accreditation or be placed on probation by the Southern Association." Zollicoffer publicly "assumed" from the testimony that accreditation would be lost, but privately he was "convinced that a loss of accreditation would seriously hamper education in North Carolina." Fisher concurred that "on the basis of the facts we've heard up to now, accreditation is certainly in jeopardy." Of all the panelists, Joyner was the sole member who seemed to come to terms with precisely what Fields's presentation had meant: that the association would likely cite any solution that did not restore the trustees' authority as "continued political interference."[45]

Chairman Britt did not believe that Fields had been open and forthright in his testimony. Britt not only believed that SACS possessed a likely scenario of what action might be taken but also refused to part with the suspicion that UNC officials and other persons in the state had brought the speaker ban to the association's attention and urged it into action. When Britt asked if the action of the Commission on Colleges was "precipitated by people in North Carolina," Fields had responded, "Yes, it was precipitated by the General Assembly in 1963." Such oblique ridicule of a body that Britt was slated to lead irritated him: "All right, sir. Was it precipitated by anyone else pursuant to the passage of the law? Did anyone else then, either the head of an institution or people connected with either one of our institutions get in touch with you or anyone that you know about and encourage you to take this action?" Fields sought to counter the suggestion: "No, at no point did any person urge me or, as far as I am aware, any other members of the Council that we act in the way that we did act." With Fields's refusal to respond to direct questions and the rambling, seeming evasiveness of many answers, Britt was not convinced.[46]

Although vexing to committee members, Fields's unwillingness to speculate or suggest a course of action for the commission to follow was understandable. The Commission on Colleges would convene in three months, and it would have been considered presumptuous and prejudicial for Fields to prescribe a decision. And had he accepted the invitation to express a personal opinion on what the commission should do, those supporting the law could have loudly proclaimed that SACS was dictating terms of surrender to the legislature through the committee. Fields went as far as he could conceivably go in suggesting SACS's objections to the law as well as those provisions with which it had no grievance.[47]

The accreditation inquiry proved that amendment was inevitable. The commission's work did not, however, signal any capitulation on the law's anti-communist features. Several commissioners remained vehemently opposed to any presence by known communists on the state's campuses. During Fields's testimony, Britt had phrased a hypothetical question assuming the law's legitimacy as a defense against the "international communist conspiracy." Added to such ideological proclivities was an unstated yet understood purpose of the commission: to find a means of placating the contending parties. If a concession on accreditation would restore campus authority to UNC trustees and administrators, then the strident anticommunism of the law's supporters would also have to be appeased. The public hearings were balanced between supporters and opponents of the law. On the first day the commission heard from SACS, whose interest implicitly reflected opposition to any such speaker law. In the afternoon of the same day, the commission invited Representative Philip Godwin, one of the law's original sponsors and ardent defenders, to make a presentation explaining his intentions and the bill's purpose as it was drafted. On the following day, August 12, the panel heard from a delegation representing the American Association of University Professors (AAUP), an organization opposing as unconstitutional any speaker law. The AAUP group was then followed in the afternoon session by witnesses representing and sponsored by the state department of the American Legion.[48]

The American Legion was a force of no small consequence. By the 1960s, World War II–era veterans came of age in North Carolina politics. Candidates for statewide office actively courted legionnaires' votes, and the keynote address at the organization's spring convention was regularly delivered by major public figures. In 1963 the speaker was Governor Terry Sanford, himself a legionnaire, and the following year Senate President Clarence Stone, a stalwart defender of the state's new anticommunist law, addressed the convention. A majority of General Assembly members also were members of the legion, and many of them had served as a commandant of a local post or held a higher statewide office. In 1963 Representative L. J. Phipps of Chapel Hill — whose local post had been instrumental in calling for legislative investigation of UNC — resigned his Assembly seat to assume his duties as the new commandant of the North Carolina American Legion. In the early and mid-1960s, the legion and state politics were closely aligned.

Like the parent organization, which proclaimed a mission of defending the nation against perceived enemies, the state department also declared its vigilance and unswerving opposition to whatever manifested itself as contrary to the legion's view of what was "American." As the national body enlisted in the war against communism by invoking the rhetoric of "100 percent American-ism," so too did its North Carolina affiliate inveigh against the depredations of the communist menace. Legion surveillance had precipitated the concern with communists at Chapel Hill. Following the passage of the bill, the legion had prominently defended the statute and encouraged those political figures identified with the speaker law.[49] It surprised no one that the legion would assume the role of coordinating defense of the speaker ban before the study commission.

The first pro–speaker ban witness to appear was Godwin. Although not representing the legion, Godwin was a veteran and a legionnaire. Godwin appeared to explain "the bill, the purpose behind the bill, and its enactment." The legislator testified that he and Ned Delamar had been "discussing the bill at great length over a period of time." Contrary to the intense grilling that the commission had directed at Fields, the questions put to Godwin were brief and cordial in tone. The panelists seemed reluctant to challenge Godwin's assumptions or account of the bill's origins. Hanes asked how broad and inclusive was the phrase "facilities of the university." The witness responded with a one-sentence answer, and Hanes acknowledged his agreement and indicated that was all he wanted to know. Swindell also asked only one question: What was Godwin's response to allegations that the law limited freedom of speech? Godwin averred that it did not. A communist could speak, he said, but not on state-owned campus property.[50]

Kirby and Zollicoffer questioned Godwin in some detail. Only Kirby, who had opposed the passage of the original bill, framed critical questions that challenged the witness: "You really don't have a definition of known Communists, do you, Representative Godwin?" Godwin replied tautologically: "I have one of my own opinion. He's a person that believes in the doctrines of Communism." Godwin said that he was willing to rely on FBI lists of "known Communist speakers" to identify who should be prevented from speaking. Godwin stipulated that in his opinion the law would prohibit any person identified as a communist from speaking, whatever the subject of the address. "You have no knowledge of where he will leave off his scientific expressions and go into a political expression." In Godwin's estimation, the law would prohibit the "Russian" ambassador from speaking as well as Soviet Premier Nikita Khrushchev, whose speech Godwin denied could possibly possess any educational merit.[51]

Godwin also departed from the focus on visiting speakers when he suggested a subtext to the law's creation: "In my personal opinion I would like to see a course taught in Marxism in all of the universities and colleges provided that course is taught by a professor that sticks to his text and does not inject any of his own philosophies." Godwin apparently assumed that an objective "text" would debunk Marxism and hence demonstrate the falsity of communism. In a broader sense, the comment suggested that he — and perhaps other speaker law supporters — perceived that "truth" was available in the social sciences and that such an exposition would confirm a particular understanding of human society; the corollary was that the professor's role was to adhere to the truth as revealed by the text. The comment, like many other statements made by Godwin, went unexplored.[52]

Thornburg asked what was potentially a most pertinent question: "I seem to recall having seen in print that perhaps something other than a consideration of Communism promoted the introduction of the bill . . . the activities going on down the street at the time." Godwin had testified that he and Delamar had discussed the need for such a bill but did not cite any context for the discussions. What social circumstances engendered the legislators' interest? Did Godwin mean to suggest that the discussion emanated from an intellectual fascination with opposing communism, without contextualized reference or grounding in any local issues? More specifically, Thornburg's query raised the possibility that ire at the constant civil rights protests had triggered a response that targeted the universities, especially UNC, as the source of the problem. Godwin simply denied the suggestion, and the matter was closed. On this question and others, the committee accepted facile responses without further probing.[53]

What explained the study commission's unwillingness to confront Godwin on the contradictions between his story and other accounts in the public record? For the most part, the members shared his anticommunist assumptions; the only problematic area was how to be sure a suspect was a "known communist." Known communists, the committee agreed, should rightfully be banned from the campuses. Thus, the committee members were intellectually and psychologically unprepared to delve more deeply into the questions surrounding the law's origin and necessity. They were willing to accept, at face value, the contention that the law was designed as a blow against communism; since everyone opposed communism, the law, whatever its flaws, possessed a redeeming character. The law was going to be amended, but the ubiquitous anticommunist imperative assured the expectation that the prohibition against certain speakers would remain.

The American Legion organized support for an unamended speaker law out of conviction but also out of a sense of duty. The legion perceived as its duty opposing any foreign threat to the United States, and no threat was seen as more real and pernicious than communism. At the legion's 1960 national convention in Miami Beach, the North Carolina department had sponsored a resolution pertaining to "Communist infiltration into institutions of higher learning." The resolution of the Chapel Hill post in September 1962 identified an obsession with the "International Conspiracy — Communism — whether it be called Marxism, Marxist-Leninism, Stalinism or by any other name as long as it was conceived in the pathological, hate-embittered brain of atheist Karl

Marx." The resolution suggested the propriety of limiting the First Amendment to combat those "who aid a conspiracy that turns academic freedom into academic license." After passage of the speaker law, the legion endorsed a resolution expressing "its sincerest praise and appreciation to the introducers of the 'ban the communists' bill and each and every member of the General Assembly who supported said bill." For those who dared oppose what the legion viewed as a wholesome, useful law, the resolution carried a defiant message: "We of the American Legion, Department of North Carolina, pledge to our departed and disabled comrades of the great wars to be ever ready to repel this latest onslaught by those who would drive a breach in our defenses against communism, for whatever reason, in North Carolina and elsewhere." [54] With the passage of the speaker ban, the legion found an issue of its own. Defense of the law was consistent with the legion's sense of mission in defending against a threat to the United States from its foremost foe.

As soon as the Britt commission was announced, the legion notified the chairman that it wanted to make a presentation and began to rally support from members throughout the state. The *North Carolina American Legion News* focused attention on the hearings and asked members to "keep in close contact with the proceedings." The state commander, J. Alvis Carver of Dunn, conferred with Britt at the commission's first meeting. Britt publicly promised that the legion would be issued a "specific invitation" to appear. "I recognize my good friend," said Britt, "the Commander of the American Legion and certainly we want to invite the Legion." In rallying its forces, the legion adopted a resolution commending the 1963 Assembly for enacting the law, praising the 1965 Assembly for refusing to alter the law, and calling for support for the study commission. [55]

On August 12, the American Legion was represented before the Britt Commission by five speakers. The first spokesman was W. Dudley Robbins of Pender County, a member of the national executive committee and a past commander of the state legion. Robbins outlined the organization's long opposition to domestic radicals and stipulated that while the legion believed it useful for universities to teach communism, such instruction should "foster and perpetuate a one hundred per cent Americanism." [56]

Robbins also raised as justification of the speaker law the widening conflict in Vietnam. When House Bill 1395 had been passed in 1963, Vietnam was not yet a part of the national lexicon and was virtually nonexistent in the minds of most Americans. The intervening period, however, had witnessed the Gulf of Tonkin Resolution and the introduction of large numbers of combat troops in the spring of 1965. These developments put the speaker ban in a new light and appeared to strengthen arguments for retaining the ban on communists. The logic was clear: why should North Carolina allow communists to speak at state-supported campuses while American soldiers were engaged in a life-and-death struggle against the communists in Vietnam? Throughout the spring and summer of 1965 supporters of the speaker law attempted to exploit the situation with a propaganda offensive. Stories of the speaker law were juxtaposed with stories and photographs illustrating the death and destruction wrought by the communist enemy. The question seemed to confound ordinary citizens, especially those with loved ones in Vietnam. A woman from Halifax County addressed a poignant telegram to the governor: "My son's life is on the altar in Vietnam, twelve thousand miles away, to oppose communism, while in North Carolina my taxes must support college forums for communist speakers. Governor can you explain this to my son?" Godwin subsequently claimed that the Vietnam War had been pivotal to his belief that a law against communists was needed. He claimed to witness the body of a young soldier being returned to a mortuary in Gatesville, Gates County, and was so disturbed that he questioned the propriety of sending American "boys" to die fighting communism while giving communists a forum at home. According to U.S. Army records, however, the soldier in question, Private First Class Ivor Ecarol Bunch, was killed in action on June 26, 1966; thus, the speaker ban law was a reality long before his death. It could not possibly have been a motive for Godwin's role in the inception of House Bill 1395.[57]

State Senator Robert B. Morgan of Harnett County, a strident speaker ban supporter, was the second legion speaker. Morgan offered a putative history of communist activities at Chapel Hill, thus providing indirect evidence that the law had been drafted with a specific campus in mind. The events and personalities described in Morgan's account largely reflected the allegations and exposés appearing in his friend and supporter Hoover Adams's Harnett County–based newspaper. Morgan stated that the "Communist Party chose North Carolina as early as the 1930s as a major launching pad for its program, printing presses for Red propaganda were set up [in Chapel Hill], and the impetus for the Speaker Ban Law was partly provided by the formation of a Chapel Hill Progressive Labor Club." Under questioning from Swindell, Morgan opined that he did not believe that the legion would be willing to see authority restored to the trustees. He complained that the record of "indifference" by the trustees, along with the reticence of UNC administrators to respond to the legion's concerns about communism, did little to evoke confidence from the legion. Much of Morgan's evidence closely resembled that appearing in Adams's principal essay on radical activities at UNC, which was reprinted in the *Charlotte Observer* in the interest of fairness. An example of the legion's erroneous allegations was Morgan's charge that the university displayed "arrogance" in not acknowledging the September 1962 resolution drafted by the

Chapel Hill post. President Friday stated that the resolutions were never transmitted to UNC officials. Friday wrote to Morgan requesting copies of letters indicating that the resolutions had been sent, but the letters and other supplemental documents promised by Morgan never arrived.[58]

The defining moment in Morgan's testimony on behalf of the legion came when Zollicoffer asked if, in the face of a massive exodus of faculty, the legion would withdraw its opposition to amending the law. On the eve of the commission's formation several hundred UNC faculty had delivered a petition to Friday promising to resign en masse should accreditation be lost. "The American Legion believes," said Morgan, "that if the services of some professors have to be purchased at the price of allowing communists to speak on our college and university campuses, then their services would not be worth the price we would have to pay."[59] The response indicated the legion's antipathy to the idea of communism and its resolve in support of the law.

Prior to the public hearings, the legion had hoped to buttress its case by securing supportive testimony from UNC-based sources. The state commander, Carver, wrote to Friday informing him that "we contemplate the use of a number of witnesses who are connected with the Greater University. I am writing to formally request that you give us in writing a guarantee that no reprisals of any sort will be taken against such witnesses at any time in the near or distant future because of such appearances in support of this law." The letter provoked outrage among those opposing the law; it blithely implied that the university was the threat to free speech when in fact the legion and its allies desired foreclosure of open forums. Friday contained any indignation he may have felt and responded with a statement of the university's and his own positions on the matter: "I am glad to say, not simply as a guarantee respecting the forthcoming hearings, but as an affirmation of established University policy, that members of the University faculty, staff, and student body have been in the past, are now, and will continue to be free to express their views on the Visiting Speakers Law and on all other issues without fear of reprisal by the University." Friday's letter was reprinted in dozens of newspapers and received very sympathetic editorial treatment from the state's newspapers, which saw Carver's request as a disreputable smear against Friday. The publication of this exchange of letters represented another masterstroke by Friday in the propaganda war swirling around the speaker law. However, there was a second, more ominous, theme in the letters as a result of Carver's request that the legion be provided the names and home addresses of the faculty members threatening resignation should accreditation be lost. Although the press failed to recognize the significance of this request, the provision of such information might have produced a campaign of intimidation and harassment.[60]

The legion did not present any UNC faculty or students as witnesses in support of the speaker ban. While testifying, Senator Morgan was asked if he had any proof that threats of intimidation had been issued against UNC faculty who supported the law. Morgan replied that he had "information in my files" from a faculty member indicating that the person was fearful of punitive action if he testified. Neither the person nor the information were revealed. The sole academician to speak on behalf of the law was A. C. Jordan, a professor of English at Duke University. Jordan had served on the Duke faculty since 1925; his contribution as a member of the legion delegation was to contend that the loss of accreditation would not produce the dire results claimed by the law's opponents. In a rambling, disjointed, and pointless monologue, Jordan contended that admission to graduate schools would not be denied to applicants from an unaccredited school.[61]

The professor also revealed his personal frustrations with campus activities and various changes taking place throughout the nation. As he closed his long-winded analysis of accreditation, Jordan suggested the need for panel members to read "Anarchy on Campus," an article appearing in a publication with the somewhat less-than-scholarly name of *Police Chief*, the magazine of the International Chiefs of Police. The article would enable the members to "see what's happening to our educational institutions as a result of Communism." Jordan also produced a copy of the 1965 Report of the California Senate Fact-Finding Committee on Un-American Activities, which sought to link the activities associated with the Berkeley Free Speech Movement to communism. Jordan claimed that the report was a "detailed account of the Communist conspiracy and how it has been built up at the University of California." The "Berkeley Rebellion," said Jordan, was the result of a united front among communist groups aided by Red China.[62]

The commission members sat in shocked embarrassment at the inept performance. Only Hanes summoned the will to ask questions. Did Jordan favor the speaker ban law? "Yes." Was Jordan a professor at Duke? "Yes." And finally there was a question that revealed Jordan's level of frustration with the state of higher education. "Do you then consider that you and your associates and the Board of Trustees at Duke University are incapable of deciding who shall or shall not speak at Duke and should therefore come under the Speaker Ban Law?" Apparently confused by the question, Jordan gave an instinctive response: "As a matter of fact, if I were to be honest, I'll say yes." And with that comment, the American Legion's star witness on accreditation was dismissed. Jordan later alleged that his statement had been falsely reported but continued to proclaim that the Duke administration was lax in preventing communist infiltration of its campus. He cited a recent case where "a Communist from the Berkeley Campus riots had spoken at Duke." The alleged communist was actually Steve Weissman of the Free Speech Movement. Jordan thought that universities were rife with communism and that "many in American high places were going soft on Communism."[63]

The final witness for the American Legion was called to offer personal testimony about both the historic and recent presence of communists at UNC. Colonel Henry E. Royall was the longtime chairman of the Americanism Committee of the Chapel Hill legion post. A retired army officer, Royall had become something of a fixture on and around the UNC campus since World War II. Over three decades, he had assumed a role of political surveillance. In the fall of 1962, Royall had drafted the resolution by the Chapel Hill legion calling for a state investigation of Marxist influences at UNC.

Royall was an ardent anticommunist, steeped in the rhetoric and Manichaean imagery of the Cold War. A student of the myriad allegations of campus subversion of the McCarthy era, Royall was convinced that UNC was a hotbed of radicalism and a source of social instability. As he began his testimony, Royall noted his "humiliation of seeing Communism make inroads into our beloved University." He recited a litany of radical speakers ranging from Carl Braden to Milton Rosen, who he alleged desired to "mold" a newer generation of students into "another Junius Scales or a Larry Phelps." Despite the paucity of campus radicals and little evidence that campus-based groups had done much organizing, Royall was convinced that elements of an "international conspiracy" were afoot and finding support from either faculty or administrators.[64]

The substance of Royall's charges and fears left much to be questioned. Much of his consternation was directed at the now defunct Progressive Labor Club, yet he had abundant opportunity to verify that there was nothing conspiratorial or subversive about the group. When members of the club or others in the New Left met or held a function, Royall was usually there. Students involved in these groups knew him as a reactionary legionnaire and expected and welcomed his presence. When Rosen spoke in Gerrard Hall in October 1962, Royall was present — one of approximately twelve audience members. His presence was never viewed with concern by the students. They assumed him to be from the "local Birch Society." But the members of the PLC, despite their rhetorical flourishes, were hardly radical in terms of activity. In the words of one member, the son of a UNC administrator, they were united by their "essential naïveté." Their idea of armed revolt was "to go out to the public shooting range near Clearwater Lake and practice shooting John Salter's pistol." The most common group activity involved "going to the movies or for pizza with [our] girlfriends or hanging out in Harry's delicatessen [rather] than any heavy-duty political organizing." These students, although ideologically sympathetic to a romanticized notion of communism, were hardly the dangerous sect portrayed by Royall and the American Legion.[65]

The questions from the commission members revealed the absence of any substance to Royall's bombastic claims. When asked the numbers of active communists at UNC, the legionnaire became vague. "I can only describe," said Royall, "that by feeling, sort of an atmosphere, and I believe that if the Commission really wanted to get into this matter, you could get students to tell you that they feel that to pass their work and get good grades they have to take a leftist tinge. . . . [T]hat is a belief and feeling." The comment stirred both panel and audience; it seemed to implicitly call for a wider investigation and raised a far more serious issue that had not previously been alleged. Thornburg quickly seized on the implication and asked for clarification. "Are you telling this Commission, Sir, that in order to pass the work that is a part of the University program, and in order for a student to get a fair grade it's necessary for him to profess leftist tendencies?" Called on to repeat such an incendiary allegation, Royall, without foundation for the claim, beat a hasty retreat: "No, I'm not saying that." On this note, the legion's presentation came to an inauspicious end.[66]

The panegyrics staged by the American Legion on behalf of the speaker law were a charade. Grossly distorting and magnifying activities that had taken place, the witnesses trooped out by the legion attempted to make a case based on "beliefs," "feelings," innuendo, and, most of all, anticommunist anxieties. In a report titled "Americanism and McCarthyism in North Carolina," the *Chapel Hill Weekly* caricatured the legion's effort as an "exercise in buffoonery."[67] Although the Chapel Hill newspaper exaggerated the episode's comedic aspects, the display resonated with many hallmarks of the worst excesses of the McCarthy era — "100 percent Americanism," lists and letters known only to the speaker, and rampant allegations of internal subversion. There was a serious side to the legion's presentation, however. The legion's argument was predicated on a visceral appeal to a melange of cultural fears. Most citizens had come to accept, almost instinctively, that communism was the embodiment of evil. By reiterating this theme and coupling it with the reality that communists and other radicals had spoken at UNC, the legion could scarcely lose regardless of how inept its witnesses might appear.

The commission held two additional days of public hearings in September at which a variety of witnesses spoke both for and against maintaining the law. Speakers included Samuel I. Parker, a Medal of Honor recipient from World War I, who labeled the law an "insult" to the intelligence of the state's youth, and State Senator White, who called a political science text used at UNC an "instrument of indoctrination." Vermont Royster, editor of the *Wall Street Journal* and a North Carolina native and UNC graduate, called the law "futile," "foolish," and therefore "bad." Former Governor Luther Hodges testified that environment for industrial development in the state would almost certainly be impaired by the continued restrictions on the university. The presence of top-flight research universities was central to various firms' decisions to locate in North Carolina. Should the reputations of these institutions be damaged, business interests might look elsewhere. Elements of the state's business and industrial sectors were also concerned that the loss of accreditation would adversely affect "the disciplines of science and technology which must be strengthened and continually improved to achieve and maintain the standards existing in other regional areas." Former North Carolina Attorney General Malcolm Seawell, who had previously called the law unconstitutional, testified that it was "poorly drafted, ineffectual in what it seeks to do, and can lead but to great mischief and damage to the University."[68]

Representatives, including students, from the state's public colleges and universities also testified that the law was poorly considered and injurious to the interests of higher education. UNC Chancellor Paul Sharp said that "faculty morale has suffered, students are restless, [and] administrators are harassed and distracted from essential duties." The highlight of Sharp's testimony was that UNC had "already lost faculty members because of this act and we expect an accelerated attrition if it remains in force." Sharp also noted that three petitions indicated an exodus of scholars should the restrictions remain in force. Nearly three hundred faculty members had signed the petitions circulated in late May. The signers included fourteen deans, associate deans, and directors; eighteen department chairs; thirteen Kenan professors; and four distinguished alumni professors. Sharp concluded that while an immediate mass exodus was unexpected, a slow but steady attrition — not to mention prospective faculty refusing offers — could gravely injure the caliber of the faculty.[69]

All that remained was for the Britt commission to give form to its solution. On the key recommendation there was unanimous agreement. According to Britt, "All members were convinced after the hearings that something had to be done to save our education institutions from serious harm." Formal authority over campus speakers would be restored to the trustees. However, it would not be returned unconditionally. A mechanism had to be devised that would insure that the trustees would be vigilant in proscribing the categories of speakers identified by the 1963 law. Although acknowledging the imperatives of the accreditation problem, the commission remained philosophically opposed to the appearance of communist speakers. Although it was widely understood that political considerations militated in favor of some anticommunist gesture, the panel members also personally desired a continued ban. Following the September hearings, the members were instructed to consider a speaker policy that the Board of Trustees would be required to adopt in exchange for a revised speaker law. The Britt commission was thus empowered to draft a solution that both supporters and opponents alike would be compelled to accept.

8 An Anticommunist Speaker Policy

On September 28, 1965, the Britt commission met in Greensboro to create a working draft of the speaker policy. Although each member contributed to the document, the principal architects of its construction were David Britt, Gus Zollicoffer, and William Joyner. The commission conceded the mandate of revising the law to preclude a loss of accreditation. The remedy, however, did not preclude a commitment to the original law's anticommunist agenda. Several days prior to the meeting, Zollicoffer informed a legal colleague of the intellectual and political task that lay before the commission: "I am convinced that a loss of accreditation would seriously hamper education in North Carolina, and to that end, I hope we can work out a solution that will not affect accreditation, but will keep the Gus Halls and Milton Rosens from speaking at Gerrard Hall at Chapel Hill. Surely such people and their speeches add nothing to the quality of the education in Chapel Hill."[1]

The revised speaker policy's primary requirement was to articulate an ideological statement of sufficient strength and clarity to pacify supporters of the law. Cognizant that amendment would placate speaker ban opponents, the panel equally understood that the language contained in the directives to the trustees would be the basis of assuaging the law's supporters. The commission was scheduled to meet with leaders fromt the state's higher education establishment on October 15. Prior to the meeting, commissioners were instructed to consider how the statement "could be strengthened" to make it "more acceptable to proponents of the law."[2]

Zollicoffer offered the revisions to strengthen the statement. The Board of Trustees would be expected to endorse a strong anticommunist position in exchange for the commission's recommendation to restore authority. Zollicoffer suggested adding the word *unalterably* before the phrase *opposed to Communism*. The other members readily agreed that rhetorical excess could be useful in selling the proposed solution. Russell Kirby, an early opponent of the original law, concurred that since "this will not be a part of the law, I see no real objection to its being strengthened to the extent necessary to please the proponents of the law." Kirby also acknowledged that anticommunism was by no means the exclusive domain of those supporting the law but was also a tenet of its opponents. "Actually," said Kirby, "a strong statement here might very well enable us to pass through the legislature a less offensive law from the standpoint of those who are against the present law."[3]

On October 15 the commission, in the interest of "strict secrecy," reconvened at the Whispering Pines Motel on the U.S. Route 1 bypass on the outskirts of Southern Pines. Also in attendance were members of the state's higher education establishment, including UNC President William C. Friday and the chancellors of the three UNC campuses. The commission had several expectations for Friday and his colleagues. Foremost among them was the unqualified acceptance of the speaker policy and assurance that the trustees would also embrace the policy as written. The commission also expected acknowledgment of the problematic character of the rising tide of student protest "riots" on the nation's campuses. Finally, the panel desired a formal statement from Friday confirming the university's commitment to anticommunism and willingness to carefully monitor the campuses to ferret out potential subversives.[4]

Realizing that the commission was fully prepared to recommend that authority be returned to the trustees, Friday had already undertaken steps to accommodate potential critics' ideological and political concerns. By the late spring of 1964, the last vestiges of the Progressive Labor Club had been eliminated from campus, and the UNC president began a series of grandiloquent public statements stressing the university's opposition to communism. Speaking before a Raleigh civic club, Friday averred, "The University is opposed to Communism. It follows that those of us who are entrusted with the administration of the University will not knowingly employ as a teacher or research investigator any person who, because of membership in the Communist Party or who because of any other commitment of mind, is not free to serve the university standard of unbiased search for truth." This statement and others similar to it were recited in many forums, and Friday occasionally included in his litany a commitment to deny admission to students who were CP members or who had some compelling political circumstance against them.[5]

The anticommunist rhetoric was not meaningless cant. Friday had long received FBI reports telling him "who every agitator was, where he was, where he came from, and when he left." The president was certain that there were no CP members employed by the university and frequently challenged critics to make public any facts to the contrary. Despite such grandstanding, Friday well understood that the absence of CP members was insufficient to placate critics and convince observers that the university was serious in its resolve. The primary criterion was not the removal of nonexistent CP members but surveillance of dissidents and insurgents — including civil rights activists —whose views fell beyond the acceptable parameters of the state's political culture.[6]

The UNC president could be certain that his demand to "show me a Red at UNC" was impervious to refutation: Friday and the rest of the Chapel Hill administration had eliminated the remnants of the small radical Left whose presence had helped instigate the charges precipitating the speaker ban. During the summer of 1965, the UNC administration, at Friday's direction, began accumulating records on suspect political speakers and former student leftists at Chapel Hill, including poet Langston Hughes, civil rights activist Anne Braden, Milton Rosen, and the first secretary of the Polish embassy as well as former students Junius Scales, Hans Freistadt, Larry Phelps, and Nicholas Bateson.[7]

The names of Phelps and Bateson carried with them the memory of PLC, whose apparent radicalism led the American Legion and Jesse Helms to call for an investigation of communist activities on the campus. With the civil rights demonstrations and the Raleigh sit-ins, PLC seemed to have been forgotten. But individual members of the group remained politically active, and several continued as members of the national PL. And the national group was involved in activities guaranteed to attract the attention and enmity of the anticommunists. On June 25, 1963, the same day that the speaker bill had been introduced and enacted, two groups of fifty-nine students and political activists, including several from UNC, left New York on a circuitous journey that would take them to London, Paris, Amsterdam, and Prague before reaching their intended destination — Cuba. PL in New York had organized the trip to familiarize the participants with a revolutionary movement in a developing country and also to defy the State Department's restrictions on travel to the island. After returning to the United States, many of the travelers were subpoenaed by HUAC, which had convened hearings on "Violations of State Department Travel Regulations and Pro-Castro Propaganda Activities in the United States."[8]

Of the Chapel Hill contingent, only Phelps was called to testify about his intent in going to Cuba. Phelps had been the principal organizer of the Chapel Hill students making the trip. He was also the most committed, at least rhetorically, to the belief that social harmony and racial equality could only be achieved by socialism. Among the students traveling to Cuba was a government informer, Barry Hoffman, who told the HUAC panel that Phelps had been a leader of the group, which probably accounts for his subpoena. Returning to the UNC campus, from which he had recently graduated, Phelps noted the popular support for the Castro government and condemned the U.S. blockade, blaming it for the rationing and shortage of goods on the island.[9]

In September Phelps spent two days facing HUAC's interrogation. Unlike an earlier generation of witnesses who cowed before the committee and sought to protect their identities as well as their careers through closed session, PL chose a strategy of defiant confrontation as its members requested open hearings. The PL members were, however, instructed not to discuss PL's activities or those of other individual members. Phelps confidently and assertively explained why he went to Cuba and linked his decision to the civil rights struggle in the Deep South and his desire to understand how certain world areas were undergoing a socialist revolution. When asked to name names and inform on the activities of other PL members, he refused and invoked the self-incrimination clause of the Fifth Amendment, thereby coming under the rubric of the North Carolina speaker law.[10]

Following his appearance before HUAC, Phelps returned to his home in Burlington before driving to Chapel Hill, where he and a fellow Cuba traveler and PLC associate arranged to talk about their Cuban experience. The meeting took place in the dormitory where Phelps had resided the previous term. The gathering was informal, and most attendees came to see and talk with their old friend and card-playing companion rather than to hear about the possibilities of revolutionary socialism.[11]

When the press discovered that Phelps, who had taken the Fifth Amendment before HUAC, had spoken on campus, the applicability of the speaker law was immediately questioned. This issue demonstrated what conundrums the statute might create. The ban sought to prevent politically undesirable outsiders from appearing on campus, and although Phelps may have been undesirable to UNC officials, he was certainly not an outsider. Still, he had used the protection of the Fifth Amendment in refusing to answer questions before a "duly constituted legislative committee," thus violating a specific provision of the law.[12]

In addressing the quandary presented by the unauthorized visit, Chancellor William B. Aycock chose to draw a distinction between "formal" and "informal" speech. The chancellor opined that "bull sessions" such as those hastily organized in the dormitory were difficult, if not impossible, to prevent. While Aycock's observation was certainly accurate, the distinction served a more compelling function: the university was thus absolved from direct responsibility and could not reasonably be held in violation of the law, which mandated enforcement by campus officials.[13]

The question of "formal" speech left Aycock with little choice. Citing the provisions of the speaker law and his responsibility to carry out the laws of the state, he announced that henceforth Phelps, a North Carolina native, resident, and recent UNC graduate, was officially proscribed and became another victim of the fear of subversion. Although "his classification is a bit hazy," the fact that Phelps was a self-defined radical was proof enough for UNC officials, who applied the law: "In view of the fact Larry Phelps has gone on record as being a communist, please deny the use of any building." It is ironic that despite the speaker law advocates' excessive paranoia concerning alleged Soviet penetration of American institutions, a Russian scientist, Dr. V. V. Petrov, professor of statistics at Leningrad State University, was given permission to speak the same week that Phelps was banned. Such an occurrence offers remarkable insight into the law's real objective. This incident would not mark the last time that Soviet or East Bloc personalities and intellectuals would be permitted to speak at campus functions while domestic radicals were turned away.[14]

The last remaining PL figure on the campus was Bateson. As a graduate student and university employee, Bateson was eminently vulnerable as officials scrambled to insure that the campus would be cleansed of those whose politics speaker law advocates deemed abhorrent. In a political culture that tended to equate communism with the foreign or external, Bateson's precarious position was further complicated by his legal status as a resident alien. A British citizen, he had graduated from Oxford and entered the United States in 1958. After spending a year at Yale, he began his studies at UNC. The difficulties accompanying life as a leftist foreign national became pronounced at Chapel Hill. Prior to joining PL, he had been visited at his campus office by federal agents, who questioned him about his political activities and admonished him to avoid suspect associations. The agents' message was thinly veiled: withdraw from such involvements or face the possibility of deportation.[15]

Disaster struck Bateson in the late summer of 1963. Although he had not participated in the trip to Cuba because of the need for caution as a result of the threat of deportation, he was nevertheless subpoenaed to testify before HUAC. The call to testify was surprising; as federal pressure intensified — especially that exerted by the immigration bureau — following public awareness of the formation of PLC, Bateson had agreed to "stop being public about my politics" and removed himself from active participation.[16]

The subpoena was prompted by Bateson's involvement several months earlier with Arnold Indenbaum. A PL member from New York, Indenbaum had stayed at Bateson's apartment while in Chapel Hill and had obtained a North Carolina driver's license. The license was procured under the name

"Jay Jacobs" and mailed to Bateson's address; it was then forwarded to Indenbaum in New York. The license was obtained under an assumed identity to facilitate the process of acquiring rebates on unused airline tickets that had been purchased on KLM and BOAC airlines in Ottawa, Canada, for the trip to Cuba. Federal authorities had been monitoring Indenbaum's activities, and when his attempt to use a false identity was discovered, Bateson was implicated. Bateson's October 16, 1963, testimony before HUAC revealed that he did not know what Indenbaum was planning to do with the license or that it was obtained under a false identity. Bateson also did not accompany Indenbaum to the license bureau, and it is likely that Bateson was unaware that "Jacobs" had given Bateson's address to the examiner. Bateson had asked Indenbaum why he wanted a North Carolina address but did not receive an answer. The extent of Bateson's complicity in this affair seems to have been that the license was mailed to his address and he in turn forwarded the license to Indenbaum in New York. The government intended to suggest that Indenbaum had committed fraud by attempting to receive money that did not belong to him, but Indenbaum or some other PL figure had deposited more than thirty-six thousand dollars with the two airlines and had a legitimate claim to more than six thousand dollars in refunds. The snafu resulted from the fact that to evade interference from federal authorities, someone, possibly Indenbaum, had purchased the tickets under the fictitious name, Jay Jacobs. Although subpoenaed by a New York state court, Indenbaum was never indicted by either state or federal authorities with regard to this matter.[17]

Consistent with his separation from PL, the young Englishman refused to engage in polemical assault on government policy or the committee. Instead, he quietly discounted as the product of gossip the volatile statements attributed to him in several newspapers. In discussing the trip to Cuba, he contended that any role he might have played was irrelevant since he was a British citizen and Britain had imposed no restrictions on travel to Cuba.[18]

For the most part, Bateson said very little. Since agreeing to quell his political activity and being subpoenaed, he had been engaged in "damage limitation"—that is, trying to abstain from any action that might result in injury to former comrades or friends. In taking this course, Bateson brought devastating consequences on himself. Time after time he invoked the Fifth Amendment, refusing to answer questions pertaining to the activities of acquaintances. This act brought Bateson to the attention of speaker ban advocates in North Carolina and created yet another difficulty for UNC administrators eager to have control of speaker policy returned to their hands. Bateson's hearing ended on an ominous note as Congressman August E. Johansen of Michigan asked that "the transcript of this testimony [be referred] to the Bureau of Naturalization and Immigration for appropriate review."[19]

Bateson never heard from the federal authorities again. Instead, he left the United States as a result of the machinations of UNC officials to pressure him out of the university. Returning to Chapel Hill, Bateson telephoned Chancellor Aycock and volunteered to meet and discuss the HUAC appearance. The chancellor agreed, and the following day the two men met for the first and only time. Despite the patina of cordiality, the seriousness of the occasion was underlined by Aycock's decision to carefully record the meeting. Believing it consonant with the chancellor's role to be familiar with any controversy involving students or personnel, Bateson assumed the meeting was of a perfunctory nature.[20]

Immediately after the meeting with Bateson, Aycock contacted Friday, and they agreed to use a faculty committee to eliminate Bateson. The UNC president remained behind the scenes but was consulted throughout the affair, and Aycock refused to act without obtaining Friday's concurrence. Although other administrators were involved, Aycock exchanged private letters with the president. A week after meeting with Aycock, Bateson received the first in a series of letters from the UNC administration. The initial missive, from the chancellor, set the stage for what was to follow over the next three months and revealed what Friday, Aycock, and the rest of the UNC administration intended: "Since talking with you on October 17, 1963, I have decided to refer to the Committee on Faculty Hearings the question of your fitness to continue in your assignment as a Senior Research Assistant in the Department of Psychology. Currently, I am preparing information to refer to the Committee with a request that it conduct an investigation and make a recommendation to me."[21]

That a faculty committee would be convened to make such a judgment was inappropriate inasmuch as Bateson was not a faculty member or involved in teaching. And the issue of his "fitness" seems equally dubious; Bateson's faculty adviser had informed Aycock that Bateson "performed his duties faithfully, conscientiously, and with considerable skill." The professor thought so highly of Bateson's ability that he had coauthored two scholarly papers with his student.[22]

But Bateson could not simply be expelled, and the administration could not risk public exposure for removing a student because of the political liability that he represented. Thus, the only route remaining was to remove an employee who was allegedly somehow derelict in performing his duties. A faculty committee would keep the matter covert and internal and present the impression of routine academic procedure.

Despite the veneer of official impartiality by the chancellor and the implementation of established review procedures by a faculty board, Aycock was unwilling to risk the possibility that Bateson might be exonerated and his "fitness" confirmed. Friday and Aycock had determined that Bateson had to be separated from the university. On December 5, the day prior to the hearing, Aycock wrote to Dr. Halbert Robinson, the acting chair of the psychology department: "Regardless of the outcome of this investigation, we shall soon be faced with the matter of the reappointment of Mr. Bateson. Please notify any person who may initiate such an appointment that no steps should be taken in that direction without first consulting me."[23] Any effort to reappoint Bateson following the expiration of his present contract would invite direct confrontation with UNC's chief executive officer and promised to bring only retribution to any faculty member foolhardy enough to interfere with the administration's purpose.

Bateson's orchestrated removal was necessitated by the administration's overweening desire to placate pro–speaker law critics. On December 4, two days before the faculty board convened, Aycock received a letter that alarmed him and pushed him to conclude that Bateson would have to go. The letter, the latest in a lengthy series following creation of the speaker law, came from newspaper editor Hoover Adams and requested clarification of several previous speaker-related issues. As the letter neared its conclusion, however, a new issue was introduced: "Also, I am wondering what action, if any, has been taken or will be taken in regard to Peter Gumpert, identified as a research assistant in the psychology department, and Nichols [sic] Bateson, who is doing graduate work there and both of whom pleaded the Fifth Amendment while testifying recently before the House UnAmerican Activities Committee." Gumpert, another UNC student, was Bateson's roommate but had no political background or loyalties.[24]

What specific action Adams might have had in mind is unknown, but the implication is clear that the editor believed that some punitive measure was warranted. What Adams, and perhaps Aycock, neglected to consider was that neither of the two students cited in the letter had violated any element of the speaker law. Neither man belonged to the Communist Party, and despite taking the Fifth Amendment, neither had used any campus facility for speaking purposes after doing so. Furthermore, there was no indication of Gumpert's involvement in any political activity, much less PL. Gumpert's complicity arose from his ferrying Indenbaum to a car rental agency and allowing his name to be used for the car rental. Gumpert did testify before HUAC, but, contrary to Adams's allegation, completely cooperated by answering the committee's questions. Not once did he invoke the Fifth Amendment and refuse to answer a question. Adams's influence on Aycock can be seen from the fact that in spite of these facts, the chancellor directed the psychology department not to "take any steps" to reappoint Gumpert without Aycock's knowledge. Gumpert apparently was not rehired.[25] The facts represented technical niceties that bore little relevance to the issues involved: the presence of a political radical on the campus, the invoking of the Fifth Amendment, and, paramount to all other considerations, the willingness of university officials to demonstrate that they would act decisively to remove those targeted by right-wing critics.

On December 6, the Committee on Faculty Hearings was convened to adjudicate the matter of Bateson's "fitness." The formality of the hearing was confirmed by the presence of law school dean Henry P. Brandis as the chair. Bateson was the first to testify and did so without the benefit of legal counsel. Accompanied only by John Schopler, his faculty adviser, Bateson apparently failed to grasp the intended purpose of the proceeding. Bateson responded to a variety of questions about the HUAC hearing, the false driver's license, the possible CP membership of his attorney before HUAC, why he invoked the Fifth Amendment before HUAC, what he knew about the PL trip to Cuba, and PLC's activities in Chapel Hill. The inquisitors also asked questions about his political beliefs and how much longer he intended to remain in the United States.[26]

On January 30, 1965, the committee submitted its findings and recommendation to Chancellor Aycock. The report reflected the twisted circumstances and political exigencies that characterized the Bateson matter. The faculty comprising the board were clearly uncomfortable with what they were expected to do. The report began by expressing a doubt that a faculty committee was the proper venue to hear and consider such a matter. Bateson was a graduate student, and the board was unsure if this was the "type of action contemplated by the trustee legislation on faculty discipline."[27]

Acknowledging the political nature of the event, a statement was included to repudiate Bateson's views. The committee was "unanimous in expressing disapproval of many of the attitudes and opinions reflected in Mr. Bateson's testimony" and noted its special displeasure with his use of the Fifth Amendment before HUAC. The committee could not, however, justify immediate termination, and in providing an explanation for this conclusion revealed the local and immediate circumstances weighing on the matter: "[We] particularly call attention to the fact that neither the Federal Immigration and Naturalization Service nor the House Committee on Un-American Activities nor any state authority has taken any steps against him."[28]

The statement could have been even more explicit about the lack of interest by federal authorities or the seriousness of Bateson's transgression of state codes. Bateson was never charged with a violation of state or federal law, and whatever his judgment in the driver's license issue, his action was not illegal under North Carolina law. State and federal authorities never charged either Bateson or Indenbaum with any offense.

Despite its uncertainty about the propriety of any of Bateson's actions, the committee would not disappoint the administration. In the end it chose to echo what Aycock had intimated as a resolution the day prior to the hearing. Without offering a clue about how it arrived at the recommendation, the board completed its work by stating tersely, "[We] believe that Mr. Bateson should not be re-employed at the end of his present term." [29]

The following day Bateson received what would be his final communication from Chancellor Aycock. The letter was brief and to the point: "You are herewith notified that the University of North Carolina will not re-employ you in any capacity after the termination of your present contract. I am giving you notice at this time in order that you may make plans accordingly." [30]

Bateson planned to pack his belongings. Without financial support and considered a pariah by the university, it became virtually pointless for him to attempt to continue his studies at Chapel Hill. In the summer of 1964, Bateson flew home to London, and with him went the last reminder of the campus radicalism that had helped initiate the North Carolina speaker law. [31]

The collection of information on leftists by UNC administrators that eventually led to a student being purged indicated a willingness to acquiesce to anticommunist expectations. Throughout the speaker ban controversy, UNC critics had emphasized that the mantle of academic freedom carried a mandate of "academic responsibility." While Friday and the state's higher education establishment maintained that the past reflected a consistent pattern of responsibility, this contention was not likely to be enough. In addition to the trustees' acceptance of the speaker policy, the Britt commission required a more definitive display of commitment to the vigilance expected by those clamoring for responsibility. In helping UNC prepare its case for the commission, Gordon Hanes had clued Friday that "nothing [would be] more effective than a presentation at this time of the responsibility which would be exercised by the University in the event that it were granted the freedom to control its own speakers." [32] Friday's increasing anticommunist rhetoric and the accumulation of data on speakers and students deemed questionable within the context of the speaker law were designed to aid UNC in convincing skeptics that it was vigilant in opposition to alleged subversion on the Left.

For those supporting a speaker law, *academic responsibility* implied that leftists should be privately monitored and publicly denounced, if not completely forbidden from setting foot on campus. As proponents of academic freedom, Friday and his colleagues would never adhere to a position that preemptively denied speaking privileges on political grounds. The president was, however, willing to compromise in pursuing his ultimate objective. At the October 15 meeting, Chairman Britt attempted to identify precisely how far Friday and the university were willing to go to demonstrate academic responsibility and fealty to the principles contained within the proposed speaker policy. Britt requested that Friday draft a statement defining the university's position on communism. In 1949 a similar position paper, drafted by William D. Carmichael, had allayed any fears that UNC was insufficient in its resolve to oppose communist influences at the campus. Carmichael's statement read in part, "The Communists are taking advantage of the unlimited freedom of our University. And if we are not realistic, prudent, and cautious, we may discover, too late, that we . . . have become unwitting 'collaborationists' of the Communists." Three important developments had transpired in the interim, however, that necessitated a recapitulation by UNC officials. First, Carmichael, a zealous anticommunist who had favored a formal anticommunist oath by prospective faculty, was no longer present. Second, on January 13, 1959, at the urging of Aycock and Friday, the Executive Committee of the Board of Trustees had approved the deletion of the question pertaining to communist affiliation on the UNC personnel form.[33] Finally, the subsequent presence of alleged communists at Chapel Hill had persuaded anticommunist critics that a renewed statement was necessary.

Much had changed since the late 1940s and early 1950s. The McCarthyite purges had ended, and dissent on the Left was again being welcomed as consistent with free universities. President Friday could not, for reasons personal as well as institutional, agree to oversee a policy that would ban radicals. Still, to secure his strategic objective, a strong statement was required. In a statement to Britt, Friday sought to update the university's previous anticommunist commitment. In "The University and Communism," Friday reasserted that no faculty or staff were CP members and that the university would not knowingly employ a CP member. He stipulated that UNC was "diligent in all matters of national security" and that it cooperated fully with the "security requirements" of all state and federal agencies.[34]

Friday would not commit himself or his institution to any policy that banned speakers solely on the basis of affiliation. He reiterated to Britt that "controversial" speakers had appeared at Chapel Hill but contended that their appearances did not constitute "approval or disapproval of them or their statements by the University." In short, Friday expressed the university's concern with "totalitarianism" but politely informed Britt that UNC administrators would not stray beyond state and federal law in monitoring radical speakers. Most important, Friday did not indicate any intent to do anything that did not comply with the new speaker policy.[35]

The apparent agreement by Friday was sufficient for Britt and his colleagues on the study commission. On November 5 the study commission made public its findings and recommendations in a report to Governor Daniel K. Moore. The governor had desired that the commission arrive at recommendations that reflected compromise: the state's commitment to anticommunism would be recognized and the institutional integrity of UNC preserved. Moore, who had reviewed an advance copy, enthusiastically endorsed the document: "I approve the report and its recommendations without any reservations." The next step in the governor's plan was to have the trustees meet and adopt, verbatim, the recommended speaker policy. It was expected that the speaker policy would have to be adopted "word for word by all state-supported institutions if the recommendations of the Study Commission are to be carried out."[36]

In his official statement, Moore indicated that the issue was not subject to negotiation: "Each board may consider and adopt the speaker policy recommended in this report." With the expectation that the trustees would perfunctorily endorse the revised speaker policy, Moore also announced his decision to call a special session of the General Assembly on November 15 to accommodate the statutory revision entailed in the recommendations. The orchestrated timing of Moore's scenario was essential to a satisfactory resolution of the controversy. SACS's Commission on Colleges was scheduled to reconvene in late November in Richmond, Virginia, and was anticipated to discuss the matter of UNC's accreditation. If all went according to plan, the changes desired by the agency would be implemented and the accreditation crisis ended.[37]

The study commission report contained no surprises. It noted that while the constitutionality of the law had been discussed, the panel agreed that the problems posed were much "broader" than the legal issue. The most immediate problems were political, so the committee decided to avoid this thorny question: "No steps are recommended to determine the validity of the statutes." The document also reported that university officials "have diligently complied with the law and the Commission received no evidence that the law has been violated since its enactment on June 26, 1963." The most compelling issue for the commission was the accreditation matter, and the report addressed the centrality of the issue: "Suffice it to say that accreditation means much, financially and otherwise. For any institution to lose accreditation would be substantially damaging. The most obvious impact would come from the loss of accreditation, inasmuch as many financial aids which our institutions now receive are not provided to unaccredited institutions. Loss of accreditation would make it much more difficult for our eleven institutions to recruit and maintain adequate faculties."[38]

The report concluded with a meandering statement attesting to the state's opposition to communism and the good intentions of those supporting the 1963 speaker law: "It is our judgment that the primary objective of the General Assembly was to prevent communist rabble rousers and their kind from using the campuses of North Carolina as a forum for their evil activities." The precise nature of who constituted "their kind" and what the "evil activities" were was not explained. One clue was the comment expressing concern about "the presence in the student bodies of students who individually, and by group activity, were active ultra-liberals." This was as close as the commission came to verifying that social and political forces other than communists were the targets of North Carolina's Red hunters.[39]

The recommendations were consistent with the imperatives engendered by the accreditation crisis and the anticommunist crusade. The pivotal component—although listed second—was the speaker policy. The entire package hinged on trustee acceptance of the policy as written. Once this acceptance had been secured, the amendment process restoring authority to the trustees could proceed. The first recommendation, detailing amendment, indicated the centrality of the revised speaker policy. "Subject to Recommendation No. 2, we recommend that Chapter 1207 of the 1963 Session Laws be amended so as to vest the Trustees of the institutions affected by it not only with the *authority* but also with the *responsibility* of adopting and publishing rules and precautionary measures relating to visiting speakers covered by said Act on the campuses of said institutions. We submit as a part of this report a proposed legislative bill to accomplish this purpose." The recommended bill identified the same categories of speakers—known members of the Communist Party and persons citing the Fifth Amendment—to whom the speaker policy and the concomitant "rules and precautionary measures" would apply.[40]

Inasmuch as the speaker policy would guide the trustees in applying and enforcing the revised law, the language needed to be precise. The document that the trustees were handed and, in effect, told to sign left no uncertainty that the Britt commission desired that the types of speakers covered by the law would still be banned from the campuses. The document began by recognizing that the university was "owned by the people of North Carolina." With ownership came control; since it had been determined that the "people of North Carolina are strongly opposed to Communism and all other forms of totalitarianism," it was deemed reasonable that the people could demand that communists be excluded. The trustees were told that North Carolinians were "unalterably opposed to Communism" and held that the "total program" of the college or university was predicated on "orderly process," "moral excellence," "objective instruction," and "respect for law." In an era of mounting campus-based activism, the speaker policy sought to preempt possible expansion of social protest and cultural criticism. Learning was to be a profoundly conservative process, reconfirming traditional values and conventions.[41]

The core feature was found in the fourth paragraph, which explained how the commission desired to handle dissenting voices from the Left: The trustees "feel that the appearance as a visiting speaker on our campus of one who was prohibited under Chapter 1207 of the 1963 Session Laws (the Speaker Ban

Law) or who advocates any ideology or form of government which is wholly alien to our basic democratic institutions should be infrequent and then only when it would clearly serve the advantage of education; and on such rare occasions reasonable and proper care should be exercised by the institution. The campuses shall not be exploited as convenient outlets of discord and strife." [42]

The use of such nebulous language was bound to invite disagreement and controversy. What did "infrequent" mean? By what standard would "clearly serve the advantage of education" be measured? What was meant by "discord and strife"? Given the private and public statements of commission members, especially Britt, Zollicoffer, and Joyner, some meaning can be assigned to the opaque phrases. The words assigned to the trustees meant that such appearances would be virtually nonexistent—that is, "rare." "Clearly serv[ing] the advantage of education" was an implicit code that only those speakers speaking on scientific or cultural subjects should be given clearance to appear. "Discord and strife" reflected the commission's concern that the activities associated with the Free Speech Movement at Berkeley would not be replicated at UNC. [43]

In concluding its work to resolve a cultural and political crisis, the Britt commission followed with remarkable exactitude the strategy of a commission created to alleviate the great crisis of the previous decade—school desegregation. During the mid-1950s the Pearsall committee crafted a plan enabling the state to avoid the appearance of extremism—that is, "massive resistance"—while insuring that most of the state's public schools would remain racially segregated. [44] In 1965 the Britt Plan to resolve the speaker ban crisis eschewed the extremism of a total ban in favor of a method that would result in very few appearances of undesired speakers.

The common factor in articulating this moderate-resistance tactic was Joyner. As the Pearsall committee's chief legal adviser, Joyner had played a key role in designing the Pearsall Plan that permitted tactical retreat while promoting strategic victory in the form of maintaining segregated schools. In arguing for limited desegregation, Joyner told a member of the reactionary Patriots of North Carolina that "The sacrifice of some children to mixed schools must be made so that many other children will not similarly be subjected to the evils of mixed schools." In 1965 Joyner supported a similar plan: allow a few, "infrequent" appearances by leftists while insuring that dissenting voices did not become generalized on the state's campuses. That such was the Britt proposal's intent was confirmed by the chairman in a letter to a supporter: "I verily believe that the action taken last week will settle a lot of unrest in our state and will result in fewer Communists rather than more." [45]

The Britt report and recommendations were greeted with wide acclaim.

Governor Moore, Lieutenant Governor Bob Scott, and House Speaker Pat Taylor quickly embraced the plan. As the proposal to return power to the trustees represented the embodiment of his strategy, UNC President Friday was immensely satisfied. "If the recommended actions are approved," he said, "they will remove any prior restraint on free discussion. I intend to give Governor Moore and Commission chairman all the support I can." The state's press also lined up solidly behind the Britt plan. The *Greensboro Daily News* viewed the proposals as "a path out of a dark thicket." The *Wilmington Morning Star* termed the plan a "sound, acceptable compromise." While contending that "outright repeal would be the most desirable course," the *Charlotte Observer* conceded that those "on both sides of the argument should accept the commission's recommendations and get this divisive matter behind the state." Perhaps the most resolute in its opposition to the speaker law, the *Chapel Hill Weekly* called the report a "tolerable solution." An informal poll of 103 UNC students conducted by the UNC News Bureau concluded that 90 percent supported the Britt proposals. Most of the students polled favored outright repeal but were resigned to the belief that the Britt plan was a compromise that was preferable to the original law. UNC student leaders also favored the recommendations, albeit without true zeal. The UNC News Bureau, however, led by director Pete Ivey, enthusiastically supported the Friday strategy for amendment that seemed realized by the Britt plan. Ivey's releases to the press were primarily intended to win support for the policies of the UNC administration — namely, those of President Friday. An important part of this effort was to obscure from public vision any suggestion that UNC professors or students harbored any views that might seem strange and radical.[46]

Representative Philip Godwin, a key sponsor and defender of the law, also indicated a willingness to accept the recommendations. Godwin was satisfied that the commission did not advocate repeal of the law and, in fact, acknowledged the good intentions of those who had voted for the original bill. Godwin had already given Britt a promise to support the recommendations, provided they were not amended. Godwin also expressed a belief that most of the law's supporters in the legislature would accept the modifications. If the legislature would adopt the recommendations as written, "probably the main opposition will go along." The road seemed clear, although there was certainly some opposition to the Britt recommendations on both sides. This opposition was premature, lacked a constituency, or seemed hopelessly obstinate. For example, Duke law professor William Van Alstyne, a specialist in constitutional law, had given compelling testimony before the Britt group that the law failed a number of constitutional tests. Van Alstyne now worried that the proposals would simply substitute the legislature's censorship with that of the trustees.[47]

Those opposing the recommendations included, not surprisingly, Helms, who labeled the report "artistic in its doubletalk." Helms was troubled by the nebulous language in the document, fearing that the language might be construed in such a way as to let some communists appear. At bottom, Helms had no faith in the trustees.[48]

On November 8, 1965, President Friday addressed a special meeting of the General Faculty in Carroll Hall. Before approximately five hundred faculty members, Friday requested formal approval of the new speaker policy. He emphasized that nothing in the document contradicted any of UNC's general operating policies and that acceptance of the policy was required to amend the speaker law and remove a yoke from the university's neck. In the discussion that followed Friday's presentation, much consternation focused on how words such as *controversial* and *infrequent* would be interpreted. Most prominent, however, was the sense of revulsion at the "apparent coercion" of the trustees. Friday responded that if the university hoped to regain oversight of its affairs, the board had "no option but to adopt the statement." The faculty members were persuaded that acceptance of the policy was largely a symbolic offering to persuade the public at large that UNC had been chastened. Physics Professor Lawrence Slivkin drew laughter and applause in commenting, "[P]eople had said 'we have been beating our wives,' and when this goes through they will say 'they have stopped beating their wives.' It's all the same but the University will once more be free." The faculty, led by Chairman Corydon Spruill, moved unanimously by voice vote to frame a resolution in support of the administration's position.[49]

By the end of the week, UNC's remaining institutional weight had swung behind unqualified endorsement of the Britt commission's speaker policy. On November 12, Governor Moore convened a special session of the UNC Board of Trustees to "urge" it to voice its approval for the new policy. After a brief statement from the governor, the seventy-plus trustees present and another twenty who "wrote, wired, or telephoned" perfunctorily adopted the speaker policy as written. In a vote of loud approval, the trustees gave formal sanction to the policy. Only a single, measured "no" was heard as the motion was called. The sole dissident vote belonged to Thomas J. White, leader of the archconservative bloc in the Senate. White objected to the proposed policy as too lenient and called for an amendment to create a special board of fifteen trustees to review speaker invitations. This action would have effectively permitted the trustees to ban political speakers on the Left while allowing nonpolitical speech. The proposal died for lack of a second.[50]

The General Assembly met in special session on November 15–17 to amend Chapter 1207 of the General Statutes. Meeting in joint session, the Senate and House heard Governor Moore summarize the purpose and report of the Britt commission. Moore emphasized that the recommendations represented a compromise between two sides in an effort to find "middle ground" and announced his support "both in letter and in spirit." The governor declared that it was time to put the divisive issue to rest because the continued controversy was bringing notoriety and damage to the state and its institutions. "Regardless of how each of us feel about the exact provisions of the existing Speaker Ban Law, the public controversy arising as a result of this law is damaging to the State of North Carolina." Moore invoked the validity of the ideological struggle against communism as he reminded the Assembly of the war in Vietnam. Still, said the governor, anticommunism alone was insufficient to justify keeping the law intact: "We must not allow our steadfast opposition to communism and totalitarianism to blind us from the facts involved in the speaker ban controversy." Terming the proposal a "reasonable and honorable settlement," Moore expressed his belief that if the Assembly would amend the law as recommended, the controversy would be ended permanently.[51]

Following Moore's opening address, the Senate and House each reconvened to receive the bill to amend the speaker ban law. Hanes and Kirby introduced Senate Bill 2; commission members Britt, Lacy Thornburg, and Zollicoffer introduced the identical House Bill 1. The proposed measure, "A bill to be entitled an act to amend the law relating to visiting speakers at state-supported institutions," differed little from the earlier bill suggested by the UNC trustees and circulated on their behalf during the past Assembly session by Senator Jennings King. The bill was simultaneously a political document and a palliative for the threat to accreditation from the Southern Association of Colleges and Schools. Instead of an outright prohibition, the new statute mandated that the Board of Trustees "shall adopt and publish regulations governing the use of facilities of such college or university for speaking purposes." The adjustment eliminated the statutory formality of prior restraint, thus assuring the attenuation of the criticisms and controversy surrounding the original law.[52]

The bill did not, however, completely eviscerate the speaker law or eliminate the anticommunist hallmarks that had infused House Bill 1395. Although a real power shift took place and the trustees were now the decisive agency, the same categories of speakers were still identified as inherently dangerous — "known members of the Communist Party," anyone "known to advocate the overthrow" of either the state or federal constitution, and anyone pleading the "Fifth Amendment with respect to Communist or subversive connections." The anticommunist excitement in North Carolina would not be easily brought to an end.

The proposed revision, along with the speaker policy, ominously suggested that short of a legal challenge, the speaker control law would exist in perpetuity. Whence would the opposition come? The trustees, UNC administrators, and the major dailies had been effectively placated by the study commission proposals. The new statute would simply transfer enforcement authority and carried an implicit mandate that the trustees, with their own hand, would place a gag in UNC's mouth. In the stampede to embrace the recommended statute, few critics grasped the political intent of the new arrangement. At best, critics assumed that the trustees were now free to restore freedom of speech to the campus. Van Alstyne, who had testified to the law's patent unconstitutionality, astutely recognized that the trustees had been placed in the awkward position of having to act as censors. "For most constitutional purposes," said Van Alstyne, "it makes no difference if censorship results from statute or regulation." [53] At this stage, however, constitutional problems were not the paramount consideration. The primary objective remained the articulation of a political compromise in which both sides could identify a measure of self-interest and agreement. All that remained was for the legislature to perfunctorily enact the statute recommended by the Britt commission.

In the special session, the Assembly was to ratify what the Britt commission and UNC officials had decided. Individual legislators had been consulted and cajoled to help resolve the persistent controversy and to eliminate the threat to the state's higher-education system. With the recommendations mirroring his personal preferences, Governor Moore personally called all 170 Assembly members and implored them to support the proposed revision. The earlier promise of support from Godwin, the nominal leader of the Assembly forces favoring oversight and restraint of "subversive" speakers, virtually assured that revision would be approved. [54]

But the pro–speaker law forces would not necessarily capitulate quietly. Given their level of ideological and rhetorical commitment, it could hardly be expected that the most ardent defenders of an unadulterated law would fail to make some effort to rally anticommunist sentiment. However, their attempt would largely be a rearguard effort of backbenchers instigated by the American Legion or mere political stubbornness. The most serious challenge came in the form of an amendment offered by Representatives Godwin, Isaac O'Hanlon, and Steve Dolley that would have put the matter to a statewide referendum. This proposal was controversial because it threatened to undo precisely what the Britt commission had intended. Rather than quell the fires of controversy, a plebiscite promised to further inflame passions. Rhetorical demagoguery could then exploit the widespread fears and resentments associated with communism in the popular mind, and all that had been gained would be summarily lost. Britt took to the rostrum and responded with an impassioned plea to ignore the diversionary measure that would only mean greater unrest. The amendment failed decisively, seventy-three to forty-two, and the last obstacle to passage of the revised bill was removed. When the final vote was taken, Godwin dutifully kept his promise to Britt and Moore and voted for the study commission's proposal. Like Godwin, by 1965 many other erstwhile supporters of the original law had tired of the endless skirmishes and constant recrimination. Representative Wayland Sermons of Beaufort County, a cosponsor of House Bill 1395, entered a personal statement into the House record attesting that while he remained "unalterably opposed to any known Communist . . . speaking on the campuses of our state-supported institutions," restoring authority to the trustees would "carry out the wishes of the general public." The final tally showed seventy-five House members endorsing a revised statute and thirty-nine continuing to support the original law.[55]

A similar scenario played out in the Senate. A small number of speaker ban supporters, led by White, Robert Morgan, and Julian Allsbrook of Halifax County, attempted to derail the revision bill with a series of amendments. Other than simple alterations involving the cosmetic elimination of unnecessary language, the amendments were decisively voted down. In addition to White's proposal for a special fifteen-member panel of trustees to rule on controversial speakers, another amendment would have had UNC administrators maintain a list of scheduled speakers and file a monthly report with the governor's office. In concert with pro–speaker ban forces in the House, White also proposed a statewide referendum before the revised law could be implemented. The results were no better than those in the House; each amendment was defeated by better than two to one. White, the most obstinate foe of any changes in the existing statute, was reduced to the long, sermonic rhetorical excursions for which he was well known. Confident of the eventual outcome, those leading the drive to revision patiently allowed White to exercise his speaking privileges. At one point, when a member attempted to invoke cloture, King interjected that nothing would be changed by giving the minority speakers all the time they wanted. White responded to King's gesture with a tacit recognition of the outcome: "It sounds like you think you got the hosses." King tersely replied, "We have."[56]

King's confidence was well founded. On November 17, the day following similar action in the House, the Senate handily endorsed the bill by a thirty-six-to-thirteen vote. The bill was enrolled, and Chapter 1207 of the General Statutes of North Carolina was revised in favor of a less draconian but still sinister law.[57]

With revision of the law restoring trustee authority came the anticipated SACS action. The swift amendment of the law had been necessitated in large part by knowledge that the accrediting agency would be meeting in late November and the expectation that the association would render a decision on the accreditation status of the North Carolina schools at this meeting. SACS officials were constantly monitoring developments in North Carolina. When the revised law eliminated the specter of "outside political interference," the accreditation issue was effectively blunted. On December 1, the association's College Delegate Assembly, "without discussion or dissent," voted reaffirmation of accreditation for North Carolina's twelve public colleges and universities.[58]

Revision of the statute on visiting speakers appeared to signal the end of the controversy. The loss of accreditation was no longer a threat, but a mechanism remained in place to screen and prohibit politically questionable speakers. With few exceptions — most notably, Helms and Adams — the state's press celebrated the elimination of the speaker ban as the "welcome end of an era." In what was expected to be a final series of editorials, the press generally emphasized the political compromises at the core of the new law. Understanding the array of forces supporting amendment, Helms merely responded with muted criticism at what he viewed as political strong-arming. Adams, however, angrily denounced the amendment with a banner headline, "N.C. Legalizes Commie Speakers," and juxtaposed a report of the Assembly action ("UNC Can Now Invite Commies, Other Enemies") with a report of a communist offensive in Vietnam ("American Troops Fight off New Commie Attacks"). In an editorial, Adams averred, "The Fight Has Just Begun!" and asked his readers to "picture the gloating at Chapel Hill — and also in the office of the Communist Party." In general, however, neither side was entirely satisfied, but the procedure offered something to each in exchange for bringing the issue to a close.[59]

Such assessments of the end of the conflict, based on hope and fatigue, were too optimistic. The answer to the most fundamental question — would communists and other leftist radicals be permitted to speak on state-supported campuses — remained ambiguous and largely unaddressed. And herein lay the potential source of continuing controversy. President Friday expected the trustees to support administration decisions concerning future speakers. Friday and campus administrators assumed that restoration of trustee authority would mean that, given proper precautionary procedures, controversial figures would be permitted to speak. The regulations would require several formal, if cumbersome, procedures. Such gatherings would be chaired by a university officer or faculty member, and the speaker would have to accept questions from the audience. It was further mandated that an "opportunity be provided at the meeting or later" to present speakers of a different viewpoint. In Friday's perspective the new regulations represented the long-standing de facto state of affairs at UNC; the new policy largely meant stricter administrative oversight.

For the Britt commission, Governor Moore, and numerous legislators, the revised law and the all-important speaker policy meant quite the opposite. While the Britt recommendations stressed restoration of trustee authority, they also reflected an adamant opposition to the appearance of communists or radicals at UNC. The report acknowledged that the legislative ban had to be abolished, but the commission fully expected the trustees to maintain the speaker ban's mandate.

Those most responsible for designing the speaker policy and drafting the revised statute clearly believed that the new arrangement meant that certain speakers would continue to be banned. In a subsequent explanation of the necessity of amendment, Britt declared that the original law had served a "good purpose" in letting UNC officials know that the people of the state "are opposed to having our youth exposed to Communist speakers." He expressed his understanding of what amendment would mean: "It is my further opinion that no Communist of the type of Gus Hall, Milton Rosen or Herbert Apthecker [sic] will speak on our campuses." Zollicoffer had similarly expressed a desire to "keep the Gus Halls and Milton Rosens from speaking at Gerrard Hall at Chapel Hill." Zollicoffer, like his colleagues, believed that "such people add nothing to the quality of the education in Chapel Hill." And such a judgment, predicated on a deep-seated cultural antagonism toward communism, became in turn prima facie evidence that radicals should not appear. During the recently concluded Senate debate, Hanes had promised amendment critic Morgan, "We won't in the future have speakers such as Gus Hall appearing on campus." The Britt recommendations, embodied in the new policy and statute, were shrewd political legerdemain. Whatever the revised procedures meant, they did not mean that communists would appear at the University of North Carolina.

At the close of the special Assembly session, both sides were satisfied with the outcome. The predominant feeling was relief. After more than two years of acrimonious charges, the speaker ban controversy appeared to finally have been put to rest. In a letter to UNC Trustee Victor Bryant, Britt basked in the satisfaction that the new statute enjoyed widespread support and predicted, "[T]his issue will soon be a dead one." But Britt's assessment was premature: even as he wrote, plans were under way to resurrect the speaker issue at UNC.[60]

9 | Freeing the University

As an organizing issue, the speaker ban was made to order for the UNC chapter of Students for a Democratic Society (SDS). Since its inception as a national organization, university reform that included challenging any restrictions of open dialogue had been at the forefront of SDS politics. And although the UNC chapter was only a few months old at the time that it came out in opposition to the speaker policy, UNC had been nominally represented in some of the earliest activities of the national body of SDS. Former UNC President Frank Porter Graham, himself a champion of liberal causes, was a vice president of the League for Industrial Democracy in 1961. The league was the parent organization of SDS. SDS had originated as the Student League for Industrial Democracy but had changed its name to eliminate any threat to the league's tax-exempt status as well as to free the new organization from the anticommunist criticisms lodged by the league's executive committee. Two members of UNC's New Left Club attended SDS's December 1961 conference in Ann Arbor. At this meeting a National Executive Committee was selected, and the committee chose one of the UNC students, Nicholas Bateson, as its regional representative.[1]

The following May, Bateson and the New Left Club hosted an SDS conference at UNC on "Race and Politics in the South." Led by SDS's Tom Hayden, Sandra Cason, and Robb Burlage, SNCC's Bob Moses, SCEF's Carl Braden, and the League for Industrial Democracy's Michael Harrington, more than seventy student leaders met for three days, conducting a series of discussion panels on how to enlist greater support from southern whites for SNCC-sponsored voter registration efforts. On the whole, the conference achieved little; attendance did not meet the organizers' expectations, and most of those who did attend were already committed activists.[2]

The Chapel Hill meeting did, however, produce one noteworthy result for the future of SDS. The National Executive Committee met to discuss the working draft of the SDS "manifesto" being prepared by Hayden, Al Haber, and Bob Ross. The meeting resulted in sharp and often heated discussion, particularly between Hayden and Steve Max. Max's principal concern centered on the draft's emphasis on "values" in defining SDS as a Left organization. Shaped by the political milieu of the Communist Party in New York, Max and a handful of supporters argued that the manifesto needed to present a clearer and more specific political program. Hoping to avoid confining the fledgling organization to a party agenda that might be perceived as sectarian, Hayden contended that SDS should remain ambiguously open to attract a wider variety of democratically minded people. Hayden's position was upheld, and in June 1962 the draft was accepted by the SDS convention as the Port Huron Statement.[3]

Despite the possibilities suggested by an SDS's early appearance in Chapel Hill, no chapter developed at UNC. The national leadership pursued the Economic Research and Action Project aimed at urban poverty in areas closer to New York and Chicago and abandoned most of the South to SNCC and the emergent Southern Student Organizing Committee (SSOC). SSOC evolved out of SNCC in 1964 as white organizers and students were encouraged to operate in predominantly white schools and in white working-class areas. SSOC also developed close, formal relations with SDS; SSOC increasingly identified with the national group's activism and came to be considered its southern affiliate. By the summer of 1962, the SDS regional representative, Bateson, was being quoted in state newspapers as a PLC spokesman as the UNC New Left Club was split by "ideological differences." For a three-year period, despite the speaker ban law as an organizing issue, there was no SDS and only a nominal Left presence in Chapel Hill.[4]

By the spring of 1965, the campus evinced little willingness to criticize or even seriously debate issues of civil liberty and foreign affairs. An attempt to create an "open forum" (a plan spiritually informed by the Free Speech Movement) where dissenting opinions about university issues could be heard ended, in the words of its organizers, James Gardner and Timothy Ray, in "significant failure." The organizers attributed the lack of any political challenge to a widespread belief among students that the university was beyond criticism. The existing liberal campus political groups — SPU, CORE, and the

NAACP—were rebuked as single-interest groups that had "no measurable effect on the thought and behavior of the larger community."[5]

With the widening of U.S. involvement in Southeast Asia and the continued presence of the pernicious speaker law, a handful of students decided to provoke their cohorts into action by bringing to UNC activists identified with the storied protests of recent months and years. In the spring of 1965, speaking engagements were planned for James Farmer, a leader of the CORE-sponsored "Freedom Rides," and Steve Weissman of the Berkeley Free Speech Movement.[6]

While Farmer received a polite response from a modest-sized audience, Weissman moved the more than one hundred people who gathered in UNC's Gerrard Hall by telling them that "students and faculty should be given control of their university." By the spring of 1965, Weissman was attached to the SDS national office as an adviser and speaker on university reform. The Chapel Hill appearance was a part of a speaking tour of southern campuses organized by Ed Hamlett of SSOC. Weissman offered an articulate representation of how students could act on their political convictions. Astutely recognizing the speaker ban as both a real and a symbolic issue that could galvanize a wide array of students, Weissman urged "an all out offensive against any deterrent to free speech." He advocated a student-led "campaign that would further controversy and discussion" about the law and called on the faculty to support the students by "stand[ing] on its own two feet" and inviting a communist speaker in direct defiance of the law. If students and faculty acted collectively, said Weissman, the legislature would be powerless to enforce the law.[7]

That evening a group of students who had been searching for an appropriate organizational vehicle met to discuss formation of an SDS chapter. On May 5, thirty-five people convened to organize UNC-SDS and "challenge the establishment's control." That same evening, in another campus venue, UNC alumnus and liberal activist Allard Lowenstein was criticizing the sending of U.S. troops to the Dominican Republic, LBJ's escalation in Vietnam, the Vietcong, Vietcong sympathizers, national SDS, "radicals," and the Berkeley Free Speech Movement. A liberal activist who spent his undergraduate years at UNC as a protégé of Frank Graham, Lowenstein encouraged student activism while denouncing any politics that smacked of radicalism. Junius Scales, a leader of the small Communist Party in Chapel Hill during the late 1940s, recalled Lowenstein as a vociferous anticommunist. On the North Carolina speaker ban, Lowenstein responded with an obfuscation that was at once humorous and ironic: "There's no question about the Speaker Ban being a terrible law," he said, "but I'm against widespread student protests unless people think they can be successful." In Gerrard Hall, UNC-SDS was beginning preparations to confront the trustees' speaker policy.[8]

From its inception, UNC-SDS was committed to direct confrontation with UNC authorities by inviting speakers banned under the law. Although the chapter was interested in other issues attending Vietnam and civil rights, the speaker law assumed immediate priority as an organizing basis for a broad student coalition. During its first ten months, the chapter consisted of as many as twenty-five or thirty members and perhaps forty to fifty supporters. Given its democratic openness and loose style, however, formal membership meant little because anyone interested in the expressed aims and political values of the group was welcome to share in the discussions, work, and conviviality.[9]

In the formative months following official recognition, the chapter's few contacts with the national office in Chicago were of a perfunctory nature. UNC-SDS was free to draft its own constitution and articulate an agenda emanating from its membership's experiences and political visions. Interestingly, the SDS constitution asserted that "members may be excluded for reasons of their political beliefs." This was a general reference to the group's belief in "democracy as a means and as a social goal." Anyone not adhering to this "commitment" was subject to exclusion. The most prominent feature of the nascent group's leadership cadre was the marked prevalence of out-of-state graduate students. The organizers of UNC-SDS were typically northern and midwestern and possessed prior records of notable academic accomplishment. The first chairman of SDS was Jim McCorkel, a graduate student in sociology from Swarthmore, Pennsylvania, and the vice chairman was Gary Waller, a sociology graduate student from Versailles, Missouri. Other core members were Chuck Schunior, an older undergraduate from Park Forest, Illinois; Ann Mayer, a graduate student in philosophy from Dayton, Ohio; and Reid Reynolds, another sociology graduate student from Chappaqua, New York. Although there were southerners and a few North Carolinians among UNC-SDS's early supporters, they were few in number and for the most part did not take vocal or influential roles in chapter activities. One prominent exception to this tendency was Jerry Carr, who at age fifteen had left Columbus, Ohio, to live with relatives in Decatur, Alabama. Like several of his SDS cohorts, Carr was a graduate student in sociology. During the latter half of the decade he would serve as chairman as the group enjoyed increasing support and subsequently began its precipitous demise.[10]

These individuals were recognized as leaders because they demonstrated the rhetorical and organizational skills needed to mobilize others. The first SDS organizers stood out for their oratorical acumen, exceptional writing skills, and previous, although limited, political experiences. Only a few had begun to develop radical sensibilities that were theoretically grounded or emanated from a broader systemic analysis. The principal catalyst influencing the minds and consciences of almost every member of the leadership was the example of the civil rights movement. While few had any prior direct involvement in civil rights work, their exposure to various components of the movement, such as civil rights training, discussions with black student activists, and witnessing the open expression of protest in marches and sit-ins, had been a profound experience in politicizing these SDS recruits.[11]

In early 1965 these students were responding to the speaker ban and other problems largely as idealists who took seriously the promises of liberal democracy in the United States. They did not envision or advocate any structural transformations of American society; at this juncture, their criticisms were grounded in a belief that personal and civic liberties were sacrosanct, untouchable by state authority.[12]

As the SDS leadership immediately recognized, the speaker ban was essentially a liberal issue. The protest could be wrapped in the esteemed guarantees of the Constitution. If those wielding authority failed to adhere to constitutional safeguards, then more direct confrontation by student-citizens was democratically justified. And public dissent against the speaker control law was, from this perspective, a moral requirement. In announcing its opposition to the speaker policy proposed by the Britt panel, the SDS appeal resonated with a defense of constitutional rights: "AS AMERICANS, THE ONLY SPEAKERS LAW ACCEPTABLE TO US IS THE FIRST AMENDMENT." Around this ideal UNC-SDS sought to enlist the support and participation of fellow students who had been largely quiescent in the face of the speaker law. SDS would seek to challenge others on the Chapel Hill campus to speak out, to choose sides, and to confront authority to restore freedom to the university.[13]

The tensions and difficulties inherent in these alternatives were apparent in the differing political styles of the two persons who became speakers for the first installment of UNC-SDS. McCorkel, the group's first chairman, came from a tradition of cautious but principled activism. His father had been a supporter of Socialist Party leader Norman Thomas and in the 1940s had campaigned for the governorship of Pennsylvania on the Socialist Party ticket. Organized politics, however, were not the sole or even the primary expression of McCorkel's social conscience. While the family abandoned the Socialists for the progressive wing of the Democratic Party, it remained deeply committed to Quaker values. While in the seventh grade in 1951, McCorkel participated in his first protest: a Quaker picketing of the White House in protest of the atmospheric testing of atomic weapons. McCorkel's religious associations and commitments accompanied him to Chapel Hill. While UNC-SDS chairman, he remained a Quaker and served as the "high school fellowship leader" at the Chapel Hill Community Church.[14]

McCorkel brought political acumen to his role as SDS chairman. He was a member of the Democratic Party and had voted for Lyndon Johnson the previous fall. A liberal critic who could "articulate a clear position,"

McCorkel's politics were shaped by his agreement with the "general political stance of the Americans for Democratic Action." As an undergraduate, he had honed his rhetorical and debating skills with the Congressional Club at the College of Wooster in Ohio. In 1959 and again in 1962 while at UNC, McCorkel had gained further political experience at National Student Association–sponsored meetings in Tunisia, Ghana, and Finland.[15]

Equally influential in the formation of his tactical politics and ideological grounding were his Quaker sensibilities of nonviolence and dissent. He was already a vocal opponent of the war in Vietnam and had applied for conscientious-objector status. For McCorkel, open and unimpeded speech in public forums was a vital mechanism for civic responsibility in a democratic society. He enjoyed a further advantage of neither sounding nor appearing radical. McCorkel's politics were cautious and rooted in American ideals, and his appearance was that of an aspiring professional. He was neatly groomed and preferred "striped collegiate ties, vests, cordovan shoes, and tweed suits." It would not be easy to castigate or caricature SDS through McCorkel.[16]

The other key leader of UNC-SDS was Vice Chairman Waller, by temperament and political style the polar opposite of McCorkel. Whereas McCorkel favored extensive discussion and limiting SDS activities to the campus, Waller envisioned SDS as the motor for a far-reaching participatory democracy that would take students into coalitions beyond the boundaries of UNC and Chapel Hill. From a rural background, he had spent his undergraduate years at Iowa's Drake University, where his fraternity included a number of liberal students active in efforts to oppose housing discrimination in Des Moines.[17]

The two leaders of the embryonic SDS chapter were poles apart in personal style as well as in their conceptions of political engagement. McCorkel insisted that "action is essential, but discussion must come first. The last thing that Students for a Democratic Society wants to see is people picketing without knowing what they're picketing for." This elitist assumption that only those possessing sophisticated comprehension or eloquent explication were qualified to picket was met by Waller's contention that democracy postulated an active citizenry. In this perspective, ordinary people were capable of understanding social circumstances and acting on them; the objective was the mobilization of students for public action that would, it was hoped, generate larger, systematic protest. By means of this participatory democracy, those in power refusing to respond to popular opposition would have to be confronted. Waller believed it necessary to "challenge the establishment's control. . . . Totalitarianism may be present in governments in the center as well as those leaning to the left or right." Here was an incipient radicalism emerging not from ideological adherence but from an indigenous source as a protest against dangerous concentrations of power.[18]

In the profiles of the two principal figures of the UNC chapter it is possible to see a replication of the conflicting political styles of the first and second generations of national SDS leadership. The founding generation of the national group tended to be eastern, with a style that highlighted rhetorical flourish and intellectualism. The second wave of national SDS leadership featured more midwesterners who favored more action-oriented politics. The changing orientation of the second wave of national leadership was represented in the ascendancy of Carl Oglesby, Carl Davidson, and Jeff Shero. Referred to as "prairie power" and associated with the "action faction" style, the second generation rejected any ideas of bureaucratic hierarchy.[19]

Arriving in Chapel Hill in 1963, Waller considered the events of the local desegregation campaign to be his epiphany, moving him to question his personal level of commitment to social change. In the process he confronted the same question that thousands of other students put to themselves during the era: Why am I on the sideline instead of in the street? Almost immediately, Waller became involved in "a lot of protesting and picketing" of the remaining restaurants around Chapel Hill refusing to desegregate.[20]

Few, if any, of the early SDS members at Chapel Hill possessed truly radical sensibilities in 1965. They were, for the most part, exemplary students who had excelled in their high school civics courses. But they were also beginning to discover that the realities of American society did not square with what they had been taught. The speaker ban, as a symbol of compromised democratic ideals, contributed in a dynamic way to the growing politicization of the students in UNC-SDS. However, it did not and could not radicalize them. As an essentially liberal issue, the speaker ban could not transcend the politics of constitutionalism. For those who would eventually become radicals, the mounting contradictions of U.S. actions in Vietnam and the rest of Southeast Asia would be the catalyst. The stakes and gravity of Vietnam far surpassed those of the speaker ban. In the case of Vietnam, "a system was at fault"; it was an "issue of imperialism."[21]

Early SDS activity against the speaker ban was slowed by the academic calendar and by the impending Britt commission investigation. With the end of the spring semester, the fledgling chapter had few members on hand, and the student population had dispersed for the summer. During the summer months, a few members began drawing up a list of possible speakers for a tentative challenge to the speaker law. At this juncture the study commission was under way, and the results of its deliberations were not yet clear. While few SDS members believed that the commission would recommend abolition of the law, it seemed prudent to wait until the panel submitted its recommendations before taking any action that might appear precipitous.[22]

The SDS chapter did not, however, sit idly and do nothing. It began activities designed to engender campus debate and give students an opportunity for political engagement. In June UNC-SDS published a series of bibliographies to "aid members of SDS in summer reading programs related to concerns they have expressed interest in" and to give others an idea of the kinds of "study and action programs SDS [was] planning for the coming year." The "preliminary" bibliographies included titles on "Problems of the University," "Race Relations," and "Foreign Policy." In November a separate bibliography was published on issues surrounding the war in Vietnam.[23]

When the fall term began on September 17, SDS began a campaign of protest against the military's presence on campus and growing evidence that U.S. actions in Vietnam were morally suspect. Waller and Schunior, who was also chairman of the moribund SPU chapter, began a two-person protest against the presence of a missile brought to campus by the UNC Air Force Reserve Officers' Training Corps as part of a recruiting promotion. The student newspaper derisively criticized the action and reported it akin to a football score: "Air Force — 106 [recruits], SPU — 0." And the UNC Young Democrats Club responded with its own sign — "We support Johnson's stand on Vietnam" — to counter those of Waller and Schunior.[24]

Even greater student opposition and scorn was directed at anti-Vietnam protests the following month when McCorkel and Schunior organized a "soup fast" in support of the International Days of Protest. Cosponsored by SDS, SPU, and the Durham chapter of the Women's International League for Peace and Freedom, the fast asked students to avoid one meal, eating only soup, while donating the savings to the Cooperative for American Relief Everywhere. The money collected was to be used in rebuilding the village of Cam Ne, which had been destroyed in a counterinsurgency operation by U.S. and South Vietnamese troops. The fast was denounced, and its organizers vilified and Red-baited. The student legislature approved a resolution asking students not to participate. The *Daily Tar Heel* ridiculed SPU as "odorous" and "the most disrespected element on this campus." In language resonant of the calumny of the McCarthy era, the editorial asked how SPU "could find the stomach to direct its bitter fanaticism against other young Americans who are dying for them in Vietnam." The student legislature and the *Daily Tar Heel* called on students to demonstrate their support for the war by signing a telegram of support that would be sent to the troops or by donating blood.[25]

The new activists of SDS and the remnants of SPU would not be deterred by the hostile and often vacuous rhetoric from those sitting on the sidelines. On October 16 a contingent marched onto the federal military base at Ft. Bragg and picketed the John F. Kennedy Special Warfare Center, the home of counterinsurgency training for the U.S. Army Special Forces (the Green Berets). Although a pacifist gesture — the eighteen demonstrators left quietly when told to do so by military authorities—the press largely viewed the action as an unnecessary provocation, and, interestingly, many UNC students agreed. One of the two campus political parties endorsed a resolution condemning both SDS and SPU for demonstrating against government policy in Vietnam. In a torrent of letters to the editor, members of the groups were branded "dastardly scum" and "stupid little boys with beards." One letter termed the actions "insipient [sic] and outrageous acts of cowardliness and treason." Another invoked the specter of Jesus standing amidst U.S. troops and called for drafting all protesters. "All talk aside," said the author, "a man who will not fight when his country calls is no man."[26]

A few intrepid writers defended SDS's and SPU's raising of legitimate issues that college youth should be discussing. At this juncture, however, the majority of student sentiment appeared to be in virtual lockstep with Johnson administration policy. The nascent antiwar movement persisted, however, as a seventy-five-person contingent including students, faculty, and townspeople made their way from Chapel Hill to Washington for the fall 1965 SDS antiwar protest.[27]

The opening weeks of the fall term indicated the difficulties SDS would have to overcome if it hoped to mobilize students on the speaker ban and other issues. The UNC campus, despite its vaunted reputation for liberalism, was mired in apathy and evinced an animosity toward any sustained critique of established authority, particularly picketing and public protest. The UNC student body was drawn largely from localities within the state. As such, it was steeped in a political culture that emphasized values that were both provincial and conservative. This situation reflected a peculiar irony—while critics charged the school with being excessively liberal, the students were often profoundly conservative. Such circumstances belied a widely held belief throughout the state that UNC was a swirling cauldron of protest and dissent. Any such "tradition" was largely apocryphal, resting on the conspicuous activities of small minorities of students and faculty. SDS was merely the most recent activist minority to challenge the elite establishment of UNC and the state of North Carolina.

If, as proclaimed by the UNC News Bureau, nine in ten students at Chapel Hill approved of the Britt plan to amend the law by simply restoring authority to the trustees, one campus group refused to acquiesce to the refurbished law and the accompanying speaker policy. On November 8, as the trustees prepared to adopt the speaker policy demanded by the Britt commission, UNC-SDS issued a press release and an open letter to the board opposing the speaker policy for the "ambiguous, arbitrary and capricious infringements on freedom of speech." Identifying itself as comprised of "liberals and radicals, activists and scholars, students, faculty, and townspeople," SDS called on the trustees to reject the proposed policy.[28]

The SDS statement emphasized the essentially political nature of the Britt plan. The proposed amendment and the new speaker policy represented an expedient compromise designed to eliminate the accreditation threat and placate both sides in the contentious issue. The SDS manifesto cited four continuing problems left unaddressed by the commission, stressing that the proposals severely compromised "essential democratic principles," most prominently the First Amendment. The commission was scored for its unwillingness to examine the constitutionality of the original law. In SDS's view, the recommendations failed to reach the root of the matter. The fundamental issue remained unaddressed, and SDS warned that the controversy would continue until freedom of speech was insured.[29]

SDS also called attention to the speaker policy's nebulous language. SDS noted that the definitions of circumstances under which controversial speakers could appear—for example, "infrequent" and "clearly serve the advantage of education"—were subject to varying interpretation and application. As the SDS position noted, it was easily possible to use such language to arbitrarily deny campus access to speakers deemed politically undesirable. The proposal was also castigated for its implicit threat that the legislature would not be asked to amend the statute unless the trustees approved the policy without delay and dissent. For the members of SDS, to demand that the trustees perfunctorily adhere to a fait accompli was entirely inconsistent with democratic principles because doing so foreclosed any possibility of open discussion of the policy and speaker law.[30]

That the trustees were commanded to sign a prescripted policy as a price for legislative action suggested an ominous precedent: the possibility that the trustees might henceforth be expected to satisfy legislative whim in fear of loss of accreditation or to avoid other forms of retribution. For SDS, the issue represented nothing less than the freedom of the university itself. If the Britt proposal was unequivocally accepted by the trustees, the elemental conditions necessary for a true university—an open atmosphere in which to contest and debate ideas and issues—would be jeopardized. "If the trustees are not free to reject what has been set before them," contended SDS, "then we do not have a free university." Implicit in the SDS critique was a commitment—a promise—to challenge any ensuing regulation or policy that compromised or denied "essential democratic principles."[31]

Although the SDS statement was presented to the trustees, they showed no apparent interest in considering its questions and criticisms. The quid pro quo embodied in the amendment strategy of the Britt recommendations had already been agreed to by William C. Friday. The UNC president had solemnly indicated his anticommunist resolve to the satisfaction of the study commission and, in return, was promised restoration of campus authority. The problem with the Britt plan, astutely identified by SDS, was that the essential question remained unaddressed: would communists and radicals be permitted the same access to campus venues as other speakers? This, the cardinal issue, was never directly confronted during the commission's deliberations. For those drafting the policy statement, primarily David Britt, William T. Joyner, and Gus Zollicoffer, the answer was a clear and emphatic no. In their perspective, adherence to the new policy guidelines would mandate that the trustees would do by campus regulation what the speaker law had done by statute. Contrary to this view was President Friday's belief that by finessing the space created by the absence of prior restraint, conditions could be created to permit controversial speakers. Here was a crisis in the making. Rather than end the controversy, the mandated speaker policy was sure to exacerbate it.[32]

The SDS statement against the putative compromise suggested by the Britt commission report attracted almost no attention from the press. Despite a stylish press release to more than a dozen papers across the state, only a single local paper saw fit to report the declaration. This lack of attention, however, was soon to end as SDS proceeded with plans to confront the law. "If SDS couldn't get press coverage by begging for it in November," remembered McCorkel, "by early February we were the cat's meow."[33]

Following the trustees' perfunctory acceptance of the speaker policy and the General Assembly's subsequent amendment of the speaker law, SDS quickly swung into action. In early December a "Dear Communist" letter was drafted and distributed to secure speakers willing to test the new policy. SDS's intent was clear: "We would like to invite to our campus several persons who fall under the Speaker Policy or whom the board of trustees would construe as falling under the Speaker Policy." The letter made clear that this effort was not merely a frivolous attempt at creating controversy but resulted from a sincere belief in freedom of speech and open debate.

By Christmas two speakers had been identified, and invitations to speak at UNC followed in early January. The first speaker would be Frank Wilkinson, the executive director of the National Committee to Abolish the House Un-American Activities Committee, and the second would be Dr. Herbert P. Aptheker, a prominent figure in the Communist Party and director of the American Institute for Marxist Studies. Both prospective speakers possessed previous histories to suggest probable applications of the speaker policy. Wilkinson had drawn scrutiny from congressional committees critical of his civil rights activism and willingness to confront the authority of governmental agencies. In 1952 he was dismissed from a position with the Los Angeles Housing Authority after refusing to answer questions about earlier political associations. In 1958, after being subpoenaed to appear before a HUAC panel in Atlanta, Wilkinson refused to answer questions and cited the First Amendment as a defense. Convicted for contempt of Congress, Wilkinson spent a year in federal prison following the U.S. Supreme Court's five-to-four vote against overturning the verdict. For several years Wilkinson had traveled the campus lecture circuit, speaking against the antidemocratic politics underpinning much of the HUAC agenda. Refusing to adhere to anticommunist dogma and denouncing the reactionary shibboleths that often characterized HUAC's work, Wilkinson would be a prime target for those in North Carolina who continued to adhere to the validity of a communist conspiracy.

Whatever the response by the state's anticommunist mavens to Wilkinson's visit, it could hardly match the potential for acrimony that would follow the announcement that Aptheker would be coming to UNC. A prominent CP figure and well-known historian of the African American experience, Aptheker had spoken at dozens of colleges and universities, including, on at least one prior occasion, the University of North Carolina. He was already something of a cause célèbre: his presence had provoked speaker issues in several other states.

Supporters of North Carolina's speaker ban had singled Aptheker out as precisely the kind of speaker that should be barred from the public campuses. During the study commission hearings, Ralph Clontz, a professional witness and FBI informant from the McCarthy era, testified that on a previous UNC visit Aptheker had called for the overthrow of the U.S. government. Aptheker had spoken on "The Roots of Negro Oppression" in Gerrard Hall on January 12, 1950. There was no suggestion of violent revolution against the state, although he expressed sympathy for earlier slave revolts. A critical reporter for the *Daily Tar Heel* noted, "Communists sound intelligent so long as they don't talk about Leninism and Marxism." Clontz's claim went unchallenged by the study commission, but an inquiry launched by President Friday produced conclusive evidence that Aptheker had made no such statement. By this point, however, Aptheker had become completely unacceptable as an invited speaker at North Carolina's public colleges and universities. Even those opposing the concept of a blanket proscription of speakers conceded that Aptheker should be banned. During the recent amendment debate in the General Assembly, Senator Gordon Hanes had solemnly promised Senator Robert Morgan that under the amended law, Aptheker would not be allowed to speak on state-funded campuses. SDS's impending invitation promised a showdown on whether free speech or anticommunism would prevail at the University of North Carolina.[34]

Beyond Aptheker's recognition as a CP figure, events were taking shape that would further infuriate anticommunist forces and make him an even more controversial presence. SDS decided to invite Aptheker shortly before Christmas, and Aptheker, historian Staughton Lynd, and SDS's Hayden defied the U.S. State Department by visiting North Vietnam, Czechoslovakia, the Soviet

Union, and the People's Republic of China over the holidays. Coming at a time of largely uncritical public support for the war against a communist foe, the visit to Hanoi could only lend further fuel to the fire when Aptheker's appearance at UNC was announced. The Hanoi visit was made unbeknownst to UNC-SDS, and the decision to invite Aptheker had already been made. Regardless of the Hanoi trip, however, SDS was not about to abandon the principle of free speech because of an individual's political views.[35]

On January 21, McCorkel notified Chancellor Paul F. Sharp of the invitations. Sharp immediately recognized the proposal as a test of the trustees' policy. The UNC administration's response was twofold: it sought to persuade SDS to withdraw the invitations and to gather additional information on Aptheker and Wilkinson. After numerous meetings, the Executive Committee of the Board of Trustees was asked to permit the talks under the new policy guidelines and strict supervision of campus officials. The meetings revealed a strong consensus among students and faculty that Aptheker should be permitted to speak. The plan called for obscuring the controversial figure by surrounding him with a panel of UNC faculty members. It is interesting that although Aptheker's talk was to be on the "Negro Movement," UNC still found it necessary to provide a rebuttal to his views. While Friday and his associates decided that they needed to inform the Executive Committee about Aptheker's visit, they carefully avoided release of the story to the press. If a means could be found to placate SDS, the impending crisis could be averted.[36]

Over several days, various UNC officials met with the SDS leaders and their faculty advisers. Much of the information was gathered by Dean of Student Affairs C. O. Cathey, who conducted a series of telephone interviews and subsequently met the students and advisers. Cathey maintained a written record of each communication concerning SDS. Usually drafted as memoranda, copies were routinely provided to the chancellor and, on occasion, were given to President Friday. One such memo carefully chronicled the responses given by McCorkel and SDS faculty advisers Norman F. Gustaveson, William H. Wynn, and Joseph W. Straley to questions about the invitations to Aptheker and Wilkinson. Although the encounters were ostensibly conducted to gather the facts, they were, in fact, part of a subtle effort to challenge SDS and locate a means to convince the group to rescind the invitations. The administration hoped to determine that the faculty advisers had been remiss in counseling the students and that the students had failed to comprehend the implications of this affair for the university.[37]

But the students had considered the implications of the visits for the university; this was the very reason that the invitations were issued. Would the University of North Carolina stand behind the principles of free speech and open expression, or would it capitulate to anticommunist hysteria and place a gag in its own mouth? Confident of the moral integrity inherent in its position, SDS was determined to stand its ground and appeal to the collective conscience of the university community. Any hope that the three faculty advisers would intercede on behalf of the administration was lost when they submitted a statement affirming that the appropriate discussions had taken place. The advisers had counseled the group to proceed with its plans to invite the speakers, inasmuch as their appearances had obvious educational merit and the legislature had seemingly eliminated any total statutory prohibition of such speakers. The advisers contended that they had "never regarded it as necessary that the organization secure [the administration's] approval of their program." They submitted that such was unnecessary because the students comprising SDS "command our respect because of their concerns, their judgment, and their integrity." In fact, the faculty advisers supported the SDS move because it would resolve the restrictions that continued to hover above the campus.[38]

UNC administrators had considered UNC-SDS a potential threat and had investigated preemptive measures against the group for some time prior to the controversial invitations. The origin of this concern and activity remains unclear; perhaps the growing prominence of national antiwar efforts led by SDS spurred concern, or the cause may have been a simple belief that the local SDS might eventually challenge the administrators' authority. Whatever the motivation, the UNC administration, led by Friday, immediately sought information that might be used to decertify SDS as an official student group by soliciting data from the two sources of anticommunist authority on which it had come to rely: the FBI and HUAC. As early as September 1965 Cathey had written FBI Director J. Edgar Hoover to inquire about whether SDS was a communist group. Hoover was noncommittal, stating that the group was being investigated but as yet had not been so identified. A similar request to HUAC chair Edwin Willis obtained no designation of SDS as CP related. In reporting these findings to the press, Cathey noted that the FBI was in "routine contact" with his office "concerning this organization and others. . . . [T]he FBI knows of the members." How did the FBI obtain such knowledge about the SDS membership? Cathey himself likely supplied the information. In December Cathey had requested and received the leaders' names from a faculty adviser. A glimpse of how the administration might have responded had either the FBI or HUAC labeled SDS as subversive or communist-inspired can be seen from Cathey's remarks about the CP-dominated DuBois Clubs. Cathey noted in a press statement his discovery that the "DuBois Society [sic] is definitely identified as a Communist recruiting device. No club has been formed at the University, and we'll nip it in the bud at the first sign of any activity. . . . [I]t certainly would be squelched."[39]

President Friday made the final attempt at averting the expected crisis. When the early efforts failed to yield the desired result, Friday invited McCorkel and Waller to his office. He implored the students for additional time to negotiate and convince trustees and legislators that the talks should be allowed to take place. For the time being, however, Friday remained unalterably opposed to SDS proceeding with its plans. He feared that the legislature would retaliate against the university if it allowed the speakers to appear. Attempting to appeal to the students' self-interest, he admonished the SDS leaders that their careers might be irreparably harmed by association with a radical group.[40]

Despite his sincerity and civility, Friday was greatly irritated by the SDS action. He continued to believe that his plan, as codified in the amended law and the trustee-guided speaker policy, had effectively resolved the controversy. In this view, the speaker policy would restore free speech and academic freedom at UNC as long as no one attempted to provide a forum for politically controversial speakers. He expressly criticized the invitations, believing they occurred only because "some people wanted to agitate the situation."[41]

While McCorkel and Waller respected Friday and understood the dilemma he faced, they were equally resolved to proceed with the invitations. They pointed out that the administration had received abundant time to eliminate the law but had failed to do so. McCorkel and Waller assured Friday that their actions, no less than his own, were motivated by a sincere concern for the university's welfare. The students believed that one way or another, the invitations would resolve the matter: either free speech would be restored, or a court test would invalidate the law.[42]

On January 28 and 29, state newspapers reported that invitations had been extended to Aptheker and Wilkinson. The news quickly touched off a welter of rumors that a radical group at Chapel Hill was bringing subversives to the campus. Identified as the spokesperson for SDS, McCorkel was now besieged by journalists seeking information on the group and its plans. Typically supportive of the UNC administration and the new policy, many state papers excoriated SDS as a "minority group" desiring to impose its will on the populace by inviting a treacherous communist to Chapel Hill. In the view of many newspapers, SDS was seeking to provoke a needless controversy by defying the properly constituted university authorities. McCorkel also received a series of letters that called him ungrateful and suggested that he return to Pennsylvania. Although several papers profiled the group fairly, they carefully distanced themselves from any approval of SDS plans to confront the speaker policy. SDS would not find support from the established institutions of North Carolina.[43]

The most substantial problem following publication of SDS plans came from an expected source: the North Carolina General Assembly. The news that a student group had invited an acknowledged communist to speak set off a firestorm of criticism among legislators. Seeing the effort as a deliberate affront to the authority of the state's lawmaking body, they responded with denunciations and demands that Friday squelch the appearances. Aggrieved legislators viewed the plan as a deliberate abrogation of the political compromise forged by the Assembly-dominated Britt commission, in which UNC administrators were to assume responsibility for preventing such activities. To allow these individuals to appear would be tantamount to nullifying the agreement.

Several of those instrumental in the Britt compromise expressed a sense of outrage and betrayal that Friday and the administrators were refusing to take immediate action. Philip Godwin pointed to the intent of the new arrangement: "I was assured by Representative Britt that it was the intention of the Commission in its recommendation that this should assist in the exchange of scientific ideas between Communist countries and ours, and not to be used by Herbert Aptheker and his fellow travelers." Godwin's view of the meaning of the agreement was informed by his support for the original speaker ban and above all by his unstinting belief that domestic communists were behind the social insurgencies taking shape in the South and around the nation. Irritation was also expressed by Hanes, who had served on the commission and worked diligently to obtain the result desired by UNC. The senator was particularly offended that Aptheker had been invited. Communicating his displeasure to Friday, Hanes termed the proposal "a supreme and arrogant insult to the Legislature and the people of North Carolina." Hanes called on the UNC president to "take a strong hand" with SDS, implying that the "small group of radicals" be compelled to desist or face expulsion from the university.[44]

The two principal legislators responsible for defining the speaker law compromise were no less aggrieved by the unexpected turn of events. In a letter to Friday, Zollicoffer disputed that either Aptheker or Wilkinson would offer anything of legitimate educational value. "If they are permitted to speak," he concluded, "then I made one hell of an error on the Commission and my confidence in you and the Executive Committee of the Board of Trustees was wrong. . . . [F]or goodness sakes don't let them speak, blame it on being of no educational value which is what I thought our amendment did." Of all the remonstrations, few were more pointed and conclusive than that coming from Britt. If anyone knew the political intent of the commission's recommendation, then surely that person was the chairman. Britt declared his "alarm and disappointment" that "two political communists" were coming to UNC. The use of the term *political* was deliberate and significant: its use denoted a carefully drawn distinction between *scientific* and *political*—that is, foreign communists who would be permitted to appear and domestic radicals who would be banned. Britt explicitly explained the commission members' intent: "[We] felt that if our recommendations were followed that University and college administrations would use the good judgment to keep communists off their campuses at least for several years."[45]

Britt was a rising figure in state politics whose political ascendancy rested in part on preserving the belief that the committee's "recommendations" included a tacit agreement to ban domestic communists and radicals. The public hearings and the subsequent report had been widely praised as fair and informative; the press and much of the populace heaped hosannas on the panel and especially its chairman. Britt was scheduled to become Speaker of the House in 1967 and was seen as a future gubernatorial candidate. The political metaphysic that enabled an agreement on amending the law after adoption of the prescribed speaker policy was the assumption that the principal parties agreed that controversial speakers would not appear in the near future. The SDS action offered a direct challenge to this assumption. When Friday and UNC leaders appeared to equivocate in their response, Britt came to believe that he and the commission had been betrayed. "I must say," he angrily concluded, "that [letting Aptheker and Wilkinson appear] is the worst case of letting down friends and rewarding enemies that I have ever seen."[46]

President Friday was alarmed and shaken by the angry tone of the letters he received. He was more concerned, however, with their suggestions, both subtle and blatant, of legislative retribution. Several communicants suggested that a referendum would certainly result in a restoration of the original statute or possibly the enactment of one carrying criminal sanction. Hanes warned of "the most grave consequences on the future of the University, consequences far out of proportion to the importance of one speaker." An indirect inference was the possibility that the legislature might impede or reduce its biennial appropriation to the university. In a personal message to Friday, Britt intoned the direst of possibilities: "Bill, forgetting your obligations to those who helped you, if you are interested in the future welfare of U.N.C. you will do something to get these schedules canceled."[47]

The hope that future controversies would be muted with the passage of time or successfully micromanaged by UNC personnel was becoming unraveled. Friday's most immediate necessity was to assuage the accusers that any agreement had been abrogated. Rather than affirm his own belief that Aptheker and Wilkinson should be allowed to speak, he attempted to transfer authority to the trustees' Executive Committee. He assured his accusers that he "did not believe that the Committee [would] approve Aptheker's appearance here. . . . [T]his will settle that problem." He also attempted to deflect the Wilkinson issue by suggesting that the speaker law, even in its original form, would not prohibit his visit. Friday's response was at best disingenuous. It obscured his preference and his belief that the committee could be persuaded to approve the invitations. Almost unmentioned were the collaborative activities of UNC officials in trying to justify banning Wilkinson.[48]

Wilkinson's case, difficult though it was, was resolved, ironically, in the same manner as that of his friend and colleague Braden the previous spring. UNC officials relied heavily and uncritically on the opinions and files of federal agencies, most notably HUAC. When HUAC delegitimated an individual or group, UNC officials accepted the report as conclusive evidence. And in terms of Wilkinson, with its own political agendas and biases under attack, HUAC could be expected to provide evidence to discredit one of its most resolute critics. The UNC officials who took charge of obtaining information on Wilkinson were Cathey and Arthur J. Beaumont, the chief of campus police. At Cathey's behest, Beaumont telephoned the Washington office of HUAC, which informed the policeman of Wilkinson's background and quickly dispatched to Chapel Hill a collection of documents purporting to establish him as a card-carrying communist. With this "evidence" in hand, UNC officials summarily decided that Wilkinson came under the auspices of the speaker policy.[49]

While HUAC needed little additional incentive to vilify Wilkinson and other radicals, Beaumont meant to leave no doubt in enforcing the speaker ban. Far from operating in a neutral manner, Beaumont was an antiradical zealot who encouraged and praised HUAC's anticommunist crusade. Following the "exposure" of Wilkinson as a communist, Beaumont sent a letter of effusive congratulations to his HUAC contact. Praising the committee's "speed and accuracy," he cited the stakes of preventing dissident speakers from the campus: "We have won the first round in this never ending battle with people who use our rights in an effort to destroy the same." UNC-SDS was ridiculed as "these vocal trouble makers." And Beaumont knew well the "trouble" that SDS sought to make: he attended every public meeting of the group, conspicuously taking notes and attendance.[50]

It was still not clear how the Board of Trustees would respond to the confrontation. The 102-member board had adopted a set of speaker regulations on January 14, 1966, that seemed to provide access for the speakers. The formalism of the regulations appeared excessive and somewhat unwieldy, but they did not impose any measure of prior restraint. Given the size of the board, however, an interim decision on the Aptheker and Wilkinson invitations would be left to the thirteen-member Executive Committee, which met on February 2. The meeting was characterized by high emotions, as several trustees expressed outrage over the invitations. Governor Dan K. Moore, attending as an ex-officio member, expressed his personal opposition, stating that the invitations had been made solely to create controversy and would not, in his opinion, serve any valid educational purpose. No formal action was taken, however, as only nine members were present and the discussion was so acrimonious that a strong majority was impossible to obtain. With the issue postponed until February 7, all sides began to marshal evidence and mobilize supporters. As Beaumont contacted HUAC, Godwin, Friday, and others called members of the Executive Committee in hopes of influencing their decisions.[51]

On February 10 Moore issued an official statement that indicated his own opinion of the two invitations and, more important, enunciated the essential compromise implicit in the Britt committee recommendations and the resulting law and policy. Domestic communists were to be banned, while scientific and cultural speakers from communist countries were to be given access under controlled academic conditions. In Moore's view, Aptheker should be banned because he "is an avowed American Communist who has just returned from a visit to North Vietnam where he gave support and encouragement to the Communists there who are killing our American servicemen every day." Conversely, said the governor, "the university does need the freedom to host international scientific conferences which would be attended by Communist scientists or to hear the ambassador or official of a Communist nation." Moore congratulated the Executive Committee for its decision to ban Aptheker and Wilkinson. Despite his own statement to the committee, Moore denied that there had been any "attempt to censor free speech at the university, no political interference in academic affairs, and no attempt to dictate a speaker policy at the university." The weight of the state's highest elected official was firmly placed against the two invitations. Along with the earlier vote of the Executive Committee, it would now take extraordinary courage and resolve to oppose the political forces demanding that the anticommunist imperative be enforced.[52]

10 Confrontation in Chapel Hill

SDS did not enjoy institutionalized access to power and influence, but it was able to effect a dramatic turn in the positions of the official student representatives. In the aftermath of the Britt committee's recommendations, both student government President Paul Dickson and *Daily Tar Heel* editor Ernest McCrary had expressed satisfaction with the amended law and the new speaker policy. Neither voiced any interest in challenging the new arrangements. Dickson, McCrary, and other official student leaders maintained positions that mirrored to an extreme degree the policies of UNC officials like President William C. Friday, with whom the students identified. The key component of both student leaders' and the university administration's endorsement of the new law and policy was that authority had been restored to the trustees. But if Dickson and McCrary expected to maintain any credibility as representatives of student opinion, however, they would have to disengage from the adult wing of the UNC establishment, of which they were a part. SDS's decision to forcefully test the boundaries of free speech at UNC left these student leaders with little choice but to openly acknowledge and support the legitimacy of the speakers' appearances.[1]

Left to their own devices, it is doubtful that either branch of the student establishment would have questioned the new arrangements. Partly as a result of SDS's obvious commitment, but more importantly out of a concern that SDS might use the issue to generate greater student support, Dickson,

McCrary, and several other established student organizations agreed to co-sponsor the invitations to Herbert Aptheker and Frank Wilkinson. Throughout the controversy, Dickson was a close confidant of President Friday and hoped to use the experience as student leader as a building block for a future in the state Democratic Party. Fearful that the leadership of the student protest might pass to others, Friday and Dickson held "clandestine" meetings at which the UNC president conveyed to his young charge a prudent course of action and Dickson reciprocated with information about student plans. "He kept me fully advised," said Friday, "and I encouraged him in every way that I could."[2]

In effect, Dickson became an agent for Friday, doing what the president could not do for himself. Having lost considerable credibility in failing to get the law repealed, Friday could not effectively contain SDS and the students. But Dickson might. Similarly, because of the political delicateness of his di-lemma, Friday was effectively restrained from a forceful enunciation of why Aptheker should be allowed to speak. Here again, Dickson stepped forward by publicly defending the legitimacy of Aptheker's appearance. In rhetoric about "defending against communism," the student leader asserted the educational value of the talk. "He is certainly qualified," noted Dickson, "as an academi-cian having received his Doctorate degree from Columbia University. He is also the author of some 17 books." At a press conference on February 3, 1966, Dickson declared that it was the "unequivocal position" of the "overwhelming majority" of the student body that Aptheker should speak.[3]

A majority of the students certainly considered the invitations valid. Their political education was the result of an SDS campaign to rally support for freedom of speech at UNC. SDS members did the legwork of the initial grass-roots organizing by going floor to floor in residence halls and using other student venues to explain why the law had to be opposed. The successful stu-dent mobilization meant that SDS could no longer be ignored. When Jim McCorkel responded to the governor's position, he was surrounded by a wall of reporters and television cameras. The SDS leader castigated Governor Dan K. Moore's statement that Aptheker's visit lacked educational merit, la-beling the governor's attitude reflective of a "tremendous amount of igno-rance." Moore's position, said McCorkel, constituted an "attack on the Uni-versity." The SDS response ratcheted up the level of emotional intensity and equated the issue with the interests of everyone who supported the school. Although hopeful that the trustees' Executive Committee would approve the invitations when it again met on February 7, the SDS leader indicated that his group was planning to organize support for a legal challenge to the law should the invitations be denied. In so doing, UNC-SDS indicated its unwillingness to accept a verdict that mandated anything less than open and equal campus access to student-invited campus speakers.[4]

Members of the Executive Committee were heavily lobbied with forecasts of devastating results for UNC if the visits were approved. The opposition was spearheaded by Philip Godwin and the members of the Britt commission, who argued that allowing Aptheker to speak would constitute a flagrant violation of the principle undergirding the compromise. Aptheker was a known communist, and there had been agreement that communists had nothing legitimate to offer the educational enterprise.

The members of the Executive Committee, deeply divided on February 2, were annoyed by the seeming effrontery of college students in openly defying university officials and the state's highest elected officials. For some members, a "yes" vote now might be perceived as a capitulation to student radicals. The trustee committee was now trapped between its own hubris and fear of antagonizing powerful legislative interests. Given these stakes there could be little doubt about what the decision would be. When the Executive Committee met in the governor's office on February 7, there was no appeal that would change its collective mind. A faculty representative and Dickson vainly argued that the invitations should be granted. President Friday, sensing the difficulty of his task, also made a plea to recognize the speakers under acceptable safeguards. Given his track record of success in persuading the trustees to accede to his judgment, Friday still believed that they might be convinced to support his position. The summary denial of his request left him shocked and dispirited. Friday's sense of being "repudiated" by a board that was supposed to follow his lead led him to "seriously consider getting out."[5]

Led by eastern conservatives Frank Taylor of Goldsboro and Judge Rudolph Mintz of Wilmington, the Executive Committee quickly moved to quash the invitations. An early vote to permanently ban the two speakers from UNC passed seven to four but was then superseded by a compromise resolution, passed by an eight-to-three margin, limiting the prohibition to the March appearances. The committee also resolved that the speaker regulations adopted on January 14 that established a procedural basis for the visits were beyond their constituted authority. Sections 116–199 of the General Statutes amending the speaker law mandated that such regulations be approved by the entire board, which was scheduled to meet on February 28. The Executive Committee voted to suspend all speakers coming under the terms of the revised statute until the full board established "rules and regulations governing visiting speakers."[6]

Prior to the Executive Committee meeting, SDS organized a campus rally attended by eight hundred students that called for trustee recognition of the invitations. Sensing that campus sentiment was swinging solidly behind the SDS effort, official student leaders had little choice but to support a call for freedom of speech. On February 7 what had originated as a SDS plan to test the speaker policy became an issue embraced by the entire student body: with few exceptions, every recognized campus political group agreed to cosponsor the appearances. Gary Waller, now the acting chairman of SDS, appealed to the sanctity of the First Amendment. "If we are denied freedom to speak," he said, "then it means little that we have differences of opinion." While stressing his opposition to SDS and to communism, Dickson called for all students to rally behind academic freedom. Although the faculty members had remained generally quiet over the first two years of the speaker ban, they were also moved by the students' example. Lewis Lipsitz, a young political science professor and informal adviser to SDS, called for a threatened mass resignation of faculty members to convince the trustees of the faculty's commitment to freedom of speech on campus.[7]

The opposition to the appearances emphasized their contrived nature and sought to arouse a general anticommunist sentiment. Governor Moore, who was personally opposed to any manifestation of communism, however symbolic, also lent his considerable political weight to the pending decision. Still smarting from the accusation that he had imposed his will on the Executive Committee's decision, the governor sought to explain his rationale throughout the controversy. In a public statement, Moore expressed his "personal conviction that their appearance would not clearly serve the advantage of education" and labeled Aptheker an "avowed American Communist" who had just returned from North Vietnam "where he gave support and encouragement to the Communists there who are killing our American servicemen everyday." Moore also laid out the centerpiece of his compromise plan that he believed had found expression in the Britt report. The university should be allowed to host scientific conventions and cultural gatherings that communist scientists or representatives of communist governments might attend. With the need to maintain the ideological polarity and a sense of clarity between "us" and "them," domestic communists and radicals were not to appear.

Among the opponents of the invitations, Jesse Helms was the most outraged. In a stinging commentary following McCorkel's criticism of the governor's statement, the editorialist called for firm action from UNC authorities. The Helms plan was simple: expel those students who questioned authority and intimidate the remainder into abject silence. Calling SDS "asinine," "arrogant," and "noisy," he hoped to stampede the trustees into precipitous action by implying that the issue was one of "backbone" and whether the trustees were afraid of this "motley organization." From Helms's perspective, the matter could be resolved in a period equal to a "short coffee break." The trustees, he said, should order the students to "cancel the invitations and extend no more." If SDS resisted this directive, the university should "kick the last one of them out" and "advise all the rest that no such further nonsense will be tolerated." Deeply suspicious of academicians, Helms's ideal university situation would reflect what he viewed as natural social hierarchies based on order and authority. The purpose of a university education was to provide proficiency within a finite body of knowledge to take one's proper place in society. Dissent and questions critical of authority were immoral and not to be allowed; those who engaged in such activities forfeited their place at the university.[8]

As the most unstinting critic of any sort of compromise, Helms continued a refrain that emphasized student culpability in general and SDS "troublemakers" in particular. Helms devoted several editorials to the Aptheker-Wilkinson controversy, calling on campus officials to "clamp down and insist upon discipline." Labeling campus protests against the policy "arrogant" and "ridiculous," Helms predicted "political tremors" unless Friday told "the troublemakers on campus, faculty members and students alike, to behave themselves or get out." In Helms's view, there was no crisis: the only problem was UNC authorities' unwillingness to "deal sternly with those students and faculty who insist on playing trick-or-treat with constituted authority." Helms hoped that Friday would simply order the students to be silent and the controversy would thus be resolved.[9]

For its part, SDS had no intention of remaining quiet or withdrawing the invitations. SDS ignored the trustees' Executive Committee's resolutions and continued making plans to mobilize the student body in support of the appearances. On the evening of the trustees' announcement, February 7, some five hundred students met to organize support for the appearances. Under the ever-present watch of Police Chief Arthur J. Beaumont, an interim Committee for Free Inquiry (CFI) was formed. With Waller presiding, the students voted to hold a mass rally in support of free speech and to invite the governor and members of the Executive Committee to address the gathering. Most of the meeting was taken up with desultory debate, but it was clear that SDS was propelling the larger student population toward confrontation over the issue of free speech. A major outcome of this meeting was the students' refusal to entrust strategy entirely to the official student government. Midway during the meeting Dickson appeared and attempted to take charge of the proceedings. Many students, particularly SDS members, were suspicious of his motives. It was well known that student government at UNC, with its organized political parties, had links to state government. In the past, student government leaders had even received surreptitious funding from the state Democratic Party. Apparently, this support had happened often enough that few students even questioned its propriety, although the radical student press did. In 1969 one publication reported, "Historically, one or even both major party candidates have been offered—and have accepted—several thousand dollars from the state Democratic Party; some years (not this one) the editor of the *Daily Tar Heel* is included in the politicos' junior g-men games." The students correctly suspected that Dickson was operating in coordination with the UNC administration, and some attendees believed that he had arrived at the meeting only after conferring with campus officials.[10]

Dickson's behavior persuaded few that he could be entrusted to implement an assertive defense of the invitations. He immediately attempted to derail the sense that immediate action was needed. Urging caution, the student body president recommended that no precipitous action be taken until the trustees met on February 28. Fearful that demonstrations or talk of student strikes might result in the trustees voiding the invitations, Dickson implored the students to take a wait-and-see approach. The students, at the urging of the SDS contingent, proceeded with plans to defy any restraint on free speech. A four-member steering committee was formed, including Dickson and Waller, to coordinate plans. On February 11 the formal CFI was created, and representatives from various campus constituencies, including the faculty, were chosen to direct the effort.[11]

The committee's plans were restrained, which was fortunate because the administration had taken steps to monitor the meeting and get the names of any student making "incendiary" statements. The committee drafted a letter to the governor explaining CFI's purpose and inviting him to Chapel Hill to address the students about why he opposed allowing Aptheker to speak. The letter was sent to Moore's office although few believed that he would accept the offer. The principal objective, however, was to mobilize student and faculty opinion and use it to pressure President Friday and the administrators to accept nothing less than unfettered freedom of speech for the campus.

The culmination of the CFI effort was a mass rally held at Memorial Hall followed by a silent walk to Friday's home. At the rally, thirteen hundred people heard several speakers denounce the speaker ban law and the policy it had spawned. The highlight of the assembly was a stinging rebuke to the law delivered by Jefferson Fordham, dean of the University of Pennsylvania Law School and himself a former UNC student body president. Asserting that "the intrusion of government into the intellectual life of a university is totally unsupportable," Fordham called on the trustees to adopt a nonrestrictive policy that would provide a forum to all who wanted to speak. In Fordham's opinion, there was only one "satisfactory disposition" to the issue: "outright repeal." Following the rally, the assembly walked in a cold rain to Friday's home, where the president and Acting Chancellor J. Carlyle Sitterson were presented with a resolution calling for, among other things, the state of North Carolina to "readopt the Constitution of the United States."[12]

Friday and Sitterson did not have to be convinced of the veracity of the students' contention: both men believed in free speech, academic freedom, and the essential harmlessness of the appearances. The immediate problem facing UNC, however, was intrinsically political. While the constitutional questions were certainly legitimate, the visits' opponents emphasized the moral imperative of opposing communists. Linked to this position was also an increasing insistence that UNC should cease its obstinacy and adhere to the will of the legislature, which ostensibly represented the wishes of the citizenry. As the leader of UNC's institutional interests, Friday had to secure a consensus from the trustees and, most difficult of all, avoid antagonizing a legislature whose leaders increasingly saw the university as a maverick political foe.

The first task was placating the trustees and winning their endorsement of procedures that would enable each constituent campus to make its own decisions about speakers. In approaching the February 28 trustee meeting, Friday and his associates left nothing to chance. Each trustee was telephoned or personally contacted and asked to support a plan that would ultimately enable the particular chancellor to decide which speaking invitations would be approved. After the disastrous Executive Committee meeting, Friday and his two closest supporters on the committee, Victor Bryant and Watts Hill Jr., both from Durham, began formulating procedures to regulate questionable appearances. The result was a highly formalistic and rigid set of requirements that could be used to summarily reject any invitations that did not come from officially recognized student groups. This policy was created to assure the trustees of administrative vigilance in monitoring speakers. The procedures were designed to slow down the process of ruling on invitations by presenting a variety of permissions and oversight requirements. The reward for UNC would be trustee affirmation of the principle that campus administrators were the appropriate and capable parties to resolve such conundrums.[13]

In pursuit of this strategy, UNC officials largely reprised their claims and position from the previous fall. The decision to apply and implement any speaker procedures, they contended, properly rested with them and their administrative agents. Still, however, the most difficult issue — permitting known communists, especially the suddenly notorious Aptheker, to speak at UNC — was quietly avoided. For the moment, this dilemma was postponed in the search for allies. When ninety trustees convened on February 28, 1966, to consider the procedures devised by Friday, Bryant, and Hill, the outcome was virtually certain. Friday, Sitterson, Bryant, and Dickson were allowed to address the assembly and register their support for the plan that would ostensibly protect UNC's reputation as a citadel of free expression and assuage fears that campus officials were being less than circumspect in identifying potential subversion. As at the February 7 meeting, SDS representatives and younger faculty members were not allowed to speak. SDS did, however, submit a paper refuting conservative allegations that allowing communists to speak represented a betrayal of American soldiers fighting in Vietnam. There is no evidence that the trustees read or considered the statement. In the minds of many trustees, SDS and its dissent from the established rules had caused the present crisis.[14]

The trustees' near-unanimous vote was the reaffirmation for which Friday and the chancellors had campaigned. Although some trustees had private reservations about the plan, only one—the irrepressible Tom White, who invoked Pontius Pilate—expressed audible opposition to the Friday-led proposals. UNC, in the person of the chancellor, had secured a clear mandate to determine if the invitations would be permitted. Given Friday and Sitterson's expressed proclivities, the road now seemed open for the appearances to take place.

CFI (which provided the aegis under which the Aptheker and Wilkinson invitations had been issued) wasted no time in renewing the invitations. On the afternoon of the trustees' decision, ten CFI representatives asked permission from Sitterson to host the two speakers. Noting that the request was in accordance with the freshly adopted procedures, the student group asserted that both appearances would serve the cause of education and were entirely consistent with the university's stated academic mission.[15]

The letter merely formalized knowledge of the speaking schedules. The UNC administration had known for some time that Wilkinson had agreed to speak on March 2 and Aptheker on March 9. The denouement had arrived: the UNC administration would either articulate and act on its stated adherence to free speech and an unfettered academic environment or capitulate to powerful political forces and gag itself.[16]

The trustees' action did nothing to persuade Governor Moore and prominent Assembly figures that the appearances should be allowed. The university found itself isolated and confronted by some of the state's most powerful political figures. In addition to Moore, the vehement opposition of David Britt, White, Robert Morgan, and Godwin promised a stormy period if the two speakers appeared on campus. And no one was more aware of the potential for negative repercussions than Friday. Despite ongoing disagreement and resentment, the General Assembly had been remarkably generous with UNC, approving increased funding as Friday embarked the school on a program of dramatic expansion. If the university failed to comply with the preferences of Moore and Assembly leaders, future institutional development might be endangered. Some kind of opposition or veiled retribution might become manifest when the Assembly reconvened for the 1967 session. And the opposition was well positioned to take action: Britt would serve as Speaker of the House, and White could expect to oversee the powerful Joint Appropriations

Committee. If Sitterson approved Wilkinson's and Aptheker's talks, UNC could expect some manner of retribution from angry and irritated Assembly members.

The decision to permit or refuse the invitations formally rested with the chancellor. A strong, confident chancellor could likely have employed the trustee mandate to enunciate the propriety of the appearances. Such a scenario was not possible, however, because UNC lacked such leadership. The school did not have a chancellor but rather an acting chancellor, a post Sitterson assumed on February 16, in the midst of the Aptheker-Wilkinson controversy. A professor of history and assistant chancellor, Sitterson replaced Paul Sharp, who had announced the previous fall his decision to accept the presidency of Drake University.

Lacking any preexisting base of support and unwilling to make a unilateral decision, Sitterson was completely reliant on a circle of UNC associates, including law school dean Henry Brandis and former chancellor William B. Aycock. Sitterson's foremost adviser, however, was Friday. In making his decision, Sitterson faithfully adhered to the procedures recently established by the trustees. He solicited the advice of a joint student-faculty advisory committee as well as others in the UNC administration. Friday, Aycock, and faculty chairman Corydon Spruill offered the decisive advice, however. As the acting chancellor polled his inner circle, "there was absolutely no dissent among them as to the decision reached under the circumstances in which it had to be made." The senior cohort, led by Friday, told Sitterson to deny the speaking requests.[17]

The UNC decision, made primarily by Friday, could have been different and certainly more in keeping with the school's desired image as a bastion of uncompromising intellectual freedom. The primary factor that prevented Friday from authorizing Sitterson to permit the speakers was a fear of retribution, especially the possible loss of appropriations during the next biennium. Reduction of funding had always been the implicit threat looming over UNC if it failed to adhere to the speaker ban. Friday simply lacked the necessary conviction that the mission of a free university was sacrosanct and a concomitant willingness to defend this belief by defying the political meddlers. A useful example of such a principled stand could be found in Michigan, where in early February the Senate passed a resolution calling on the state university presidents to ban communist speakers from their campuses. The resolution did not carry the force of law, Senate Majority Leader Raymond Dzendzel of Detroit noted, "but we hold the purse strings." Despite this threat, the university presidents promptly ignored the resolution. Citing policy adopted by the state's Council for Higher Education, the presidents of Wayne State and Michigan State notified the Senate that they would not comply with such wanton political interference in university affairs. Two hours after the resolution was passed, Aptheker spoke to a student group at Wayne State, and he addressed a standing-room-only crowd the following evening at Michigan State.[18]

Sitterson's personal desire to preserve the institution was conspicuous in his official statements during the days leading up to March 2. In taking office on February 16, he noted the "increasing financial support from the Governors and General Assemblies" and the increased national prestige that such monetary support had made possible. When Sitterson addressed the trustees on February 28 his statement was a glowing paean that described the university as a holy shrine to be revered. UNC, he reminded them, was "venerable and distinguished," and it was the trustees' responsibility to "protect, preserve, and promote" the school's "greatness" by restoring campus authority to the administration. Although well positioned to make a decision reaffirming the historic academic principles to which he alluded in his public statements, Sitterson was swayed by the same sentiment held by those whose opinions he sought — institutional loyalty and preservation.[19]

On the morning of March 2, Sitterson informed Dickson that Wilkinson could not speak. In a public statement, Sitterson stipulated that although the trustees had given him procedural authority to decide, he still regarded the Executive Committee's decision of February 7 as binding. With this explanation, Sitterson rendered pointless the trustees' February 28 vote. The statement of refusal was short and to the point but devoid of any clarification of the factors that led to the decision.[20]

On March 1 Wilkinson addressed a gathering of two hundred persons at Duke University in Durham. The subject of his talk was HUAC and its history of violating constitutional safeguards of personal liberty. The event was civil and informative, and Wilkinson readily responded to questions put to him by his audience.[21]

The following day Wilkinson came to the UNC campus for the scheduled 1:00 P.M. talk. The speech was to be held in McCorkle Place, a spacious area adjacent to downtown Chapel Hill adorned by ancient oak trees and statuary commemorating hallowed UNC figures. Events, as they unfolded, were not left to happenstance. Friday and Dickson, with Sitterson's knowledge, agreed that the ban would be approached but not broken. Such a strategy would serve two purposes: it would give symbolic display to the absurdity of the restriction, and, more important, it would prevent any further embarrassment to the university such as would come with the arrest of Wilkinson and the scuffling and violence that might ensue.[22]

Instead of speaking on campus grounds, Wilkinson addressed a crowd of some twelve hundred students sitting and standing behind a low stone wall along Franklin Street at the perimeter of the campus. In a scene of grand political theater, Wilkinson stood on a public sidewalk in front of a sign reading "Gov. Dan K. Moore's (Chapel Hill) Wall," suggesting an obvious parallel with the Berlin Wall, which had come to symbolize U.S. Cold War commitment. The talk itself lasted a mere ten minutes. Wilkinson noted that the law banning him was a willful violation of constitutional principles and promised to appear on campus later that evening.[23]

The Franklin Street appearance attracted considerable media attention, but it did not confront the speaker ban. To establish grounds for a court test, banned speakers would have to be led onto the campus and then compelled to leave by university authorities. When Wilkinson and the students arrived at Carroll Hall that evening they were met by Police Chief Beaumont, the same official who had sought evidence from HUAC that could be used to ban Wilkinson. The students had hoped to reenact a scenario similar to the afternoon's episode that would demonstrate the absurdities of the speaker law. Knowing that the police had been instructed to prohibit any effort by Wilkinson to address the audience, the students came armed with a tape recorder. The plan was to play a tape of Wilkinson speaking while Wilkinson himself sat mute on the platform. This scheme was overruled, however, when Beaumont informed Dickson that the tape could be played on the steps but not inside the building itself. Following an impromptu speech by Dickson and expressions of irritation from the crowd, the next phase of the plan proceeded with Wilkinson being led to the Hillel House, where he gave his intended talk. In introducing Wilkinson, Jim McCorkel commented on the significance of the day's activities: "The outcome of today's happenings is going to be a court case, [and] it will certainly be backed by the Civil Liberties Union." McCorkel also informed the audience of several hundred that Wilkinson had agreed to join the suit as a plaintiff when the time came.[24]

As significant as the ban on Wilkinson was, the apogee of the speaker ban crisis at Chapel Hill did not occur until the following week. Aptheker had come to symbolize the kind of speaker that supporters of the law desired to ban from the public campuses. Here was an issue on which both sides of the legislative debate found plausible agreement: Aptheker should not be allowed to speak at UNC. In the minds of both friends and foes of the speaker law, he was a dangerous figure. Aptheker not only was a member of the national committee of the CPUSA but also advocated the kind of black assertiveness that many white North Carolinians found threatening. As the author of *American Negro Slave Revolts*, Aptheker had long been recognized as a historical authority on slave rebellion in the antebellum South. The announced title of his planned address, "The Negro Movement—Reform or Revolution?" could scarcely assuage the anger of UNC critics.[25]

There was no possibility that Aptheker would be permitted to speak: in the minds of UNC administrators, the political exigencies of the moment mandated that the appearance be denied. On March 4 Sitterson notified Dickson that Aptheker would not be allowed to speak. In a brief letter, the acting chancellor was as vague and evasive in stating the reasons for his decision as he had been in the earlier refusal to permit Wilkinson to speak. Sitterson reasserted his contention that the February 7 action of the Executive Committee took precedence over the subsequent vote of the entire Board of Trustees.[26]

Sitterson was no less circumspect in privately articulating the precise considerations influencing his decision to refuse the invitations. The acting chancellor lamented the decision as "painful" because it violated his own "basic principles and concept of what a university should be." He sought to justify his decision by labeling Aptheker and Wilkinson "emotional symbols"; permitting them to visit would be a "disservice" to the university. The precise character of this "disservice" went undefined, but if the denials produced so much anguish for the chancellor, then UNC's concerns about possible legislative reprisal and vindictiveness must have been palpable indeed.[27]

In a March 4 communication addressed to a faculty group, Sitterson sought again to provide some coherent reason for his decision. He acknowledged that "the decision by the Board of Trustees on February 28 did, indeed, return responsibility for decision-making to the Chancellor [and] in theory this may well have included the invitations to Wilkinson and Aptheker, but I reluctantly came to the conclusion that, in fact, the invitations were not really in that category." The primary problem, in Sitterson's viewpoint, was not the threat to free speech engendered by his refusals but the demand by an "active few" students that the university reaffirm its commitment to constitutional liberties and academic freedom.[28]

What was the "fact" that overruled the "theory" of the trustees' vote? And why were Aptheker and Wilkinson in another "category"? The source of UNC's dilemma was practical politics. Because of its consistent failure to address the antidemocratic assumptions as well as the simplest question at the core of the issue, UNC found itself politically isolated. At the point of denouement, influential trustees, notables from the state's business elite (especially the traditional extractive, labor-intensive industries), and, most prominently, a majority of legislators expected the invitations be denied. These ranks were not the pro–speaker bill conservatives who wanted to punish the university. This group included self-conscious friends of the university, some of whom had earlier called for repeal of the speaker law. The implicit "category" that applied to Wilkinson and Aptheker was one reserved for domestic radicals. An influential bloc of North Carolina's business and political elite agreed with the speaker law's core assumption: leftist activists should not speak at UNC. Sizing up these political circumstances, Friday and Sitterson opted to preserve the university's long-term interests. Constitutional principles and free speech would have to await a more favorable day.

After announcing his decision to ban the speakers, Sitterson received the praise of many outside the university as he simultaneously heard faculty disappointment. Appearing on television, former governor and textile executive Luther Hodges congratulated Sitterson for his action and labeled the controversy at Chapel Hill one of authority versus anarchy. Hodges was not alone in this criticism of the students who were challenging their elders' authority. Fearful that UNC might "appear like Berkeley, California," supporters of Sitterson's decision ridiculed the students for provoking the issue. Judge Rudolph Mintz of Wilmington, a member of the trustees' Executive Committee, condemned the students as "bent on defying all legal and constituted authority." What was paramount in the mind of Judge Mintz and undoubtedly others was clearly the preservation of the status quo and generational authority.[29]

The acting chancellor also received the legislature's plaudits. Lavish praise came not only from UNC critics like White but from those who had sided with the university administration throughout the controversy. C. W. Phillips, a House member from Guilford County, identified himself as "very active in an attempt to repeal the Speaker Ban Law." Like many other UNC supporters, Phillips believed it best to "leave this sort of activity in the hands of the College and college officials." While this objective had been achieved, it had not alleviated the threat to free speech at UNC. The assemblyman closed by endorsing Sitterson's action with an awkward rationale: "I'm for free speech, but feel that the cause [of free speech] will be better served to have it acted upon as you have done." As throughout the controversy, free speech had many advocates but few defenders.[30]

Among the faculty members, reaction to Sitterson's decision was somewhat mixed. A few individuals expressed loyalty to the administration or personal sympathy for the difficulty of the chancellor's position and thought the decision correct. Most faculty members, however, were angry and disappointed by what had taken place. They could not believe that the university itself would ban speakers and were aghast that the administration had capitulated to perceptions of public opinion and to political threats. Having believed previous assurances from the administration that it would never ban speakers, they considered the result a "grave violation of trust." The only way to rectify the damage to the university's commitment to openness would be for Sitterson to take a "firm stand" and affirm the invitation.[31]

For its part, the administration, led by President Friday, adamantly refused to acknowledge the authority that it had received from the trustees. The problem was not that Friday and Sitterson had yielded to concerted political pressure from nonuniversity sources but that the students—namely, the members of SDS—had compelled UNC officials to take a stand in defense of academic liberty. "This particular problem, agitated as it was by the actions of the SDS Chapter in inviting these men prior to affording the administration and

Trustees the time to comply with legal requirements upon us, forced Trustee consideration of the invitations and we were bound by the intent of their decision." This complaint sounded hollow, and it unnecessarily begged the question of why Friday had advised Sitterson to turn down the invitations. The administration had had a relatively placid two and a half years to eliminate the impediment to the stated principles and mission of UNC. And the administration had had more than a month to address the invitations that had been carefully drawn to meet existing policy guidelines.[32]

Several professors stoutly defended the educational significance of the announced subjects of both Wilkinson and Aptheker. In so doing, the faculty members extended their criticism to the issue that the administration had long avoided. After hearing Wilkinson speak at Duke, one critic proclaimed that he was "convinced that this is a dedicated American who has done nothing more than take a strong stand on the Bill of Rights. He . . . generally impressed me as being the kind of person who *very much needs to be heard.*" And these criticisms were not coming from younger, junior faculty members. Robert Gallman, a distinguished historian of nineteenth-century southern economy, asserted that after hearing Aptheker speak, he felt "more strongly than ever that he should have been afforded a University platform." Such expressions did not reflect latent faculty radicalism but an intellectual honesty based on the articulation of the speaker's thoughts.[33]

Despite the often compelling complaints and criticisms by faculty, students, and others, Sitterson had arrived at a decision. Unlike his faculty cohorts who had lived and trained elsewhere and whose academic values typically transcended institutional constraints, the acting chancellor was nothing if not a university man. Sitterson's devotion to what he believed to be UNC's larger interests overrode all residual considerations of academic principle. In this respect, he was a ready recipient of Friday's admonishment that the university's interests would not be served by admitting Wilkinson and Aptheker. The persistent challenges of students and their faculty allies could not impede the university's growth and expansion as an institution. The matter came down to an equation of relative political power: the UNC administration decided that the legislature and its implied threats had to be placated.

On March 9 the final act of the atavistic drama that was the speaker ban played out. Shortly after noon, Dickson, Waller, and other student leaders led Aptheker onto campus grounds, with the speaker wired for sound by a national television network, which apparently believed that he would be arrested, although he was not. Aptheker proceeded to the base of a prominent statue of a Confederate rifleman in McCorkle Place. As Aptheker mounted the base of the statue to begin his talk, Beaumont's voice interrupted: "Paul, I want you to tell Dr. Aptheker that if he speaks he is breaking the law." Adamant that his instructions be obeyed, the chief of police also threatened to have Dickson charged with violation of UNC's honor code if Aptheker attempted to speak. Aptheker seemed unfazed by the directive and asked what law he was breaking. A brief exchange between communist and policeman followed: "I thought I had my rights as a citizen of the United States," said Aptheker. "You do," answered Beaumont. "You have a right to obey the law." [34]

At this impasse, Dickson quickly took charge and directed the next act. President Friday had impressed on the student that whatever the outcome, the university had to be spared further embarrassment. While the spectacle of refusing Aptheker had to be played out to establish the basis for the incipient court test, the arrest of Aptheker and the resulting chaos was not to be allowed. Aptheker himself, for political reasons, was willing to challenge the ban and invite arrest. Not wanting to upstage the students, however, he quietly followed Dickson to the same stretch of Franklin Street sidewalk to which Wilkinson had retreated the previous week. [35]

In a brief address before more than two thousand students gathered on the fringe of the campus, Aptheker apologized that his appearance had "turned into a spectacle . . . some kind of circus." Calling the campus policy "medieval and absurd," he contended that the trustees and chief of police were violating the law by abrogating the Bill of Rights. Later that evening, Aptheker delivered his prepared address — a critique of U.S. actions in Vietnam — to a standing-room-only crowd at Chapel Hill's Community Church. In introducing Aptheker, Waller noted, "It is ironic that a few centuries ago, the universities had to free themselves from repressive church control. Now, we are refugees from a repressive university." [36]

With the Aptheker debacle, momentum accelerated toward a court test and closure of the speaker ban conflict. Knowing that the administration would not change its position and pressured by SDS, which had begun picketing South Building, which housed Sitterson's office, Dickson met with those quietly planning the legal challenge. Led by Greensboro attorney McNeill Smith, the lawyers advised the student body president to exhaust every possibility for the university to reverse itself, thereby creating certifiable evidence that the law, the trustees' policy, and the administrative action violated constitutional standards. [37]

On March 14 CFI renewed its request that Aptheker and Wilkinson be permitted to speak on campus. Although Sitterson had on two previous occasions denied the requests, such a step was necessary to establish that the denials were not merely for a particular date. Sitterson and the UNC administration would be given a final opportunity to remedy the students' complaint by allowing the speakers to appear. Between the March 4 administrative veto of Aptheker and Sitterson's response to the final appeal, both students and administrators continued to take steps and make plans that reflected the presence of the speaker ban. On March 6 the Carolina Forum, a student-run campus organization responsible for bringing speakers to the campus, announced that Robert Welch of the John Birch Society would be appearing on March 13. Although the leaders of the Carolina Forum participated in CFI and supported the Aptheker and Wilkinson invitations, Welch's invitation was not another attempt to test the speaker policy. Welch was definitely not a communist, and he had never pled the Fifth Amendment. Furthermore, he had been born in the state and was a UNC graduate. The invitation demonstrated the capricious and discriminatory nature of the speaker policy. A right-wing extremist was welcome at Chapel Hill, while anyone from the Left might be banned at the chancellor's whim. This circumstance suggested that the policy and the law itself might run afoul of the Fourteenth Amendment's equal-protection clause.[38]

Believing a lawsuit to be imminent, Sitterson made a final attempt to restore the impression that UNC was committed to freedom of speech. On March 4, as part of the same statement that formally denied the invitation to Aptheker, Sitterson announced that two "communist scholars" had been invited to speak and that he had approved the invitations. The chancellor's action, coming when it did, served two important purposes. First, it seemed to offer a means to repair UNC's image as a free and open academic institution at the very time when the school's reputation was being sullied by craven capitulation to external political forces. Second, the new invitations offered Sitterson a putative rationale for his decision to ban Wilkinson and Aptheker. In triumphantly announcing the visits, Sitterson contended that because these "scholars" came within the parameters established by the trustees, they were permissible. Conversely, Wilkinson and Aptheker belonged in nebulous "certain categories" of speakers proscribed by the trustees. Thus, Sitterson had acted properly in administering the policy. Sitterson never defined the criteria for assessing membership in these "certain categories."[39]

Plans for the two new invitations had been initiated in the week prior to the Wilkinson showdown. The marginalia on correspondence related to the invitation, initialed by Sitterson, clearly demonstrate that UNC officials were hoping to use these visits to offset the negative publicity of the bans on Wilkinson and Aptheker. The UNC News Bureau issued two press releases on March 4; both sought to provide information while offering a rationale suggesting that Sitterson's judgments on Aptheker and Wilkinson had been fair and even-handed.[40]

Sitterson's distinctions between the "scholars" and Aptheker and Wilkinson were, at best, disingenuous. First, the trustees had not explicitly mandated that any category of speaker be denied campus privileges. Despite whatever personal inclinations and strong reservations the trustees may have had about Aptheker and others, the February 28 procedures and proclamation clearly left the matter in the chancellor's hands. But Sitterson understood quite well the implicit imperatives driving the speaker issue. Political speakers, especially those on the Left and from the United States, had to be banned. Speakers from communist countries, regardless of party membership, were never really at issue. In congratulating Sitterson for his decision to ban Wilkinson and Aptheker, Britt acknowledged the political distinction inherent from the speaker ban's inception: "I voice no objection to your approving the appearances of the two communists from other countries. In my mind there is a distinct difference between a group represented by Aptheker on the one hand and Communist scholars from behind the Iron Curtain on the other hand. Suffice it to say, American Communists are traitors to our country." [41]

The two speakers, Professor Vladimir Alexandrov, a political scientist from Moscow State University, and Dr. Hanus Papousek, a behavioral psychologist from Prague, were quickly approved without any invocation of the speaker policy procedures. In an irony, approval was granted despite the faculty sponsor's acknowledgment that Papousek was a member of the Czech Communist Party and that Alexandrov was a specialist in the history of the Soviet Party and a fulsome defender of the Soviet system. Sitterson quickly understood that since both speakers had obvious scholarly merit and would not expressly criticize American society, the occasion offered an excellent chance to raise the university's sagging reputation as well as his own. When presented with the invitations, Sitterson approved them and attempted to orchestrate notification to coincide with the Aptheker and Wilkinson cases in hopes of diffusing criticism of his veto. [42]

The weakness in this scenario was that few people took notice. The political character of the Wilkinson and Aptheker cases and the distinction between them and the "communist scholars" was well understood. Alexandrov and Papousek were visiting scholars, already in the country to discuss scholarly matters removed from any political critique of American society. Papousek was doing work in the "learning processes in the neonatal and infant human." Although a nominal member of the Czech party, he was "a rather nonpolitical one" according to the faculty sponsor. A visiting professor at Indiana University, Alexandrov could speak with authority and conviction about the Soviet system but was known to be a vocal critic of the United States. Both speakers were scheduled to address graduate student colloquia chaired by faculty. [43]

In admitting the speakers, Sitterson made an easy decision that drew complaint from virtually no one. Both men were legitimated by faculty and departmental sponsors as scholars. Both speakers came and went practically unnoticed and with scant criticism of their presence. It may have provided a more difficult moment and revealed the inherent hypocrisy had a faculty member invited Aptheker to address a class. A Columbia University Ph.D. and the author of seventeen books on American history, Aptheker was clearly a scholar and a "communist scholar" at that. What made his case unique and placed him in a "certain category" apart from the other esteemed "communist scholars" were his political commitments—his open criticism of American capitalism, racism, and foreign policy. Coupled with his American citizenship, these reasons constituted the compelling factors in his being banned from the University of North Carolina.[44]

On March 31 Sitterson submitted his response to the final CFI request for administrative approval of speaking invitations to Aptheker and Wilkinson. The statement resonated with much the same reasoning and rhetoric as the earlier denial. The acting chancellor assured the students that procedures had been followed and that the advisory committees had been "virtually unanimous." He prefaced his judgment by emphasizing that the speakers had already spoken in Chapel Hill, and thus a return would be of "no educational purpose." Sitterson defended the viability of the procedures, claiming the invitations to Alexandrov and Papousek proved that the existing policy served UNC's interests. He correctly argued that Alexandrov and Papousek could not have spoken under the vague prohibitions of the 1963 law. Sitterson concluded that when he ruled against the invitations on March 2, he considered "the matter closed for [the remainder of] this academic year." The chancellor held out hope that the invitations could be reconsidered sometime in the future.[45]

The students were not surprised or mollified by Sitterson's remarks. Within an hour of receipt of the letter, Dickson filed papers in U.S. Middle District Court in Greensboro. The complaint, signed by twelve students and Aptheker and Wilkinson, named Chancellor Sitterson, President Friday, and the Board of Trustees as defendants. The suit sought "interlocutory and permanent injunctive relief and for a declaratory judgment." The students demanded nothing less than a declaration that the speaker law and its trustee policy were illegal and unconstitutional.[46]

The long-expected court test was under way. The North Carolina speaker control law, persistent and durable, had entered the final phase of its life.

11 The Speaker Ban Goes to Court

The one issue that united all strands of opposition to the speaker ban law was its conspicuous lack of adherence to constitutional standards. On face value, even the revised statute appeared to infringe on First Amendment liberties. Furthermore, one clause of the speaker law permitted the proscription of any person who had invoked the protection of the Constitution by use of the Fifth Amendment. Finally, and perhaps most important, the law seemed to violate the equal-protection clause of the Fourteenth Amendment. By creating a law applicable solely on the basis of political identity, the North Carolina speaker law appeared to run counter to a body of legal precedent. Despite numerous differences among themselves, university officials, student government leaders, and SDS activists all believed that a court test would inevitably result in the statute being declared invalid.

From the moment it had conceived the invitations to Herbert Aptheker and Frank Wilkinson, the leaders of UNC-SDS realized that a federal lawsuit was a possibility. While desiring to avoid the expensive and drawn-out process of litigation, SDS's members comprehended that political suasion would likely be insufficient to reverse the ban. But the issue of First Amendment rights was so compelling that SDS was willing to participate in such a suit if it became the ultimate recourse. After the student government became a party to the invitations, it too emphasized the constitutional principles that the speaker law flagrantly violated. In a February 14, 1966, letter to President

William C. Friday and in his address before the trustees on February 28, Paul Dickson identified the "unnecessary constitutional risks" the university incurred as it sought to enforce the speaker regulations. In Dickson's view, the law and its concomitant regulations violated the First Amendment as well as the due-process components of the Fifth and Fourteenth Amendments.[1]

Friday was no less sanguine about the prospects once a suit was initiated: "I knew that the minute that we got this thing in the federal courts, school was out. We would win." Following the Aptheker and Wilkinson debacles, a defeat and embarrassment for the university elite, all that remained was a lawsuit. For Friday, who had quietly encouraged Dickson's efforts to establish the basis for a court case, the legal challenge was the last possibility after all political avenues had been exhausted. Afraid that a premature legal challenge would merely result in a tighter, more draconian statute, Friday had sought resolution by political maneuver and by placating the Assembly with anticommunist homilies. When SDS and the students pressed ahead with their test of the new speaker law and policy, Friday and the administrators found themselves trapped. They felt forced to acquiesce to the demands of the political compromise hatched by the Britt commission. With the failure of his own political strategy, Friday could only support the student-driven court test.[2]

Despite the blatant constitutional questions raised by the law, the Britt commission had largely ignored the issue. The commission's deliberations had been primarily devoted to consideration of the political dilemma—specifically, how to construct a compromise amenable to both sides. The study commission left unquestioned the findings of Deputy Attorney General Ralph Moody in his early memorandum asserting the speaker law as a "constitutional, valid and a proper exercise of the authority vested in the legislative branch of the state government." The initial announcement that the law met constitutional muster was made by Attorney General T. Wade Bruton. Bruton himself had not researched the constitutional questions but had rested his opinion entirely on the claims of his deputy, Moody. Bruton's assertion, however, did not convince critics, who termed the ruling "absurd." Hailed by the law's defenders as compelling evidence of statutory viability, the memorandum failed to address the free-speech, due-process, and equal-protection concerns raised by critics. In his analysis, Moody asserted that the statute was entirely consistent with the constitutional right of the legislature to oversee and establish regulations for the use of state property.[3]

Deputy Attorney General Moody's August 2, 1963, brief defending the constitutionality of General Statute 116-119 ignored an extensive body of case law and recent court decisions. It was also questionable whether the decisions cited had proper application to the speaker law. A substantial portion of Moody's opinion rested on the ruling of a lower court in the state of New York,

Egan v. Moore, that enjoined the Regents of the State University of New York at Buffalo from permitting Herbert Aptheker, a member of the Communist Party, to speak. The decision was reversed by an appeals court the following year. The Moody brief also did not mention *Buckley v. Meng*. In this case, regulations restricting the use of an auditorium at Hunter College in New York to speakers "compatible" with the views of the college administration were overturned on Fourteenth Amendment grounds. Moody also failed to discuss the Supreme Court's ruling in *Slochower v. Board of Education*, which declared that the dismissal of a college professor solely for invoking Fifth Amendment rights was an unconstitutional infringement of due process.[4]

Instead of citing federal and state court decisions on First Amendment cases and equal access to public venues, Moody referred to a spate of decisions affirming the right of state legislatures to regulate the property and grounds of its public universities. The North Carolina case cited as the most applicable was more than a hundred years old — an 1852 decision, *University v. Maultsby*. When the document did discuss the applicability of the Bill of Rights' protection of free speech, it did not cite a body of pertinent court decisions but simply cited "The Opinion of the Committee of the Bill of Rights of the American Bar Association." The only case law cited to sustain the assertion that communists could be barred from speaking at public universities was a New York decision that affirmed the legality of the State University of New York at Buffalo barring Aptheker. The brief made no mention that the decision had been recently overturned by a New York appeals court.[5]

Fully a third of the Moody brief was devoted to a rambling exposition on "The Nature and Characteristics of Communism." And Moody was nothing if not a believer in the real and palpable threat of an international communist conspiracy. Citing numerous McCarthy-era anticommunist rulings, Moody asserted that although predicated on a relationship between legislative oversight and state property, the North Carolina law was entirely in line with a host of precedents defining the Communist Party as a conspiracy aimed at the overthrow of government. Interestingly, Moody could not cite the validity of the North Carolina statute as within the legislature's power to combat sedition by controlling the Communist Party. In a response to a group of Corvallis, Oregon, high school students who wrote to inquire if "the Communist Party of the United States [should] be outlawed by *state* law," Moody responded in the negative. While going to great lengths to define the CP as less a political party than a criminal conspiracy, he responded that "the states do not have any constitutional right to pass any such laws" because the Supreme Court had, in effect, declared that Congress should "occupy the whole field" with regard to sedition and that any state law would be superseded by federal law. Thus, in defending the speaker ban, Moody was largely compelled to base his contentions on the property issue. Strict reliance on federal decisions pertaining to communist speakers would have been difficult, if not impossible, to sustain.[6]

The position of the state's attorney on the speaker ban law was more sharply defined by the political psychology of its chief defender than by any body of legal precedent. A longtime member of the attorney general's staff, Moody had briefly attended UNC as an undergraduate and "shunned all curriculums," taking only those courses that "caught his fancy." Returning to UNC after service in World War I, he began taking law courses but dropped out after passing the state bar examination. The state's chief advocate in defending the speaker ban against the intricacies of constitutional requirements never received a college degree.[7]

Before embarking on his odyssey as an anticommunist warrior, Moody had earned a reputation as a defender of segregation. During the middle and late 1950s, Moody served as the state's counsel as black plaintiffs brought suit after suit seeking to eliminate racial segregation from North Carolina's public schools. As the lead attorney for the state, Moody took charge of the legal strategy that sought to circumvent the Supreme Court's ruling in the *Brown v. Board of Education* case. Seeking to support the Pearsall Plan, Moody created arguments that emphasized the token integration of a limited number of school districts. In this manner he sought to confirm that the state was in compliance with the federal court mandate. Moody's work resulted in several short-term victories in cases originating in Charlotte and Greensboro.[8]

Moody's interest in the segregation cases transcended his enjoyment of the legal maneuvers of the state's response to the federal courts. Moody was a committed segregationist who fought the legal battles with a conviction that blacks should be kept subordinate to whites. In his view, the stakes of the struggle were nothing less than which race would exercise the power of civil governance. He defended the propriety of literacy tests, arguing that "the colored people think that if they can get this position of theirs sustained they will be able to control their voters until they will have the balance of power in the state." For Moody, the barriers of race were natural and eternal. The southern racial hierarchy that had formed his worldview had to be defended. After a two-year absence, Moody took a salary cut to return to the attorney general's staff in 1957 as the lead counsel on integration cases.[9]

Like many of his contemporaries, Moody also believed that communism was responsible for much of the insurgency aimed at overturning Jim Crow laws and practices. In a 1968 letter to a law student commenting on the Supreme Court's invalidation of antimiscegenation statutes, Moody held responsible the nefarious workings of communism. "As desired by the Communists," he said, "we are well on the way to the production of a polyglot race of morons!" The hybridization of these two themes — segregation and anti-communism — defined Moody's association with the speaker ban law from start to finish. As his drafting of the original statute, his meandering brief attesting to its constitutionality, and his participation in the federal suit show, Moody viewed communism as a surreptitious threat to a natural order of social relations that was nowhere more evident than in matters of racial tradition.[10]

The anti–speaker ban forces had to look no farther than the local law faculties to find legal thinkers specializing in First Amendment and other issues of constitutional law. UNC and Duke Law School faculty members were concerned about the speaker law from the outset. Opposing Moody were two of the most respected constitutional lawyers in the country. William Van Alstyne had only recently come to Duke from Ohio State University, where he had participated in the legislative hearings on the Ohio speaker law that had served as the model for House Bill 1395. At UNC Professor Daniel Pollitt was, like his Duke colleague, a recognized authority on constitutional issues that involved civil liberties. These two legal scholars immediately recognized the speaker law's flawed character and offered assistance to those working to seek its repeal.[11]

Immediately prior to passage of the North Carolina speaker law, Van Alstyne had published a comprehensive and compelling article on the constitutional rights of political speakers at public universities. Noting that such speakers were protected by provisions of both the First and Fourteenth Amendments, the Duke professor emphasized that the body of federal rulings mandated that any decision to bar a speaker must be based on the actual content of the speech and its probable effect rather than on the speaker's affiliation. The applicable constitutional standards, said Van Alstyne, were the First Amendment and the equal-protection clause of the Fourteenth Amendment. While a public university was under no legal requirement to provide a forum for outside speakers, once it made provision to do so it could not discriminate on the basis of affiliation. "With respect to speeches of a political character," he concluded, "the Constitution permits a state to ban only those who would exhort their audience to unlawful action." Since the North Carolina statute instituted a ban on the basis of affiliation rather than on actual speech content, the pertinent precedents suggested that the law was unconstitutional.[12]

Pollitt had also weighed in with an opinion that the North Carolina law was unconstitutional. Writing in the *North Carolina Law Review* shortly after passage of the bill, Pollitt cited and reviewed many of the same decisions as his Duke colleague. The applicable state and federal court decisions, he contended, clearly prohibited bans based on affiliation or failing to provide equal protection to all would-be speakers. Pollitt also had the advantage of examining the specific language and ostensible intent of the recently enacted North

Carolina statute. For Pollitt, the law was yet another form of censorship, which, he noted, had a lengthy and dishonorable history in American academic life. Pollitt found most problematic the law's failure to meet the requirements of due process. The law was so vaguely worded that people of "reasonable" intelligence would likely draw different meanings from reading it. In particular, the UNC professor took issue with the nebulous character of the phrase banning speakers on the basis of "Communist or subversive connections, or activities." This language was, concluded Pollitt, "vagueness with a vengeance." [13]

A close observer of repeal efforts, Pollitt had by the summer of 1964 concluded that political efforts to effect repeal of the statute were doomed. At this time, almost two years before the suit was filed, he suggested a legal scenario on which a case could be erected. It would be necessary "that a litigant must be denied an alleged right which he specifically asserts." With remarkable prescience, Pollitt predicted the route that would ultimately bring the speaker ban into court, although there were, of course, limits to Pollitt's prognostication. He did not foresee the pivotal role played by student groups, assuming instead that the AAUP would be the "logical organization to bring a suit." [14]

When the Britt commission held its public hearings on the speaker law, Van Alstyne offered testimony and presented a memorandum on the constitutional issues inherent in the statute. (Pollitt did not participate in the Britt commission proceedings because he was away at the University of Oregon on a visiting professorship.) The Van Alstyne memorandum was an intellectual high point of the entire controversy. The document presented a compelling review of those decisions that resembled the issues of the North Carolina law. The memorandum also offered evidence strongly suggesting that the cases cited by the Moody memorandum as providing viable limitations on the First Amendment were almost exclusively limited to situations where the violent overthrow of government was involved. As such, Van Alstyne asserted, "they are irrelevant to the constitutionality of the speaker ban law." [15]

The memorandum also noted that the Moody document had omitted a plethora of relevant decisions bearing on the North Carolina case. Of these omissions, none was more egregious than that of *Egan v. Moore*. The *Egan* case seemed ideal for the deputy attorney general. A New York trial court had upheld the State University of New York at Buffalo's decision not to permit Aptheker to speak. Resonating with McCarthy-era judicial reasoning, the decision held that a constitutional limitation on free speech was enforceable since CP membership automatically denoted an advocacy of armed violence aimed at governmental overthrow. Handed down in 1962, the decision was highlighted by Moody as the most applicable for speaker bans at public universities. In his memorandum, Van Alstyne revealed that the lower court decision had been reversed in a unanimous decision by an appellate court. Even the most promising ruling cited as precedent by Moody had been struck down. Following the adoption of the new trustee policy and the General Assembly's enactment of the statutory revisions suggested by the Britt commission, Van Alstyne continued to see the modifications as unconstitutional. In his view, proscription of a speaker because of political affiliation or for having invoked Fifth Amendment privileges was unconstitutional whether it was by the statutory authority of a legislature or the regulatory agency of campus administrators.[16]

The Van Alstyne memorandum raised several crucial questions about the longevity of a speaker law. The memorandum reaffirmed and accelerated the momentum already gathering to reconstruct the statute. It did not, however, convince the conservative anticommunists at the core of the commission's activity to accept a contention that any anticommunist speaker law was unconstitutional. The law remained, for the commissioners, a political problem. The reversal in the *Egan* case and other federal and state precedents, however, presaged problems for any speaker law. Anticipating this issue, the Britt commission had already requested that Moody update his memorandum in consideration of recent federal court rulings concerning the CP and subversive activities. The deputy attorney general continued to maintain that the speaker ban was not an antisubversion statute but an "expression of a proprietor or landowner" to keep certain people off property. Any attempt to refuse the legislature, as a proprietor of a form of property, control of its property was to advocate socialism. Moody's view conflated private and public interests, with legislators able to exercise rights as owners. In reasserting the application of the 1852 *University v. Maultsby* decision, Moody ruminated about the political meaning of an invalidated speaker law. "Perhaps no rights of private property," he lamented, "remain any longer or are available to a landowner in this socialistic world."[17]

In responding to the Van Alstyne memorandum, Moody reversed his position on the similarity between private property and a public institution. He attempted to argue a curious distinction between public and nonpublic by claiming the memorandum irrelevant because of its author. Since Van Alstyne was a professor at Duke, a private, formerly ecclesiastical institution, there was "no reason [for him] to display such interest." Here was a conspicuous attempt at diversion. No one would accept the specious contention that the document was compromised or irrelevant because its author's employer was a private entity. Obsessed with the necessity of making a political statement about communists, Moody speculated that the attempt to condemn the anticommunist law was inconsistent with Duke's interests in funding the university. "One wonders whether the members of the Duke family, who derived their fortune from private enterprise, would be interested in hard core

Communists speaking on the campus of their university." The explanation of the reversal in *Egan v. Moore* was equally hollow. The New York court had ruled against a regulation of the Board of Regents, and since the North Carolina ban was a state statute, the decision did not apply.[18]

In addressing Van Alstyne's contention that the statute's vagueness rendered it unconstitutional, Moody revealed how intertwined anticommunism and racial politics were in his legal thought: "As to the attack made by Professor Van Alstyne on this statute, upon the theory that it is void for vagueness, [it] is no more vague than the various Federal Civil Rights Acts." The deputy attorney general's response to the Van Alstyne memorandum largely evaded the legal questions in favor of a polemic that inveighed against liberals, socialism, communists, and civil rights activists. For Moody, political exigency overrode constitutional considerations.[19]

The extent to which Moody ignored the constitutional questions raised by Britt's request for clarification was revealed further by his open advocacy of the General Assembly's withholding university appropriations should the statute be overturned. Moving from a legalistic position to a purely political one, Moody expressed a desire that even if the law were invalidated, a new statute should be enacted to ban dissident speakers: "We still think the people of the State will find some method of controlling the situation and we still believe that the General Assembly has the right to control the allocation of funds that it makes to institutions of higher learning." Moody would not retreat from his endorsement of the statute; its provisions reflected too clearly his own sentiments. To have acknowledged the statutory inadequacies of the speaker law would have required acceptance of the flaws in his own worldview. As might have been expected, publication of the contents of Moody's letter engendered a torrent of criticism of its improper political speculations. One Assembly member sternly rebuked Moody for having "used [his] office in an exceedingly unbecoming manner."[20]

Given the polemical cast of Moody's position and his refusal to consider the problems of First and Fourteenth Amendment protections, it was not surprising that the state decided to seek additional counsel as *Dickson v. Sitterson* began. In addition to Moody and Andrew Vanore from the attorney general's staff, the state retained William T. Joyner and his son, William T. Joyner Jr., to assist in making a defense that a federal court would find reasonable. In securing the elder Joyner, the state obtained counsel from a staunch conservative who had experience in creating judicial obstacles that would buy time for new political arrangements to be made.

With McNeill Smith of Greensboro representing the plaintiffs, the case against General Statutes 116-199 and 116-200 and the trustees' regulations closely followed the arguments put forth in the articles by Pollitt and Van

Alstyne. Along with the suit filed by Smith were amicus curiae briefs filed by Pollitt and others on behalf of the North Carolina Civil Liberties Union and by Van Alstyne for the AAUP. The reply briefs from the defendants attempted to persuade the court that the cardinal issue at stake in the suit was anticommunism. They sought to circumvent the plaintiffs' contention that the statute and its regulations violated constitutional standards by arguing that the amended law did not absolutely ban anyone. Discretion was left to the trustees and chancellors to adjudicate each invitation on the basis of its clear service to the "advantage of education." The bans of Aptheker and Wilkinson, the briefs argued, were not final; Chancellor J. Carlyle Sitterson's denial had left open the possibility that the invitations would be permitted during the next academic year. The claims of the plaintiffs were invalid, the state argued, because they were "predicated upon the existence of an active, absolute, *continuing* ban on such speakers." This legal strategy emphasized what the law's supporters viewed as a dramatic transformation in the statute's character following the 1965 amendment. Since formal proscription was supplemented by policy-based judgments, the criticism of constitutional violations was inapplicable.[21]

In place of precedent-setting decisions that involved communists speaking in state-supported venues, Moody and Joyner offered the sacrosanct legitimacy of statutory opposition to communism and communists. The essence of this anticommunist critique was an attempt to articulate a definition of communism as something foreign from and hostile to the university: the university was for education, while the CP was about "world domination." One brief contained a full thirteen pages of quotes culled from the youth report for the Eighteenth National Convention of the CPUSA. The CP material, while radical in tone and positing an opposition to capitalism and fascism, in no way advocated violent subversion or unlawful conduct. The document was augmented by extensive quotations from three "experts" in communism — in this case, from people who previously belonged to the party and now found service providing testimony on the insidious nature of the so-called communist conspiracy. The brief also quoted extensively from anticommunist standards of the Cold War, including Frank Kluckhohn's *The Naked Rise of Communism* and Dr. Fred Schwarz's *You Can Trust the Communists (to Be Communists)*. The defendants offered the court familiar terrain in which to ground the arguments and frame the appropriate precedents. The case, Moody and Joyner argued, did not concern constitutional rights but involved a legitimate right of legislators and educators to prevent a foreign and malicious group of conspirators from penetrating the university for their own sinister purposes.[22]

After a lengthy series of briefs and replies, the court heard final oral arguments on February 21, 1967. Smith emphasized that the statute imposed a "licensing system" for speakers through prior restraint and thus ran afoul of the Fourteenth Amendment. Speaking for the defense, William Joyner Jr. reiterated that the communists intended to "take over the university." The law and the regulations, he maintained, were entirely appropriate given the well-documented nature of communists. He argued that the plaintiffs' contentions were false by the "fact" that Chancellor Sitterson had "never denied one person the right to speak at UNC."[23]

Despite the defense's legerdemain in attempting to redefine the meaning of the suit, the body of judicial precedent appeared to support the plaintiffs' contention that constitutional safeguards had been broached. The statute continued to identify CP members as well as those taking the Fifth Amendment, and, most conspicuously, Aptheker and Wilkinson had been banned from speaking on the UNC campus. Prior decisions in a plethora of cases offered strong indication that simple CP membership was insufficient grounds for denying due process or equal protection of the law. And the decision in *Slochower v. Board of Education* suggested that use of the Fifth Amendment could not be the basis for denial of civil liberties.[24]

With the staggering body of precedent and case law, why did it take almost two years for the litigation process to run its expected course? The length of the deliberations had far more to do with contemporary politics and the familiar siren of anticommunism than with judicial reasoning. Furthermore, *Dickson v. Sitterson* coincided with intensification of U.S. involvement in Vietnam. Joyner and Moody hoped this set of political and ideological circumstances would enable the statute to survive judicial scrutiny. These two lawyers, who had earlier attempted to salvage the remnants of segregation as its ideological edifice was crumbling, now hoped to preserve a familiar political and cultural order by appealing to widely accepted assumptions of anticommunism.

The personal backgrounds of the three judges hearing the case were also a contributing factor. Since the suit challenged the constitutionality of a state statute, a three-judge panel was required. Judge Edwin M. Stanley of Greensboro, chief judge of the Middle District for North Carolina, selected judges Algernon L. Butler of Clinton, North Carolina, and Clement F. Haynsworth of Greenville, South Carolina, to assist in hearing the case. As the chief judge of the district in which the suit was filed, Stanley became an automatic member and presiding judge of the panel.

From the Eastern District, Butler had no personal or judicial background indicative of how he might respond to a case pitting constitutional issues against anticommunist ideals. There was, however, genealogical baggage that suggested that Butler might be inclined to overturn a law banning specified categories of speakers. Butler was the nephew of Marion Butler, a turn-of-the-century Populist leader and U.S. senator. In calling this information to Smith's attention, Frank Porter Graham revealed an interesting and possibly useful tidbit of information: Marion Butler had been denied speaking privileges at the university because he belonged to a dangerous political organization — the Republican Party. In his closing arguments, Smith related this sordid history to the panel, including how many well-known North Carolina jurists had opposed the earlier de facto speaker ban.[25]

The impact of the recitation of his famous uncle's earlier ban on Judge Butler cannot be known. But there was little in his past to indicate any intellectual or judicial embrace of the anticommunist imperatives offered by the defendants. However, such was not the case with his two colleagues. Their histories indicated a profoundly conservative temperament in one instance and a thorough acceptance of Red Scare ideology in the other. Haynsworth, a close associate of South Carolina Senator Strom Thurmond, had over the previous decade written numerous decisions defending racially segregated schools by barring application of the Supreme Court's decision in *Brown v. Board of Education*. A jurist who took a dim view of civil rights applied within a racial context, Haynsworth was intellectually inclined to accept the contention that civil liberties were not paramount in *Dickson v. Sitterson*.

Judge Stanley was most likely to be sympathetic to the anticommunist appeal. A significant portion of the trajectory of Stanley's career resulted from his zealous participation in North Carolina's most memorable McCarthy-era moment: the Smith Act trial of Junius Scales. Appointed to the federal bench by President Dwight Eisenhower, Stanley had gained public exposure as the federal attorney in the 1955 trial that convicted the former CP regional chairman to a six-year prison term. In his opening statement, Stanley had announced that the foundation of his case would be the party's alleged violent orientation. "Communism," said Stanley, threatened the "American way of life" and was little more than "a plot to destroy the government of this country." Stanley was not the only actor from the earlier anticommunist episode to reappear in the speaker ban trial. At the Scales trial, prosecutor Stanley had offered robust praise for the government's "expert" witnesses, including Ralph Clontz, who had also testified falsely before the Britt commission. Another witness in the Scales trial was John Lautner, whose authoritative expertise was now copiously displayed by the defendants in the speaker ban case.[26]

At the 1955 trial, Stanley had inveighed against the presence of Aptheker, a court spectator, daring the defense to call the CP figure as a witness. Now, more than a decade later, Stanley was presiding over a trial in which the state asked the court to validate its denial of Aptheker's right to speak. In Stanley's view, the issue in the earlier trial had not been Scales's guilt or innocence but whether the public approved of communism. In asking the jury to find Scales guilty, he implored the members to "show the world that Communism has no place in our own North Carolina." For Stanley, who had demonstrated an unstinting opposition to any manifestation of communism, the legal and political conundrums implicit in the speaker ban suit undoubtedly presented a personal intellectual dilemma. He would have to resolve his commitment to anticommunism with an almost certain understanding that the statute was constitutionally flawed. Furthermore, like Haynsworth, Stanley possessed an early record of judicial support for defending segregated schools. Stanley's appointment to the federal bench was enthusiastically endorsed by prosegregationist Democrats, principally U.S. Senator Sam J. Ervin Jr. and Representative Harold Cooley. After the Johnson administration's vigorous support of desegregation, Stanley's decisions displayed a marked bent toward enforcement of Supreme Court rulings, a transformation that suggests that his views on racial matters were largely political. However, anticommunism remained politically and ideologically potent.[27]

The unexpected lengthy delay in a ruling touched off speculation that the case was headed to the Supreme Court. This conjecture inferred that the district court might actually uphold the law. The state's attorneys expressed no intent or desire to pursue the constitutionality of the statute should their current effort fail. The most zealous defender of the statute, Moody, had called for a political response, stipulating that the legislature should enact a more stringent version. The fundamental factor, however, in the state's refusal to consider pursuit of the intrinsic constitutional issues was that its case had been predicated on a denial that any such issues existed in the case. Only a ruling in favor of the state would extend the suit to a possible review by the high court, as the plaintiffs alone would pursue appeal.[28]

Despite speculation about a Supreme Court hearing, a more plausible explanation for the delay was political rather than judicial. The delay suggested that the judges were conferencing about the language and tone of the ruling. Would it be limited to an exploration of the precedents presented by the plaintiffs? Would it offer a ringing endorsement of civil liberties and reiterate the constitutional limitations placed on the state in regulating behavior covered by the Bill of Rights? Or, most important, how would the decision address the anticommunist imperative emphasized by the state? Given the panel members' prior records, especially that of Judge Stanley, the ruling would almost certainly address the last of these questions.

On February 19, 1968, the panel handed down its decision. The court found North Carolina General Statutes 116-119 and 116-200 and the procedures and regulations adopted to enforce them "facially unconstitutional because of vagueness." The panel concluded that the revised 1965 speaker control law and its accompanying procedures were "null and void." The

constitutional objections long raised by opponents of the law had been validated. What opponents had not been able to achieve politically was now
accomplished by the rule of law.[29]

The university, the students, and most of the state's press immediately interpreted the ruling as a vindication. The Daily Tar Heel called the judgment a
victory for the university and academic freedom. In a brief statement, Friday
and Sitterson expressed a shared hope that the decision "brings this long and
costly controversy to an end." The Asheville Citizen, like many other dailies,
saw the ruling as confirmation that the statute had been a "bad law." Many
editorials echoed the tone of the Raleigh News and Observer in proposing how
the state should respond — "let it alone." The district court had issued its opinion that the statute was constitutionally flawed; any attempt to create an acceptable measure would be fraught with political acrimony and wrangling. In
the view of most of the press as well as the public, the Assembly's attention
would be better devoted to more practical issues.[30]

Despite the accolades and admonitions offered by the press, the opinion
was not an unmitigated condemnation of the statute. In its discussion, the
court clearly and unequivocally endorsed the cause of anticommunism. "This
Court is not blind to world affairs," it began, "the record in this case clearly
establishes that the communist conspiracy is dedicated to the destruction of
freedom." In language and reasoning resonating with contempt for student
activism, the panel accused the students of deliberately seeking "sensational-
ism" in inviting Aptheker and Wilkinson. Dismissing any possibility that the
students were motivated by faith in American ideals, the ruling claimed they
had pursued their strategy to the "neglect of academic responsibility." Conversely, the actions of the 1963 General Assembly and the special session of
1965 were held to be consistent with the "utmost good faith" in their concern
for the students' welfare and the "vexing problem" posed by visiting speakers.[31]

The ruling seemed to affirm the reasoning of legislators and trustees by stipulating that invitations to certain kinds of speakers might not serve the university's educational purposes: "One does not acquire an understanding of important racial problems by listening successively to a Stokeley [sic] Carmichael or
an H. Rap Brown and an officer of the Ku Klux Klan. Countering a Herbert
Aptheker with an official of the American Nazi Party may furnish excitement
for young people, but it presents no rational alternatives and has but dubious
value as an educational experience."[32]

In proclaiming certain kinds of speakers irrational extremists and dismissing
any possible educational value in their ideas, the rhetoric of the ruling closely
paralleled the political logic imposed on the UNC trustees in the fall of 1965.
The court implied that it was possible to objectively determine whether a
speaker would "serve the advantage of education." Ultimately, the court went

little beyond the "vagueness" of the law in its commentary. It went to un-
usual lengths, however, to reaffirm the ideological motive that had given rise
to the speaker ban law. In choosing Carmichael and Brown as its notorious
examples, the court inadvertently acknowledged that political context and
especially issues of race were pertinent in the law's formulation. The commentary did not stop here. It went on to offer implicit suggestions about a
satisfactory resolution of the constitutional difficulties raised by the law. Any
future statute, the judges noted, would need to contain more precise language
identifying the specific targets and intent.[33]

A close reading of the commentary offered no small measure of encouragement to supporters of continued anticommunist legislation to regulate the
universities. From his editorial booth at WRAL, Jesse Helms quickly and accurately concluded that the ruling had "commended the principle of keeping
communists off the campus." With obvious pleasure, Helms noted that the
federal panel's language resonated with the language and logic of those defending the fundamental integrity of the speaker law. "The federal judges," he
concluded, "differed with the legislature only in the wording of the law, not
with its principle and intent."[34]

Helms believed that the ruling had pinpointed alternative possibilities for
the construction of a new law. Although it voided the statute, the court's language was muted by its reaffirmation of the need to battle a sinister "conspiracy." The conservative editorialist used his review of the decision to call
on the legislature to quickly draft a new measure consonant with the court's
instructions: "Now it is a whole new ball game. The federal judges have upheld, even commended, the spirit of the law, and have given fairly precise
instructions as to how it should be rewritten in order to withstand constitutional tests in the future. Almost any schoolboy could take the old law, insert
a few words of definition, and hand it to a state legislator for introduction in
the next session of the legislature." Although the state attorney general's office
did not call explicitly for legislative action on a new measure, Bruton's response echoed Helms's conclusions. The attorney general issued a statement
that concluded, "We think the Court has approved our positions and objectives but has simply said that we do not have the proper statutory and regulatory procedures to carry out these objectives."[35]

That Helms had accurately assessed the political character of the ruling was
confirmed by Van Alstyne. Although relieved that the capricious law had been
overturned, the Duke law professor termed the outcome a "marginal, almost
Pyrrhic, victory" for those seeking an affirmation of constitutional rights and
academic freedom. Van Alstyne recognized that contemporary political concerns—student dissidence and growing opposition to authority—as well as
personal ideology profoundly influenced the thinking of the three judges. He

acknowledged the larger implications of the decision with understatement: the panel, he noted, was "not wildly enthusiastic about our case." Van Alstyne found evidence of the court's political proclivity in its criticism of the student plaintiffs who were the nominal beneficiaries of the judgment. Political values produced the odd commentary because the issue of student dissent was unnecessary to the merits of the case, and, as the Duke professor astutely recognized, the students had been "models of restraint."[36]

Any response to the ruling from the state would be enunciated by Governor Dan K. Moore, who met with his advisers and with the attorneys to assess the possibility of further legal action. He also briefly considered requesting a revised statute from the General Assembly. Eager to end the acrimonious controversy, Moore quickly decided to pursue neither avenue. In a public statement on February 22, the governor announced that the decision in *Dickson v. Sitterson* would not be appealed. He noted, however, the court's confirmation of the trustees' right to establish speaker regulations. The governor's response was aimed at resolution of two political problems: it avoided a potentially nasty and protracted legislative battle while adopting the court's call for restraint of political speakers. Moore called on the trustees and UNC administrators to "adopt reasonable rules and regulations within the framework of this opinion." While there would be no speaker law, there would be a speaker policy to marginalize radicals and regulate political behavior within parameters considered acceptable to the trustees.[37]

President Friday and the trustees did not require prodding from Moore to begin immediately considering a new speaker policy. Recognizing the political opportunity and vacuum created by the voiding of the statute and its procedures, Friday quickly moved to have the trustees draft a policy acknowledging conservative concerns about control and order. At the same time, Friday and the trustees insured that the new policy would contain no form of prior restraint by refusing to deny any specified group or persons access to the campus.[38]

Within a week of the decision, the trustees had approved interim guidelines for regulating visiting speakers. Friday and his principal allies on the Executive Committee, most notably Victor Bryant and George Watts Hill, hoped to gain approval of a new policy that would effectively end the matter. If a new policy could be constructed with preemptive dispatch, it would throw UNC critics on the defensive. More specifically, it would deny conservative, pro–speaker law forces an opening to call for a revised statute.[39]

The Friday maneuver did not go according to plan. Two trustees, former State Senator Cameron Weeks of Tarboro and Tom White, contended that a new statute — one capable of banning undesirable speakers — was still needed. Weeks and White argued for delay by warning that precipitous action would likely set off a firestorm of criticism in the next session of the legislature. The usually vociferous White urged "calm deliberation" and called for careful study and construction of a new policy. The legislators sought to move the policy issue into the Board of Trustees' Executive Committee, where it might still be possible to create regulations barring communists and other radicals.[40]

The crucial problem in creating a new statement of policy, however, lay in an evolving recognition by conservatives that visiting speakers were not the cause of the political agitation emanating from the campuses. A new policy would need to reflect this realization and bridge the distance between a concern with external speakers — that is, "outside agitators" — and protests indigenous to the campus. White himself continued to call for strict disciplinary measures against dissident faculty. He alleged that "the power or duty to discipline members of the faculty for such actions that are bad for the University . . . hasn't been exercised and I think that's bad." With the governor ruling out further legal action in defense of the speaker ban and prospects fading for a new statute, a restrictive speaker policy was the last best hope for conservatives.[41]

The conservatives' plan to forestall expeditious approval of a new policy was met with growing irritation at the lack of action. Trustees H. L. Riddle of Morganton and Virginia Lathrop of Asheville demanded immediate action. "If we start again down the path of studying the speaker ban and not doing anything about it," exclaimed Lathrop, "we're not getting anywhere." Faced with a possible impasse, the trustees adopted a motion by former State Senator Lunsford Crew to adopt the interim regulations. The temporary guidelines were virtually identical to the regulations adopted in 1965 but lacked mention of any specific category of speakers. Conspicuously absent was any reference to communists or those taking the Fifth Amendment. The regulations stressed a commitment to "balance" public addresses to insure that "all sides" would be presented.[42]

Adoption of the interim guidelines was a momentary victory for White; the policy issue went to the Executive Committee, as he had desired, but conservative hopes faded as the committee was unable to create a statement devoid of the restrictive language invalidated by the court case. The committee was supplanted by a special ad hoc committee appointed by Governor Moore to study the problem and bring a recommendation to the executive board. After several months of deliberation, the special committee presented its recommended "Policy and Regulations Regarding Visiting Speakers." The Executive Committee unanimously endorsed the proposal verbatim and sent it on to the full board for final approval.[43]

On May 27, 1968, with scant dissent, the Board of Trustees approved the new policy and regulations. Although shorn of the explicit anticommunism of the prior policy, the new document was no less a political statement. It resonated with the thought and rhetoric of those who had conceived, promulgated, and defended North Carolina's contribution to American anticommunism. While refusing to identify or summarily reject any particular category of speaker, the new policy echoed the language and assumptions of the recently nullified version: "[V]isits of speakers who represent any ideology or form of government that is alien to our basic institutions shall be infrequent, and on such occasions necessary care shall be exercised to insure that the campuses shall not be exploited as convenient outlets of discord and strife."[44]

In articulating and approving this statement, those responsible for governing the university capitulated to political anxiety and to provincial fears of difference and heterogeneity. That which was culturally familiar and dominant was privileged by an institution ostensibly devoted to the professed values of eclecticism. The restrictive components of the policy, along with the still-cumbersome regulations for inviting speakers, offered implicit acknowledgment of political defeat by the university. As UNC had been unsuccessful in mobilizing legislative support for abolition of a vindictive law, it now moved in fearful reaction to what its leaders believed might become manifest as another speaker law or, worse still, direct retribution in the form of reduced appropriations. The policy language limiting controversial speakers and attempting to constrict political protests reflected tacit acceptance of conservative fears of political mobilization on the campus. The restrictive language was taken almost verbatim from White's proposal. As a member of the special ad hoc policy committee, White could be outvoted, but he could not be ignored.[45]

In releasing the new policy statement, President Friday expressed relief and sought to put a gloss on the political character of the language. As he announced that the new policy "brings to an end the Speaker Ban controversy in North Carolina," Friday disingenuously claimed that the status quo ante had been restored on terms favorable to UNC. Such an optimistic conclusion was only partially accurate. There was no longer a speaker ban, but the university acknowledged the cultural politics of antiradicalism. Equally important, UNC recognized the power of the General Assembly to compel surveillance of campus activities. No less than before, UNC would be expected to adhere to the political expectations of legislators and the cultural values of a public mistrustful of intellectuals.[46]

The conclusion of the speaker ban era found the university battered, with its sense of institutional autonomy badly compromised. UNC was no longer confident of its role as a cultural agent and arbiter within the state. The controversy firmly established Helms's bona fides as a spokesman for cultural conservatism. The incipient political career of the editorialist resulted in no small part from his adroit exploitation of the multifaceted issues of the speaker ban and his portrayal of UNC as an institution at odds with the cultural mores of many North Carolinians.

Helms's victory in asserting the propriety of legislative control of campus political activity also reflected the weakness of North Carolina liberalism in defending academic freedom and political dissent. No less than much of the state's "progressive" leadership, UNC leaders throughout the period refused to confront those forces attempting to subject the campus to stringent political controls. Preferring power to principle, UNC administrators compromised the academy's standards to preserve what they believed to be long-term institutional interests.

During the ensuing decade, UNC would experience prodigious growth as its physical plant and academic programs were continually expanded from the largesse of the state treasury. But something had been lost during the 1960s. As an alternative source of authority, UNC had slipped from the position it had nurtured and occupied since the 1930s. And the course of the speaker ban debacle traced the university's decline as a force within the state's political culture. While Helms celebrated the outcome of the controversy and continued to fulminate that UNC be "cleaned up," UNC could only offer a curious praise for its foremost critic. As a Raleigh civic club honored Helms in 1971 as its man of the year, President Friday commended the recipient: "Nothing is more essential to the maintenance of freedom and the security of our nation than the right to express one's views openly and freely. Jesse Helms has long been committed to this democratic principle." Coming in the aftermath of the speaker ban, this was a strange accolade inasmuch as Helms had been at the forefront of the effort to muzzle dissenting expression. After a decade of compromise and occasional collaboration with forces not committed to academic liberty, UNC was having difficulty recognizing the opposition.[47]

12 Beyond the Speaker Ban

The creation of a new speaker policy did not put the issue of radical speakers to rest. During the 1969 session of the General Assembly a spate of bills were introduced that expressed a desire to curtail campus radicalism. One attempted to revive the speaker ban; others sought to suspend, expel, and rescind grants from students who participated in activities deemed disorderly and disruptive. The General Assembly bills that would "regulate the use of sound-amplifying equipment" and allow campus officials to "designate periods of time" during which the campus would be "off-limits and subject to curfew" would apply to anyone who was not a student, a faculty or staff member, or, most pointedly, a national guardsman. House Bill 985, one of the few that was enacted, revoked all state financial aid to students convicted of any charges resulting from campus unrest. Associating political behavior with personal order and cleanliness, the legislature also adopted a resolution asking the chancellors of the state-supported universities to require students to keep their dormitory rooms clean. Although the legislature avoided the draconian speaker ban, the 1969 General Assembly remained no less determined than its predecessors to scrutinize and regulate political behavior at the state's public campuses. The sponsors of the various bills came predominantly from the rural eastern counties or from counties with substantial black populations and included J. F. Mohn of Onslow, Julian Allsbrook of Halifax, Julian Fenner of Edgecombe, William Watkins of Granville, and Allen Barbee of Nash, who had also been one of the cosponsors of the speaker ban bill in 1963. The legislature considered these measures as the President's Commission on the Causes and Prevention of Violence, chaired by Dr. Milton Eisenhower, was warning against such laws. In its first statement, the commission noted that "such efforts are likely to spread, not reduce the difficulty."[1]

If the bills enacted indicated the legislature's growing concern with campus activism, those measures that were defeated demonstrated the depth of its acrimony and obsession. A centerpiece of this effort was a bill requiring all students and their parents to sign a "good behavior" contract prior to enrolling in classes. If involved in campus "disturbances," a student could be expelled or suspended for violation of the pledge. This bill, of dubious legal weight, was quickly voted down by a House committee. The most charged measure, one reminiscent of the speaker ban bill, was an attempt to remove all discretionary authority from campus administrators in dealing with student protests. Proposed by Representative Watkins, House Bill 551 mandated a four-year expulsion for any student refusing to obey an order from "any administrative officer or employee" to vacate a university facility. Any student charged with violating the statute would be allowed to appeal to the Executive Committee of the Board of Trustees. Other than the "duty to make written report of the offense within twenty-four hours," the campus administration would be bypassed entirely. The Watkins bill passed in the House by a narrow two-vote margin but died in a Senate committee following objections to its lack of due process for students and its elimination of any intermediary role for administrators.[2]

Although failing to mention communists or to identify any groups for proscription, the campus control measures generated by the 1969 Assembly emanated from a concern similar to that which led to the now notorious speaker ban law. Both measures were implicit statements of mistrust by conservative politicians who did not believe campus officials to be sufficiently zealous in monitoring and forestalling student activism on the Left. Echoing Jesse Helms's remonstrations, critics charged that administrators were permitting students to run roughshod, disrupting the university's educational functions. One such critic was Henderson attorney Robert G. Kittrell. In a letter to UNC President William C. Friday, Kittrell noted "the consensus of opinion in our county" and called for "a firm hard line with both students and faculty." In March 1969 one of the sponsors of the good-conduct bill, Representative Worth Gentry of Stokes County, submitted a questionnaire to the trustees that attempted to assess their views about handling campus disorder. The questionnaire was politically coded and suggested that the trustees should support a get-tough response. These concerns had their effect. Governor Robert Scott increasingly adopted a hard line, warning the trustees to take decisive action to end the "indecision, delay, and vacillation and gain control of the situation" in his address to a closed meeting of the trustees' Executive Committee on March 14. The committee subsequently publicized the text of the address.[3]

This new challenge to campus autonomy closely approximated the concerns that had fueled the speaker ban law's conception. In each case, restrictive and punitive legislation followed highly publicized activities that challenged core assumptions of political culture. Both responses spoke fundamentally to issues of racial etiquette and hierarchy and a generationally coded threat to vested authority. The speaker ban resulted from the conspicuous involvement of students and faculty in civil rights demonstrations before the vengeful eyes of the 1963 General Assembly. The efforts of the 1969 legislature to censor and control campus radicalism came in the aftermath of student participation in an acrimonious and protracted March strike by black food-service workers at UNC. As the strike intensified and student leaders enforced a boycott of Lenoir Hall, the center of the strike, North Carolina's civil authorities grew restive at the students' increased militancy and UNC authorities' recalcitrance to crush the protest. Assembly members and UNC critics were outraged that no students had been suspended or expelled for their involvement in "disrupting" the university. Responding to the increasing political pressure, in March Governor Scott adopted a tough law-and-order stance. When minor scuffling broke out and students set up an alternative eating spot in a campus building, Scott ordered sixty state troopers onto the campus. More than a hundred faculty and graduate students threatened a walkout unless the troops were withdrawn. Despite the fact that no serious violation of the law had occurred, UNC was occupied by armed troops. Echoes of the concerns that had spawned the speaker ban resonated in the rhetoric of legislators incensed by the apparent unwillingness of UNC officials to forcefully end student disquiet. Representative R. C. Soles of Columbus County encapsulated a theme permeating the various measures: a bill requiring mandatory expulsion of troublemakers and other measures "have let the college officials know how we feel." Many legislators believed that their proprietary obligation as representatives of the "owners" of the university had been violated. Here again was the contention that a public institution was akin to private property. In this view, the managers of the property, the UNC administration, had failed to deal sternly with those abusing the property. Another potent consideration was student support for the demands of black food-service workers for a collective bargaining agreement and recognition of their union. In a political culture that valorized the sanctity of the right to work, strikes by obdurate workers were anathema, especially when those workers were black. Not only were the students seen as unruly and disrespectful of adult authority, but they were also supporting political actions that symbolically struck at the state's system of racial authority and class power. Regardless of the fact that no laws had been violated, such a threat could not be tolerated.[4]

Worth Gentry, one of the sponsors of the good-behavior bill, was incensed by UNC officials lobbying against the bill, which would have mandated expulsion of disobedient students: "We felt like and the public feels like some legislation is necessary. The people are disappointed in the way the administrators handled those who have taken over buildings and interfered with normal campus activities. They didn't even reprimand them. They didn't suspend any."[5]

While few of the bills became law, the torrent of campus control legislation achieved its strategic purpose. It was a none-too-subtle reminder to UNC administrators of the Assembly's power to intervene and bring the campus into line with hegemonic expectations. Once again, campus officials were placed on notice by anxious and angry legislators. The University of North Carolina was neither free nor independent; it belonged to the taxpayers, who had a sacrosanct right to expect cultural conformity from those benefiting from the property. The Assembly's spring 1969 message was a clear reminder of the drastic action that had been taken six years earlier. Either the administrators would cooperate in identifying and controlling dissident students, or the legislature would once again assert its power.[6]

During the remainder of 1969 and into the following spring, UNC officials had the opportunity to demonstrate their readiness to cooperate in clamping down on student protesters. As student opposition to the widening war in Southeast Asia intensified, police and intelligence agencies stepped up their efforts to monitor and preempt campus radicalism. The State Bureau of Investigation (SBI) sought and received formal assistance from the university in carefully monitoring student dissidents. President Friday designated a "campus contact" at each UNC school to provide "ready reference" as SBI officials conducted a campaign of political intelligence. The agency published a weekly "Civil Intelligence Calendar" of campus political activities that was circulated to various police agencies and university officials.[7]

The result of this collaboration was stepped-up surveillance of legitimate political activity, an action guided by the inference that the protests were subversive. In several instances, the SBI intelligence calendar stated that student radicals were using campus facilities to openly offer instruction in violence, vandalism, and wanton campus disorder. This "civil intelligence" focused almost exclusively on two forms of activity: African American liberation protests at the historically black colleges and antiwar mobilizations at the state's predominantly white campuses. In this manner, the SBI alleged that an orientation workshop for high school students by the Afro-American Student Organization at Fayetteville State University should be closely watched. At the same time, a similar workshop at North Carolina A&T State University was alleged to be for the purpose of holding "classes on disruption of schools, fire bombing and so forth."[8]

The first faculty antiwar gesture to become a public issue was deftly handled by President Friday and Chancellor J. Carlyle Sitterson in a manner suggesting that radical sentiment would be protected at UNC. When political science professor Lewis Lipsitz publicly remarked in early 1968 that the "worst possible outcome of the Vietnam War would be an American victory," his words were eagerly seized by Reese Gardner, a congressional candidate desperately searching for an issue. Gardner quickly dispatched a telegraph to Friday demanding that Lipsitz be fired.[9]

Sensing an emotional issue, the questionable patriotism of the University, Helms attempted to exploit it as yet further evidence of UNC's deviance from cultural norms. In so doing, Helms sought to expand the matter's significance beyond the professor's words. What really mattered, according to the editorialist, was not Lipsitz's "crackpot statement" but the university's "posture." In this instance, Helms was concerned that the university did not make a political statement of its own. Since "countless thousands of taxpayers" shared Gardner's sentiment, campus officials were duty bound to make a statement putting UNC on the side of this putative majority.[10]

Fresh from the embarrassments of the speaker ban debacle, Friday and Sitterson quickly dismissed any suggestion that Lipsitz be punished. The institution's leaders also did not want to insinuate their endorsement of a foreign policy that increasing numbers among the campus community considered a failure, immoral, or both. In responding to the telegram, Friday and Sitterson issued a simple statement defending the professor's right, as a citizen and as a member of an intellectual community, to express his opinion. The problem with that response, in Helms's view, was not that the university was improperly engaging in politics but, ironically, that it was being insufficiently political. The failure to disclaim the professor's statement, Helms contended, offered implicit encouragement for radicals. The university was thus "bound — in the long run — to encourage other noisy left-wing extremists on the faculties to feel free to downgrade America, and give aid and comfort to communism, in the implicit name of the University." This message carried a familiar refrain: once again, UNC was betraying its public trust by providing a safe haven for those with views foreign and dangerous to the body politic.[11]

Helms and other UNC critics did not need to be inordinately concerned about the lack of a decisive response from the administration. While opposed to any restrictions or punitive responses to dissenting speech from faculty, officials had initiated steps to oversee and prohibit faculty and student activities that were deemed disruptive. In the aftermath of the speaker ban, President Friday and the trustees identified behaviors that would not be tolerated. In response to complaints that insurgent faculty members were missing classes to organize protests, steps were taken that mandated that faculty face disciplinary action and possible termination if they missed or canceled classes for political reasons.

On March 14, 1969, the Executive Committee of the Board of Trustees passed a resolution defining "the offense of disruption of [the] educational processes of the University." The resolution was an interim attempt to define conduct and identify the requisite grounds for suspension and/or dismissal. For both students and faculty, involvement in "activities impairing, impeding, or disrupting the educational processes of the University" was declared an appropriate reason for suspension, expulsion, or termination. The resolution also declared that "neglect of duty" and "misconduct of a nature as to indicate that the faculty member is unfit to continue as a member of the faculty" were grounds for termination. The trustees' resolution was clearly prompted by campus political conditions. And the nebulous character of definition left open the possibility for misapplication and abuse.[12]

Cognizant that younger faculty were more inclined to support and engage in political protest, a screening process was installed that would foreclose the hiring of activist faculty. All department heads received a directive that instructed them to investigate the prior political activities of prospective appointments. New appointees were to answer a questionnaire about whether they had been involved in "disruptive activity" elsewhere. The certification would be required of all new hires. Although all ranks would be affected, most of the new appointees would be assistant professors, graduate teaching assistants, and part-time instructors, all of whom were typically younger and potentially more sympathetic to protest politics. Although the department heads recognized the impropriety of such a litmus test, few openly complained. To be sure, there was concern about and opposition to the implications of certifying political behavior prior to a hire. The Faculty Senate at North Carolina State University adopted a resolution opposing the trustee directive. For the most part, however, department heads dutifully provided assurances that their new appointments were free of disruptive tendencies.[13]

On July 7 the trustees approved the formal policy, which mandated the discharge of any faculty member "who willfully fails or refuses to carry out validly assigned duties." With students and faculty placed on notice to moderate their behavior, the university committed itself to a policy of policing campus political activity. Under penalty of dismissal, faculty members were prohibited from canceling or missing class for political reasons. If a boycott or strike was called to facilitate a mass antiwar action, it would be difficult if not impossible for faculty members to participate. Also implicit was an affirmation that faculty members should contain students with course activities, thus further crippling any efforts at campuswide mobilization.[14]

The critical test of the university's resolve to enforce the policy came with Vietnam Moratorium Day on October 15. On campuses across the nation, students and sympathetic faculty were planning a massive demonstration of opposition to the war. Students were asked to boycott classes and attend rallies intended to convince the Nixon administration of the depth of popular anti–Vietnam War feeling. UNC faculty members — along with several thousand students — did participate in the moratorium, but it is unlikely that many missed or canceled classes to do so. Aware of the event's public exposure, UNC officials were eager to prove to restive critics their resolve in enforcing the disruption policy. Prior to the event, faculty members were warned that missing class would result in disciplinary action. The university threatened to make an example of any faculty member violating the letter or spirit of the policy. Friday and Sitterson announced their intention to investigate possible violations of the policy.[15]

Shortly after the implementation of the new disruption policy on September 12, Gerhard Lenski, chair of the sociology department, complained to Friday about the severity of the penalty for violation. In the professor's view, automatic dismissal was far out of proportion to the nature of the violation. It was, said Lenski, "a matter of simple justice, the punishment seems disproportionate to the offense. It is like sending a man to jail for stealing a loaf of bread." While Lenski's point was undoubtedly apt, the severe punishment was obviated by the political predicament that Friday faced. The trustees, no less than the Assembly, were determined to clamp down on campus protests. Fairness was not a part of the solution to what they perceived to be wanton disorder.[16]

Professor Lenski's concern was soon borne out. David Blevins, a part-time instructor in the School of Social Work at UNC-Charlotte, had informed his class of his intended absence on October 15. It was difficult to hold that he had neglected his duty, however; he had made arrangements with the students for "alternative ways to insure that course work would not be interrupted." Nevertheless, a faculty hearing committee, which included two students and the superintendent of the local water-filtration plant, voted four to three that Blevins was guilty of willful violation of the policy. Friday promptly notified Blevins that he would not be rehired. Charging that the policy was "overbroad, chilling political conduct," Blevins contended that it not only violated standards of academic freedom but constitutional principles as well. The young instructor appealed to the AAUP to support his reinstatement, but the organization was loathe to defend someone who was not actually dismissed but simply not rehired. Despite the overtly political character of UNC's action and its excessively punitive tenor, the AAUP remained on the sidelines.[17]

Believing the action a violation of due process and refusing to allow it to possibly jeopardize his academic career, Blevins filed suit in federal court. On

September 8, 1971, federal District Judge Eugene Gordon issued a ruling that denied Blevins's claim for reinstatement and, more important, explicitly validated the disruption policy. The ruling concluded that the disciplinary measure had not deprived the plaintiff of any constitutional rights and that the "resolution and the procedures utilized to implement the same . . . are in harmony with the First and Fourteenth Amendments." [18]

In the end, Blevins was dismissed by the university for exigencies similar to those that militated the quiet elimination of Nicholas Bateson during the speaker ban. In both instances, the university's larger interests — retention of power and authority in its own hands — resulted in the elimination of political elements offensive to conservative critics. There were, to be sure, important differences between the two episodes. Bateson's employment was discontinued as a preemptive measure — to forestall conservative criticism that UNC was knowingly employing a communist radical. The Blevins case was, first and foremost, an example to both angry legislators and campus protesters. The stern and punitive application of the policy offered clear demonstration to the General Assembly of UNC's willingness to aggressively enforce the disruptions policy. This result would service an important political objective: it would preclude any legislation circumventing the authority of Friday and the chancellors.

By the time of the moratorium, UNC officials were determined to remedy the humiliation of seeing themselves bypassed and their authority ignored by politicians seeking to bring to a halt virtually every expression of campus radicalism and insurgency at the state's public colleges and universities. The speaker ban, the occupation of UNC by state police, and the frenzied series of campus control bills had taken their toll on an embattled and weary UNC administration. In no mood to tolerate willful violation of its policies, regardless of how politicized those policies had become, UNC officials wheeled into line with the expectations of those who demanded conformity from the university. At the end of a tumultuous decade, UNC was enunciating a clear demarcation between political speech and political behavior. Having survived the speaker ban, UNC officials were determined to preserve the appearance of academic integrity. They were, however, equally adamant that student and faculty political activism would not threaten institutional interests vis-à-vis the General Assembly.

A refractory faculty, however, was not the source of UNC's continuing difficulties with the legislature and aroused citizens like Charles H. Reynolds, a prominent textile manufacturer and past president of the North Carolina State University Alumni Association, who demanded that the school "blow the whistle on this kind of activity." An increasingly restive student body, angered by the duplicity of Nixon administration policy in Southeast Asia and growing awareness of the callous exploitation of American racism, posed problems for UNC authorities. Because students could not be fired, other means of checking their behavior had to be devised. Although the disruption policy contained clauses applicable to students, it could not carry punitive measures for skipping classes to take part in demonstrations and other forms of protest. And despite the demise of SDS and SSOC, there remained nascent efforts to restore a radical presence at UNC, including the Chapel Hill Revolutionary Society; the New University Conference, a faculty affiliate of SDS; the Black Student Movement; the women's liberation movement; and the *Protean Radish*, a publication whose mission was to "convey the leftist political ideas of its writers to the university community." [19]

Unwilling to be so illiberal as to blatantly prohibit dissidence, the university administration opted for surveillance. The result was a collaboration with police agencies who cared little about the legitimacy of protest and who were, in many instances, actively attempting to disrupt and destroy leftist organizations. Much of this effort at UNC focused on SDS. Although becoming increasingly fragmented and enjoying little support from other students, UNC-SDS, like chapters elsewhere, had been ensnared by the FBI's Counterintelligence Program. Devised by J. Edgar Hoover, the program was launched in 1967 to "neutralize"—that is, destroy—black nationalist and, eventually, New Left organizations. At UNC collaboration and informing by various personnel took a grievous toll as students were spied on, lost employment, and acquired secret dossiers that continued to follow them after they left Chapel Hill. [20]

Spying on SDS began soon after the chapter was formed. Arthur Beaumont, the head of campus police, was present at most of its meetings and campus actions, and Dean C. O. Cathey sought information on the group and carefully compiled a record of its activities. While there is little evidence that Cathey shared his documentation of UNC-SDS with federal authorities, by the spring of 1966 sources within the UNC administration and possibly the faculty were supplying information to the FBI. When SDS sought permission to hold a campus rally, an informer told the agency and provided a description of the event. When SDS and SSOC organized a sit-in and picketing of a Dow Chemical recruiter, the FBI was tipped off, and agents were dispatched to watch developments. [21]

As the Nixon administration's obsession with student opposition grew, simple surveillance evolved into a campaign to discredit and punish. By 1969 the financial resources of UNC-SDS members had become a focal point of FBI interest. The agency was particularly concerned with the possibility of federal funds supporting SDS students. If such funding, in the way of employment or scholarship, could be identified, its withdrawal would further the

FBI's political agenda. The loss of employment income or scholarship money might compel a student to limit or withdraw from political activity. In a more pernicious manner, the loss of funding might derail a career within the academy. At the very least, however, the loss of financial resources would punish students by making life more difficult. This objective was affirmed by the political assumption that animated the program: the federal government should not be "subsidizing persons who are not supporting that government."[22]

Much of the FBI's scrutiny of UNC-SDS was targeted at its most conspicuous activist. Leslie Gerald "Jerry" Carr had joined the chapter shortly after its formation in 1965 and by the fall of 1966 was its most visible figure, publishing letters and newspaper articles and organizing antiwar activities. The FBI had long been aware of Carr's SDS activism, and following his involvement and arrest in the Dow Chemical protest stepped up its effort to harass him. In December 1969 a UNC informant reported that Carr was the recipient of indirect funding from a federal source. The agent in charge informed his superiors that the "established source advised subject is currently employed as a graduate assistant in the School of Library Science and being paid $2,520 (tax exempt) for 12 months work. He is being paid entirely from federal funds."[23]

The special agent in the Charlotte office reported the exposure of Carr's employment directly to the FBI director's office. The information, along with other documentation establishing Carr as a New Left activist, was then sent to a variety of federal agencies, foremost among them NASA, which, it had been learned, provided the funds used to employ Carr. The FBI's objective became explicit: to have the funding withdrawn. Filing the report as a "Pending Counterintelligence Action," the special agent notified Hoover's office that a letterhead memorandum had been sent to NASA "with the objective that perhaps CARR's employment and source of funds will be terminated." In early April the agent reported "tangible results." He noted that the memo had been sent "and apparently it got results inasmuch as on 4/3/70 [a UNC source] advised as of 2/1/70, his employment paid for by NASA funds was terminated." The report cited the difficulties Carr would likely incur as he was forced to accept a part-time position that paid only $375 for the entire semester. The outcome served perfectly the agency's political objective: "This action has not only placed financial pressures on this New Leftist, but has resulted in a savings to the Federal Government."[24]

One result of this pattern of harassment was that by mid-1970 organized student activism at UNC had waned noticeably. The remnants of the two principal radical groups, SDS and SSOC, were in disarray. The UNC chapter of SSOC had been formed in the fall of 1968. Its leading figure was George Vlasits, a graduate student from Hackensack, New Jersey. Editing the newsletter, Vlasits devoted considerable space to his own involvement and his increasing problems with the selective service system. Another organizer was Lyn Wells, who had been active in SNCC and SSOC for some time. Of college age herself, Wells had not attended college but had left high school in Maryland to go South as a full-time organizer. She became one of SSOC's most effective workers. The transitional problems of replacing leaders and members also produced organizational stagnation in SDS. By early 1970 Carr and Gary Waller, the two remaining figures from SDS's speaker ban origins, had departed UNC, Waller to Oregon and Carr to California. Left behind was a younger, newer cohort of students without the experienced leadership and political skills needed to perpetuate a viable organizational presence. While these activists were eager, the absence of seasoned leadership undermined any hope of continuity. It is ironic that the events of the spring of 1970 demonstrated the remaining possibilities for student mobilization. Following exposure of the Vietnam War's expansion into Cambodia and Laos and the killing of students at Kent State University, a brief but successful student strike did occur at UNC. However, the radicalism of the action was blunted by support from an unlikely source, the UNC administration. Like many other Americans, the administration agreed with the students that the war was morally flawed and issued a criticism of the Cambodian invasion. For the first time during the era, the UNC administration, led by President Friday, took a public stand on a partisan issue. Friday and the chancellors sent a telegram to the state's congressional delegation expressing serious reservations about the war and sympathy for the student protest.[25]

The Cambodia–Kent State protests, however, failed to provide a basis for student activism by SDS or any other group. In the end, UNC-SDS suffered much the same fate as national SDS; its last partisans were swept into a vortex of factional and sectarian disputes. Members of SDS-SSOC, the last New Left formation at UNC, participated in the internecine warfare that occurred as Progressive Labor sought an internal takeover of SDS. In doing so, the PL members increasingly became ideologically rigid and eventually endorsed the abolition of SSOC rather than allowing it to remain independent and thus vulnerable to PL influences. UNC-SDS had originated with a nonsectarian commitment to social justice, civil liberties, and nonviolence. It ended in a cauldron of federal surveillance and harassment, strident sectarianism, and a more-radical-than-thou polemics.

The demise of the New Left, nationally and at UNC, was not as apparent to the state's chief conservative critic. Still believing UNC politically suspect, Helms continued to advocate repression as the only way to control the institution. In a letter to Tom White, his fellow conservative and longtime friend, Helms observed, "I have the feeling that no college or university — be it UNC or Duke, or any other — is ever going to be cleaned up piecemeal. It's going to require a big broom." [26] But contrary to Helms's absolutist contention, the university had been "cleaned up." Although unwilling to silence speech, it had taken clear and decisive steps to circumscribe the political behavior of students and faculty. With UNC staff members supplying vindictive police agencies with information on activists, the open political space at the campus was badly eroded.

The ravages of the decade, including a series of political reversals, convinced UNC officials to find some means of accommodating their critics. The battles of the 1960s threw UNC into a defensive posture, and the university's relative autonomy to operate apart from the influences of the larger political culture was compromised in ways that would not be easily rectified.

CONCLUSION

As in many states and localities throughout the country, North Carolina endured a contentious period in the 1960s as opposing social forces struggled for cultural hegemony. The decade witnessed the demise of the ideological underpinnings that had governed the state's social relations and political life since the turn of the century. North Carolina's political economy and demographic structure had been greatly transformed after World War II, and the corresponding shifts in political culture became open and pronounced as the edifice of Jim Crow crumbled in the early 1960s. Unquestioning adherence to racial separatism remained a core value of the rural, small-town conservatives who continued to exercise overweening power in the state legislature. Beginning with the momentous implications of the *Brown v. Board of Education* decision in 1954, the elements of traditional politics started to become unglued. This process accelerated with the direct-action phase of the civil rights movement that began in Greensboro in 1960. Urban blacks, with youth in the vanguard, took decisive steps to overturn the racial practices and laws that forced them into second-class citizenship. During the spring of 1963, Jim Crow entered the terminal phase of its notorious career.

As the segregation system that had buttressed the political power of small-town conservatives faced the juggernaut of civil rights protests, it also became apparent that other elements of the state's political culture were ascending. The major urban areas stepped forward to claim their rightful share of representation in the legislature. The satisfaction of this demand dramatically reconfigured the nature of public discourse; new issues that concerned urban classes would command increasing attention. The death of Jim Crow brought political fear and disorder to North Carolina. Although the state witnessed comparatively little of the racial demagoguery, mayhem, and violence that occurred in other southern states, the end of segregation marked a critical juncture in North Carolina's history. The decline of the tattered ideology of white supremacy left a vacuum for a new political trajectory. Segregationist politics were no longer openly viable, and conservatives had been deprived of a critical component of traditional ideology. Racist politics did not end in North Carolina with the death of Jim Crow, but an alternative ideological vehicle capable of reflecting the fears and beliefs of white conservatives had to be located. That vehicle, flexible and seemingly unassailable, was anticommunism.

The end of segregation meant transitional politics for conservatives. The national Democratic Party embraced the civil rights movement's agenda, and the party's liberal wing gained ascendancy. As North Carolina's conservative Democrats grew alienated with the national party, they seized on the politics of anticommunism to rally disaffected whites and provide a basis for continuity. Anticommunism was an amazingly flexible signifier that could be used to explain or exploit any number of concerns of southern whites who were feeling increasingly estranged from the actions and policies of the liberal wing of the Democratic Party. Jesse Helms astutely recognized and exploited the political potential of anticommunism. As the nation sent its young men to war against a communist foe in Southeast Asia, such politics gained an even greater audience and legitimacy. The great irony was that as conservatives used anticommunism to perpetuate their influence, the issues to which it spoke were almost completely distanced from the politics of the speaker ban law's origin: the demise of Jim Crow and its ideological supports.

The anticommunist politics reflected in North Carolina's speaker ban law also illustrates an important dimension of the political realignment taking shape in the South in the wake of the civil rights movement. As the Republican Party articulated a race-conscious "southern strategy," the unstintingly militant anticommunism of the party's right wing offered a comfortable ideological home for alienated southern white Democrats. As Helms changed party affiliation and moved from the editorial booth into the U.S. Senate, his anticommunist pedigree appeared to have found its proper home in the party of Richard Nixon and Barry Goldwater. If anything, Helms and the conservative Democrats who served as his core constituency were even more committed to an expansive application of anticommunist principles than were many traditional Republicans. As the origins of the speaker ban law demonstrated, communism was most visibly expressed by the social disorder associated with black protest politics. A staple of Helms's rhetorical arsenal had been that the civil rights crusade was the product of a decades-old communist conspiracy. As the movement gathered steam and won decisive victories in the mid-1960s, Helms led the charge, claiming that many of the movement's leaders, including Martin Luther King Jr., were communists.[1]

If the anticommunist reaction in North Carolina signaled a phase of political realignment, it also suggests the university's vulnerability as a target for political opportunists. This situation appears to hold especially for public universities with traditions of active political involvement. With established connections to the public interest as well as the public treasury, publicly funded institutions can readily be subjected to hostile political pressure. In the case of the University of North Carolina, a coterie of radicals became the means by which a full-scale assault was launched on the school's academic tolerance and spirit of liberal inquiry. The anticommunist campaign against the liberal university ultimately failed for two important reasons. First, the ruling elite of the urban Piedmont realized that UNC, as a leading research institution, was simply too vital to the state's political economy. The future of the state's economic development and its place within larger economies might be seriously jeopardized if the speaker ban and its latent anti-intellectualism were not brought to an end. A second factor was that institutionally UNC shared many of the anticommunist sympathies of its critics. In this sense, the university mirrored a culturally dominant ideology. The school and its administration consistently followed both the letter and spirit of the speaker law and enthusiastically cooperated in law-enforcement organizations' monitoring of campus activists. The University of North Carolina eventually escaped the ignominy of a speaker control law but did not do so without having its potential as an alternate source of authority within the political culture of North Carolina seriously compromised.

As a vehicle of political repression, the speaker ban symbolized the 1960s in North Carolina: reaction to democratic insurgency and social change. And reaction came at an early date, June 1963, when the infrastructure of segregation that had underpinned the state's political culture since the turn of the century came crashing down. The spring of 1963 marked the passage of cultural authority and political power to the hands of an urban bourgeoisie willing to accommodate a nonracial civil equality because its interests did not require the strictures of Jim Crow. Reeling from a surprising defeat on segregation and an impending defeat on apportionment, rural conservatives and small-town traditionalists sought to broaden their political appeal by supplanting segregation with a still-vital anticommunism that could service a variety of interests.

The speaker ban served its intended purpose: to put a temporary brake on political agitation and democratic activism. While other states witnessed the emergence of political forces that pressed the boundaries of social change, much energy in North Carolina was spent — wasted — in a protracted discussion of the circumstances of political speech. The speaker ban and the ideological imbroglio that it touched off enabled the perpetuation of conservative power at a critical juncture. Despite its eventual repeal, the speaker ban was a victory for conservative forces. They were able to present themselves as the guardians of public institutions and vulnerable youth against a silent but menacing threat. The verdict in the court case reaffirmed the legitimacy of the anticommunist agenda while striking down the law. As the ban's chief proponent, Helms interpreted the ruling as a victory; the liberal opposition's dominant feeling was one of relief.

If the speaker ban represented the continuation of conservative power, it correspondingly denoted the comparative weakness of liberalism in the state. The leadership of the anti–speaker ban forces, primarily officials of the liberal university, was unable to persuade the legislature or a considerable part of the public that the law should be repealed. This result, at least in part, followed from many liberals' acceptance of the anticommunist imperative. It was difficult, if not impossible, for liberals to contend that such a law was undesirable when they also believed that radicals had no legitimate place at the university. Even the greatest of the Chapel Hill liberals, Frank Porter Graham, contended that communists should not be employed as faculty. President William Friday extended Graham's principle by declaring that UNC would not tolerate communist faculty or students. The decision to purge Nicholas Bateson for his political beliefs symbolized Friday's commitment to this principle.

The willingness of public officials in North Carolina to tolerate and defend a speaker control law targeted at a public institution on which much of the state's progressive reputation rested suggests that the state was far less progressive than it appeared. Almost every assessment of North Carolina's progressive reputation, from V. O. Key's *Southern Politics in State and Nation* to more recent studies, has emphasized the role of UNC in promoting regional self-analysis and social change. The vindictive presence of the speaker ban indicated a rejection of this role by the forces of traditionalism. Despite the potential for broader social change emanating from the momentum of the civil rights movement, at the end of the era North Carolina was perhaps the least changed of all the southern states. This stasis persisted even as the state preserved its national image for moderation. The speaker ban represented a definitive flaw in this carefully constructed appearance. And herein lies the key reason for the dearth of social renewal in North Carolina during an era given to transformation: the politics of anticommunism, as expressed in the speaker ban, were never fueled by the actual presence of communists but by a fear of change. The speaker ban's goal was to forestall social change, not communism.

Despite the power of anticommunist ideology, it was not inevitable that the speaker ban would be a victory of conservative reaction. Forceful leadership against a measure that negated a basic American liberty might have provided Governor Terry Sanford with a vital platform on which to continue his political ascent. Neither Sanford nor any other leader in the liberal, progressive mold came out actively against the law. Richardson Preyer and Robert Scott, candidates for governor and lieutenant governor, respectively in 1964, both refused to endorse repeal. Preyer was a liberal, the heir designate to Sanford, and Scott was the son of former governor and U.S. senator Kerr Scott, who had appointed Graham to the U.S. Senate in 1949. The university's leadership quickly acknowledged the weakness of liberalism and worked to secure the authority to administer the law rather than to effect its repeal. The weakness of liberal forces allowed the student Left at UNC to easily co-opt what was essentially a liberal issue. Beyond the university, there was no consistent or sustained leadership opposing the speaker ban as an assault on democratic values. Ostensibly progressive leaders abandoned the speaker ban as an issue to be exploited by those whose political values were rooted in the past.

The speaker ban gave public exposure to those conservatives ready and willing to reap the political benefits of an issue that they believed had a solid measure of popular support. Dan Moore, the business conservative whose candidacy galvanized the opposition to both the Kennedy and Sanford administrations, came out solidly in favor of the law. The Moore years were a cautious reaction to the portent that further changes might occur in the aftermath of desegregation. Moore appointed his young protégé David Britt, a vehement anticommunist who had supported the original speaker ban, to head the commission that amended the law into a form that would assuage critics while preserving its essential character. His public exposure as chairman of the study commission made Britt an apparent rising star in state politics. There was immediate speculation that Britt might be a future governor. While serving as Speaker of the House, Britt was appointed to the State Court of Appeals by Moore and eventually became a justice on the State Supreme Court.

Although much of the core of the legislative leadership that created the speaker ban was of advanced age and preparing to retire from public life, several of the younger pro–speaker ban cohort benefited from the exposure. They prolonged their careers and reinvented themselves politically to assume leadership roles. Philip Godwin, who helped initiate the speaker ban measure, was chosen Speaker of the House in 1971 by his colleagues. Robert B. Morgan, the protégé of segregationist I. Beverly Lake and perhaps the most visible defender of the speaker ban, effected an impressive political transformation. Morgan was elected attorney general in 1968 on a platform that stressed consumer protection; he also added black attorneys to the office's staff.

He publicly distanced himself from his earlier association with Lake, claiming to have been motivated by loyalty to his former law professor rather than by an affinity to segregationist politics. Morgan was never a conservative but was a populist who carried a long aversion to entrenched economic and political power. By the late 1960s, Morgan made the transition from a right-wing variety of populism burdened by race to a democratic populism that opposed concentrations of power and wealth.[2]

In 1974, Morgan resigned as attorney general to run for the U.S. Senate seat being vacated by Sam Ervin. Morgan won election by fashioning a Democratic coalition comprised of blacks, white liberals, and the eastern conservatives that formed his traditional base. In the Senate, Morgan continued to espouse populist ideas such as higher taxes on the wealthy and support for beleaguered farmers. On foreign policy, Morgan retained the kernel of his earlier anticommunism, supporting President Nixon's war against communism in Vietnam even after the war had become politically unpopular. Morgan was considered by some observers to be the future of Democratic politics in a North Carolina that was breaking from the past. That future lasted until 1980, when John East, a conservative political science professor from East Carolina University, upset Morgan in his reelection effort. A key component in Morgan's defeat was charges that he was "soft on communism" for supporting the Panama Canal Treaty and for supporting U.S. aid to Nicaragua following the Sandinista victory there. In Morgan's defeat lay a notable irony: a centerpiece of his early career had been his conspicuous support for an anticommunist law; now he himself was victimized, his political career prematurely ended by anticommunist demagoguery.[3]

The person who orchestrated the campaign against Morgan in 1980 was the same person who drew the most political benefit from the speaker ban episode, Helms. The politics of anticommunism encapsulated the fear, anger, and anxiety that many people felt in an era of social change, economic uncertainty, and political upheaval. Where liberal politicians backed away from the issue lest they find themselves labeled sympathetic to communism, Helms saw an ideologically driven issue and rushed to make it his own. Helms commandeered the central question of whether communists should appear on state-supported college campuses and answered it with an unequivocal "no." Virtually every speaker ban critic, with the exception of UNC-SDS but including UNC officials, carefully evaded this issue and allowed Helms to exploit it. This unwillingness to forcefully address this question gave Helms confidence, as the liberal opposition appeared inept and afraid. More important, the critics' inability to make headway against the speaker ban reaffirmed for Helms the staying power of anticommunism. And Helms would exploit strident anticommunism as one means of moving straight from the editorial booth to the U.S. Senate in 1972.

For many observers, Helms's stunning victory over Congressman Nick Galifianakis was the result of the editorialist's successful association of his opponent with Democratic presidential nominee George McGovern. And Helms's indiscreet use of racially coded attacks was certainly instrumental in his victory. But the anticommunist campaign gave Helms a sense of victory, perhaps the first of his career, and helped make him a highly popular figure among conservatives, many of whom were disaffected white Democrats. The speaker ban's success, a reaction to the anger and frustration caused by liberal change, reinforced Helms's understanding of the effectiveness of these feelings as political levers. Success in exploiting the speaker ban gave Helms a momentum that would carry him into the U.S. Senate.[4]

By the end of the speaker ban era, Key's "progressive plutocracy" had been amended to a more appropriate "progressive myth." It was now evident that North Carolina's commitment to its national appearance obscured a reality of economic inequality, racism, and, as the speaker ban symbolized, political repression. In the words of one political observer, "The farther you get away from North Carolina, the more progressive it looks."[5]

There remain reasons for a more optimistic future. After all, in a state with the motto "Esse Quam Videri" (To be rather than to seem) there is always the possibility that at some future time the state will construct a progressive reality that approaches the image it cultivates. Any hope of such a realization, however, will of necessity involve a free university in a leading role.

NOTES

Introduction

1. Chafe, *Unfinished Journey*, 146. On the Greensboro sit-ins and the wave of student-generated protests they touched off, see Wolff, *Lunch*; Dykeman and Stokely, "Sit Down Chillun"; and Walzer, "Cup of Coffee."
2. Ashby, *Frank Porter Graham*; Sosna, *In Search of the Silent South*; Sitkoff, *New Deal*, 129, 135.
3. Pleasants and Burns, *Frank Porter Graham*; Lubell, *Future*, 106–13; Luebke, *Tar Heel Politics*, 15–17.
4. Key, *Southern Politics*, 205–18.
5. Ibid., 207.
6. Chafe, *Civilities*. See also Chafe, "Greensboro."
7. Chafe, *Civilities*, 67–82.
8. Severson, "Promised Land," 11, 52; *Durham Morning Herald*, September 2, 1956; *Greensboro Daily News*, October 6, 1956; William W. Taylor Jr. to Herman Talmadge, October 11, 1954, Pearsall Papers, Southern Historical Collection (hereafter cited as SHC); Lefler and Newsome, *North Carolina*, 302–3, 323; Furgurson, *Hard Right*, 93; Greenhaw, *Elephants*, 161–69.
9. "Clontz Tells of over 20 N.C. Reds," *Daily Tar Heel*, January 15, 1954; "Innocent of Wrong, Ab Says," *Daily Tar Heel*, March 15, 1954. See also Scales and Nickson, *Cause at Heart*.
10. U.S. House Committee on Un-American Activities, *Investigation*, 3505–80.
11. Schrecker, *No Ivory Tower*, 89; "University of California Rescinds Its Ban on Red Speakers," *New York Times*, June 22, 1963; and "Freedom Unlimited" (editorial),

New York Times, June 22, 1963. The *Raleigh News and Observer* noted the irony between the California and North Carolina actions; see "Throwback to McCarthyism," *Raleigh News and Observer*, June 29, 1963.

12. Woodward, *Thinking Back*, 17.

Chapter 1. The "Speaker Ban" Law

1. "White, High Swap Verbal Brickbats," *Raleigh News and Observer*, June 21, 1963; "For Grave Bill—A Deep Six," *Raleigh News and Observer*, June 26, 1963; Thomas J. White Jr., interview with author, Kinston, North Carolina, September 17, 1986. White requested and received permission from close friend Clarence Stone to speak, on point of personal privilege, to the Senate and explain the events. A text of White's remarks is located in the *Journal of the Senate*, 1963 sess., 693, and can also be found among his personal papers (1963 Assembly, White Papers, SHC). Much of the sequence of events described in this chapter is based on a series of oral history interviews with members of the 1963 Assembly, state officials, university officials, and UNC faculty and students. The senators interviewed (with their home counties indicated in parentheses) include: White (Lenoir), Perry Martin (Northampton), Lindsay Warren Jr. (Wayne), John Jordan Jr. (Wake), and Robert B. Morgan (Harnett). Interviewees from the House are: Ned E. Delamar (Pamlico), Philip Godwin (Gates), David M. Britt (Robeson), J. Raynor Woodard (Northampton), and Algernon Augustus Zollicoffer Jr. (Vance). University officials interviewed include: William C. Friday, president of the consolidated University of North Carolina; William B. Aycock, chancellor, UNC–Chapel Hill; John Caldwell, chancellor, North Carolina State University at Raleigh. Additional interviews were conducted with Thad Eure, North Carolina secretary of state, and Dennis King and Nicholas Bateson of the Progressive Labor Club at UNC–Chapel Hill, 1962–63.

2. "Super Court Bill Killed in Senate," *Raleigh News and Observer*, June 21, 1963; "3 Amendments Fail in North Carolina," *New York Times*, June 21, 1963. The "Super Court" proposal was one of three states'-rights amendments introduced in the North Carolina Assembly. For more on these amendments, see chapter 4.

3. *Journal of the Senate*, 1963 sess., 762.

4. This reconstruction of the handling and introduction of H.B. 1395 is based on oral history interviews with Eure, Delamar, and Godwin (Thad Eure, interview with author, Raleigh, North Carolina, August 13, 1986; Philip Godwin, interview with author, Gatesville, North Carolina, August 19, 1986; Ned E. Delamar, interview with author, Bayboro, North Carolina, August 20, 1986).

5. *An Act to Regulate Visiting Speakers at State Supported Colleges and Universities*, *Laws of the General Assembly*, 1963 sess., 1688–89.

6. Godwin interview; David M. Britt, interview with author, Raleigh, North Carolina, August 9, 1986; Delamar interview; *Charlotte Observer*, June 28, 1963; *Greensboro Daily News*, June 27, 1963.

7. Godwin interview; Delamar interview; *Raleigh News and Observer*, June 27, 1963.

8. Godwin interview; *Raleigh News and Observer*, June 26, 1963; *Greensboro Daily News*, June 26, 1963.

9. *Raleigh News and Observer*, June 26, 1963; Perry Martin, interview with author, Ahoskie, North Carolina, August 19, 1986.

10. *Charlotte Observer*, June 26, 1963. Martin interview; John Jordan interview with author, Raleigh, North Carolina, August 15, 1986.

11. Chafe, *Unfinished Journey*, 187.

12. Dan T. Carter, *Politics of Rage*, 133–51; E. Culpepper Clark, *Schoolhouse Door*.

13. Dan T. Carter, *Politics of Rage*, 151–55.

14. Civil rights activist Anne Braden assembled a pamphlet chronicling the increasing linkage between anticommunist rhetoric and the diehard defense of segregation. See Braden, *House Un-American Activities Committee*; Dan T. Carter, *Politics of Rage*, 158–60.

15. *Engel v. Vitale*, 370 U.S. 421 (1962); *School District of Abingdon Township v. Schempp*, 374 U.S. 203 (1963).

16. Martin interview.

17. Jordan interview.

18. *Raleigh Times*, September 12, 1963.

19. Ibid., June 27, 1963.

20. Terry Sanford to G. Grenville Benedict, December 13, 1963, Chancellor's Records, Aycock Series, University Archives (hereafter cited as Aycock Series).

21. For accounts of the Smith-Graham primary, see Lubell, *Future*; Pleasants and Burns, *Frank Porter Graham*. For Sanford's involvement, see Pleasants and Burns, *Frank Porter Graham*, 53, 107, 270; Terry Sanford, interview with author, Durham, North Carolina, December 7, 1988.

22. *North Carolina American Legion News*, July 1949, copy in possession of author.

23. The resolution is attached to A. C. Stephenson to R. B. House, June 8, 1949, Chancellor's Records, House Series, University Archives (hereafter cited as House Series).

24. *North Carolina American Legion News*, July 1949, copy in possession of author; C. Leroy Shuping Jr. to Robert B. House, November 21, 1949, House Series. A copy of the resolution passed on June 21 is attached to the letter.

25. William Donald Carmichael to Terry Sanford, June 24, 1949, General Administration, Vice President for Finance Records (William Carmichael), University Archives; "If We Would Keep the University Free, We Must Keep It from Those Who Would Destroy It: A Report to the Board of Trustees 'on Communism and the University' by the Committee of Chancellors," May 24, 1949, General Administration, Vice President for Finance Records (William Carmichael), University Archives.

26. On Sanford's approach to race relations and civil rights and its reception, see Chafe, *Civilities*, 143–48; Earl Black, *Southern Governors*, 109, 110; Bass and DeVries, *Transformation*, 229–31.

27. *Raleigh News and Observer*, June 27, 1963.

28. Ibid.

29. "A Word for Clarence Stone," December 6, 1963, in *Messages of Sanford*, ed. Mitchell, 386.

30. Ibid.; P. D. Midgett Jr. to Terry Sanford, December 11, 1963; Philip Godwin to Sanford, December 9, 1963; Edgar Gurganus to Sanford, December 10, 1963, all in T. Clarence Stone Papers, SHC; Thomas J. White Jr. to T. Clarence Stone, December 8, 1963, White Papers, SHC. See also "Sanford Statement on Senator Stone Brought Surprise," *Raleigh Times*, December 11, 1963.

31. WRAL-TV Viewpoint #748, December 10, 1963, North Carolina Collection (hereafter cited as NCC). On Helms's meteoric rise from an obscure television personality to prominent U.S. senator, see Furgurson, *Hard Right*.

32. "Senate Refuses to Recall Bill Banning Red Speakers," *Raleigh Times*, June 26, 1963; "Last Ditch Try to Nullify Act on Reds Fails," *Greensboro Daily News*, June 27, 1963; "Senate Rejects Attempts to Recall Ban on Red Talks," *Winston-Salem Sentinel*, June 26, 1963.

33. *Raleigh Times*, June 26, 1963.

34. Luther Hamilton et al. to T. Clarence Stone, June 26, 1963, T. Clarence Stone Papers, SHC. The document, signed by fourteen senators, appears in *Journal of the Senate*, 1963 sess., 763–64. A similar statement of dissent was also entered into the House record (*Journal of the House*, 1963 sess., 1225–26).

35. Key, *Southern Politics*, 205–6.

36. The best account of CP activities at Chapel Hill and Scales's involvement is in his autobiography, *Cause at Heart*. On the commuting of his sentence in 1962 and its reception by conservatives in North Carolina, see Furgurson, *Hard Right*, 78; WRAL-TV Viewpoint #513, December 28, 1962; #518, January 4, 1963; #631, June 14, 1963, NCC.

37. "Investigation Call Said Based on Organization of 'Labor Club' at UNC," *Raleigh Times*, October 9, 1962; "'Red Nest' at UNC? Reporters Find Nothing More Than a Few Young Left-Wingers," *Durham Morning Herald*, October 21, 1962; "University Officials Stick to Stand on 'Red Nest,'" *Raleigh News and Observer*, June 23, 1963. PL's existence was initially made public during the summer of 1962; see "UNC Students Form Labor Club along Marxist Lines," *Charlotte Observer*, August 2, 1962. This story later reappeared when HUAC subpoenaed three UNC students to testify in Washington. The activities of and the response to PLC at UNC is discussed more fully in chapter 2.

38. "Legion Asks Study at UNC," *Charlotte Observer*, June 23, 1963; *Raleigh News and Observer*, June 23, 1963.

39. *Raleigh News and Observer*, June 23, 1963. The determination of membership in the American Legion and/or the Veterans of Foreign Wars is taken from biographical data supplied by the legislators themselves. See "Delamar, Ned Everett," "Wilson, Edward Howell," "Barbee, Allen Crowell," and "Calder, Robert Edward," all in *Biographical Dictionary*, ed. Massengill. See also *North Carolina American Legion News*, July 1963.

40. WRAL-TV Viewpoint #502, December 12, 1963; #582, April 5, 8, 1963, NCC.

41. WRAL-TV Viewpoint #591, April 18, 1963; #593, April 22, 1963, NCC; Furgurson, *Hard Right*, 79.

42. Castigation of academic freedom as a conduit by which unpopular political speak-
    ers would be allowed to appear or radical ideas expressed had been a staple in
    Helms's arsenal almost from the beginning of his "Viewpoint" commentaries on
    November 21, 1960 (WRAL-TV Viewpoint #67, February 24, 1961; #125, May 17,
    1961; #282, January 12, 1962; #313, February 28, 1962, NCC). A sample of a
    critique of alleged abuse of academic freedom can be found in #333, March 28,
    1962, in which the professorate is scored for criticism of "decadent capitalism."
43. WRAL-TV Viewpoint #587, April 12, 1963, NCC.
44. WRAL-TV Viewpoint #636, June 21, 1963, NCC.
45. Ibid.
46. Ibid., #640, June 27, 1963.
47. Ibid., #542, April 5, 8, 1963. WRAL President A. J. Fletcher sent a copy of the
    editorial to UNC President William C. Friday and to the Board of Trustees prior
    to its airing. This event occurred several months after the brief furor over the le-
    gion's call for investigation had died down. Fletcher to Board of Trustees, April 3,
    1963, Friday Records, University Archives.
48. WRAL-TV Viewpoint #466, October 18, 1962, NCC.
49. "UNC's 'Liberalism,' Speaker Ban Traced to Graham and Politics," *Charlotte Ob-
    server*, August 9, 1965.
50. Ibid.
51. Ibid.

Chapter 2. Student Radicalism and the University

1. "9,600 Students Anticipated as UNC Enters 169th Year," *Daily Tar Heel*, September 18, 1962; "Enrollment Jumps to Highest Point in History: 9,604," *Daily
   Tar Heel*, October 3, 1962. Two studies that chronicle the first sit-ins in North
   Carolina are Wolff, *Lunch*, and Chafe, *Civilities*. On the involvement of white
   students in the civil rights movement and the eventual tensions that followed, see
   Carson, *In Struggle*, 52–53, 72–73, 98–103.
2. The paper's position on the Meredith incident can be found in a September 27
   editorial simply entitled "Ignorance." Student opinion solidly supported James
   Meredith's admission; see "UNC Urges Ole Miss Relent, Telegram Sent to Kennedy," *Daily Tar Heel*, September 28, 1962; "Most UNC Students Condemn Barnett Action," *Daily Tar Heel*, October 2, 1962; and "400 Students Wire Meredith
   Support," *Daily Tar Heel*, October 2, 1962.
3. *Daily Tar Heel*, November 31–December 2, 1962.
4. See "YAF Meeting Scheduled Today," *Daily Tar Heel*, October 18, 1962; "YAF
   President Backs Kennedy," *Daily Tar Heel*, October 27, 1962; Gitlin, *The Sixties*,
   89, 99.
5. "Carolina Political Panorama," *Daily Tar Heel*, May 19, 1963.
6. For examples of the younger Maupin's views, see "A View from the Hill: Conservatives Supported JFK," November 2, and a December 4, 1962, essay bashing new
   Massachusetts senator Edward Kennedy.
7. Schultz and Schultz, eds., *It Did Happen Here*, 13–21; "Pete Seeger Sings to over

1,000 Despite YAF & Independent Pickets," *Daily Tar Heel,* December 6, 1962; "Demonstrators Burn Fidel, Shout Anti-Cuba Protests," *Daily Tar Heel,* October 27, 1962.

8. All 2,762 editorials are available in hard copy and microfilm in the NCC. For examples of the above, see WRAL-TV Viewpoint #478, November 7, 1962; #502, December 12, 1962, NCC.

9. Isserman, *If I Had a Hammer,* 194–202.

10. The best indicator of SPU activities on the UNC campus is the resolution linking world peace with civil rights and basic human freedoms. This manifesto also includes a list of the local segregated establishments to be boycotted. See "A Resolution of the UNC Chapter of the Student Peace Union," March 17, 1963, UNC Student Government Association Records, University Archives.

11. Ehle, *Free Men,* 6–9.

12. Ibid., 4.

13. Ibid. See also "Resolution," March 17, 1963, UNC Student Government Association Records, University Archives.

14. "SPU to Demonstrate against Foreign Policy in Vietnam," *Daily Tar Heel,* October 9, 1963. For campus protests during the Madame Nhu tour, see Zaroulis and Sullivan, *Who Spoke Up?* 15; Powers, *Vietnam,* 35; Dennis King, telephone interview with author, September 26, 1989.

15. "Peace Group Joins with National," *Daily Tar Heel,* December 15, 1962.

16. Ibid; Isserman, *If I Had a Hammer,* 194.

17. Isserman, *If I Had a Hammer,* 194.

18. "Resolution," March 17, 1963, UNC Student Government Association Records, University Archives.

19. Waynick, Brooks, and Pitts, eds., *North Carolina,* 29–30.

20. Ibid.

21. "Ohioan Hero or Villain at N.C.," *Cleveland Plain Dealer,* May 21, 1963; "Dunne Is Released; Will Return Monday," *Daily Tar Heel,* May 18, 1963.

22. "Concerning John Dunne," *Daily Tar Heel,* May 18, 1963.

23. Ibid.

24. Ibid.

25. Walter Spearman to Harold and Emmeline Dunne, May 18, 1963, Dunne Papers, SHC.

26. Charles Henderson Jr. to Mrs. John B. Dunne, May 20, 1963, Dunne Papers, SHC.

27. Waynick, Brooks, and Pitts, eds., *North Carolina,* 29–33. See also Barksdale, "Civil Rights Organization."

28. Waynick, Brooks, and Pitts, eds., *North Carolina,* 49–50; Ehle, *Free Men;* "Community Help Is Sought in Desegregation Movement," *Chapel Hill Weekly,* May 8, 1963; *Chapel Hill Weekly,* December 18, 1963; "Sit-in Arrests Total Passes 90 Persons," *Durham News,* December 19, 1963.

29. "That SPU Cartoon Was Good for Our Livers, but What about Our Lives?" *Daily Tar Heel,* October 15, 1963; "Concerning John Dunne," *Daily Tar Heel,* May 18, 1963.

30. On the impact of the Red Scare on academic communities, see Schrecker, *No Ivory Tower*; Diamond, *Compromised Campus*.

31. Scales and Nickson, *Cause at Heart*; Richard Nickson, "Junius Irving Scales," in *Encyclopedia*, ed. Buhle, Buhle, and Georgakas, 676–77; Junius Scales, interview with author, Chapel Hill, North Carolina, November 14, 1988.

32. On the historic relevance of the Greensboro sit-ins, see Wolff, *Lunch*; Chafe, *Civilities*, 109–20; Branch, *Parting*, 271–73; Morris, *Origins*, 291–93.

33. Jezer, *Dark Ages*, 308–9; Isserman, *If I Had a Hammer*, 188–89; Gitlin, *The Sixties*, 82–83; Miller, "Democracy," 46.

34. King interview; Nicholas Bateson, telephone interview with author, September 27, 1989; "New Leftist Club 'Solidifies' Views," *Daily Tar Heel*, September 25, 1962.

35. King interview.

36. *Daily Tar Heel*, December 6, 1962.

37. King interview. Cusick withdrew from participation in the New Left Club precisely for its lack of practical activity ("New Left Member Ends Membership," *Daily Tar Heel*, November 10, 1962).

38. "New Left Club 'Solidifies' View," *Daily Tar Heel*, September 25, 1962; Bateson interview; King interview.

39. The best source on the ideological orientation and programmatic creed of the national group is its journal *Progressive Labor*, beginning in 1962. For a glimpse at the makeup of the Chapel Hill group, see "UNC Students Form Labor Club along Marxist Lines," *Charlotte Observer*, August 2, 1962; "'Red Nest' at UNC? Reporters Find Nothing More than a Few Young Left-Wingers," *Durham Morning Herald*, October 21, 1962. On May 19, 1963, the *Daily Tar Heel* reported that the UNC club was "the only group of its kind within a four hundred mile radius of Chapel Hill."

40. *Progressive Labor* 1 (July–August 1962): 1–5. For analysis of PL and its co-optation of SDS, see Miller, "Democracy," 284–85, 311; Gitlin, *The Sixties*, 382–83; Fraser, ed., *1968*, 301–12.

41. King interview.

42. Ibid.

43. Ibid.

44. *Progressive Labor* 1 (July–August 1962): 5; *Charlotte Observer*, August 2, 1962; King interview.

45. King interview. For King's views in 1962, see "'Red Nest' at UNC?" *Durham Morning Herald*, October 21, 1962. Phelps was a sincere and committed socialist.

46. Bateson interview; King interview. For more on Bateson's views, see "'Red Nest' at UNC?" *Durham Morning Herald*, October 21, 1962; "New Left Club 'Solidifies' View," *Daily Tar Heel*, September 25, 1962.

47. "UNC Students Form Labor Club along Marxist Lines," *Charlotte Observer*, August 2, 1962.

48. "New Left Club 'Solidifies' View," *Daily Tar Heel*, September 25, 1962.

49. Ibid.

50. On Lake's animosity toward the university's support for more liberalized race rela-

tions, see "Lake Sees Threat to Public Schools," *Raleigh News and Observer*, April 9, 1960; "Morgan Hits Governor Hodges," *Raleigh News and Observer*, May 15, 1960; "Universities and Race for Governor," *Winston-Salem Journal*, June 11, 1960. For more on the challenge posed by Lake and the segregationists, see Chafe, *Civilities*, 69, 144, 228; Bass and DeVries, *Transformation*, 229–34.

51. *Raleigh News and Observer*, October 5, 1962; *Daily Tar Heel*, October 5, 7, 1962.

52. *Raleigh News and Observer*, October 5, 1962. See also "Leftist Educators," *Winston-Salem Journal*, June 11, 1960; WRAL-TV Viewpoint #313, February 28, 1962; #461, October 11, 1962; #502, December 12, 1962, NCC.

53. The complete text of the resolution appears in the *Durham Morning Herald*, October 9, 1962.

54. "Statement by Chancellor William B. Aycock, in reply to request by the Associated Press," October 9, 1962, Aycock Series; William B. Aycock, interview with author, Chapel Hill, North Carolina, July 21, 1992.

55. "Chancellor Says UNC Not 'Pink,'" *Charlotte Observer*, October 10, 1962.

56. *Daily Tar Heel*, October 17, 1962; Charles Henderson Jr. to Nicholas Bateson, December 7, 1962, Aycock Series.

57. WRAL-TV Viewpoint #461, October 11, 1962, NCC.

58. Ibid.; #466, October 18, 1962, NCC.

59. Ibid.; #466, October 18, 1962, NCC.

60. Chafe, *Civilities*, 77–78.

61. William B. Aycock, "Freedom of the University," June 6, 1960, Aycock Series. See also Frank Graham to William B. Aycock, June 14, 1960; Robert M. Hutchins to Anne Queen, June 14, 1960, both in Aycock Series.

62. "Legion's Shameful Red Nest Slap in Face for Fine Tar Heels," *Raleigh Times*, October 9, 1962.

63. "A New Red Scare at UNC," *Winston-Salem Journal*, October 11, 1962.

64. "Hunting a Gnat with a Shotgun," *Durham Morning Herald*, October 13, 1962.

65. *Raleigh News and Observer*, October 10, 1962.

66. WRAL-TV Viewpoint #582, April 5, 8, 1963; #587, April 12, 1963; #591, April 18, 1963; #593, April 22, 1963, NCC.

67. On the use of anticommunism by defenders of segregation, see Braden, *House Un-American Activities Committee*.

68. "University Officials Stick to Stand on 'Red Nest'" and "Legion Condemns University Club," both in *Raleigh News and Observer*, June 23, 1963. The anticommunist law was introduced and passed on June 25.

Chapter 3. The Streets of Raleigh

1. Branch, *Parting*, 690–705, 822, 834; Fairclough, *To Redeem*, 111–27, 145–47; Garrow, *Bearing*, 248–52, 305–6. The events of Birmingham received abundant coverage in the North Carolina press; see "Dogs Used against Birmingham Negroes: Fire Hoses Also Turned on Crowds," *Raleigh News and Observer*, May 4, 1963.

2. Wolff, *Lunch*; Chafe, *Civilities*, 99, 112–20. On the impact of the Greensboro action on similar protests elsewhere, see Morris, *Origins*, 188–89.

3. The best study of the formation and internal dynamics of SNCC remains Carson, *In Struggle*, 9–12, 19–20. On the sit-ins and the formation of SNCC, see also Morris, *Origins*, 197–200, 215–21. A readable account on SNCC is Zinn, *SNCC*.

4. *Winston-Salem Journal*, February 9–10, 1963; Carson, *In Struggle*, 10–11; Patrick, *Lunch-Counter Desegregation*. For a personal account of the incidents in Monroe, see Robert F. Williams, *Negroes*; these events are also covered in "Swimming Pool Showdown."

5. Chafe, *Civilities*; Key, *Southern Politics*, 205–28; Hodges, *Businessman*; Bartley, *Rise*, 23, 141–44; Chafe, *Civilities*, 67–82.

6. A useful overview of desegregation in selected North Carolina cities can be found in Waynick, Brooks, and Pitts, eds., *North Carolina*; see also Jacoway and Colburn, eds., *Southern Businessmen*.

7. *Durham Morning Herald*, May 28, June 3–6, 1963; *New York Times*, June 5, 1963.

8. *Durham Morning Herald*, June 2, 1963; Waynick, Brooks, and Pitts, eds., *North Carolina*, 63–76.

9. Waynick, Brooks, and Pitts, eds., *North Carolina*, 63–76. See also Chafe, *Civilities*, 202, 208–9; Morris, *Origins*, 190.

10. *Winston-Salem Journal*, June 8, 1963; *New York Times*, June 5, 1963; Waynick, Brooks, and Pitts, eds., *North Carolina*, 180–87.

11. Chafe, *Civilities*, 197–206; Waynick, Brooks, and Pitts, eds., *North Carolina*, 87–103.

12. Chafe, *Civilities*, 207–12.

13. Spence, *Making*; Chafe, *Civilities*, 144.

14. The history of the campaign to desegregate Raleigh has yet to be written. Waynick, Brooks, and Pitts, eds., *North Carolina*, 138–43, provides a general overview of some of the more noteworthy events. Few documents from the campaign are extant, although a newsletter was published. The best source on the daily events is the *Raleigh News and Observer*.

15. "Declaration of Principles and Intentions of the Citizens Coordinating Committee, Raleigh, North Carolina, May 11, 1963"; *Newsletter*, June 21, 1963, both in Lowenstein Papers, SHC.

16. "Declaration of Principles and Intentions of the Citizens Coordinating Committee, Raleigh, North Carolina, May 11, 1963."

17. "2 Negroes Guilty of Trespassing"; "Pickets, Pickets, Pickets," both in *Raleigh News and Observer*, May 4, 1963.

18. "92 Negroes Arrested Here," *Raleigh News and Observer*, May 9, 1963; "Negroes Refuse to Leave Jail, Protest Continuing," *Raleigh News and Observer*, May 10, 1963. For Lyons's remarks, see "Talks Begin to Resolve Race Issues," *Raleigh News and Observer*, May 10, 1963.

19. "Talks Begin to Resolve Race Issues," *Raleigh News and Observer*, May 10, 1963; Waynick, Brooks, and Pitts, eds., *North Carolina*, 139.

20. "Talks Begin to Resolve Race Issues," *Raleigh News and Observer*, May 10, 1963.

21. "Negroes Boo Gov. at Mansion," *Raleigh News and Observer*, May 11, 1963.
22. Chafe, *Civilities*, 144–49.
23. *Raleigh News and Observer*, June 18, 1963; *Durham Morning Herald*, June 23, 1963.
24. "Statement of North Carolina Demonstration Leaders Presented to Governor Terry Sanford at Conference in Raleigh, North Carolina," June 25, 1963, Lowenstein Papers, SHC.
25. Harris, *Dreams*, 9–10, 23. For more on Lowenstein's early career in North Carolina, see Pleasants and Burns, *Frank Porter Graham*, 53, 83, 166, 230; Ashby, *Frank Porter Graham*, 260–61. An interesting treatment of Lowenstein's political activism is found in Harris, *Dreams*.
26. WRAL-TV Viewpoint #631, June 14, 1963, NCC.
27. Lowenstein published his observations and reflections on the racial situation in South West Africa (Namibia) in *Brutal Mandate*.
28. "UN Official Turned Away," *Raleigh News and Observer*, May 1, 1963.
29. "U.S. Agency Apologizes for Incident Here," *Raleigh News and Observer*, May 2, 1963.
30. "Diplomacy and Agitation," *Raleigh News and Observer*, May 2, 1963.
31. Robert Pace to Angie Brooks, May 1, 1963, Lowenstein Papers, SHC; *Raleigh News and Observer*, May 10, 11, 1963; John Caldwell to T. Clarence Stone, May 9, 1963, T. Clarence Stone Papers, SHC; John Caldwell, interview with author, Raleigh, North Carolina, November 9, 1988; T. Clarence Stone to David L. Hardee, March 2, 1964, T. Clarence Stone Papers, SHC. UNC President Friday confirmed that Stone inquired about Lowenstein's tenure and suggested that he should not be continued (William C. Friday, interview with author, Raleigh, North Carolina, August 21, 1986).
32. "State Troopers Eject Negroes at Statehouse," *Raleigh News and Observer*, May 10, 1963.
33. Ibid.
34. For stories detailing activities outside the hotel as well as inside its lobby, see *Raleigh News and Observer*, May 4, 9, 10, 15, June 11, 12, 1963.
35. "Negroes 'Sit-in' at Sir Walter," *Raleigh News and Observer*, June 11, 1963; Britt interview.
36. "Under the Dome," *Raleigh News and Observer*, June 12, 1963.
37. "He'd Strengthen State House Rules," *Raleigh News and Observer*, May 29, 1963; "Legislation Aimed at Integrators," *Raleigh News and Observer*, June 12, 1963; "House Yells Approval of Negro Bills," *Raleigh News and Observer*, June 13, 1963; *Journal of the Senate*, 1963 sess., 657, 720.
38. *Southern School News* (March 1963): 13; "Sit-in Issue Raised in Money Committee," *Raleigh News and Observer*, February 20, 1963; "Legislator Gives A&T Warning," *Greensboro Daily News*, February 20, 1963. See also "Representative Kerr on College Funds" (editorial), *Greensboro Daily News*, February 21, 1963.
39. *Raleigh News and Observer*, June 11, 1963; "Marchers' Footsteps Echoed in Assembly," *Raleigh News and Observer*, June 29, 1963.

40. *Raleigh News and Observer,* June 10, 1963.

41. Eure interview. By the time of his retirement in 1988, Eure had become the longest-serving state official in the nation, having spent fifty-two consecutive years as secretary of state ("'Oldest Rat' Begins 50th Year in Office," *Wilmington Morning Star,* December 23, 1985).

42. Delamar interview; Eure interview. Chapter 7 explores thoroughly each of the bill's possible trajectories.

43. *Raleigh Times,* November 11, 1963; Eure interview.

44. "House OK's Red Speakers Bill," *Cleveland Plain Dealer,* May 30, 1963; "Move to Ban Red Campus Orators Stirs up a Storm," *Cleveland Plain Dealer,* June 1, 1963; "Legislature OK's Speaker Bill," *Cleveland Plain Dealer,* June 28, 1963; Eure interview.

45. Eure interview. The likelihood that Moody designed the bill's language is indicated by his strong personal defense of the measure following its passage into law. No other member of the attorney general's staff showed much interest.

46. "Plain Truth from the Horse's Mouth," *Chapel Hill Weekly,* December 11, 1963.

47. Jordan interview, August 15, 1986.

48. "Marchers' Footsteps Echoed in Assembly," *Raleigh News and Observer,* June 29, 1963; "The Gag Law: Racial Bias by Any Other Name Smells Just as Rank," *Chapel Hill Weekly,* June 30, 1963.

49. "About Origins of the Ban Law," *Raleigh Times,* July 23, 1965.

50. The movement from segregationist to anticommunist ideology in condemning the civil rights movement is noted in Braden, *House Un-American Activities Committee.* This tendency is also described and evaluated in Branch, *Parting,* 681, 853–56, 861–62, 904, 911, 919; O'Reilly, *Racial Matters,* 140.

51. *New Bern Sun Journal,* June 28, 1963.

Chapter 4. The 1963 General Assembly

1. Chafe, *Civilities,* 72–82; McMillen, *Citizens' Council,* 111–15, 130–31; Bartley, *Rise,* 96–97; "N.C. 'Patriots' Name Leaders at Closed Greensboro Meeting," *Raleigh News and Observer,* September 11, 1955; "Statement on Segregation by Representative Tom White," *Kinston Free Press,* May 27, 1954; Stone to R. Hunt Parker, February 11, 1956; Stone to Governor Orval Faubus, August 2, 1958; Stone to Senator Sam J. Ervin Jr., June 4, 1956, all in T. Clarence Stone Papers, SHC.

2. "Little Counties vs. Big Counties," *Charlotte Observer,* March 17, 1963; "2 Old, 2 New Redistricting Plans Offered," *Charlotte Observer,* February 17, 1963; "General Assembly Fully Aware Senate Redistricting Is 'Must,'" *Charlotte Observer,* March 10, 1963. On the impact of the Court's reapportionment rulings, especially in *Baker v. Carr* (369 U.S. 186 [1962]), see Murphy, *Constitution,* 354–55, 384–91.

3. "Lt. Gov. Passes at Twin City," *Greensboro Daily News,* August 20, 1961; "TV Reporter Says Stone Cussed Him," *Charlotte Observer,* March 29, 1963. On Stone's social background, see "Stone, Thomas Clarence," in *Biographical Dictionary,* ed.

Massengill. On the close relationship to and support from Helms and WRAL, see T. Clarence Stone to Paul D. Hastings, April 10, 1963; Stone to Alan Newcomb, April 16, 1963; Jesse A. Helms to Clarence E. Stone Jr. [*sic*], February 11, 1963; Stone to A. J. Fletcher, January 12, 1963; Helms to Stone, January 15, 1963; Stone to Helms, January 12, 1963, all in T. Clarence Stone Papers, SHC; WRAL-TV Viewpoint #609, May 14, 1963, NCC.

4. T. Clarence Stone to Sam J. Ervin Jr., June 4, 1956, T. Clarence Stone Papers, SHC. Stone had been an eager proponent of the Pearsall Plan (see Stone to Thomas J. Pearsall, April 7, 1956; Stone to Luther H. Hodges, April 7, 1963, both in T. Clarence Stone Papers, SHC).

5. *Raleigh News and Observer*, May 4, July 5, 1963.

6. See, e.g., T. Clarence Stone to Herman E. Talmadge, March 5, 1968, Stone to Sam J. Ervin Jr., March 3, 1958, both in T. Clarence Stone Papers, SHC. The T. Clarence Stone Papers contain a wealth of correspondence between the North Carolinian and segregationist governors and politicians. Much of it seems to have been initiated by Stone and often takes the form of cheerleading.

7. T. Clarence Stone to Justice R. Hunt Parker, February 11, 1956, T. Clarence Stone Papers, SHC.

8. T. Clarence Stone to Sam J. Ervin Jr., July 12, 1957, T. Clarence Stone Papers, SHC.

9. T. Clarence Stone to Mrs. Clyde Claybrook, May 8, 1963, T. Clarence Stone Papers, SHC; White interview. See also "Senate Strong Man Gives His Views," *Charlotte Observer*, March 3, 1963; "Tom White Dominates Senate, Meets House Detour," *Charlotte Observer*, February 7, 1963; "Tom White Is Mr. Big in General Assembly," *Charlotte Observer*, March 3, 1963; "White, Thomas Jackson, Jr.," in *Biographical Dictionary*, ed. Massengill.

10. *Charlotte Observer*, February 7, March 3, 1963.

11. T. Clarence Stone to Sam J. Ervin Jr., June 4, 1956, T. Clarence Stone Papers, SHC.

12. Scott Jarrett to Thomas J. White Jr., March 5, 1963; White to Mrs. L. S. Raker, March 20, 1963, both in White Papers, SHC. See also "Conduct of General Assembly So Far Isn't Too Impressive," *Charlotte Observer*, March 31, 1963.

13. *Charlotte Observer*, March 28, 1963; "TV Reporter Says Stone Cussed Him," *Charlotte Observer*, March 29, 1963; "House Members Defend Stone in His TV Hassle," *Charlotte Observer*, March 30, 1963.

14. "Sen. White Fights with UPI Newsman during Argument," *Charlotte Observer*, April 7, 1963; "Sen. Tom White Denounces N.C. Press," *Charlotte Observer*, April 17, 1963; Jesse A. Helms to Earl J. Johnson, April 18, 1963, White Papers, SHC; White interview; *Raleigh News and Observer*, March 28, April 20, 1963.

15. The term *ultraconservative* is used guardedly. In surveying the political attitudes of her colleagues, Representative Rachel Davis, a physician from Lenoir County, concluded, "there is a stronger ultra-conservative group than ever before" ("Historic Week of Racial Progress in State," *Raleigh News and Observer*, June 9, 1963). Thus, at least one member made public use of the term. The problem is how to

define *ultraconservative*. Since it is largely an ideological designation, there are no objective criteria to assess. For the purposes of this study, *ultraconservatism* is used to connote radical conservatism in terms of rhetoric and support for certain measures. Avowed support for segregation and a willingness to radically alter the constitutional arrangements between federal and state governments are two indicators of such identification. White and Stone were exemplars: both publicly supported efforts to prevent the implementation of federal mandate in a number of areas.

16. "Little Counties vs. Big Counties," *Charlotte Observer*, March 17, 1963; "Small County Bloc Can 'Show Teeth,'" *Charlotte Observer*, March 17, 1963; "Why Did East Get Turtle-Hold?" *Charlotte Observer*, March 17, 1963. See also Chafe, *Civilities*, 72.

17. Lindsay Warren Sr. to T. Clarence Stone, May 24, 1963, T. Clarence Stone Papers, SHC; "2 Old, 2 New Redistricting Plans Offered," *Charlotte Observer*, February 17, 1963.

18. Murphy, *Constitution*, 385–91.

19. "Small County Bloc Can 'Show Teeth,'" *Charlotte Observer*, March 17, 1963; Matthews and Prothro, *Negroes*, 148–55; Goldfield, *Black, White, and Southern*, 167; Stanley, *Voter Mobilization*, 90; Lawson, *Black Ballots*, 312.

20. "Small County Bloc Can 'Show Teeth,'" *Charlotte Observer*, March 17, 1963.

21. Ibid.

22. "Bill Asks Revamped N.C. Representation," *Charlotte Observer*, March 20, 1963; see also "One Week Is Left — Or Special Session," *Charlotte Observer*, June 13, 1963; "A Proclamation by the Governor," October 10, 1963, T. Clarence Stone Papers, SHC.

23. "Hopes Soar at Opening of Session," *Charlotte Observer*, October 15, 1963; "Tighter Grip on House Is Small Counties' Goal," *Charlotte Observer*, October 16, 1963; "Redistricting Measure Is Passed by House," *Charlotte Observer*, October 17, 1963; "Constitutional Amendment, Senate Redistricting OKd," *Charlotte Observer*, October 18, 1963.

24. In the days prior to the constitutional referendum, Helms devoted five editorials to support of the Little Federal Plan (see WRAL-TV Viewpoint #766, January 6, 1964; #767, January 7, 1964; #768, January 8, 1964; #771, January 13, 1964; #774, January 16, 1964, NCC). For a statewide summary of the outcome of the vote, see "Voters Kill Little Federal Plan," *Charlotte Observer*, January 15, 1964.

25. Edsall and Williams, "North Carolina," 408.

26. The *Jeffers v. Whitley* case originally had been filed in 1956 as a test of the North Carolina Pupil Assignment Law. See "Six-Year Old Desegregation Suit in Caswell County Is Reopened," *Southern School News* (May 1962): 16–17; "Negro Father Gets 90–Day Term for Shooting in School Disorder," *Southern School News* (December 1962): 12; "Special Bus Service Denied Negro Children," *Southern School News* (May 1963): 26.

27. "Caswell Solon Hits Integration," *Raleigh News and Observer*, February 21, 1963; "N.C. Legislator Blasts Action of Federal Court," *Charlotte Observer*, February 21, 1963. On the Pearsall Plan (Pupil Assignment Law), see Chafe, *Civilities*, 72–82.

28. "Caswell Solon Hits Integration," *Raleigh News and Observer*, February 21, 1963.
29. H.R. 1341 and 1342, *Journal of the House*, 1963 sess., 1069.
30. Lefler and Newsome, *North Carolina*, 302–3, 326, 323. On John H. Kerr Sr., see Badger, *Prosperity Road*.
31. "Sit-in Issues Raised in Money Committee," *Greensboro Daily News*, February 20, 1963; "Legislator Scolds A&T Prexy for Sit-in Action," *Durham Carolina Times*, February 23, 1963. For a rebuttal to Kerr's tirade, see "Disgraceful Representation in the Legislature" (editorial), *Durham Carolina Times*, February 23, 1963; "Representative Kerr on College Funds," *Greensboro Daily News*, February 21, 1963. See also the letter from former A&T President Warmoth T. Gibbs to T. Clarence Stone asking for his support (February 22, 1963, T. Clarence Stone Papers, SHC). There was also a petition signed by members of the Greensboro chapter of CORE protesting Kerr's "verbal attack" ("Petition of Protest" to T. Clarence Stone, T. Clarence Stone Papers, SHC).
32. "Abusing Fiscal Authority," *Greensboro Daily News*, February 23, 1963. For other responses to Kerr, see "Us White People," *Greensboro Daily News*, February 24, 1963; "Days Numbered?" *Greensboro Daily News*, February 23, 1963.
33. *Raleigh News and Observer*, June 12, 1963; "Wallace Yields to Troops; Negroes Enter University," *Southern School News* 10 (July 1963): 1. T. Clarence Stone to Governor George C. Wallace, June 4, 1963, T. Clarence Stone Papers, SHC.
34. *Journal of the House*, 1963 sess., 1200; "Gettysburg to See N.C. Units in July," *Charlotte Observer*, March 22, 1963.
35. *Journal of the House*, 1963 sess., 436; *Raleigh News and Observer*, April 24, 1963.
36. "High Court, N&O Bombed by 2 Solons," *Raleigh News and Observer*, May 11, 1963. For an editorial response, see "Whose Disgrace?" *Raleigh News and Observer*, May 11, 1963. See also T. Clarence Stone to Governor George C. Wallace, July 2, 1963, T. Clarence Stone Papers, SHC.
37. *Journal of the Senate*, 1963 sess., 126; "Guard Color Bar Dropped by Assembly," *Raleigh News and Observer*, April 2, 1963; "Senate Group Approves Guard Integration Bill," *Charlotte Observer*, March 21, 1963.
38. *Journal of the Senate*, 1963 sess., 81, 245, 347.
39. "'Americanism' Class Bill Dies," *Raleigh News and Observer*, May 3, 1963.
40. *Journal of the House*, 1963 sess., 996, 1002, 1035, 1182; "Legislation Aimed at Integrators," *Raleigh News and Observer*, June 12, 1963; "House Yells Approval of Negro Bills," *Raleigh News and Observer*, June 13, 1963.
41. *Journal of the House*, 1963 sess., 715, 959, 960, 1052, 1053. On Knowland's address, see "Under the Dome," *Raleigh News and Observer*, June 2, 1963; *Journal of the House*, 1963 sess., 847.
42. "Amending the Constitution." For more on the states'-rights amendments, see "10 States Ask Amendment to Gain Districting Rights," *New York Times*, April 14, 1963; "Upsetting the Constitution" (editorial), *New York Times*, April 15, 1963; "Warren Is Critical of Lawyer Silence," *New York Times*, April 28, 1963; Charles L. Black Jr., "Proposed Amendment," 957–66; Murphy, *Constitution*, 478–79, 483.
43. Waynick, Brooks, and Pitts, eds., *North Carolina*, offers a basic overview of the

process of desegregation in a number of North Carolina cities during this period. See also "Merchants Here Urge End to Segregation," *Raleigh News and Observer*, May 14, 1963; "34 Negroes Arrested as Truce Talks Begin," *Raleigh News and Observer*, May 15, 1963; "Mass Demonstrations Hit 4 Cities in State," *Raleigh News and Observer*, May 19, 1963; "Charlotte Acts to Lift Racial Ban," *Raleigh News and Observer*, May 24, 1963; "Negotiating Integration at Durham," *Raleigh News and Observer*, June 3, 1963; "Bans Lifting at Durham," *Raleigh News and Observer*, June 5, 1963; "Twin Cities Dropping Barriers," *Raleigh News and Observer*, June 6, 1963; "Business Firms Drop Racial Barriers Here," *Raleigh News and Observer*, June 20, 1963. For the restructuring of traditional power relations as a result of business leaders' role in desegregation, see Jacoway and Colburn, eds., *Southern Businessmen*.

44. *Raleigh News and Observer*, May 15, 1963.

45. "Picket Beaten in High Point," *Raleigh News and Observer*, May 29, 1963; "One Killed, Another Wounded in Lexington Racial Outbreak," *Raleigh News and Observer*, June 7, 1963; "Lexington Is Quiet as Troopers Patrol," *Raleigh News and Observer*, June 8, 1963; "Oxford Marchers Stage Small Riot," *Raleigh News and Observer*, June 16, 1963. See also Waynick, Brooks, and Pitts, eds., *North Carolina*.

46. E.g., "400 Whites Jeer as Negroes March," *Raleigh News and Observer*, May 23, 1963; "1,000 Whites Watch Negro Demonstrators," *Raleigh News and Observer*, May 24, 1963. The pro-Wallace letter is found in "Wallace Stand," *Raleigh News and Observer*, May 25, 1963; see also the letters titled "Government" and "Demonstrations," in *Raleigh News and Observer*, June 20, 1963.

47. The American Legion, Department of North Carolina, Forty-Second Annual National Convention, Miami Beach, Florida, October 19, 1960, "Resolution — Subject: 'Communist Infiltration into Institutions of Higher Learning,'" copy in J. Gordon Hanes Papers, SHC.

48. For a synopsis of UNC's role in fostering more equitable race relations and the university's impact in the spring of 1963, see "UNC's 'Liberalism' Traced to Graham," *Greensboro Daily News*, August 9, 1965.

49. On May 20 the Court handed down its sit-in decision. *Peterson v. City of Greenville* (373 U.S. 244 [1963]) joined five similar cases from four states. *Avent v. North Carolina* (373 U.S. 375 [1963]) involved several protesters who had been arrested during peaceful sit-in demonstrations in Durham. In a landmark decision, the Court invalidated a variety of means, including trespass laws and disturbing-the-peace ordinances, that had been capriciously used to maintain segregation. See "Supreme Court Legalizes Sit-ins in Cities Enforcing Segregation," *New York Times*, May 21, 1963; "Sit-in Laws Struck Down," *Raleigh News and Observer*, May 21, 1963. See also Murphy, *Constitution*, 361–62.

50. Murphy, *Constitution*, 392; *School District of Abingdon Township v. Schempp*, 374 U.S. 203 (1963). See "Supreme Court, 8 to 1, Prohibits Lord's Prayer and Bible Reading as Public School Requirements," *New York Times*, June 18, 1963. A survey of North Carolina clerics indicated that many viewed the decision as an appropriate separation of church and state (see "Lord's Prayer Barred from U.S. Class-

rooms: Practice Called Unconstitutional," *Raleigh News and Observer,* June 18, 1963; "Tar Heel Pastors Comment," *Raleigh News and Observer,* June 18, 1963).

51. On the American Legion's actions, see "Legion Chaplain Indirectly Attacks Bible-Reading Ban," *Charlotte Observer,* June 24, 1963; "Legion Asks Study at UNC: University Group Termed Atheistic," *Charlotte Observer,* June 23, 1963. The proto–speaker ban resolution (resolution #6) had been drafted on June 13 by Raleigh Post 1. Copy in possession of author.

52. "Historic Week of Racial Progress in State," *Raleigh News and Observer,* June 9, 1963.

53. *Raleigh News and Observer,* June 16, 1963.

54. Martin interview; Lindsay C. Warren Jr., interview with author, Goldsboro, North Carolina, August 15, 1986; "Two States' Rights Bills Die in House," *Raleigh News and Observer,* June 14, 1963; "Rights Group Has Leaflet for Senators," *Raleigh News and Observer,* June 21, 1963.

55. "Super Court Bill Killed in Senate," *Charlotte Observer,* June 21, 1963; "Under the Dome," *Raleigh News and Observer,* June 21, 1963; "3 Amendments Fail in North Carolina," *New York Times,* June 21, 1963.

Chapter 5. Making a Case for Revision

1. The standard biography of Haldane's life and scientific accomplishments is Ronald W. Clark, *J. B. S.* On the speaker controversy, see "New Statute Cancels Lecturer's UNC Visit," *Charlotte Observer,* September 13, 1963.

2. "New Statute Cancels Lecturer's UNC Visit," *Charlotte Observer,* September 13, 1963; "'It's a Great Shame—Prof,'" *Charlotte Observer,* September 13, 1963.

3. "New Statute Cancels Lecturer's UNC Visit," *Charlotte Observer,* September 13, 1963.

4. Ibid.

5. WRAL-TV Viewpoint # 692, September 17, 1963, NCC.

6. Ibid.

7. *Charlotte Observer,* September 13, 1963; Paul F. Sharp to Dr. Arnold Nash, January 20, 1965, Chancellor's Records, Sharp Series, University Archives (hereafter Sharp Series).

8. "Aycock Tells Lawyers: 'Bomb the Ban,'" *Daily Tar Heel,* November 22, 1963.

9. "Gag Law Crimps National Meeting," *Chapel Hill Weekly,* January 8, 1964.

10. Ibid.

11. "Ban Scores Another 'Victory,'" *Durham Morning Herald,* January 12, 1964.

12. A copy of the report can be found in Aycock Series.

13. *North Carolina American Legion News,* July 1963; L. J. Phipps to William Haisley, October 12, 1964, Aycock Series.

14. Frederick S. Barkalow Jr. to Senator Gordon Hanes, July 19, 1965, Hanes Papers, SHC.

15. Gordon Hanes to Frederick S. Barkalow Jr., July 21, 1965, Hanes Papers, SHC.

16. "The Impact of the 'Visiting Speakers' Law," Aycock Series. It is ironic that Williams had come to North Carolina from Ohio State University, where a similar

law was being considered. See chapter 3 for a discussion of the anticommunist bill in Ohio.

17. Lawrence Slifkin to Dan K. Moore, May 11, 1965, Moore Papers, North Carolina State Archives (herafter cited as NCSA).

18. Jacques Berger to David M. Britt, July 23, 1965, Chairman's Correspondence, Speaker Ban Study Commission Records, NCSA.

19. Salton is mentioned in Frederick P. Brooks Jr. to Paul F. Sharp, July 28, 1965, Sharp Series.

20. Yates Bailey to T. Clarence Stone, July 30, 1963, T. Clarence Stone Papers, SHC; Harding is quoted in *Newsweek*, July 12, 1965, 73–74.

21. On the Chapel Hill demonstrations and the participation of UNC students and faculty, see Ehle, *Free Men*.

22. Robert W. Spearman, UNC student government president, to L. J. Phipps, March 17, 1965, UNC Student Government Association Records, University Archives.

23. See Navasky, *Naming Names*, 61, 224, 420. At Miller's May 1957 trial for contempt of Congress, HUAC prosecutor Richard Arens claimed that Miller had belonged to the CP for four years during the 1940s, but Arens refused to identify the source of the allegation (Caute, *Great Fear*, 100, 536–37).

24. "Academic Freedom"; Caute, *Great Fear*, 536–37.

25. Paul F. Sharp to Wayne A. Bowers, May 18, 1965, Sharp Series.

26. A brief overview of the Bradens' lives and careers appears in Buhle, Buhle, and Georgakas, eds., *Encyclopedia*, 103–5. On the sale of the house in Louisville and the subsequent racist violence, police harassment, and sedition trial, see Braden, *Wall*. For additional commentary on Carl Braden, see Caute, *Great Fear*, 167, and Scales and Nickson, *Cause at Heart*, 358.

27. Caute, *Great Fear*, 100, 167; Scales and Nickson, *Cause at Heart*, 358–59.

28. WRAL-TV Viewpoint #1108, May 24, 1965, NCC; C. O. Cathey to Paul F. Sharp, May 13, 1965, Carl Braden to C. O. Cathey, May 7, 1965, Sharp Series.

29. C. O. Cathey to Paul F. Sharp, May 13, 1965, Sharp Series. This letter contains a three-page addendum marked "Confidential Memorandum." On p. 1, Cathey's conversation with Walter Anderson of the SBI is summarized.

30. Ibid. The memorandum also summarizes an apparent telephone conversation between Cathey and a Mrs. Valenti, a HUAC staffer in Washington, about the fact that "Mr. Braden has been identified as a member of the Communist Party by a woman, Mrs. Alberta Ahearn." Cathey underlined every suggestion that indicated that Braden had been a CP member and that pertained to his refusal to answer HUAC questions pertaining to the CP. A portion of the "public" files on Braden and SCEF are attached to Edwin E. Willis to C. O. Cathey, May 13, 1965, Sharp Series.

31. "Exhibit 'C', excerpts of telephone conversation between Dean Cathey and Mr. Ralph Moody, Attorney General, Raleigh," May 12, 1965, Sharp Series; C. O. Cathey to Paul F. Sharp, May 13, 1965, Sharp Series; "Speaker Ban Cited to Halt Braden's Speech On Campus," *Durham Morning Herald*, May 18, 1965.

32. C. O. Cathey to Paul F. Sharp, May 13, 1965, Sharp Series.

33. Ibid.

34. *Durham Morning Herald*, May 18, 1965; "Ban Law Prevents UNC Speech," *Raleigh Times*, May 18, 1965.

35. The following editorials demonstrate the intense scrutiny that Helms devoted to speaker-related issues at UNC: WRAL-TV Viewpoint #1099, May 11, 1965; #1103, May 17, 1965; #1106, May 20, 1965, NCC. Helms's vilification of Braden and SCEF is featured in #1108, May 24, 1965.

Chapter 6. The Accreditation Threat

1. "Report of the Special Committee in Connection with H.B. 1395 of the 1963 General Assembly (So-Called Speaker Ban Law)," April 24, 1965, Records of the UNC Board of Trustees, University Archives.

2. Fred Weaver to members of the special committee, January 15, 1965, Sharp Series.

3. "Trustees to Consider Law," *Winston-Salem Journal*, May 22, 1965; "UNC Trustees to Ask Amendment of Speaker Ban," *Durham Morning Herald*, May 25, 1965.

4. "White: Ban Law Won't Be Repealed," *Raleigh Times*, May 14, 1965.

5. "Opposition Sees No Chance of Repealing Speaker Ban," *Greensboro Record*, May 22, 1965; "Speaker Ban Law Repeal Is Said Dead Issue," *Asheville Times*, May 15, 1965.

6. "Democratic Chief Says Gag to Be Repealed or Amended," *Chapel Hill Weekly*, March 8, 1964; W. Lunsford Crew to William B. Aycock, March 13, 1964, Aycock Series.

7. "Scott to Seek Second Post of State," *Greensboro Daily News*, January 14, 1964. For the full text of Scott's position, see "Statement by Bob Scott, Candidate for Lieutenant Governor, Carolina Hotel, Raleigh, North Carolina, January 13, 1964." A copy is attached to Robert W. Scott to William B. Aycock, January 24, 1964, Aycock Series.

8. "Statement by Bob Scott, Candidate for Lieutenant Governor, Carolina Hotel, Raleigh, North Carolina, January 13, 1964," in Robert W. Scott to William B. Aycock, January 24, 1964, Aycock Series.

9. "Opposition Sees No Chance of Repealing Speaker Ban," *Greensboro Daily News*, May 22, 1965.

10. "Gag Law Not Needed, Candidate Moore Says," *Raleigh News and Observer*, March 4, 1964; see also "Sly Way Can Be as Ruinous as Ban" (editorial), *Durham Morning Herald*, March 5, 1964.

11. In the second primary, Preyer's total increased by a meager 12,433 votes, while Moore's ballooned by 222,559. Lake had polled 217,172 votes in the first primary. For a description of the campaign's activities and the Moore forces' successful outreach to Lake's supporters, see Spence, *Making*; Luebke, *Tar Heel Politics*, 110, 158. C. A. Dillon, Moore's finance chairman, reported, "[I]t is amazing and most encouraging to see the large number of Lake supporters who are ready and willing to help Judge Moore" (Dillon to T. Clarence Stone, June 11, 1964, T. Clarence Stone Papers, SHC).

12. WRAL-TV Viewpoint #890, June 29, 1964, NCC.
13. *A Bill to Be Entitled an Act to Amend Chapter 1207 of the 1963 Session Laws (Now Incorporated into the General Statutes as Sections 116-199 and 116-200 of Article 22)*. A copy of the bill can be found attached to Gordon Hanes to David M. Britt, July 9, 1965, in Speaker Ban Study Commission Records, NCSA. The bill is given contextualized description in "Drive to Loosen Gag Is Slated Next Week," *Raleigh News and Observer*, May 22, 1963.
14. "The Long Watch and Wait on the Gag," *Chapel Hill Weekly*, May 9, 1965.
15. Ibid.
16. "Dan K. Moore Supports Speaker Ban," *Winston-Salem Journal*, April 7, 1964.
17. The full text of the telegram is found in Moore's statement, "On the Threat to Institutions of Higher Learning," May 20, 1965, in *Messages of Moore*, ed. Mitchell, 606–11. See also "Moore Says Gag Law Threatens College," *Raleigh News and Observer*, May 21, 1965. Copies of the telegram were also sent the following day to Friday, Dees, and Sharp.
18. "Moore Says Gag Law Threatens College," *Raleigh News and Observer*, May 21, 1965. See also "Accreditation of Colleges Threatened," *Greensboro Daily News*, May 8, 1965; "College Group Discussed Ban with Governor," *Greensboro Daily News*, May 17, 1965.
19. "College Group Discussed Ban with Governor," *Greensboro Daily News*, May 17, 1965.
20. "The Loss of Accreditation Would Be a Major Disaster for the Entire State" (editorial), *Chapel Hill Weekly*, May 23, 1965. This editorial provided perhaps the most comprehensive analysis of the dangers posed by loss of accreditation.
21. "Accreditation of Colleges Threatened," *Greensboro Daily News*, May 8, 1965. For Archie's view of the stakes involved in the speaker ban issue, see William C. Archie to Robert A. Kuettner, August 5, 1963, Aycock Series; Archie to Gerald W. Johnson, August 9, 1965, Speaker Ban Study Commission Records, NCSA.
22. "Opposition Sees No Chance of Repealing Speaker Ban Law," *Greensboro Daily News*, May 22, 1965.
23. "The Threat to Our Institutions of Higher Learning," May 20, 1965, Moore Papers, NCSA.
24. "The Loss of Accreditation Would Be a Major Disaster for the Entire State" (editorial), *Chapel Hill Weekly*, May 23, 1965.
25. William Medford to Dan K. Moore, April 24, 1965, Sharp Series. The Medford Report was attached to the letter. For the trustees' resolution, see "UNC Trustees Vote to Ask Amendment of Speaker Ban," *Durham Morning Herald*, May 25, 1965.
26. Karl Bishopric (Spray, North Carolina) to Dan K. Moore, May 27, 1965, Moore Papers, NCSA.
27. Wesley Critz George to Dan K. Moore, May 31, 1965, Moore Papers, NCSA; James W. Painter and Kathleen S. Painter to Moore, May 31, 1965, Moore Papers, NCSA; letters also came from a retiring faculty member of the School of Textiles at North Carolina State University, the director of athletics at North Carolina

State University, two members of the medical faculty at Duke University, and a mathematics professor at Wilmington College; all can be found in the Moore Papers, NCSA.

28. Godwin interview; "'Smokescreen' Charged by Speaker Ban Author," *Raleigh News and Observer*, May 11, 1965; "Drive to Loosen Gag Is Slated Next Week," *Raleigh News and Observer*, May 22, 1965; "Speaker Ban Backer Gives His Views," *Charlotte News*, June 24, 1965; Garland S. Garriss to Dan K. Moore, May 22, 1965, Moore Papers, NCSA.

29. "Accreditation of Colleges Threatened," *Greensboro Daily News*, May 8, 1965; Hoover Adams to Dan K. Moore, May 23, 1965, Moore Papers, NCSA.

30. "Friday: Didn't Know Association's Action," *Raleigh Times*, May 25, 1965.

31. Ibid.

32. William C. Friday to Elizabeth Swindell, July 16, 1965, Speaker Ban Study Commission Records, NCSA.

33. Friday interview; "Friday: Didn't Know Association's Action," *Raleigh Times*, May 25, 1965.

34. Friday interview; "Speaker Ban Backer Gives His Views," *Charlotte News*, June 24, 1965.

35. Friday interview; Paul F. Sharp to Rex W. Warner, June 14, 1965, Sharp Series; J. Carlyle Sitterson to William V. North, July 2, 1965, Sharp Series. Admissions officials received numerous inquiries about the legitimacy of the threat (see, e.g., Dell F. Pendergrast [Brookline, Massachusetts] to Sally Denton Coe, director of graduate admissions, June 8, 1965, Sharp Series).

36. WRAL-TV Viewpoint #1109, May 25, 1965, NCC.

37. Eure interview; "Sounding the Old Tocsin against Freedom of Speech on the Campus," *Chapel Hill Weekly*, September 29, 1963. On the Eure-Moody investigation of the SACS, see "Legality of Group Studied," *Greensboro Daily News*, June 24, 1965. For Eure and Moody's involvement in drafting H.B. 1395, see chapter 3.

38. "No Secrets Here," *Greensboro Daily News*, June 25, 1963; "Legislator Asked Secretary of State to Probe Group," *Raleigh Times*, June 23, 1965.

39. "Eure Says Let State Accredit Schools Itself," *Charlotte Observer*, August 22, 1965; "Southern Accrediting Unit Labeled 'Monster' by Eure," *Durham Morning Herald*, August 22, 1965. See also the following editorial takes on the Eure effort: "Accreditation Does Matter," *Winston-Salem Journal*, August 24, 1965; "Eure, Bruton Still Tilting at Accreditation Windmills," *Charlotte Observer*, September 26, 1965.

40. "From Law Office, Legal Artillery," *Durham Morning Herald*, September 26, 1965; "A Stroke of Genius" (editorial), *Winston-Salem Journal*, September 24, 1965; "A Disgraceful Attack" (editorial), *Greensboro Daily News*, August 23, 1965.

41. Hoover Adams to Dan K. Moore, May 23, 1965, Moore Papers, NCSA.

42. Hoover Adams to J. Edgar Hoover, March 27, 1965, Sharp Series.

43. J. Edgar Hoover to Hoover Adams, April 2, 1965, Sharp Series.

44. Hoover Adams to J. Edgar Hoover, May 10, 1965; Hoover to Adams, May 14, 1965,

both in Sharp Series. For a sample news story, see "FBI Chief Backs Speaker Ban Law," *Greensboro Daily News*, May 17, 1965.

45. "Statement Doesn't Bear on Ban" (editorial), *Durham Morning Herald*, June 2, 1965; J. Edgar Hoover to Hoover Adams, April 2, 1965, Sharp Series.

46. Arnold Nash to Hoover Adams, June 8, July 6, 1965; Adams to Nash, July 8, 1965; Lewis Lipsitz to Nicholas Katzenbach, June 3, 1965, all in Sharp Series.

47. WRAL-TV Viewpoint #1099, May 11, 1965, NCC.

48. Ibid.

49. Friday interview.

50. "The Gag, Accreditation and Jesse Helms," *Chapel Hill Weekly*, May 30, 1965.

51. "On Authorization of a Special Commission to Study the Speaker Ban Law," in *Messages of Moore*, ed. Mitchell, 615–17; "Moore Moves to Forestall Action on Speaker Ban," *Greensboro Daily News*, June 2, 1965.

52. "Commencement Program of the University of North Carolina at Chapel Hill," June 7, 1965, in *Messages of Moore*, ed. Mitchell, 164–68. See also "The Night the Governor Came to Ask for Understanding of His Abdication," *Chapel Hill Weekly*, June 9, 1965. The governor's announcement, as expected, unleashed a torrent of editorial ink. The *Raleigh News and Observer* labeled it a "retreat from duty" (June 8, 1965); the *Asheville Citizen* termed it "the politic way" (June 9, 1965); and the *Greensboro Daily News* titled its editorial "An Uncertain Trumpet" (June 8, 1965). A sampling of editorials from throughout the state appears in "Moore and the Speaker Ban," *Winston-Salem Journal*, June 15, 1965.

53. *A Joint Resolution Creating a Commission to Study the Statutes Relating to Visiting Speakers at State Supported Educational Institutions*, June 16, 1965, *Session Laws*, 1699–1700. H.R. 1068 had been passed on June 10, while S.R. 85 was a duplicate of the House measure. See "House Okays Bill to Study Speaker Ban," *Charlotte Observer*, June 10, 1965.

54. Friday interview.

Chapter 7. Rethinking the Speaker Ban

1. *Joint Resolution, Session Laws*, June 16, 1965, 1699–1700; "Speaker Ban Study Group Announced by Gov. Moore," *Greensboro Daily News*, June 25, 1965; "Nine Will Study Speaker Ban Law," *Winston-Salem Journal*, June 25, 1965.

2. "Moore Expected to Name Gag Law Study Panel Today," *Raleigh News and Observer*, June 24, 1965.

3. "Lt. Gov. Scott Says Tar Heels Want to Retain Speaker Ban," *Winston-Salem Journal*, June 26, 1965.

4. "Taylor: Ban Compromise Imperative," *Raleigh News and Observer*, June 22, 1965; "Speaker Ban Solution May Be Found in Court," *Greensboro Daily News*, June 22, 1965; see also "Speaker Taylor Speaks Up" (editorial), *Greensboro Daily News*, June 24, 1965.

5. "Speaker-Ban Study Unit to Be Appointed Soon," *Charlotte Observer*, June 18, 1965.

6. Dan K. Moore, June 24, 1965, as quoted in "Speaker Ban Study Group Announced by Gov. Moore," *Greensboro Daily News*, June 25, 1965.

7. Ibid.

8. Chafe, *Civilities*, 228, 395.

9. *Raleigh News and Observer*, March 3, 1963; *Journal of the House*, 1963 sess., 1226).

10. "A Good Commission" (editorial), *Greensboro Daily News*, June 26, 1965.

11. "Gordon Hanes Will Seek Forsyth's Senate Seat," *Raleigh News and Observer*, February 13, 1962; "Gordon Hanes: Senator, Manufacturer," *Raleigh News and Observer*, April 4, 1965; Powell, ed., *North Carolina Lives*, 540. Hanes's early support for the law is indicated in Joseph S. Sloane to Gordon Hanes, May 1, 1965, Sharp Series; Hanes to Lindsay C. Warren Jr., July 26, 1965, Hanes Papers, SHC; "Nine Will Study Speaker Ban Law," *Winston-Salem Journal*, June 25, 1965.

12. *Journal of the Senate*, 1963 sess., 763–64; "Nine Will Study Speaker Ban Law," *Winston-Salem Journal*, June 25, 1965.

13. "Thornburg, Lacy Herman," "Taylor, Hoyt Patrick, Jr.," and "Zollicoffer, Algernon Augustus, Jr.," all in *Biographical Dictionary*, ed. Massengill; "Speaker Ban Study Group Announced by Gov. Moore," *Greensboro Daily News*, June 25, 1965; Algernon Augustus Zollicoffer Jr., interview with author, Henderson, North Carolina, August 18, 1986; "Nine Will Study Speaker Ban Law," *Winston-Salem Journal*, June 25, 1965.

14. WRAL-TV Viewpoint #1134, June 29, 1965, NCC.

15. Ibid.

16. "Dan K. Moore Supports Speaker Ban," *Winston-Salem Journal*, April 6, 1964.

17. Britt interview. See also "Nine Will Study Speaker Ban Law," *Winston-Salem Journal*, June 25, 1965; "Speaker Ban Study Group Announced by Governor Moore," *Greensboro Daily News*, June 25, 1965. For a more detailed profile, see "Now Here's a Man Who Likes His Work—And Why Not?" *Raleigh News and Observer*, May 7, 1972.

18. "Commissioner," *Raleigh News and Observer*, June 29, 1965; "Ben C. Fisher: Big Booster for Carolina Baptists," *Raleigh News and Observer*, February 10, 1963.

19. WRAL-TV Viewpoint #1134, June 29, 1965, NCC.

20. *Raleigh News and Observer*, October 14, 1945; "Tarheel of the Week: Elizabeth G. Swindell," *Raleigh News and Observer*, May 6, 1951; WRAL-TV Viewpoint #662, August 6, 1963, NCC; "Wilson Editor Heading Press," *Raleigh News and Observer*, August 4, 1963.

21. Furgurson, *Hard Right*, 52–55; Pleasants and Burns, *Frank Porter Graham*, 198–99, 238, 98, 132–33, 197, 199, 254. See also "Address by Colonel William T. Joyner in Behalf of U.S. Senatorial Candidate Willis Smith, Wednesday Night, May 10, 1950, over a State-Wide Radio Hook-Up," William T. Joyner Papers, SHC; Hoover Adams to William T. Joyner, July 5, 1950; Joyner to Adams, July 20, 1950, both in Joyner Papers, SHC. In 1970 Joyner was featured on Helms's WRAL-TV Viewpoint as the commentator read a statement from Joyner denouncing the use of busing to eliminate racially segregated schools (#2281, February 24, 1970, NCC; Joyner to Jesse A. Helms, February 25, 1970; Helms to Joyner,

February 26, 1970, both in Joyner Papers, SHC). In 1972 Joyner was among the first and most prominent conservative Democrats to endorse Helms's candidacy for the U.S. Senate. The pivotal issue in Joyner's support was race and public education, specifically, an obstinate opposition to court-ordered busing, which Helms made a cornerstone of his campaign. See Joyner to Helms, July 5, 1972; "Helms News" (news release), July 6, 1972, both in Joyner Papers, SHC.

22. Chafe, *Civilities*, 92, 371.
23. William T. Joyner to J. H. Burke, August 1, 1963; J. M. Hunt Jr. to Joyner, March 11, 1964, both in Joyner Papers, SHC; "Nine Will Study Speaker Ban Law," *Winston-Salem Journal*, June 25, 1965.
24. Britt's support was confirmed in interviews with three members of the 1963 House, including Britt himself (Britt interview; Delamar interview; Zollicoffer interview). Britt's approval of H.B. 1395 was also mentioned, with a mild apology, in "Nine Will Study Speaker Ban Law," *Winston-Salem Journal*, June 25, 1965.
25. "Nine Will Study Speaker Ban Law," *Winston-Salem Journal*, June 25, 1965; Hoover Adams to David M. Britt, June 24, 1965, Speaker Ban Study Commission Records, NCSA.
26. "'R.F.D. Lawyer,'" *Greensboro Daily News*, August 15, 1965; Britt interview.
27. Gordon Hanes to Lindsay C. Warren Jr., July 26, 1965, Hanes Papers, SHC; "Minutes," meeting no. 1, July 14, 1965, Speaker Ban Study Commission Records, NCSA. The constitutional issues will be examined in greater detail in chapter 11.
28. A. D. Holt, president of the University of Tennessee, to Gordon Hanes, July 2, 1965; Thomas F. Jones to Gordon Hanes, July 2, 1965, both in Hanes Papers, SHC.
29. Elizabeth G. Swindell to N. G. Fawcett, August 20, 1965; Fawcett to Swindell, August 24, 1965, both in Speaker Ban Study Commission Records, NCSA.
30. "Alabama Nixes Speaker Ban," *Raleigh Times*, August 20, 1965; "'Bama Gag Reaction Instructive," *Hertford County Ledger*, September 3, 1965.
31. The responses to the inquiry were excerpted and summarized for the commission. See "The Significance of Regional Accreditation with Reference to Federal Higher Education Programs," Speaker Ban Study Commission Records, NCSA. On the private foundations, see Frank Bowles to David M. Britt, July 26, 1965; Florence Anderson to Britt, July 29, 1965, both in Speaker Ban Study Commission Records, NCSA.
32. Francis J. Colligan, director of policy review, State Department Bureau of Educational and Cultural Affairs, summarized in "Significance of Regional Accreditation."
33. Peter P. Muirhead, associate commissioner for higher education, Department of Defense, summarized in "Significance of Regional Accreditation."
34. Cecile Hillyer, chief, Division of Training, Vocational Rehabilitation Administration, summarized in "Significance of Regional Accreditation."
35. Testimony of Emmett B. Fields before the Speaker Ban Law Study Commission, August 11, 1965, Speaker Ban Study Commission Records, NCSA (hereafter cited as Fields testimony).
36. Ibid.

37. Ibid.
38. Ibid.
39. Ibid.
40. Ibid.
41. Ibid.
42. Ibid.
43. Ibid.
44. Testimony of Howard Boozer before the Speaker Ban Law Study Commission, August 11, 1965, Speaker Ban Study Commission Records, NCSA.
45. "Accreditation Loss Is Feared by Sen. Kirby," *Charlotte Observer*, August 19, 1965; "Ban Law Probers Find Witness Disappointing," *Winston-Salem Sentinel*, August 17, 1965; "Panel Members Fear Accreditation Loss," *Raleigh News and Observer*, August 19, 1965; William T. Joyner to Charles H. Young, September 16, 1965, Speaker Ban Study Commission Records, NCSA. For an elaboration of Zollicoffer's private concern, see A. A. Zollicoffer Jr. to E. C. Brooks Jr., September 17, 1965, Speaker Ban Study Commission Records, NCSA.
46. William T. Joyner to Charles H. Young, September 16, 1965, Speaker Ban Study Commission Records, NCSA; Fields testimony.
47. "You Can't Blame Dr. Fields for Evading Direct Answers," *Charlotte Observer*, August 15, 1965.
48. "Transcript of Hearings," August 12, 1965, Speaker Ban Study Commission Records, NCSA.
49. Copies of various American Legion resolutions can be found in the Gordon Hanes Papers, SHC. See the July 10, 1963, resolution endorsing the speaker law and the June 18, 1965, resolution calling for support for the study commission.
50. Testimony of Philip Godwin before the Speaker Ban Law Study Commission, "Transcript of Hearings," August 12, 1965, Speaker Ban Study Commission Records, NCSA.
51. Ibid.
52. Ibid.
53. Ibid.
54. "Resolution — Subject: "Communist Infiltration into Institutions of Higher Learning," Hanes Papers, SHC; "A Resolution and Recommendation by American Legion Post no. 6," Chapel Hill, North Carolina, September 17, 1962, Hanes Papers, SHC; Resolution of the American Legion, Department of North Carolina, July 10, 1963, Hanes Papers, SHC.
55. "Commander's Message"; "Legion Is Invited"; Nash D. McKee to David M. Britt, October 7, 1965, Speaker Ban Study Commission Records, NCSA. The legion resolution, dated June 18, is attached.
56. Testimony of W. Dudley Robbins before the Speaker Ban Law Study Commission, August 12, 1965, "Transcript of Hearings," Speaker Ban Study Commission Records, NCSA (hereafter cited as Robbins testimony).
57. Robbins testimony; Mrs. J. R. Fisher (Enfield, North Carolina) to Dan K. Moore, November 17, 1965, White Papers, SHC; Godwin interview. For examples of Viet-

nam rhetoric from both supporters and opponents of the law, see "Speaker Ban Praised and Berated by N.C. Leaders," *Charlotte Observer,* August 12, 1965; "While Yanks Die in Viet War, Southern Assn. Coddles Reds," *Concord (N.C.) Tribune,* November 17, 1965. See also "Special Speaker Ban Issue" of the *North Carolina American Legion News,* November 1965.

58. Testimony of Robert B. Morgan before the Speaker Ban Law Study Commission, August 12, 1965, "Transcript of Hearings," Speaker Ban Study Commission Records, NCSA (hereafter cited as Morgan testimony; "UNC Offers Platform to Radicals, *Charlotte Observer,* July 2, 1965; William C. Friday to David M. Britt, September 1, 1965; Britt to Friday, September 2, 1965, both in Speaker Ban Study Commission Records, NCSA.

59. Morgan testimony.

60. Alvis Carver to William C. Friday, July 26, 1965; Friday to Carver, July 28, 1965, both in Friday Records, University Archives. For press accounts of the exchange of letters, see "Questionable Query, Proper Reply," *Charlotte Observer,* July 29, 1965; "Low Blow," *Raleigh News and Observer,* July 29, 1965; "Insult, Misconception in Demand," *Durham Morning Herald,* July 29, 1965; "Free Speech: Plank or Splinter?" *Greensboro Daily News,* July 30, 1965.

61. Morgan testimony; testimony of A. C. Jordan before the Speaker Ban Law Study Commission, August 12, 1965, Speaker Ban Study Commission Records, NCSA (hereafter cited as Jordan testimony).

62. Jordan testimony. Each member of the study commission had access to the report on Berkeley to which Jordan referred, and Joyner made the report part of the official record. See *Thirteenth Report.* See also Schrecker, *No Ivory Tower,* 117, 279.

63. Jordan testimony; A. C. Jordan to David M. Britt, August 17, 1965, Speaker Ban Study Commission Records, NCSA; Jordan to Thomas J. White Jr., November 27, 1965, White Papers, SHC.

64. Testimony of Henry B. Royall before the Speaker Ban Law Study Commission, August 12, 1965, "Transcript of Hearings," Speaker Ban Study Commission Records, NCSA (hereafter cited as Royall testimony).

65. King interview; Dennis King to author, October 5, 1989.

66. Royall testimony.

67. "Americanism and McCarthyism in North Carolina," *Chapel Hill Weekly,* August 18, 1965.

68. Testimony of Samuel I. Parker before the Speaker Ban Law Study Commission, September 8, 1965; testimony of Thomas J. White Jr. before Speaker Ban Law Study Commission, September 9, 1965; testimony of Vermont Royster before the Speaker Ban Law Study Commission, September 9, 1965; testimony of Luther H. Hodges before the Speaker Ban Law Study Commission, September 9, 1965; testimony of Malcolm B. Seawell before Speaker Ban Law Study Commission, September 9, 1965; all in "Transcript of Hearings," Speaker Ban Study Commission Records, NCSA; E. A. Bescherer, Greensboro Chamber of Commerce, to Dan K. Moore, June 1, 1965, Speaker Ban Study Commission Records, NCSA. See also "Medal of Honor Winner Says Law Insults People," *Raleigh Times,*

September 8, 1965; "White Calls University Text 'Instrument of Indoctrination,'" *Raleigh News and Observer*, September 10, 1965; "2 UNC Authors Cite Ike, Others," *Raleigh Times*, September 10, 1965; "Speaker Ban Called Unconstitutional," *Raleigh News and Observer*, August 5, 1965; Charles F. Myers to David M. Britt, September 11, 1965, Speaker Ban Study Commission Records, NCSA.

69. Testimony of Paul F. Sharp before the Speaker Ban Law Study Commission, September 9, 1965, "Transcript of Hearings," Speaker Ban Study Commission Records, NCSA.

Chapter 8. An Anticommunist Speaker Policy

1. A. A. Zollicoffer Jr. to E. C. Brooks Jr., September 17, 1965, Speaker Ban Study Commission Records, NCSA.
2. David M. Britt, memorandum to members of the commission studying the Speaker Ban Law, October 1, 1965, Speaker Ban Study Commission Records, NCSA.
3. A. A. Zollicoffer Jr. to David M. Britt, September 29, 1965; J. Russell Kirby to David M. Britt, October 4, 1965, both in Speaker Ban Study Commission Records, NCSA.
4. David M. Britt, memorandum to members of the commission studying the speaker ban law, October 1, 1965; William T. Joyner to Britt, October 5, 1965, both in Speaker Ban Study Commission Records, NCSA.
5. *Raleigh News and Observer*, November 24, 1964.
6. Friday interview; "Does the University Really Need a Crier to Proclaim Its Anti-Communist Stand?" *Winston-Salem Journal*, July 11, 1965; "'Show Me a Red at UNC,' Friday Challenges State," *Gastonia Gazette*, October 15, 1965.
7. J. Carlyle Sitterson, memorandum to William C. Friday, "Subject: Visiting Speakers," August 20, 1965, Sharp Series.
8. U.S. House Committee on Un-American Activities, *Violations*, pt. 2; "Students Crash 'Kennedy Curtain'"; "Students See Cuba."
9. U.S. House Committee on Un-American Activities, *Violations*, pt. 2, 780–87. See also *Durham Morning Herald*, September 6, 1963.
10. See U.S. House Committee on Un-American Activities, *Violations*, pt. 2, 655.
11. *Durham Morning Herald*, November 1, 1963; *Winston-Salem Journal*, November 2, 1963.
12. *Durham Morning Herald*, November 1, 1963.
13. Ibid.
14. *Winston-Salem Journal*, November 2, 1963; William G. Long to Howard Henry, November 1, 1963, Aycock Series.
15. The essential source for documentation on the matter of Nicholas Bateson is the file marked "Nicholas Bateson," Aycock Series. Biographical information and his academic record can be found in a report from his adviser, John Schopler, to Chancellor Aycock (Schopler to Aycock, November 7, 1963, Aycock Series). Evidence of interrogation by the Immigration and Naturalization Service is provided

in "Summary of Testimony at the Hearing on December 6, 1963, before the Committee on Faculty Hearings in the Matter of Nicholas Bateson," Aycock Series (hereafter cited as "Summary of Testimony"). Bateson confirmed and elaborated this record in a telephone interview with the author, September 27, 1989.

16. U.S. House Committee on Un-American Activities, *Violations*, pt. 4, 847–57. Bateson's quid pro quo with the Immigration and Naturalization Service is mentioned in "Summary of Testimony," 3; Bateson interview.

17. U.S. House Committee on Un-American Activities, *Violations*, pt. 4, 811–17; Bateson interview.

18. U.S. House Committee on Un-American Activities, *Violations*, pt. 4, 850–52.

19. Ibid, 857. Bateson's motives in taking the Fifth are presented in "Summary of Testimony." For a response from speaker law advocates, see the editorial statement of WBTV in Charlotte, "The F.B.I. and Bateson," October 22, 1963, Friday Records, University Archives. The quote on "damage limitation" as his purpose is from Bateson's interview with the author.

20. Much of the material in this passage is provided in the Bateson interview. It is corroborated by three additional documents. The first is Aycock's handwritten notes of his October 17, 1963, meeting with the student. The second is the "Summary of Testimony," which confirms that Aycock released the information Bateson volunteered despite an apparent agreement that the contents of the discussion would remain confidential. Finally, the October 17 meeting is cited in William B. Aycock to Nicholas Bateson, October 21, 1963. All these documents are in Aycock Series.

21. William B. Aycock to Nicholas Bateson, October 21, 1963, Aycock Series. Friday's role is confirmed by the correspondence between the president and chancellor and by two subsequent letters to Bateson, the latter of which notified him that he would be stripped of university employment (Aycock to Bateson, November 12, 1963, January 31, 1964, Aycock Series). The "information" about which Aycock desired investigation is presented in a memorandum from the chancellor to the chairman of the hearing board. It consisted of Bateson's HUAC testimony, statements made by Bateson's roommate, and an itemized list of "the facts volunteered" by the student to Aycock (William B. Aycock to Henry Brandis, November 4, 1963, Aycock Series).

22. John Schopler to William B. Aycock, November 7, 1963, Aycock Series.

23. William B. Aycock to H. B. Robinson, November 5, 1963, Aycock Series. A blind copy of the letter went to Friday.

24. Hoover Adams to William B. Aycock, November 4, 1963, Aycock Series.

25. U.S. House Committee on Un-American Activities, *Violations*, pt. 4, 838–43; William B. Aycock to H. B. Robinson, December 4, 1963, Aycock Series.

26. William B. Aycock to Henry P. Brandis, November 4, 1963; Aycock to Bateson, November 12, 1963, both in Aycock Series; "Summary of Testimony"; Bateson interview. That the highest echelon of the UNC administration was both aware of and encouraging the move against Bateson is confirmed by Friday's endorsement of Aycock's action.

27. Henry Brandis et al. to William B. Aycock, January 30, 1964, Aycock Series.

28. Ibid.

29. Ibid.

30. William B. Aycock to Nicholas Bateson, January 31, 1964, Aycock Series.

31. Bateson interview.

32. Gordon Hanes to William C. Friday, July 26, 1965, Hanes Papers, SHC. Invocation of the need for "academic responsibility" was a hallmark of Helms's anti-UNC commentary preceding passage of the speaker law. The ambivalent term eventually became a staple of those supporting the law.

33. "If We Would Keep the University Free, We Must Keep It Free from Those Who Would Destroy it," May 24, 1949, General Administration, Vice President for Finance Records (William Carmichael), University Archives; William C. Friday to William B. Aycock, December 2, 1958; Aycock to Friday, December 19, 1958, Aycock Series.

34. "The University and Communism," attached to William C. Friday to David M. Britt, October 19, 1965, Speaker Ban Study Commission Records, NCSA. Friday's response to Britt's request for a UNC position paper on communism was marked *Personal.*

35. Ibid.

36. "On Report of Speaker Ban Law Study Commission," November 5, 1965, in *Messages of Moore*, ed. Mitchell, 628–30; Watts Hill Jr., chairman, State Board of Higher Education, memorandum to presidents of state-supported institutions of higher education, November 8, 1965, Sharp Series.

37. "On Report of Speaker Ban Law Study Commission," November 5, 1965, in *Messages of Moore*, 629.

38. Untitled report, Speaker Ban Study Commission Records, NCSA.

39. Ibid.

40. "Policy and Regulations of the Board of Trustees Regarding Visiting Speakers," November 12, 1965, Records of the UNC Board of Trustees, University Archives.

41. Ibid.

42. Ibid.

43. See Joyner to David M. Britt, October 5, 28, 1965, Speaker Ban Study Commission Records, NCSA.

44. Chafe, *Civilities*, 72–82.

45. Ibid., 92, 371; David M. Britt to Otto K. Pridgen Sr., November 26, 1965, Speaker Ban Study Commission Records, NCSA.

46. "UNC Students Favor Amendment Offered on Speaker Ban Law," *Raleigh Times*, November 11, 1963; "Student Leaders Generally Favor Decision on Ban," *Raleigh Times*, November 6, 1965. The poll was described as "casual."

47. Britt interview; *Winston-Salem Journal*, November 7, 1965; "Speaker Ban Critic Fears 'Censorship' by Trustees," *Fayetteville Observer*, November 7, 1965.

48. See WRAL-TV Viewpoint #1224, November 10, 1965, NCC.

49. "Minutes of the Special Called Meeting of the General Faculty Held November 8, 1965, in Carroll Hall, at 4 P.M.," Sharp Series; "Remarks by President Friday at the Special Called Meeting, November 8, 1965," Sharp Series.

50. Minutes of November 12, 1965, meeting, Records of the UNC Board of Trustees, University Archives; "University Adopts New Campus Speaker Policy," *Raleigh News and Observer*, November 13, 1965; "UNC Board Okays Ban Policy at Brief Meeting Here Today," *Raleigh Times*, November 12, 1965; "Amendment to Speaker Policy Proposed by Thomas J. White," November 12, 1965, White Papers, SHC.

51. Mitchell, ed., *Messages of Moore*, 63, 64.

52. *Journal of the Senate*, 1965 extra. sess., 845; *Journal of the House*, 1965 extra sess., 13; "Britt Is All Things to All Men in Effort to Get Ban Amended," *Raleigh News and Observer*, November 16, 1965. A copy of King's bill is attached to Gordon Hanes to David M. Britt, July 9, 1965, Speaker Ban Study Commission Records, NCSA.

53. "Speaker Ban Critic Fears 'Censorship' by Trustees," *Fayetteville Observer*, November 7, 1965.

54. Britt interview.

55. "Dolley to Fight Speaker Ban Amendment," *Raleigh News and Observer*, November 11, 1965; Britt interview; "Statement by Member," November 16, 1965, in *Journal of the House*, 1965 extra sess., 29; "House Approves Ban Overhaul; Final Action Today in Senate," *Raleigh News and Observer*, November 17, 1965.

56. "Teeth Extracted from State's Troublesome Speaker Ban Law," *Raleigh News and Observer*, November 18, 1965; *Journal of the Senate*, 1965 extra sess., 849, 850–52; *Charlotte Observer*, November 16, 1965.

57. *Journal of the Senate*, 1965 extra sess., 852–53; General Statutes of North Carolina, art. 22, "Visiting Speakers at State-Supported Institutions," chaps. 116–199 and 116–119, 1965, ex. sess., c.1, s.1.

58. "Accrediting Plea to Be Presented," *Raleigh News and Observer*, November 28, 1965; "Accrediting Crisis over for Schools," *Raleigh News and Observer*, December 2, 1965.

59. For examples of editorial treatment, see "The Welcome End of an Era," *Greensboro Daily News*, November 18, 1965; "The Governor's Achievement," *Winston-Salem Journal*, November 18, 1965; "State Can Breathe Easier with Speaker Ban Amended," *Charlotte Observer*, November 18, 1965; "Legislature Resolves the Speaker Ban Stew," *Asheville Citizen*, November 18, 1965; "Speaker Ban Amendment," *Warren Record*, November 19, 1965; "Fight Ends on a Familiar Note," *Durham Morning Herald*, November 19, 1965; WRAL-TV Viewpoint #1233, November 23, 1965, NCC; *Dunn Daily Record*, November 17, 18, 1965.

60. David M. Britt to Victor S. Bryant, November 27, 1965, Speaker Ban Study Commission Records, NCSA.

Chapter 9. Freeing the University

1. On the formation and early agenda of SDS, see Sale, *SDS*, esp. 40; Miller, "*Democracy.*" See also "Individuals to Be Invited to SDS Evaluation Meeting Proposed for Dec. 26–27–28, 1961," November 27, 1961, Students for a Dem-

ocratic Society (SDS) Papers (Microfilm), ser. 1, no. 3 (hereafter cited as SDS Microfilm).

2. On the role played by Bateson and the UNC New Left Club in organizing the conference, see Tom Hayden to Robb Burlage, November 16, 1961, SDS Microfilm, ser. 1, no. 4; Hayden, newsletter addressed "Dear Friend," n.d., SDS Microfilm, ser. 1, no. 3. For descriptions of the conference, see Sandra Cason to Al Haber, April 17, 1962, SDS Microfilm, ser. 1, no. 4; Sale, *SDS*, 44–46; Miller, *"Democracy,"* 102–5.

3. Sale, *SDS*, 44–45; Miller, *"Democracy,"* 103–4.

4. On the Economic Research and Action Program, see Sale, *SDS*, 120–29; Miller, *"Democracy,"* 192–95, 212–13. On SSOC's involvement with SNCC and SDS, see Carson, *In Struggle*, 102–3; Evans, *Personal Politics*, 44–47; Simon, "Southern Student Organizing Committee." Information regarding Bateson's involvement with PL is based on his interview with the author.

5. Gardner and Ray, "Attempt at 'Open Forum' Was a Significant Failure," *Daily Tar Heel*, April 29, 1965.

6. Ibid.

7. On Weissman's Free Speech Movement activity, see Rorabaugh, *Berkeley*, 24, 30–31, 97–99. For the southern speaking tour, see Steve Weissman to Clark Kissinger, SDS national secretary, March 26, 1965, SDS Microfilm, ser. 2A, no. 33; Sale, *SDS*, 175–76. Weissman's speech in Chapel Hill was announced and covered in "Rebels Set Campus Talks," *Daily Tar Heel*, May 2, 1965; "Control of University Urged by FSM Spokesman," *Daily Tar Heel*, May 4, 1965.

8. On the formation of SDS, see "'To Challenge the Establishment' Given as Purpose of New SDS Group," *Daily Tar Heel*, May 7, 1965; on Lowenstein's critique, see "Lowenstein Says U.S. Action in Viet Nam 'Humiliating,'" *Daily Tar Heel*, May 7, 1965; Scales and Nickson, *Cause at Heart*, 327. Further commentary on Lowenstein's anticommunism can be found in Harris, *Dreams*, 315–16.

9. Given its loose organizational structure, there is scant documentation confirming membership and affiliate figures. The best such indicator is a questionnaire returned to *New Left Notes*. Although undated, it suggests the state of the group during the spring of 1966. The form reports "circa 30" members, equally divided between undergraduates and graduate students. UNC-SDS's organizational dimension was limited: "Have tried active recruiting—feel doomed to fail," the reporter lamented. See UNC-SDS questionnaire, SDS Microfilm, ser. 3, no. 55. The other available indicator is a letter from chapter treasurer Reid Reynolds to SDS, November 18, 1965[?], SDS Microfilm, ser. 3, no. 55. The best sources for information on UNC-SDS are the members themselves: for this book, oral history interviews were conducted with several former SDS activists.

10. "Constitution of the University of North Carolina at Chapel Hill Chapter of Students for a Democratic Society," Friday Records, University Archives. See also Joseph W. Straley to C. O. Cathey, December 21, 1965, Friday Records, University Archives. A professor of physics, Straley was a faculty adviser for the SDS chapter. On the early history of UNC-SDS, see "The Controversial SDS," *Chapel Hill Weekly*, February 6, 1966. Much of the description and analysis of UNC-SDS in

this chapter is based on interviews and correspondence with members: R. James McCorkel Jr., telephone interview with author, November 18, 1991; McCorkel to author, December 7, 1991; Gary E. Waller, telephone interview with author, December 13, 1991; Reid Reynolds, telephone interview with author, June 25, 1992; Reynolds to author, July 11, 1992; Chuck Schunior, interview with author, Chapel Hill, North Carolina, July 27, 1992; Jerry Carr, telephone interview with author, January 7, February 19, 1992; Carr to author, March 13, 1992.

11. McCorkel interview; Waller interview; Reynolds interview; Carr interview.

12. McCorkel interview; Waller interview; Reynolds interview; Carr interview.

13. Waller interview. See also "An Open Letter to the UNC Board of Trustees," UNC-SDS, November 8, 1965; "Statement to Press," November 8, 1965, both in Frank Porter Graham Papers, SHC.

14. McCorkel interview; McCorkel to author, December 7, 1991. See also "He Has No 'Vietnik' Image," *Winston-Salem Journal*, February 4, 1966.

15. McCorkel interview; McCorkel to author, December 7, 1991. See also "He Has No 'Vietnik' Image," *Winston-Salem Journal*, February 4, 1966.

16. "He Has No 'Vietnik' Image," *Winston-Salem Journal*, February 4, 1966.

17. Waller interview; "SDS Leader Waller Has Interesting Past," *Daily Tar Heel*, December 4, 1966; "SDS: Carolina's Strange Creature of the New Left," *Daily Tar Heel*, November 6, 1966; "The Controversial SDS," *Chapel Hill Weekly*, February 6, 1966.

18. "'To Challenge the Establishment' Given as Purpose of New SDS Group," *Daily Tar Heel*, May 7, 1965; McCorkel interview; Waller interview; Schunior interview.

19. The best sources on the intellectual origins of SDS and the style of the Port Huron generation are Miller, "*Democracy*," and Isserman, *If I Had a Hammer*. For the second generation, see Sale, *SDS*, 305–6; Gitlin, *The Sixties*, 258–59. The UNC profiles are based on interviews with McCorkel and Waller and "SDS Leader Waller Has Interesting Past," *Daily Tar Heel*, December 4, 1966; "SDS: Carolina's Strange Creature of the New Left," *Daily Tar Heel*, November 6, 1966; "The Controversial SDS," *Chapel Hill Weekly*, February 6, 1966.

20. McCorkel interview; Waller interview; "SDS Leader Waller Has Interesting Past," *Daily Tar Heel*, December 4, 1966.

21. Waller interview.

22. McCorkel interview.

23. Bibliographies in possession of author.

24. Schunior interview; Waller interview; "Protests Begin Again at UNC: SPU Pickets Hound Dog Missile," *Daily Tar Heel*, September 17, 1965. See also Schunior's response to the story in "Letters," *Daily Tar Heel*, September 23, 1965.

25. McCorkel to author, December 7, 1991; "Group Collects $97 and Heckles," *Daily Tar Heel*, October 16, 1966; "They Wouldn't Understand" (editorial), *Daily Tar Heel*, October 15, 1965; "Student Legislature Votes against 'Soup Fast' Day," *Daily Tar Heel*, October 16, 1965. On the national effort, see "Battle of Vietnam Day." Background on SPU at UNC and student response to the soup fast is found in Thorpe, "Study," 26, 37–38.

26. Schunior interview; Sale, *SDS*, 230; "SPU, Others Demonstrate at Special Forces

Post," *Daily Tar Heel*, October 17, 1965; "University Party Condemns SPU for Peace Policy," *Daily Tar Heel*, October 20, 1965; "SPU Activities: Right or Wrong?" *Daily Tar Heel*, November 12, 1965.

27. "Chapel Hill Represented in March," *Daily Tar Heel*, November 30, 1965.
28. "UNC Students Favor Amendment Offered on Speaker Ban Law," *Raleigh Times*, November 11, 1963; "Students for a Democratic Society, University of North Carolina at Chapel Hill, Statement to Press for Immediate Release," November 8, 1965; "Students for a Democratic Society, University of North Carolina at Chapel Hill, Open Letter to the UNC Board of Trustees," November 8, 1965, both in Graham Papers, SHC.
29. "UNC Students Favor Amendment Offered on Speaker Ban Law," *Raleigh Times*, November 11, 1963.
30. Ibid.
31. Ibid.
32. "Friday Says He's Satisfied with Proposed Speaker Law," *Winston-Salem Journal*, November 6, 1965; Friday interview.
33. McCorkel to author, December 7, 1991.
34. William C. Friday to David M. Britt, October 11, 1965; Wayne A. Bowers to Friday, October 2, 1965, both in Friday Records, University Archives; "Aptheker Isn't Apathetic," *Daily Tar Heel*, January 13, 1950; "Dr. Aptheker Misses Topic, Praises Reds," *Daily Tar Heel*, January 13, 1950.
35. For a personal account of the visit to North Vietnam, see Hayden, *Reunion*, 175–97. See also Miller, *"Democracy,"* 264–69; Gitlin, *The Sixties*, 264–74.
36. Paul F. Sharp to William C. Friday, January 27, 1966, Sharp Series; McCorkel interview; McCorkel to author, December 7, 1991.
37. "Re: Students for a Democratic Society, Invitations to Mr. Aptheker and Mr. Wilkinson, Answers to questions from Dean Cathey to Messers. Norman Gustaveson, William Wynn, Joseph Straley and Jim McCorkel," January 21, 1966, Friday Records, University Archives.
38. Ibid.; Joseph W. Straley, Norman F. Gustaveson, and William H. Wynn to C. O. Cathey, February 2, 1966, Friday Records, University Archives; Straley, interview with author, Chapel Hill, North Carolina, July 18, 1992.
39. "Invited Speakers Causing Concern," *Raleigh News and Observer*, January 29, 1966; William C. Friday to T. M. Andrews, February 7, 1966, Friday Records, University Archives; Friday interview; Joseph W. Straley to C. O. Cathey, December 21, 1965, Friday Records, University Archives; C. O. Cathey press statement, reported in *Raleigh News and Observer*, January 28, 1966.
40. McCorkel interview; Waller interview; McCorkel to author, December 7, 1991.
41. Friday interview. In this interview, Friday never mentioned his meeting with the SDS students but frequently cited his numerous meetings with student body president Paul Dickson.
42. McCorkel interview; Waller interview. The response of the two SDS leaders is further elaborated in McCorkel to author, December 7, 1991.
43. "Invited Speakers Causing Concern," *Raleigh News and Observer*, January 29,

1966; "Controversial Speakers Asked to Chapel Hill," *Raleigh Times*, January 28, 1966; "Student Group Leader Says Red Speaker Victim of Press Errors," *Greensboro Daily News*, February 1, 1966; "Barring of Aptheker Will Simply Help Leftist Cause," *Charlotte Observer*, February 1, 1966; McCorkel interview; McCorkel to author, December 7, 1991.

44. Philip P. Godwin to William C. Friday, February 1, 1966, Friday Records, University Archives; Gordon Hanes to Friday, February 2, 1966, Friday Records, University Archives. See also "Academic Freedom."

45. A. A. Zollicoffer Jr. to William C. Friday, February 2, 1966; David M. Britt to Friday, February 4, 1966, both in Friday Records, University Archives.

46. David M. Britt to William C. Friday, February 4, 1966, Friday Records, University Archives.

47. Gordon Hanes to William C. Friday, February 2, 1966; David M. Britt to Friday, February 4, 1966, both in Friday Records, University Archives.

48. Friday interview; William C. Friday to Philip P. Godwin, February 7, 1966, Friday Records, University Archives.

49. Arthur J. Beaumont to C. O. Cathey, February 4, 1966, Sharp Series.

50. Arthur J. Beaumont to Mrs. Valenti, February 8, 1966, Sharp Series. Interviews with former UNC-SDS members revealed Beaumont's presence and activity at student gatherings; most recalled a trademark cigar (McCorkel interview; Waller interview; Reynolds interview).

51. "Regulations adopted by the Board of Trustees of the University of North Carolina, January 14, 1966," Friday Records, University Archives; "On Invitations to Known Communists to Speak at University," in *Messages of Moore*, ed. Mitchell, 636–38; "Governor Slams University Door on Red Speaker," *Chapel Hill Weekly*, February 2, 1966; "Governor Should Stick to Rule of Not Being Censor in Future," *Raleigh Times*, February 2, 1966; "Who Should Run University?" *Fayetteville Observer*, February 9, 1966; "Red Speaker Backer Is 'Shocked,'" *Raleigh News and Observer*, February 3, 1966.

52. Mitchell, ed., *Messages of Moore*, 636–38.

Chapter 10. Confrontation in Chapel Hill

1. "Student Leaders Generally Favor Decision on Ban," *Raleigh Times*, November 6, 1965; "Friday Says He's Satisfied with Proposed Speaker Law," *Winston-Salem Sentinel*, November 5, 1965; "UNC Campus Leaders Join Bid for Red's Appearance," *Greensboro Daily News*, February 4, 1966.

2. Friday interview. Following graduation from UNC, Dickson took a position with a printing firm in Fayetteville and continued his climb within the ranks of the state Democratic Party. At the time of his death in 1972, he was serving as the state Young Voters Campaign chairman in James B. Hunt Jr.'s gubernatorial effort ("Political Worker, Two Others Killed," *Raleigh News and Observer*, April 30, 1972).

3. *Daily Tar Heel*, February 4, 1966.

4. "McCorkel Resigns Office amidst Speaker Flare-Up," *Daily Tar Heel*, February 3,

1966; C. O. Cathey, "Memorandum to File: Students for a Democratic Society," February 2, 1966, Sharp Series. At the same press conference, McCorkel announced his decision to resign as chairman of SDS, ostensibly to devote more time to completion of his Ph.D. (McCorkel interview; McCorkel to author, December 7, 1991). See also "SDS May Test Denial of Aptheker in Court," *Raleigh Times*, February 2, 1966.

5. Friday interview.

6. "Trustee Committee Bars Red Speaker from UNC," *Charlotte Observer*, February 8, 1966. C. O. Cathey to Gary Waller, February 11, 1966, Sharp Series.

7. *Daily Tar Heel*, February 8, 1966; *Winston-Salem Journal*, February 8, 1966; Waller interview.

8. WRAL-TV Viewpoint #1290, February 10, 1966, NCC.

9. Ibid.

10. "Students Back Free Speech," *Winston-Salem Journal*, February 8, 1966; Waller interview; *Protean Radish*, April 14–20, 1969, Anti-War Materials, NCC.

11. "UNC Rally for Free Speech Set," *Winston-Salem Journal*, February 9, 1966.

12. *Chapel Hill Weekly*, February 26, 1966; Jefferson B. Fordham to William C. Friday, February 25, 1966, Friday Records, University Archives.

13. See Executive Committee Minutes, January 14, 1966, Friday Records, University Archives.

14. "Statement to UNC Board of Trustees from UNC-CH SDS," February 28, 1966, Chancellor's Records, Sitterson Series, University Archives (hereafter cited as Sitterson Series); *Greensboro Daily News*, March 1, 1966; Executive Committee Minutes, January 28, 1966, Friday Records, University Archives.

15. Paul Dickson et al. to J. Carlyle Sitterson, February 28, 1966, Sitterson Series.

16. Ibid.

17. J. Carlyle Sitterson, interview with author, Chapel Hill, North Carolina, July 20, 1992.

18. The situation involving Aptheker in Michigan was reported in several North Carolina newspapers (see, e.g., "Aptheker Speaks in Michigan," *Durham Sun*, February 2, 1966).

19. Sitterson interview; *Raleigh News and Observer*, February 29, 1966.

20. J. Carlyle Sitterson press release, March 2, 1966, Sitterson Series.

21. *Durham Morning Herald*, March 2, 1966; *Raleigh News and Observer*, March 2, 1966; Frank Wilkinson, interview with author, Los Angeles, California, March 22, 1987.

22. Sitterson interview; Friday interview.

23. "UNC Bans Wilkinson Speech; He Talks over Campus Wall," *Charlotte Observer*, March 3, 1966; Wilkinson interview; Waller interview. For the text, see "Remarks of Frank Wilkinson Made from the Public Sidewalk on East Franklin Street in Chapel Hill, North Carolina, at 1:00 P.M., March 2, 1966," Frank Porter Graham Papers, SHC.

24. McCorkel interview; McCorkel to author, December 7, 1991; Wilkinson interview; "Students Eager for Court Test of UNC Policy," *Winston-Salem Sentinel*,

March 3, 1966; "Students Plan Wilkinson Ban Test in Court," *Greensboro Daily News*, March 3, 1966.

25. Herbert Aptheker to Stuart Matthews, February 13, 1966, Frank Porter Graham Papers, SHC.
26. J. Carlyle Sitterson to Paul Dickson, March 4, 1966, Sitterson Series.
27. J. Carlyle Sitterson to Victor Bryant, March 5, 1966, Sitterson Series.
28. J. Carlyle Sitterson to B. F. Ullman et al., March 10, 1966, Sitterson Series.
29. Rudolph I. Mintz to J. Carlyle Sitterson, March 2, 1966, Sitterson Series.
30. C. W. Phillips to J. Carlyle Sitterson, March 3, 1966, Sitterson Series.
31. John Honigman to J. Carlyle Sitterson, March 2, 1966; Robert Gallman to Sitterson, March 2, 1966, both in Sitterson Series.
32. *Winston-Salem Journal*, March 3, 1966.
33. John Honigman to J. Carlyle Sitterson, March 2, 1966, Robert Gallman to Sitterson, March 2, 1966, both in Sitterson Series.
34. "Halted by UNC Policeman, Aptheker Speaks over Wall," *Charlotte Observer*, March 10, 1963; "Aptheker Talks off Campus after Threat of Arrest Made," *Durham Morning Herald*, March 10, 1966; Herbert Aptheker, interview with author, San Jose, California, November 14, 1985. The whereabouts of any tape recordings are unknown.
35. "Halted by UNC Policeman, Aptheker Speaks over Wall," *Charlotte Observer*, March 10, 1963; "Aptheker Talks off Campus after Threat of Arrest Made," *Durham Morning Herald*, March 10, 1966; Aptheker interview.
36. "Halted by UNC Policeman, Aptheker Speaks over Wall," *Charlotte Observer*, March 10, 1963; "Aptheker Talks off Campus after Threat of Arrest Made," *Durham Morning Herald*, March 10, 1966; Aptheker interview; "Aptheker Speaks at Chapel Hill," *Raleigh News and Observer*, March 10, 1966; Waller interview. For a text of Aptheker's comments, see "Remarks of Herbert Aptheker Made from the Public Sidewalk on East Franklin Street in Chapel Hill, North Carolina, at 12:00 Noon, March 9, 1966," Frank Porter Graham Papers, SHC.
37. *Raleigh News and Observer*, March 11, 1966.
38. "Radio-Television News Release," Carolina Forum, March 4, 1966; "Press Release," Carolina Forum, March 6, 1966, both in UNC Student Government Association Records, University Archives; Paul Dickson et al. to Chancellor J. Carlyle Sitterson, March 14, 1966, Sitterson Series.
39. J. Carlyle Sitterson press release, March 4, 1966, Sitterson Series.
40. Frederic N. Cleaveland to J. Carlyle Sitterson, February 26, 1966; John W. Thibaut to Sitterson, February 24, 1966; "Copy of University News Bureau Dispatch Phoned to News Media at 3 P.M. March 4, 1965"; "Dispatch by University News Bureau for P.M. News Media Friday, March 4, 1966," all in Sitterson Series.
41. David M. Britt to J. Carlyle Sitterson, April 1, 1966, Sitterson Series.
42. Frederic N. Cleaveland to J. Carlyle Sitterson, February 26, 1966; John W. Thibaut to Sitterson, February 24, 1966, both in Sitterson Series. The Thibaut letter has a handwritten note explaining how the invitation would be handled. For coverage of the Alexandrov visit, see "Communist Talks to UNC Classes," *Burlington*

Daily Times-News, March 23, 1966. The public announcement of Papousek's addressing a graduate colloquium is found in "Communist Scientist Will Speak," *Chapel Hill Weekly,* May 8, 1966.

43. "Communist Scientist Will Speak," *Chapel Hill Weekly,* May 8, 1966.

44. A brief résumé including Aptheker's publications and university lecturing is available in Herbert Aptheker to Stuart Matthews, February 13, 1966, Frank Porter Graham Papers, SHC. The timing of the refusal also confirmed the political character of Sitterson's action. Aptheker had spoken at UNC on two previous occasions without any difficulty (Aptheker interview). See also "Aptheker Isn't Apathetic," *Daily Tar Heel,* January 13, 1950; Wayne A. Bowers to William C. Friday, October 2, 1965, Friday Records, University Archives.

45. J. Carlyle Sitterson to Paul Dickson, March 31, 1966, Sitterson Series; Speaker Ban File, Sitterson Series, March 1966; J. Carlyle Sitterson, interview with author, Chapel Hill, North Carolina, November 18, 1987.

46. *Dickson et al. v. Sitterson et al.,* Civil Action No. C-59-G-66, U.S.D.C., Middle District of North Carolina. On the students' motivations and principles, see McNeill Smith to Frank P. Graham, May 30, 1966, Graham Papers, SHC. For news commentary, see "Speaker Ban Annulment Sought in Student Suit," *Raleigh News and Observer,* April 1, 1966; "Speaker Ban Suit Is Filed," *Chapel Hill Weekly,* April 3, 1966; "AAUP Supports Students' Lawsuit," *Greensboro Daily News,* April 8, 1966.

Chapter 11. The Speaker Ban Goes to Court

1. "SDS May Test Denial of Aptheker in Court," *Raleigh Times,* February 2, 1965; McCorkel interview; Paul Dickson to William C. Friday, February 11, 1966, Friday Records, University Archives; Paul Dickson, "Statement to Board of Trustees," February 28, 1966, UNC Student Government Association Records, University Archives.

2. Friday interview.

3. Ralph Moody to T. W. Bruton, "Memorandum: Constitutionality of Chapter 1207 of the Session Laws of 1963 (H.B. 1395) entitled: 'An Act to Regulate Visiting Speakers at State Supported Colleges and Universities,'" August 2, 1963, Attorney General Records, NCSA; "Mr. Bruton and the Campus Speakers," *Greensboro Daily News,* June 29, 1963.

4. Ralph Moody to T. W. Bruton, "Memorandum," August 2, 1963, Attorney General Records, NCSA; *Egan v. Moore,* 235 N.Y.S. 2d 995 (1962); *Egan v. Moore,* 245 N.Y.S. 2d 622 (1963); *Buckley v. Meng,* 230 N.Y.S. 2d 924, 35 Misc. 2d 467 (1962); *Slochower v. Board of Education,* 350 U.S. 551 (1956).

5. Ralph Moody to T. W. Bruton, "Memorandum," August 2, 1963, Attorney General Records, NCSA; *University v. Maultsby,* 43 N.C. 254 (1852) (one of the rare instances in which the brief cited the year in which a ruling was issued); *Egan v. Moore,* 235 N.Y.S. 2d 955 (1962); *Egan v. Moore,* 245 N.Y.S. 2d 622 (1963).

6. Ralph Moody to T. W. Bruton, "Memorandum," August 2, 1963, Moody to Patricia Malone, May 1, 1963, both in Attorney General Records, NCSA.

7. "Took Salary Cut to Return to Scene of Court Battles," *Raleigh News and Observer,* August 24, 1958.

8. Ibid.; William T. Joyner to Thomas J. Pearsall, December 4, 1959; Joyner to Ralph Moody, November 13, 1959, both in Attorney General Records, NCSA.

9. "Took Salary Cut to Return to Scene of Court Battles," *Raleigh News and Observer,* August 24, 1958; Ralph Moody to Thomas J. Pearsall, September 5, 1958, Attorney General Records.

10. *Raleigh News and Observer,* November 23, 1968.

11. William W. Van Alstyne, "Memorandum on the North Carolina Speaker Ban Law," Speaker Ban Study Commission Records, NCSA (hereafter cited as Van Alstyne memorandum).

12. Van Alstyne, "Political Speakers." See also "Symposium," which concludes that Wilkinson would have been constitutionally eligible to speak at UNC under 1963 speaker ban.

13. Pollitt, "Campus Censorship."

14. Daniel H. Pollitt to John Oliver Cook, July 24, 1964, American Association of University Professors Records, North Carolina State University Archives.

15. Van Alstyne memorandum. Of the numerous decisions relevant to the speaker ban, five were highlighted as decisive. In *DeJonge v. Oregon* (299 U.S. 353 [1937]), the U.S. Supreme Court overturned a state statute making it a criminal offense to speak under CP auspices without taking into account the actual content of the speech. *Danskin v. San Diego School District* (28 Cal. 2d 536 [1946]) overturned a California statute forbidding the use of school auditoriums by "subversive elements" on grounds that the law represented a violation of the equal-protection clause of the Fourteenth Amendment. A recent decision, *Buckley v. Meng* (230 N.Y.S. 2d 924, 35 Misc. 2d 467 [Sup. Ct. 1962]), invalidated a Hunter College regulation restricting the use of the college auditorium to speakers deemed "compatible with the interest of Hunter College in higher education." In *Slochower v. Board of Education* (350 U.S. 551 [1956]), the Supreme Court held that the dismissal of a college professor on the basis of his invoking the Fifth Amendment before the Senate Subcommittee on Internal Security was unconstitutional. The fifth case was *Egan v. Moore* (245 N.Y.S. 2d 622 [1963]), a discussion of which follows.

16. Van Alstyne memorandum, 3; William W. Van Alstyne to Wesley H. Wallace, August 17, 1965, Wallace Papers, SHC; "Professor, Lawmakers Give Views on Speaker Ban Move," *Raleigh News and Observer,* November 7, 1965; "Van Alstyne on the Speaker Ban Law," *Chapel Hill Weekly,* October 6, 1965.

17. Ralph Moody to David M. Britt, August 4, 1965; Britt to Moody, August 5, 1965, both in Chairman's Correspondence, Speaker Ban Study Commission Records, NCSA.

18. Ralph Moody to David M. Britt, September 7, 1965, Chairman's Correspondence, Speaker Ban Study Commission Records, NCSA.

19. Ibid.

20. Ibid.; "Moody Sees Reply by Electorate If Ban Law Held Unconstitutional," *Greensboro Daily News,* September 15, 1965; "Legal Logic Lost," *Raleigh News*

and Observer, September 16, 1965; Thomas H. Woodard to Ralph Moody, September 16, 1965, Chairman's Correspondence, Speaker Ban Study Commission Records, NCSA.

21. Memorandum re. *Dickson et al. v. Sitterson et al., re. Plaintiff's Reply Brief,* January 3, 1967, Sitterson Series.

22. Ibid.

23. "Judges Hear Ban Law Arguments," *Raleigh News and Observer,* February 22, 1967; "Judges Study Speaker Ban Case Decision," *Greensboro Daily News,* February 22, 1967.

24. *Slochower v. Board of Education,* 350 U.S. 551 (1956).

25. Commentary on the introduction of the earlier banning of Marion Butler from speaking at UNC is found in Ashby, *Frank Porter Graham,* 315–16.

26. *Dickson v. Sitterson* (M.D.N.C. C-59–G–66), "Brief for the Defendants." For commentary on the presence of *Dickson v. Sitterson* personae at the Scales trial, see Scales and Nickson, *Cause at Heart,* 237–40, 267–79. See chapter 9 for a discussion of Clontz's testimony before the Britt commission.

27. Scales and Nickson, *Cause at Heart,* 279. On Stanley's early school-integration judgments, see Peltason, *Fifty-Eight Lonely Men,* 79–81; Chafe, *Civilities,* 109, 156, 313–14.

28. "Ban Law Opinion Delayed," *Winston-Salem Sentinel,* October 24, 1967.

29. *Dickson v. Sitterson,* 280 F. Supp. 486 (1968).

30. "State Speaker Ban Ruled Unconstitutional," *Daily Tar Heel,* February 20, 1968; "Speaker Ban Decision: Score One for UNC," *Daily Tar Heel,* February 20, 1968; J. Carlyle Sitterson and William C. Friday, "Statement on Opinion Concerning Speaker Ban Law," February 19, 1968, Sitterson Series; "Free Speech Triumphs and a Gag Is Lifted," *Asheville Citizen,* February 21, 1968; "Leave it Alone," *Raleigh News and Observer,* February 24, 1968; "Judges Suggest Pitfalls of Speaker Ban," *Winston-Salem Sentinel,* February 21, 1968. Not every urban paper applauded the decision. For a sample critical editorial, see "Reds Receive Green Light," *Rocky Mount Telegram,* February 23, 1968.

31. *Dickson v. Sitterson,* 280 F. Supp. 486 (1968).

32. Ibid.

33. Ibid.

34. Ibid.; "Judges Suggest Pitfalls of Speaker Ban," *Winston-Salem Sentinel,* February 21, 1968; WRAL-TV Viewpoint #1792, February 22, 1968, NCC.

35. WRAL-TV Viewpoint #1792, February 22, 1968, NCC; "Statement of T. W. Bruton, Attorney General," February 20, 1968, Attorney General Records, NCSA.

36. "Speaker Ban Decision Termed 'A Pyrrhic Victory,'" *Chapel Hill Weekly,* March 20, 1968.

37. Mitchell, ed., *Messages of Moore,* 672–73.

38. Friday interview; "Speaker Code Urged at UNC," *Charlotte News,* February 26, 1968; "Policy Asked for University to Govern Disruptions," *Raleigh News and Observer,* February 27, 1968.

39. Friday interview; "Interim Set of Regulations on UNC Speakers Adopted," *Ra-*

leigh News and Observer, February 27, 1968; "Interim Speaker Rules Are Adopted by UNC," *Chapel Hill Weekly*, February 28, 1968.

40. William C. Friday, memorandum to chancellors, March 11, 1968, Sitterson Series; White interview; Friday to Frank Strong, March 13, 1968, Sitterson Series; "Trustee Meet Keeps Speaker Ban Alive," *Charlotte Observer*, February 27, 1968; "Interim Set of Regulations on UNC Speakers Adopted," *Raleigh News and Observer*, February 27, 1968.

41. "Trustee Meet Keeps Speaker Ban Alive," *Charlotte Observer*, February 27, 1968.

42. "Interim Guides Accepted," *Charlotte Observer*, February 27, 1968; "Interim Set of Regulations on UNC Speakers Adopted," *Raleigh News and Observer*, February 27, 1968.

43. "Policy and Regulations of the Board of Trustees Regarding Visiting Speakers," May 2, 1968, Friday Records, University Archives; Arch T. Allen to members of the Board of Trustees, May 20, 1968, Sitterson Series.

44. "Policy and Regulations of the Board of Trustees Regarding Visiting Speakers," May 2, 1968, Friday Records, University Archives.

45. White interview.

46. William C. Friday to Jefferson B. Fordham, May 29, 1968, Friday Records; Friday to Jordan E. Kurland, May 28, 1968, Friday Records, University Archives; *Raleigh News and Observer*, May 28, 1968.

47. Jesse A. Helms to Thomas J. White Jr., February 12, 1972, White Papers, SHC; William C. Friday to Raleigh Exchange Club, May 10, 1971, Friday Records, University Archives.

Chapter 12. Beyond the Speaker Ban

1. "Speaker Ban Bill Killed," *Raleigh News and Observer*, May 22, 1969; "New Speaker Ban Bid Fails in House," *Charlotte Observer*, May 22, 1969; *Journal of the House*, 1969 sess., 345, 744; "Bill Denying State Aid to Rioters Approved," *Raleigh News and Observer*, June 18, 1969; "College Curfew Bill Gets Okay," *Raleigh News and Observer*, May 23, 1969; "Clean Dorms Bill Passed by House," *Raleigh News and Observer*, May 20, 1969; *Journal of the House*, 1969 sess., 457, 620, 632, 725, 757, 966, 1023, 1119, 1145; *Journal of the Senate*, 1969 sess., 610, 644, 674, 691, 725, 759, 772, 797; "Report Warns against Laws to Punish Students," *Raleigh News and Observer*, June 10, 1969.

2. "Anti-Disruption Pledge Defeated," *Raleigh News and Observer*, June 26, 1969; "Student Conduct Bill Dies in House," *Charlotte Observer*, June 26, 1969; "Expulsion Bill Dies," *Raleigh News and Observer*, June 25, 1969; "Watkins Expulsion Bill Apparently Dies — Quietly," *Charlotte Observer*, June 25, 1969; *Journal of the House*, 1969 sess., 353, 983. University officials were understandably concerned about the authoritarian character of the bills, as can be observed from the university's legal evaluation of them. See Richard Bardolph, memorandum to University Advisory Council, April 21, 1969, General Administration, Vice President for University Relations, North Carolina State University Archives, which gives an over-

view of the problematic character of the Watkins bill and Gentry and Jack L. Rhyne's good-conduct bill (H.B. 808).

3. Robert G. Kittrell to William C. Friday, March 21, 1969, Friday Records, University Archives; memorandum to members of the Board of Trustees of the University of North Carolina, n.d., and trustee response, Frank Taylor to J. Worth Gentry, March 25, 1969, both in Taylor papers, SHC; "Governor Robert Scott's Warning to the University," *Chapel Hill Weekly*, April 13, 1969. See also Scott, memorandum to presidents of state-supported institutions of higher learning, "Procedures Relative to the Seizure of Buildings and Disturbances on the Campus of State Institutions of Higher Learning," February 20, 1969, Friday Records, University Archives.

4. "Procedures Relative to the Seizure of Buildings and Disturbances on the Campus of State Institutions of Higher Learning," February 20, 1969, Friday Records, University Archives; "Anti-Disruption Pledge Defeated," *Raleigh News and Observer*, June 26, 1969; "Student Bill Dies in House," *Charlotte Observer*, June 26, 1969. For a brief description of the food workers' strike and the Lenoir Hall incidents, see Snider, *Light*, 281–83. A former editor of the *Greensboro News and Record*, Snider provides a celebratory record of the handling of these conflicts by UNC administrators. The best source for information on the strike and occupation is the *Daily Tar Heel*, March 1–15, 1969. See also Daniel H. Pollitt, UNC-AAUP, to Robert W. Scott, March 6, 1969, Friday Records, University Archives.

5. *Daily Tar Heel*, March 15, 1969.

6. J. Carlyle Sitterson, memorandum to members of the faculty and student body, "Resolution Defining the Offense of Disruption of Educational Processes and Other Activities of the University," April 3, 1969, Sitterson Series.

7. William C. Friday to Charles J. Dunn Jr., director, SBI, November 26, 1969, and attachment, UNC Campus "Contacts"; State Bureau of Investigation "Weekly Bulletin," October 2, 1969, all in Friday Records, University Archives.

8. State Bureau of Investigation "Weekly Bulletin," October 2, 1969, Friday Records, University Archives.

9. Reese Gardner to William C. Friday, January 9, 1968, Friday Records, University Archives.

10. WRAL-TV Viewpoint #1766, January 15, 1968, NCC.

11. Ibid.; William C. Friday and J. Carlyle Sitterson to Reese Gardner, January 10, 1968, Friday Records, University Archives.

12. "Resolution Defining the Offense of Disruption of Educational Processes and Other Activities of the University," March 14, 1969, Records of the UNC Board of Trustees, University Archives.

13. "New Profs Must Reveal 'Violations,'" *Chapel Hill Weekly*, May 18, 1969; "A Resolution of the Faculty Senate of the North Carolina State University," May 20, 1969, General Administration, Vice President for University Relations, North Carolina State University Archives. For an individual complaint from the UNC faculty, see Wilton Mason, music department, to J. Carlyle Sitterson, May 14, 16, 1969, Sitterson Series; William C. Friday to Charles Morrow, July 18, 1969, Friday Records, University Archives.

14. "A Resolution Amending the By-Laws of the Board of Trustees to Provide for Handling the Offense of Disruption of the Educational Process and Other Activities of the University and Clarifying Responsibility for Student Discipline," July 7, 1969, Records of the UNC Board of Trustees, University Archives.

15. Nationally, the moratorium was observed at nine hundred sites with millions participating (see Zaroulis and Sullivan, *Who Spoke Up?* 245–47, 264–80). See also "Moratorium Plans Laid," *Daily Tar Heel*, September 23, 1969. For the administrators' response to the moratorium, see "Moratorium Investigated," *Daily Tar Heel*, September 25, 1969; "Faculty Told to Follow Regular Duties Oct. 15," *Daily Tar Heel*, September 26, 1969. On moratorium activities within the UNC system, see "Support Vietnam War Moratorium Today; Cut Classes, Participate in Activities," *Daily Tar Heel*, October 15, 1969; "7,000 Participate in Moratorium Here," *Daily Tar Heel*, October 16, 1969.

16. Gerhard Lenski to William C. Friday, September 26, 1969, Friday Records, University Archives.

17. "UNC-Charlotte Professor Defies Trustees: Abolishes Class," *Daily Tar Heel*, October 16, 1969; David G. Blevins to Dr. Bertram A. Davis, AAUP general secretary, April 14, 1970, Friday Records, University Archives.

18. *Blevins v. University of North Carolina*, C-21-D-70, "Conclusions of Law," September 8, 1971, Friday Records, University Archives.

19. Charles H. Reynolds to Pat Taylor, May 15, 1970, Sitterson Series; "Radicals Organize," *Daily Tar Heel*, September 30, 1969; "Both Left and Right Find Home in Chapel Hill," *Daily Tar Heel*, October 3, 1969.

20. On the program's origin as a campaign against black activists and the New Left, see O'Reilly, *Racial Matters*, 261–70, 285–87; Gitlin, *The Sixties*, 413.

21. Interviews with former UNC-SDS members, particularly McCorkel, Waller, and Carr, reveal regular, although informal, surveillance by UNC personnel at chapter functions. Carr obtained the information on FBI surveillance and harassment through the Freedom of Information Act (FBI, "Leslie Gerald Carr, AKA. Jerry," June 17, 1968, 1–19; copies in possession of author). On the picketing and arrests following the Dow protests, see "SDS to Picket Dow Recruiter," *Daily Tar Heel*, March 18, 1968; "Fifteen Arrested in Dow Demonstration," *Daily Tar Heel*, March 19, 1968; "50 Dow Protesters Present Request to Administration," *Daily Tar Heel*, March 19, 1968; Sale, *SDS*, 541.

22. FBI, SAC, Charlotte, to FBI director, "Leslie Gerald Carr SM-SDS," January 5, 1970, p. 2.

23. Carr interview; FBI, SAC, Charlotte, to FBI director, "Leslie Gerald Carr, aka Jerry, SM-SDS," November 14, December 12, 1969. On Carr's leadership in UNC-SDS, see "Peace Group Plans March, Conference," *Daily Tar Heel*, October 4, 1967; "D.C. Mobilization Defended by Carr" (letter), *Daily Tar Heel*, October 14, 1967; "Has SDS Become Too Mainstream?" *Daily Tar Heel*, January 7, 1968; "SDS to Picket Dow Recruiter, Carr Announces," *Daily Tar Heel*, March 16, 1968.

24. FBI, SAC, Charlotte, memorandum to FBI director, "Counterintelligence Program, Internal Security, Disruption of the New Left," January 5, April 9, 1970.

25. See Sitterson's May 5, 1970, public statement on the "tragedy of the war in Indochina," which implicitly approved of a protest action (Sitterson Series); William C. Friday et al. to Sam J. Ervin Jr., telegram, May 6, 1970; Simon, "Southern Student Organizing Committee," 87, 98. On Lyn Wells, see Evans, *Personal Politics*, 46–47, 173.
26. Jesse A. Helms to Thomas J. White Jr., April 15, 1970, White Papers, SHC.

Conclusion

1. Furgurson, *Hard Right*; Phillips, *Emerging Republican Majority*; Sale, *Power Shift*; Crawford, *Thunder*.
2. Bass and DeVries, *Transformation*, 233–34; Lamis, *Two-Party South*, 136–37; Luebke, *Tar Heel Politics*, 134.
3. Lamis, *Two-Party South*, 141–43; Luebke, *Tar Heel Politics*, 135, 167; Furgurson, *Hard Right*, 140–43.
4. Daniel, *Standing*, 209, 212–16; Luebke, *Tar Heel Politics*, 124–25, 129–30, 141; Furgurson, *Hard Right*, 210–14. see also Crawford, *Thunder*; Kincaid and LaMountain, "Interview."
5. Ferrel Guillory, quoted in Bass and DeVries, *Transformation*, 218–19.

BIBLIOGRAPHY

PRIMARY SOURCES

Southern Historical Collection, University of North Carolina at Chapel Hill

John Dunne Papers
Frank Porter Graham Papers
James Gordon Hanes Jr. Papers
William T. Joyner Papers
Allard K. Lowenstein Papers
Howard W. Odum Papers
Thomas Jenkins Pearsall Papers
T. Clarence Stone Papers
Olive Stone Papers
Terry Sanford Papers
Tillett Family Papers
Thomas J. White Jr. Papers

University Archives, University of North Carolina at Chapel Hill

Chancellor's Records, William B. Aycock, Robert B. House, Paul Sharp, and J. Carlyle
    Sitterson Series
William C. Friday Records
General Administration, Vice President for Finance Records (William Carmichael)
Records of the President, Gordon Gray Series
Records of the UNC Board of Trustees, 1959–71
UNC Student Government Association Records

North Carolina Collection, University of North Carolina at Chapel Hill

Anti-War Materials from the University of North Carolina at Chapel Hill, 1967–70
Jesse Helms Editorial Collection
WRAL-TV Viewpoints

Manuscripts Department, Duke University, Durham, North Carolina

J. B. Matthews Papers

North Carolina State Archives, Raleigh

Attorney General Records, 1963–68
Luther Hodges Papers
Nell Battle Lewis Papers
Daniel Killian Moore Papers
Terry Sanford Papers
Robert Scott Papers
Speaker Ban Study Commission Records

North Carolina State University Archives, Raleigh

American Association of University Professors Records
General Administration, Vice President for University Relations

SECONDARY SOURCES

"Academic Freedom: Futile Ban on Ideas." *Time,* June 11, 1965, 74, 77.
"Amending the Constitution to Strengthen the States in the Federal System." *State Government* 36 (winter 1963): 10–15.
Anderson, Eric. *Race and Politics in North Carolina, 1872–1901: The Black Second.* Baton Rouge: Louisiana State University Press, 1981.
Aptheker, Herbert. *American Negro Slave Revolts.* New York: Columbia University Press, 1943.
Ashby, Warren. *Frank Porter Graham: A Southern Liberal.* Winston-Salem, N.C.: John F. Blair, 1980.
Badger, Anthony J. *Prosperity Road: The New Deal, Tobacco, and North Carolina.* Chapel Hill: University of North Carolina Press, 1980.
Barksdale, Marcellus C. "Civil Rights Organization and the Indigenous Movement in Chapel Hill, N.C., 1960–1965." *Phylon* 17 (March 1986): 29–42.
———. "The Indigenous Civil Rights Movement and Cultural Change in North Carolina: Weldon, Chapel Hill, and Monroe: 1946–1965." Ph.D. diss., Duke University, 1977.
Bartley, Numan V. *The Rise of Massive Resistance: Race and Politics in the South during the 1950s.* Baton Rouge: Louisiana State University Press, 1969.

Bass, Jack, and Walter DeVries. *The Transformation of Southern Politics: Social Change and Political Consequence since 1945.* New York: Basic Books, 1976.

"Battle of Vietnam Day." *Newsweek,* October 25, 1965, 98.

Bello, Thomas M. "The Student Strike at the University of North Carolina at Chapel Hill (May 1970): An Eyewitness Historical Memoir." Honors thesis, University of North Carolina at Chapel Hill, 1971.

Bennett, David H. *The Party of Fear: From Nativist Movements to the New Right in American History.* Chapel Hill: University of North Carolina Press, 1988.

Beyle, Thad L., and Merle Black, eds. *Politics and Policy in North Carolina.* New York: MSS Information, 1975.

Billings, Dwight B. *Planters and the Making of a "New South": Class, Politics, and Development in North Carolina, 1865–1900.* Chapel Hill: University of North Carolina Press, 1979.

Black, Charles L., Jr. "Proposed Amendment of Article V: A Threatened Disaster." *Yale Law Journal* 72 (April 1963): 957–66.

Black, Earl. *Southern Governors and Civil Rights: Racial Segregation as a Campaign Issue in the Second Reconstruction.* Cambridge: Harvard University Press, 1976.

Blanshard, Paul. "Communism in Southern Mills." *Nation* 128 (1929): 500–501.

Bondurant, William, et al. "The North Carolina Speaker Ban Law: A Study in Context." *Kentucky Law Journal* 55 (1966–67): 225–49.

Boyd, Harold K. "Louis Austin and the *Carolina Times.*" Master's thesis, North Carolina College, 1966.

Braden, Anne. *House Un-American Activities Committee: Bulwark of Segregation.* Los Angeles: National Committee to Abolish the House Un-American Activities Committee, 1963.

——. *The Wall Between.* New York: Monthly Review Press, 1958.

Branch, Taylor. *Parting the Waters: America in the King Years, 1954–1963.* New York: Simon and Schuster, 1988.

Brazil, Wayne D. "Howard W. Odum: The Building Years, 1884–1930." Ph.D. diss., Harvard University, 1975.

Brinkley, Joel. "Helms and Rightists: Long History of Friendship." *New York Times,* August 1, 1984.

Buhle, Mari Jo, Paul Buhle, and Dan Georgakas, eds. *Encyclopedia of the American Left.* New York: Garland Publishing, 1990.

Burns, Augustus M., III. "Graduate Education for Blacks in North Carolina, 1930–1951." *Journal of Southern History* 46 (May 1980): 195–218.

——. "North Carolina and the Negro Dilemma." Ph.D. diss., University of North Carolina, 1968.

Butler, Lindley, and Alan D. Watson, eds. *The North Carolina Experience: An Interpretive and Documentary History.* Chapel Hill: University of North Carolina Press, 1984.

Buttitta, Tony. *After the Good Gay Times.* New York: Viking Press, 1974.

Carleton, Don E. *Red Scare! Right-Wing Hysteria, Fifties Fanaticism, and Their Legacy in Texas.* Austin: Texas Monthly Press, 1985.

Carson, Clayborne. *In Struggle: SNCC and the Black Awakening of the 1960s*. Cambridge: Harvard University Press, 1981.

Carter, Dan T. *The Politics of Rage: George Wallace, the Origins of the New Conservatism, and the Transformation of American Politics*. New York: Simon and Schuster, 1995.

Carter, Luther J. "Speaker Ban: Controversy Is Revived at UNC." *Science*, April 1, 1966, 50–52.

———. "Speaker Ban: State Assembly Kills Law Denying Forum to Communist; UNC's Status Is Believed Safe." *Science*, November 26, 1965, 1141, 1194.

———. "Speaker Ban (I): North Carolina Law Stirs Unrest at University." *Science*, October 29, 1965, 589–91.

———. "Speaker Ban (II): Controversial Law Endangers UNC's Standing; Move to Abolish It Expected Soon." *Science*, November 5, 1965, 725–28.

Cash, W. J. *The Mind of the South*. New York: Alfred A. Knopf, 1941.

Caute, David. *The Great Fear: The Anti-Communist Purge under Truman and Eisenhower*. New York: Simon and Schuster, 1978.

———. *The Fellow-Travellers: Intellectual Friends of Communism*. New Haven: Yale University Press, 1988.

Cell, John W. *The Highest Stage of White Supremacy: The Origins of Segregation in South Africa and the American South*. New York: Cambridge University Press, 1982.

Chafe, William H. *Civilities and Civil Rights: Greensboro, North Carolina and the Black Struggle for Freedom*. New York: Oxford University Press, 1980.

———. "Greensboro, North Carolina: Perspectives on Progressivism." In *Southern Businessmen and Desegregation*, ed. Elizabeth Jacoway and David R. Colburn, 42–69. Baton Rouge: Louisiana State University Press, 1982.

———. *The Unfinished Journey: America since World War II*. New York: Oxford University Press, 1986.

Christensen, Rob. "Helms Courting Latin Right: 'To Keep Communism Out.'" *Raleigh News and Observer*, April 25, 1982.

Clark, E. Culpepper. *The Schoolhouse Door: Segregation's Last Stand at the University of Alabama*. New York: Oxford University Press, 1993.

Clark, Ronald W. *J. B. S.: The Life and Work of J. B. S. Haldane*. London: Hodder and Stroughton, 1968.

Clark, Wayne A. "An Analysis of the Relationship between Anti-Communism and Segregationist Thought in the Deep South, 1948–1954." Ph.D. diss., University of North Carolina, 1976.

Coates, Albert. *Edward Kidder Graham, Harry Woodburn, Frank Porter Graham: Three Men in the Transition of the University of North Carolina at Chapel Hill from a Small College to a Great University*. Chapel Hill, N.C.: Institute of Government, 1988.

Cobb, James C. "Beyond Planters and Industrialists: A New Perspective on the New South." *Journal of Southern History* 104 (February 1988): 45–68.

Cohn, David L. "Durham: The New South." *Atlantic Monthly*, May 1940, 614–19.

"Commander's Message." *North Carolina American Legion News* 30 (August 1965): 1, 5.

Cox, Monty Woodall. "Freedom during the Fremont Campaign: The Fate of One North Carolina Republican in 1856." *North Carolina Historical Review* 45 (April 1968): 357–83.

Cramer, M. Richard. "School Desegregation and New Industry: The Southern Community Leader's Viewpoint." *Social Forces* 41 (May 1963): 384–89.

Crawford, Alan. *Thunder on the Right: The "New Right" and the Politics of Resentment.* New York: Pantheon Books, 1980.

Crow, Jeffrey J., and Robert F. Durden. *Republican in the Old North State: A Political Biography of Daniel L. Russell.* Baton Rouge: Louisiana State University Press, 1977.

Dabney, Virginius. "Reds in Dixie." *Sewanee Review* 42 (fall 1934): 418–22.

Daniel, Pete. *Standing at the Crossroads: Southern Life since 1900.* New York: Hill and Wang, 1986.

Daniels, Jonathan. *Tar Heels: A Portrait of North Carolina.* New York: Dodd, Mead, 1941.

Daniels, Josephus. *Editor in Politics.* Chapel Hill: University of North Carolina Press, 1941.

Degler, Carl N. "Academic Casualty." *New Republic,* July 10, 1965, 10.

Diamond, Sigmund. *Compromised Campus: The Collaboration of Universities with the Intelligence Community, 1945–1955.* New York: Oxford University Press, 1992.

Du Bois, W. E. B. "The Upbuilding of Black Durham." *World's Work* 23 (January 1912): 334–38.

Durden, Robert F. *The Dukes of Durham, 1865–1929.* Durham: Duke University Press, 1975.

Dykeman, Wilma, and James Stokely. "Sit Down Chillun, Sit Down!" *Progressive* (June 1960): 23–29.

Eagles, Charles W. *Jonathan Daniels and Race Relations: The Evolution of a Southern Liberal.* Knoxville: University of Tennessee Press, 1982.

Edmonds, Helen. *The Negro and Fusion Politics in North Carolina, 1894–1901.* Chapel Hill: University of North Carolina Press, 1951.

Edsall, Preston W., and J. Oliver Williams. "North Carolina: Bipartisan Paradox." In *The Changing Politics of the South,* ed. William C. Havard, 366–423. Baton Rouge: Louisiana State University Press, 1972.

Ehle, John. *The Free Men.* New York: Harper and Row, 1965.

Emery, Sarah Watson. *Blood on the Old Well.* Dallas, Tex.: Prospect House, 1963.

Escott, Paul D. *Many Excellent People: Power and Privilege in North Carolina, 1850–1900.* Chapel Hill: University of North Carolina Press, 1985.

Evans, Sara. *Personal Politics: The Roots of Women's Liberation in the Civil Rights Movement and the New Left.* New York: Vintage Books, 1980.

Evans, William M. *Ballots and Fencerails: Reconstruction on the Lower Cape Fear.* Chapel Hill: University of North Carolina Press, 1967.

Fairclough, Adam. *To Redeem the Soul of America: The Southern Christian Leadership Conference and Martin Luther King Jr.* Athens: University of Georgia Press, 1987.

Fields, Barbara J. "Ideology and Race in American History." In *Region, Race, and Re-*

construction: *Essays in Honor of C. Vann Woodward*, ed. J. Morgan Kousser and James M. McPherson, 26–44. New York: Oxford University Press, 1982.

Floren, Gillian Dae. "Speaking Freely: UNC-CH Administrators Respond to Freedom of Expression, 1963–1970." Master's thesis, University of North Carolina at Chapel Hill, 1989.

Fraser, Ronald, ed. *1968: A Student Generation in Revolt.* New York: Pantheon Books, 1988.

Frazier, E. Franklin. *Black Bourgeoisie.* Glencoe, Ill.: Free Press, 1957.

———. "Durham: Capital of the Black Middle Class." In *The New Negro*, ed. Alain Locke, 333–40. New York: Albert and Charles Boni, 1925.

Fredrickson, George M. *The Black Image in the White Mind: The Debate on Afro-American Character and Destiny, 1817–1914.* New York: Harper and Row, 1972.

Fried, Richard M. *Nightmare in Red: The McCarthy Era in Perspective.* New York: Oxford University Press, 1990.

Furgurson, Ernest. *Hard Right: The Rise of Jesse Helms.* New York: W. W. Norton, 1986.

Gaillard, Frye. *The Dream Long Deferred.* Chapel Hill: University of North Carolina Press, 1988.

Gardner, David P. *The California Oath Controversy.* Berkeley: University of California Press, 1967.

Garrow, David J. *Bearing the Cross: Martin Luther King Jr. and the Southern Christian Leadership Conference.* New York: W. Morrow, 1986.

Gatewood, Willard B., Jr. "Embattled Scholar: Howard W. Odum and the Fundamentalists, 1925–1927." *Journal of Southern History* 31 (November 1965): 379–92.

———. *Preachers, Pedagogues, and Politicians: The Evolution Controversy in North Carolina, 1920–1927.* Chapel Hill: University of North Carolina Press, 1966.

Gatton, T. Harry. *Banking in North Carolina: A Narrative History.* Raleigh: North Carolina Bankers' Association, 1987.

Gellhorn, Walter. *Security, Loyalty, and Science.* Ithaca: Cornell University Press, 1950.

Genovese, Eugene D. *In Red and Black: Marxian Explorations in Afro-American and Southern History.* New York: Pantheon Books, 1968.

———. *Roll, Jordan, Roll: The World the Slaves Made.* New York: Pantheon Books, 1974.

Gitlin, Todd. *The Sixties: Years of Hope, Days of Rage.* New York: Bantam, 1987.

Goldfield, David R. *Black, White, and Southern: Race Relations and Southern Culture, 1940 to the Present.* Baton Rouge: Louisiana State University Press, 1990.

Greenhaw, Wayne. *Elephants in the Cottonfields.* New York: Macmillan, 1982.

Gunter, Timothy Lee. "No Reds in Blue Heaven: A Discourse of the Passage, Amendment and Repeal of the North Carolina Communist Speaker Ban Law." Honors thesis, University of North Carolina at Chapel Hill, 1985.

Hall, Jacquelyn, James Leloudis, Robert Korstad, Mary Murphy, Lu Ann Jones, and Christopher B. Daly. *Like a Family: The Making of a Southern Cotton Mill World.* Chapel Hill: University of North Carolina Press, 1987.

Harris, David. *Dreams Die Hard.* New York: St. Martin's, 1982.

Havard, William, ed. *The Changing Politics of the South.* Baton Rouge: Louisiana State University Press, 1974.

Hayden, Tom. *Reunion: A Memoir.* New York: Random House, 1988.

Helms, Jesse. *When Free Men Shall Stand.* Grand Rapids, Mich.: Zondervan, 1976.

Himmelstein, Jerome L. *To The Right: The Transformation of American Conservatism.* Berkeley: University of California Press, 1990.

Hodges, Luther. *Businessman in the Statehouse: Six Years as Governor of North Carolina.* Chapel Hill: University of North Carolina Press, 1962.

Horowitz, David A. "White Southerners' Alienation and Civil Rights: The Response to Corporate Liberalism, 1956–1965." *Journal of Southern History* 54 (May 1988): 173–200.

Isserman, Maurice. *If I Had a Hammer: The Death of the Old Left and the Birth of the New Left.* New York: Basic Books, 1987.

Jacoway, Elizabeth, and David R. Colburn, eds. *Southern Businessmen and Desegregation.* Baton Rouge: Louisiana State University Press, 1982.

Jezer, Marty. *The Dark Ages: Life in the United States, 1945–1960.* Boston: South End Press, 1982.

Johnson, Guy B., and Guion G. Johnson. *Research in Service to Society: The First Fifty Years of the Institute for Research in Social Science at the University of North Carolina.* Chapel Hill: University of North Carolina Press, 1980.

Journal of the House of Representatives of the General Assembly of the State of North Carolina, Session 1963. Winston-Salem, N.C.: Winston Printing, 1963.

Journal of the House of Representatives of the General Assembly of the State of North Carolina, Session 1965 and the Extra-Session 1965. Winston-Salem, N.C.: Winston Printing, 1965.

Journal of the House of Representatives of the General Assembly of the State of North Carolina, Session 1969. Winston-Salem, N.C.: Winston Printing, 1969.

Journal of the Senate of the General Assembly of the State of North Carolina, Session 1963. Winston-Salem, N.C.: Winston Printing, 1963.

Journal of the Senate of the General Assembly of the State of North Carolina, Session 1965 and the Extra-Session 1965. Winston-Salem, N.C.: Winston Printing, 1965.

Journal of the Senate of the General Assembly of the State of North Carolina, Session 1969. Winston-Salem, N.C.: Winston Printing, 1969.

Joyce, Bob. "Reds on Campus: The Speaker Ban Controversy." *Carolina Alumni Review* 72 (spring 1984): 4–11, 25.

Kaplan, Craig, and Ellen Schrecker, eds. *Regulating the Intellectuals: Perspectives on Academic Freedom in the 1980s.* New York: Praeger Publishers, 1983.

Key, V. O., Jr. *Southern Politics in State and Nation.* New York: Knopf, 1949.

Kincaid, Cliff, and Richard F. LaMountain. "Interview: Senator Jesse Helms on America's Retreat from Communism." *New Guard* (fall 1979): 61–62.

King, Arnold K. *The Multicampus University of North Carolina Comes of Age, 1956–1986.* Chapel Hill: University of North Carolina Press, 1987.

Kirby, Jack Temple. *Media-Made Dixie: The South in the American Imagination.* Athens: University of Georgia Press, 1986.

Kluckhohn, Frank L. *The Naked Rise of Communism*. Derby, Conn.: Monarch Books, 1962.

Kluger, Richard. *Simple Justice: The History of* Brown v. Board of Education *and Black America's Struggle for Equality*. New York: Vintage Books, 1977.

Kneebone, John T. *Southern Liberal Journalists and the Issue of Race, 1920–1944*. Chapel Hill: University of North Carolina Press, 1985.

Knight, Douglas M. *Street of Dreams: The Nature and Legacy of the 1960s*. Durham: Duke University Press, 1989.

Koeppel, Barbara. "Something Could Be Finer Than to Be in Carolina." *Progressive* 40 (June 1976): 20–23.

Korstad, Robert R. "Daybreak of Freedom: Tobacco Workers and the CIO in Winston-Salem, North Carolina, 1943–1950." Ph.D. diss., University of North Carolina, 1987.

Kousser, J. Morgan. "Progressivism—For Middle-Class Whites Only: North Carolina Education, 1880–1910." *Journal of Southern History* 46 (May 1980): 169–94.

———. *The Shaping of Southern Politics*. New Haven: Yale University Press, 1964.

Kovel, Joel. *Red Hunting in the Promised Land: Anti-Communism and the Making of America*. New York: Basic Books, 1994.

Krueger, Thomas A. *And Promises to Keep: The Southern Conference for Human Welfare*. Nashville, Tenn.: Vanderbilt University Press, 1967.

Lamis, Alexander P. *The Two-Party South*. New York: Oxford University Press, 1984.

Latham, Earl. *The Communist Controversy in Washington: From the New Deal to McCarthy*. Cambridge: Harvard University Press, 1966.

Lawson, Steven F. *Black Ballots: Voting Rights in the South, 1944–1969*. New York: Columbia University Press, 1976.

Lazarsfeld, Paul, and Wagner Thielens. *The Academic Mind*. Glencoe, Ill.: Free Press, 1958.

Lefler, Hugh T., ed. *North Carolina History Told by Contemporaries*. Chapel Hill: University of North Carolina Press, 1956.

Lefler, Hugh T., and Albert Ray Newsome. *North Carolina: The History of a Southern State*. 3d ed. Chapel Hill: University of North Carolina Press, 1973.

"Legion Is Invited to Testify at Ban Hearings." *North Carolina American Legion News* 30 (August 1965): 1, 4.

Leloudis, James L., 2d. "School Reform in the New South: The Woman's Association for the Betterment of Public School Houses in North Carolina, 1902–1919." *Journal of American History* 69 (March 1983): 886–909.

Lemmon, Sara M. "The Ideology of the 'Dixiecrat' Movement." *Social Forces* 30 (December 1951): 162–71.

Lewis, Lionel S. *Cold War on Campus: A Study of the Politics of Organizational Control*. New Brunswick, N.J.: Transaction Books, 1988.

Lewis, Nell Battle. "Anarchy versus Communism in Gastonia." *Nation* 129 (February 1929): 321–22.

Link, William A. "William Friday and the North Carolina Speaker Ban Crisis, 1963–1968." *North Carolina Historical Review* 72 (April 1995): 198–220.

————. *William Friday: Power, Purpose, and American Higher Education*. Chapel Hill: University of North Carolina Press, 1995.

Lisio, Donald J. *Hoover, Blacks, and Lily-Whites: A Study of Southern Strategies*. Chapel Hill: University of North Carolina Press, 1985.

Lockmiller, David A. *The Consolidation of the University of North Carolina*. Chapel Hill: University of North Carolina Press, 1942.

Logan, Frenise. *The Negro in North Carolina, 1876–1894*. Chapel Hill: University of North Carolina Press, 1964.

Logan, Raymond W., ed. *What the Negro Wants*. Chapel Hill: University of North Carolina Press, 1944.

Lowenstein, Allard K. *Brutal Mandate*. New York: Macmillan, 1962.

Lubell, Samuel. *The Future of American Politics*. New York: Harper and Brothers, 1952.

Luebke, Paul. *Tar Heel Politics: Myths and Realities*. Chapel Hill: University of North Carolina Press, 1990.

Massengill, Stephen W., ed. *Biographical Dictionary: General Assembly of North Carolina, 1929–1980*. Raleigh: North Carolina State Department of Archives and History, 1982.

Mathews, Donald G., and Jane DeHart Mathews. *The Equal Rights Amendment and the Politics of Cultural Conflict: Feminists and Traditionalists in North Carolina*. New York: Oxford University Press, 1984.

Matthews, Donald R., ed. *North Carolina Votes*. Chapel Hill: University of North Carolina Press, 1962.

Matthews, Donald R., and James W. Prothro. *Negroes and the New Southern Politics*. New York: Harcourt Brace and World, 1966.

McAuliffe, Mary S. *Crisis on the Left: Cold War Politics and American Liberals*. Amherst: University of Massachusetts Press, 1978.

McMillen, Neil R. *The Citizens' Council: Organized Resistance to the Second Reconstruction*. Urbana: University of Illinois Press, 1971.

Miller, James. *"Democracy Is in the Streets": From Port Huron to the Siege of Chicago*. New York: Simon and Schuster, 1987.

Mitchell, Memory F., ed. *Messages, Addresses, and Public Papers of Daniel Killian Moore, Governor of North Carolina, 1965–1969*. Raleigh: North Carolina State Department of Archives and History, 1971.

————, ed. *Messages, Addresses, and Public Papers of Terry Sanford, Governor of North Carolina, 1961–1965*. Raleigh: Council of State, State of North Carolina, 1966.

Morris, Aldon D. *The Origins of the Civil Rights Movement: Black Communities Organizing for Change*. New York: Free Press, 1984.

Morrison, Joseph L. *Josephus Daniels: The Small-d Democrat*. Chapel Hill: University of North Carolina Press, 1966.

Morton, Hugh, Jr. *The University of North Carolina at Chapel Hill: The First Two Hundred Years*. Raleigh: Capitol Broadcasting, 1987.

Murphy, Paul L. *The Constitution in Crisis Times, 1918–1969*. New York: Harper and Row, 1972.

Murray, Pauli. *Proud Shoes: The Story of an American Family*. New York: Harper and Brothers, 1956.

Myerson, Michael. *Nothing Could Be Finer*. New York: International Publishers, 1978.

Navasky, Victor S. *Naming Names*. New York: Penguin, 1981.

Nordhoff, Grace, ed. *"A Lot of Human Beings Have Been Born Bums": Twenty Years of the Words of Senator No, Jesse Helms*. Durham: North Carolina Independent, 1984.

Odum, Howard W. *Race and Rumors of Race: Challenge to American Crisis*. Reprint, New York: Negro Universities Press, 1969.

O'Reilly, Kenneth. *Hoover and the Un-Americans: The FBI, HUAC, and the Red Menace*. Philadelphia: Temple University Press, 1983.

———. *Racial Matters: The FBI's Secret File on Black America, 1960–1972*. New York: Free Press, 1989.

Oshinsky, David. *A Conspiracy So Immense*. New York: Free Press, 1983.

Patrick, Clarence. *Lunch-Counter Desegregation in Winston-Salem, North Carolina*. Winston-Salem, N.C.: Wake Forest College[?], 1960.

Peltason, J. W. *Fifty-Eight Lonely Men: Southern Federal Judges and School Desegregation*. Urbana: University of Illinois Press, 1971.

Penegar, Kenneth L. "Who's for Academic Freedom?" *New Republic*, December 4, 1965, 15–17.

Phillips, Kevin B. *The Emerging Republican Majority*. New Rochelle, N.Y.: Arlington House, 1969.

Pitts, Nathan A. *The Cooperative Movement in Negro Communities of North Carolina*. Washington, D.C.: Catholic University of America Press, 1950.

Pleasants, Julian M., and Augustus M. Burns III. *Frank Porter Graham and the 1950 Senate Race in North Carolina*. Chapel Hill: University of North Carolina Press, 1990.

Pollitt, Daniel H. "Campus Censorship: Statute Barring Speakers from State Educational Institutions." *North Carolina Law Review* 42 (fall 1963): 179–99.

Pope, Liston. *Millhands and Preachers*. New Haven: Yale University Press, 1942.

Powell, William S. *North Carolina through Four Centuries*. Chapel Hill: University of North Carolina Press, 1989.

———, ed. *Dictionary of North Carolina Biography*. Chapel Hill: University of North Carolina Press, 1987.

———, ed. *North Carolina Lives: The Tar Heel Who's Who*. Hopkinsville, Ky.: Historical Record Association, 1952.

Powers, Thomas. *Vietnam, the War at Home: Vietnam and the American People, 1964–1968*. Boston: G. K. Hall, 1984.

Rampersad, Arnold. *The Life of Langston Hughes*. Vol. 1, *1902–1941: I, Too, Sing America*. New York: Oxford University Press, 1986.

Rankin, Carl E. *The University of North Carolina and the Problem of the Cotton Mill Employee*. New York: Columbia University Press, 1936.

Record, Wilson. *The Negro and the Communist Party*. Chapel Hill: University of North Carolina Press, 1951.

Reed, John Shelton. *The Enduring South: Subcultural Persistence in Mass Society*. Chapel Hill: University of North Carolina Press, 1972.

Reeves, Thomas C. *The Life and Times of Joe McCarthy*. New York: Stein and Day, 1982.

Reinhard, David W. *The Republican Right since 1945*. Lexington: University Press of Kentucky, 1983.

Robinson, Blackwell P., ed. *The North Carolina Guide*. Chapel Hill: University of North Carolina Press, 1955.

Rogin, Michael Paul. *Ronald Reagan: The Movie and Other Episodes in Political Demonology*. Berkeley: University of California Press, 1987.

Rorabaugh, W. J. *Berkeley at War: The 1960s*. New York: Oxford University Press, 1989.

Ross, Malcolm. "North Carolina, Dixie Dynamo." *National Geographic*, February 1962, 140–83.

Royster, Vermont. "Change and Controversy in Chapel Hill." *Carolina Alumni Review* 67 (September 1978): 16–17.

Sale, Kirkpatrick. *Power Shift: The Rise of the Southern Rim and Its Challenge to the Eastern Establishment*. New York: Vintage Books, 1975.

———. *SDS*. New York: Random House, 1973.

Sanders, Jane. *Cold War on the Campus*. Seattle: University of Washington Press, 1979.

Sawyer, Albert. "Anti-Communism: Its Effects on Academe." Master's thesis, University of North Carolina at Chapel Hill, 1988.

Scales, Junius Irving, and Richard Nickson. *Cause at Heart: A Former Communist Remembers*. Athens: University of Georgia Press, 1987.

Schrecker, Ellen. *No Ivory Tower: McCarthyism and the Universities*. New York: Oxford University Press, 1986.

Schultz, Bud, and Ruth Schultz, eds. *It Did Happen Here: Recollections of Political Repression in America*. Berkeley: University of California Press, 1989.

Schwartz, David. "U.S. Senate Gains a Controversial Voice: Paul Wellstone '65 Launches Campaign for Social Issues." *Carolina Alumni Review* (summer 1991): 29–35.

Schwarz, Frederick Charles. *You Can Trust the Communists*. Englewood Cliffs, N.J.: Prentice-Hall, 1960.

Secor, Phillip B. "Academic Freedom in Political Context: The North Carolina Speaker Ban Law." In *Law and Justice: Essays in Honor of Robert S. Rankin*, ed. Carl Beck, 207–25. Durham: Duke University Press, 1970.

Session Laws and Resolutions Passed by the General Assembly at the Regular Session 1963. Winston-Salem, N.C.: Winston Printing, 1965.

Session Laws and Resolutions Passed by the General Assembly at the Regular Session 1965 and the Extra-Session 1965. Winston-Salem, N.C.: Winston Printing, 1965.

Severson, Harold. "Promised Land for Tenants." *Southern Agriculturalist* 76 (May 1946): 4–6.

Simon, Bryant. "The Southern Student Organizing Committee: A New Rebel Yell in Dixie." Honors thesis, University of North Carolina at Chapel Hill, 1983.

Singal, Daniel J. *The War Within: From Victorian to Modernist Thought in the South, 1919–1945*. Chapel Hill: University of North Carolina Press, 1982.

Sitkoff, Harvard. *A New Deal for Blacks: The Emergence of Civil Rights as a National Issue*. New York: Oxford University Press, 1978.

Snider, William D. *Helms and Hunt: The North Carolina Senate Race, 1984.* Chapel Hill: University of North Carolina Press, 1985.

————. *Light on the Hill: A History of the University of North Carolina at Chapel Hill.* Chapel Hill: University of North Carolina Press, 1992.

Sosna, Morton. *In Search of the Silent South: Southern Liberals and the Race Issue.* New York: Columbia University Press, 1977.

Spence, James R. *The Making of a Governor: The Moore-Preyer-Lake Primaries of 1964.* Winston-Salem, N.C.: John F. Blair, 1968.

Stanley, Harold W. *Voter Mobilization and the Politics of Race: The South and Universal Suffrage, 1952–1984.* New York: Praeger, 1987.

Stewart, Alva, "North Carolina's Gag Law." *Christian Century,* October 10, 1964.

Stewart, William A. "The North Carolina Speaker Ban Episode: Its History and Implications for Higher Education." Ed.D. diss., University of North Carolina at Greensboro, 1988.

"Students Crash 'Kennedy Curtain.'" *Progressive Labor* 2 (July–August 1963): 1, 7.

"Students See Cuba, State Dept. Sees Red, Washington Launches Attack against PL." *Progressive Labor* 2 (September 1963): 1, 4.

"The Swimming Pool Showdown." *Southern Exposure* 8 (summer 1980): 70–72.

"Symposium: Students' Rights and Campus Rules." *California Law Review* 54 (March 1966): 1–22.

Theoharis, Athan. *Seeds of Repression: Harry S. Truman and the Origins of McCarthyism.* Chicago: Quadrangle Press, 1971.

Theoharis, Athan, and Robert Griffith, eds. *The Specter.* New York: Franklin Watts, 1974.

Thirteenth Report of the [California] Senate Factfinding Subcommittee on Un-American Activities. Sacramento?: California Senate, 1965.

Thorpe, Judith L. "A Study of the Peace Movement at the University of North Carolina at Chapel Hill Viewed within the Context of the Nation, 1964–1971." Master's thesis, University of North Carolina at Chapel Hill, 1972.

Tindall, George B. *The Emergence of the New South, 1913–1945.* Baton Rouge: Louisiana State University Press, 1967.

————. "The Significance of Howard W. Odum to Southern History: A Preliminary Estimate." *Journal of Southern History* 24 (August 1958): 285–307.

Tushnet, Mark V. *The NAACP's Legal Strategy against Segregated Education, 1925–1950.* Chapel Hill: University of North Carolina Press, 1987.

U.S. House Committee on Un-American Activities. *Investigation of Communist Activities in the North Carolina Area.* 84th Cong., 2d sess. Washington, D.C.: U.S. Government Printing Office, 1956.

————. *Violations of State Department Travel Regulations and Pro-Castro Propaganda Activities in the United States.* 88th Cong., 1st sess. Washington, D.C.: U.S. Government Printing Office, 1965.

Van Alstyne, William W. "Judicial Trends toward Student Academic Freedom." *University of Florida Law Review* 20 (winter 1968): 1–37.

————. "Political Speakers at State Universities: Some Constitutional Considerations." *University of Pennsylvania Law Review* 3 (fall 1963): 328–42.

———. "A Study of Academic Freedom and the Rule Making Powers of Public Universities: Some Constitutional Considerations." *Law in Transition Quarterly* 2 (winter 1965): 1–34.

Vance, Rupert B., and Katherine Jocher. "Howard W. Odum." *Social Forces* 33 (March 1955): 203–17.

Walzer, Michael. "A Cup of Coffee and a Seat." *Dissent*, September 1960, 22–25.

Waynick, Capus M., John C. Brooks, and Elsie W. Pitts, eds. *North Carolina and the Negro*. Raleigh: North Carolina Mayor's Co-Operating Committee, 1964.

Weare, Walter B. *Black Business in the New South: A Social History of the North Carolina Mutual Insurance Company*. Champaign: University of Illinois Press, 1976.

Wells, H. M. "The Speaker Ban Law." *Christian Century*, July 14, 1965, 3, 4.

Wheaton, Elizabeth. *Codename GREENKILL: The 1979 Greensboro Killings*. Athens: University of Georgia Press, 1987.

Whiteley, Michael. "Helms Honed Beliefs on TV, City Council." *Raleigh Times*, November 1, 1984.

Wiener, Jonathan M. "Class Structure and Economic Development in the American South, 1865–1955." *American Historical Review* 84 (October 1979): 970–92.

———. *Social Origins of the New South: Alabama, 1860–1885*. Baton Rouge: Louisiana State University Press, 1978.

Williams, J. Derek. "'It Wasn't Slavery Time Anymore': Foodworkers' Strike at Chapel Hill, Spring 1969." Master's thesis, University of North Carolina at Chapel Hill, 1979.

Williams, Robert F. *Negroes with Guns*. New York: Third World Press, 1962.

Wilson, Louis R. *The University of North Carolina, 1900–1930: The Making of the Modern University*. Chapel Hill: University of North Carolina Press, 1957.

Wolff, Miles. *Lunch at the Five and Ten: The Greensboro Sit-ins, a Contemporary History*. New York: Stein and Day, 1970.

Wood, Phillip J. *The Political Economy of North Carolina, 1880–1980*. Durham: Duke University Press, 1986.

Woodward, C. Vann. *Origins of the New South*. Baton Rouge: Louisiana State University Press, 1951.

———. *Thinking Back: The Perils of Writing History*. Baton Rouge: Louisiana State University Press, 1986.

Wright, Gavin. *Old South, New South: Revolutions in the Southern Economy since the Civil War*. New York: Basic Books, 1986.

Zaroulis, Nancy, and Gerald Sullivan. *Who Spoke Up? American Protest against the War in Vietnam, 1963–1975*. New York: Holt, Rinehart, and Winston, 1984.

Zinn, Howard. *SNCC: The New Abolitionists*. Boston: Beacon Press, 1964.

INDEX

Malone, Vivian, 6
Mao Tse-tung, 33
Martin, Perry, 4, 8, 86
Matthews, Carl, 46
Maupin, Armistead J., xiv
Maupin, Armistead J., Jr., 25
Max, Steve, 171
McCarthy, Joseph, ix
McCorkel, R. James, 173–75, 177, 180,
    182, 184, 190, 192, 199
McCrary, Ernest, 189–90
McGovern, George, 243
McLean, Hector, 13
Mecklenburg County, 73, 76
Medford, William, 103, 112, 115
Meredith, James, 23
Merzbacher, Eugen, 91
Michigan, 197
Michigan State University, 197–98
Miller, Arthur, 97–98
Mintz, Rudolph, 191, 201
Mohn, J. F., 225
Monroe (N.C.), 46
Moody, Ralph, 100, 101, 116, 208–10,
    212, 213–16, 218
Moore, Dan K., 103, 105–8, 110–13,
    117, 121, 123–30, 159, 160, 162,
    164–66, 168, 187–94, 196, 198, 221,
    222, 241
Morgan, Robert B., 143, 144–45, 167,
    169, 181, 196, 241–42
Morris, Aldon, 48
Moscow State University, 205
Moses, Bob, 170
Myers, Charles, 125

Nash, Arnold, 119
National Association for the
    Advancement of Colored People
    (NAACP), 29, 31, 47, 172
National Committee to Abolish the
    House Un-American Activities
    Committee, 99, 180
New University Conference, 233

News and Observer, 55
Ngo Diem Nhu, Madame, 27
Nixon, Richard, 238
North Carolina A & T State University,
    45, 49, 59, 228
North Carolina, and civil rights, 46–47
North Carolina Civil Liberties Union,
    215
North Carolina College, 46, 47
North Carolina General Assembly, ix, 1,
    2, 3, 14, 53, 55, 57, 58–64, 65–87,
    123, 127–28, 131, 160, 184–85, 196,
    213, 214, 219, 232; 1969 Session,
    225–28; and reapportionment, 65, 72,
    75–76; Special session (1965),
    164–66, 180
North Carolina State University, 50, 230,
    232

Oglesby, Carl, 176
O'Hanlon, Isaac, 166
Ohio, 62
Ohio State University, 17, 18, 132, 211.
    See also Fawcett, Novice G.
Outland, Joseph, 55

Panama Canal Treaty, 242
Papousek, Hanus, 205–6
Parker, Samuel I., 147
Patriots of North Carolina, 66, 112, 162
Pearsall, Thomas Jenkins, xiii
Pearsall Plan, xiii, 66, 77, 162, 210
People's Republic of China, 182
Petrov, V. V., 153
Phelps, Larry, 33, 35, 90, 146, 151–53
Phillips, C. W., 201
Philpott, Cloyd, 67
Phipps, L. J., 15, 61, 92, 139
Pollitt, Daniel, 211–12, 214
Port Huron Statement, 171. *See also*
    Students for a Democratic Society
Pound, Ezra, xiv
President's Commission on the Causes
    and Prevention of Violence, 226

State Bureau of Investigation (SBI), 228
States'-rights Resolutions, 81–82, 86–87
State University of New York at Buffalo, 212
Stone, T. Clarence, 1, 3, 4, 8, 11, 12, 13, 56–58, 66–70, 80, 81–82, 139
Story, Thomas, 80
Straley, Joseph W., 182
Strong, Charles, 3, 80, 81
Student League for Industrial Democracy (SLID), 170
Student Nonviolent Coordinating Committee (SNCC), 45, 171
Student Peace Union (SPU), 26–31, 171, 177, 178
Students for a Democratic Society (SDS), 170–80, 182–87, 189–93, 195–96, 201, 203, 207–8, 233–35, 242
Subversive Activities Control Board, xiv
Supreme Court, U.S., 7, 72, 74
Sweet, Gordon, 109, 111, 128, 134–35. See also Southern Association of Colleges and Schools
Swindell, Elizabeth G., 125, 128–29, 132, 137, 140, 143

Talmadge, Herman, 68
Taylor, Frank, 191
Taylor, Pat, 122, 124, 125, 126, 127, 162
Taylor, W. W., xiv
Thomas, Norman, 174
Thornburg, Lacy, 125, 127, 141, 147, 165
Thurmond, Strom, 217
Tuck, William, 68
Tyrrell County, 75

Ullman, B. L., 90
University of Alabama, 83
University of California, xv, 112, 145. See also Berkeley; Free Speech Movement
University of Mississippi, 23

University of North Carolina at Chapel Hill (UNC), x, xi, xiv, xv, 4, 10, 16, 18, 19, 26, 88, 91, 135, 181, 195, 223–24, 228, 232, 239; administration, 36, 38, 100, 104, 116, 119, 134, 152–58, 163, 182, 183–84, 187, 194, 199, 203, 235–36, 242; Board of Trustees of, 3, 41, 103, 104, 112, 137, 148, 150, 160, 161, 164, 165, 168, 180, 182, 185–88, 190–95, 200, 206, 219, 222, 226–27, 230, 231; and civil rights demonstrations, 28, 29, 32, 42, 44, 60, 62; Daily Tar Heel, 23, 25, 29, 30, 31, 36, 38, 177, 178, 189, 219; faculty, 94–95, 148, 157, 164, 192, 201–2, 229–31; Lenoir Hall Strike, 227; and liberalism, 20, 40, 45, 84, 170–71; New Left Club, 28, 32, 33, 39, 170, 171; students, 22, 24, 25, 27, 40, 172, 177, 178, 189–91, 194, 231
University of South Carolina, 131
University v. Maultsby, 209, 213
Uzzell, George, 59, 61, 63, 81

Van Alstyne, William, 163, 166, 211–15, 220
Vanore, Andrew, 214
Vietnam War: and speaker ban, 142–43, 165, 181, 182, 188, 192, 242; and UNC, 172, 176, 196, 203, 228–32, 235
Vlasits, George, 234
Vocational Rehabilitation Administration, 134

Wallace, George C., 6, 7, 8, 68, 79, 80, 83, 132
Waller, Gary, 173, 175, 176–77, 184, 192, 193–94, 202–3, 235
Warren County, 78
Warren, Earl, 7. See also Supreme Court, U.S.
Warren, Lindsay, Jr., 86
Watkins, William, 225, 226